CITY ON A HILL

CITY ON A HILL

A History of Ideas and Myths in America

✶

LOREN BARITZ

JOHN WILEY & SONS, INC.

New York · London · Sydney

To Phyllis

PREFACE

American intellectual history is an unstructured field. There has been long debate and discussion about both the proper ground and the boundaries of the subject. The one most general agreement about the nature of this area of study has made for greater, rather than less confusion. Scholars concerned with America, unlike many of those who think and write about Europe, have virtually identified intellectual with social history.

Criteria of intellectual significance have usually been social criteria, and the importance of an idea has usually been defined in terms of its popular influence. In adopting a social hierarchy of significance scholars represent the constituency of the past. They follow the man who was once on the street. If that man did not know the seminal minds of his own time, those minds presumably may be dismissed as uninfluential, as, of course, they were in this limited sense.

The use of this social standard of significance has also encouraged the writing of rather abstract history, and has contributed to the sense that forces, patterns, and movements constitute the stuff of intellectual history. Abstractions do not think; individual men do. It is important to understand the man who thinks in order to understand what he thinks. True, the fullest possible knowledge of a man's place in and response to his milieu, and that milieu's assessment of him, add to our understanding of any historical figure. But American historiography has stressed abstractions unwarrantably. It is time now to view individuals, not in some reversion to a hero or devil theory of history, but as a way to continue a serious study of ideas.

There are two main approaches to America's intellectual tradition in this book: narration and analysis. I know that narration is never "pure," that even the simplest statement of presumed fact is itself an interpretation. There is no help for that, and no alternative either. I have tried to display the thought of each of the principal subjects in his own terms, or in terms as nearly his own as I could manage. It is my view that the substance of America's intellectual history is not yet in sufficiently clear focus for an exclusively analytical treatment. Because the reader must know what is being analyzed before he can evaluate the analysis, I have shown what the principals' intellectual system was as each understood it. I have not reconstructed any total intellectual system in any case; I have focused only on the larger and most vital aspects of any individual's thought.

It is the intention of this book to try to clarify the American qualities of thought in America. Such an intention must fail because it is impossible to know the intellectual history of all other times and places, and the judgment about what is unique in American thought must obviously be a comparative judgment. I make such judgments with a wince, but it seems better to make them than not.

One American characteristic has always been an uncertainty about what it meant to be an American. There has always been some one analyzing this nation of immigrants in order to find out what made these people different from what they had been before they had sailed, or different from those who would not or those who had not yet sailed. There has always been some one at hand to ask how it was that quite ordinary people could build or sustain a quite extraordinary new nation in the New World. An American, Americans were repeatedly told, was a new man—different in kind, some said, from others. Something in the American setting had supposedly transformed weary and broken Europeans into vibrant and proud builders of the western way. Perhaps it was, as others said, that there was a magic in the forests or air of America that stripped a European of his psychological and cultural heritage and forced him to grow into a new and strong man under the western sun. Still others suggested that those who came were different from those who stayed, that only those who were strong or wise or good enough had dared to hazard the ocean in the first place.

Or perhaps Americans merely deluded themselves by asking the question. Perhaps Americans were not new men in any significant sense, and hid from that fact by asking what it was that had supposedly made them new. Perhaps the question was designed to disguise the fact that America had in some sense failed, and that the failure was precisely that Americans were ordinary and usual men, neither the saviors of the race nor the builders of a new tomorrow, but simply ordinary and usual men. That possibility has also always been suggested by and to Americans, but it has generally been thought a subversive idea, and has been not so much attacked as simply drowned in the swelling chorus of American voices singing other songs.

Every so often, an American asked or answered these questions in a relatively new or significant way. Some of them are the subjects of this book. They are not the only men who turned their minds to the meaning of America, and that was naturally not their only question. An augmented or altered cast of characters could have been assembled and would have resulted in a somewhat different, and happier, book, one that should also be written. But the men I have selected are those who, in my opinion, developed the most complex and interesting view of America, men whose definitions of the nation were subtle enough to include both success and failure. The body of thought which they produced is not the most sanguine but it is, again in my opinion, the best that an earlier America had to offer.

It cannot be said that the subjects of this book deserve inclusion in a study of that elusive thing sometimes nervously called "the American mind" because they were influential in their own days. If "influence" means impact on popular thought and action, it can be said that at least Winthrop and Emerson were somewhat influential. Edwards and Adams were influential in that sense at one period of their lives and not at others, though other contemporaries were more influential than either. Taylor and Melville, as both unhappily knew, were voices crying in the wilderness, and were not only without influence but also without an audience, at least for their most mature work. Intellectual rather than social significance was among the criteria by which this particular cast of characters was assembled. Finally, then, my own judgment of the quality of thought of each of the men I have selected contributed to the final decision.

The six subjects and chapters of this volume illustrate three intellectual modes. The first two subjects were concerned with Puritanism, which I understand to have been both a political and a theological movement. I chose Winthrop to illustrate the political and Edwards the theological aspects of Puritanism. The next two subjects were concerned with power and politics. In selecting John Adams as the best illustration of the thought of the founding fathers I open myself to the charge of ignoring Franklin and Jefferson and Madison and a literal host of others whose intellectual systems deserve the highest respect. But Adams was certainly the most systematic of that remarkable group of political thinkers, and he was in my judgment the most interesting. That Adams was in Europe while the Constitution was being framed says exactly nothing about either the substance or quality of his thought. John Taylor was selected as an illustration of agrarian and Southern thought because, again, he achieved in my opinion the highest level of quality of the Southern thinkers. That means, obviously, that I believe his thought was more significant in an intellectual sense than that of Calhoun, who is more often selected as the "mind of the South." Taylor was certainly the most extreme and consistent of the early defenders of the South's sense of itself, and though it is perfectly clear that Calhoun was more important politically, I hope that the chapter on Taylor will show that almost all of Calhoun's most important ideas were articulated first and better by Taylor. The next two subjects should occasion less disagreement. I chose Emerson and Melville as the best illustrations of Romanticism in its philosophical and creative aspects.

A word is necessary about one important matter of style. I have tried to allow the subjects to say what they said in the way that they said it. There are, as a result, very many usually brief quotations here. I wanted to keep as much of the flavor of a man's thought as possible, and that often meant that his words, rather than mine, would serve best. There is another equally compelling reason. The text under consideration is always the most relevant and pertinent evidence in intellectual history. Wherever I interpret an important idea, I try to show the reader the text of the idea itself.

I have identified the source of every direct quotation, but I have not usually given explicit credit where I have learned from other scholars. In the select bibliographies following each chapter I have listed the works which were most useful to me.

Grants-in-Aid from the Social Science Research Council and the American Council of Learned Societies provided funds for investigating specific sections of this volume. The Committee on Research of Roosevelt University granted funds to type sections of an early draft.

My thanks to Marian A. McClintock, Executive Assistant to the Deans of the College of the University of Rochester, who supervised and expedited the typing of the manuscript, and to Mr. James G. Snyder who helped to prepare the typescript for the printer.

I owe my usual debt to Professor Michael Cherniavsky of the University of Rochester for reading the entire manuscript and for making literally hundreds of suggestions, queries, guarded threats, and amused discoveries of some lapse or other on my part. Professor William R. Taylor of the University of Wisconsin put his intelligence and learning at my service, and the entire manuscript benefited from his suggestions. Both men helped to make this a better book than it was before they saw it, and, naturally, neither should be thought responsible for anything weak, bad, or evil that may yet remain.

I happily thank William L. Gum of John Wiley and Sons. He is a creative editor who continually encouraged me when he was depressed, who demonstrated on dozens of occasions as difficult and trying as I could make them that he has raised patience and good humor to an art.

August 1964   LOREN BARITZ
Rochester, New York

ACKNOWLEDGMENTS

To Constable and Co., Ltd., for permission to quote from *The Works of Herman Melville*.

To the Belknap Press of Harvard University Press, for permission to quote from *Diary and Autobiography of John Adams*, L. H. Butterfield et al., eds. © by Massachusetts Historical Society; from *The Journals and Miscellaneous Notebooks of Ralph Waldo Emerson*, William H. Gilman et al., eds. © by the President and Fellows of Harvard College.

To Houghton Mifflin Co., for permission to quote from *The Journals of Ralph Waldo Emerson*, Edward W. Emerson and Waldo E. Forbes, eds.

To the Massachusetts Historical Society, for permission to quote from *The Papers of John Winthrop*, A. B. Forbes, ed.

To Yale University Press, for permission to quote from *A Treatise Concerning Religious Affections* by Jonathan Edwards, J. E. Smith, ed.; from *Freedom of the Will* by Jonathan Edwards, Paul Ramsey, ed.; and from *Herman Melville Letters*, M. R. Davis and W. H. Gilman, eds.

To the *American Historical Review* for permission to use extended passages from my article, "The Idea of the West," which first appeared in the *American Historical Review*, LXVI, 3 (April, 1961).

CONTENTS

CITY ON A HILL

I

POLITICAL THEOLOGY ✱ *John Winthrop*

> Men shall say of succeeding plantacions: the
> lord make it like that of New England: for wee
> must Consider that wee shall be as a Citty
> upon a Hill, the eies of all people are uppon us.
>
> *1630*

In the middle of the sixteenth century, a London cloth merchant
named Adam Winthrop bought the monastery lands at Bury St.
Edmonds in the county of Suffolk. The policy of confiscation and
subsequent sale of such land by Henry VIII thus allowed this
tradesman, and others like him, to use his wealth to change his
status, to become the country squire of the manor of Groton, and
to allow his son, also named Adam, to become lord of the manor.
The younger Adam became a lawyer and established himself as a
solid and respectable representative of landed wealth in the England of Shakespeare. His first wife bore him four daughters, and
his second, Anne Browne, also took up the profession of breeding
that was characteristic of the time, place, and rank. On January
22, 1588, the year of the great Armada, Adam's only son, John,
was born.

Very little is known of John Winthrop's childhood. He entered
Trinity College, Cambridge in 1603. When he was seventeen he
left college before he had qualified for a degree, and married Mary
Forth who, in time, presented him with his first six children. She
died shortly after their tenth anniversary; he remarried within six

months, and that wife died, along with her newborn infant, one year later. When Winthrop was thirty he married his third wife, Margaret Tyndal, who lived through eight children to 1647. Near sixty, he married for the last time, and had enjoyed, in his way, two years with this fourth wife when he died in 1649.

During his years at Trinity College, Winthrop was seized by a spirit which, despite his frequent protestations to the contrary, was not to release him until the day he died. It must be that he was already prepared to be seized before he rode from Groton to Cambridge. But once there, among the new joys of Trinity, Winthrop seems to have learned how to suffer, and how to do a proper job of it; he later recalled the process: "About fourteen years of age, being in Cambridge, I fell into a lingering fever, which took away the comforts of my life: for, being there neglected and despised, I went up and down mourning with myself; and, being deprived of my youthful joys, I betook myself to God, whom I did believe to be very good and merciful, and would welcome any that would come to him, especially such a young soul, and so well qualified as I took myself to be; so as I took pleasure in drawing near to him."[1] He was beginning to exhibit the peculiar symptoms which indicated that he had caught Puritanism.

That affliction had already reached epidemic proportions in his England, and was raging most fiercely in the eastern counties from which he came and at Cambridge where he was. Puritanism in England was a state of mind, a moral commitment, and a general theology. It always acknowledged some definite ecclesiastical polity whose content, however, varied widely from place to place. It defined purity, and sought to purge men and institutions of the corruption which presumably had befouled them. Puritans believed that they understood their inscrutable God, and that they were on His side. Though no man could be certain of his own place in the cosmic drama, the Puritans believed that, as a group, they would taste the fruits of victory even if, as individual men, most of them would be damned. Both personal pessimism and cosmic optimism were necessary deductions of their theological system.

The Puritans were Calvinists in theology. This should be taken to mean no more than that they went to Calvin for instruction, while they went to St. Augustine and St. Paul for inspiration. The English Puritans, at least, thought of themselves as belonging to a tradition which was as old as Christianity, a tradition to which Calvin had also belonged and which he had helped to systematize. They went to Calvin for explanations, not for dogma, and when they found him lacking they looked elsewhere.

Their theological system was reduced to five essential points at the Synod of Dort, which met through the winter of 1618–1619. The Synod had been called to counteract a growing number of heresies, but especially to refute Arminianism, the theology of the Establishment, with its doctrines of freedom, salvation, and the influence of human behavior on God's decisions. The five points of orthodox Calvinism were defined as unconditional election, limited atonement, total depravity, irresistible grace, and the perseverance of the saints:

1. Election was willed by God before the creation of the world.
2. The efficacy of Christ's atonement extended only to the elect.
3. The Fall left man in a state of corruption and helplessness; his natural powers were of no help in salvation.
4. Regeneration was a rebirth of soul and will, and was a result of God's mercy and His love, not of anything men did or could do.
5. God preserved the saints so that, despite their inevitable sins, they would not eventually fall from grace.

As an organized movement, Puritanism in England may be said to have been started during Elizabeth's reign by men who had been driven out of England by Mary, and many of whom had found refuge in Calvin's Geneva. With Elizabeth's accession these reformers returned to England, now armed with the English translation of God's word, the Geneva Bible, and a clearer view of what work was at hand and what the finished product should look like. Elizabeth's policy of general inaction in ecclesiastical matters drove a group of these men to demand a cleansing of the established church. In the slang of the day, they were derisively called Puritans, a label the first generation resented but subsequent ones accepted. Elizabeth seemed willing enough to allow quiet requests for moderate change, but demands for radical change were discouraged. A few professors of divinity at Cambridge were dismissed, some were exiled, and a few others were jailed, but the sun still shone on England.

The Stuarts brought clouds from Scotland. The absolute failure of the Hampton Court Conference in 1604 to resolve differences between the Crown and the dissenters meant that the high hopes engendered by the accession of a presumably orthodox Calvinist were false. When James I threatened to send them all into exile, the Puritan preachers returned to their pulpits with a purpose made firmer by a sense of betrayal. Perhaps they could have been controlled for a time longer had an even firmer resolution been set against theirs, but James could not or would not go far enough. His ability to irritate was masterful, but he could not rise either to frustration or to repression; and the preachers increased in numbers and influence with each passing year.

They preached the five-pronged system of Calvinism, but they had an enormously complicated society with which to contend and therefore could not expect the appealing victories won at Geneva or in Scotland. Whether to remain within the structure of established English institutions in the hope of purifying them, or to flee from corruption out of a fear of contagion became a crucial question. As Puritans, these men did not expect perfection in this world, and they thought of themselves as an advance guard sent by the Lord to combat, not fly from, evil. Others who shrank from Satan's handiwork might sail off to Holland or the New World, or wherever; the Puritan could not separate himself from sin because he had a commission similar to the Jesuits' to fight the good fight. According to the English Puritan preachers, the business of the Christian was relentless war against the forces of evil.

Christ as the first new man, rather than in the manger or on the cross, was the meaningful Christ to them. Thus both Easter and Christmas were stricken from their calendar as pagan celebrations. In the eternal war with Satan, the preachers, as the special intelligence branch of the Christian armies, sought to persuade their congregations to arm in time, to deploy effectively, and to close ranks. Unconditional surrender was not to be hoped for, because this was England, not heaven.

Evil and this world were coterminous. But out of His mercy God would justify and regenerate and sanctify those whom He arbitrarily chose. God's soldiers would be formed from those who had faith as a result of their prior election by the Lord. Because evil was universal, was in the flesh, God's grace was unmerited and free. Winthrop put it this way: "I could only mourn, and weep to think of free mercy to such a vile wretch as I was."[2] With the strength that came from that grace, a mere man could stand with Christ and do battle in His name. In the autumn of 1617 Winthrop expressed his understanding of this, and implied that Christ would have men stand and fight, and not go sailing off in quest of quiet or peace:

> he which would have suer peace and joye in christianitye, must not ayme at a condition retyred from the world and free from temptations, but to knowe that the life which is most exercised with tryalls and temptations is the sweetest, and will prove the safeste. For such tryalls as fall within compasse of our callings it is better *to arme and withstande them* then to avoide and shunne them.[3]

So far from retiring from the world of affairs in order to protect his faith through isolation, Winthrop became increasingly involved in it. Following the lead of his father, he became a lawyer, and had been a justice of the peace at Groton since he was twenty-one years old. In 1619 he took over the lordship of the manor, while improving his legal practice in London. In mid-January, 1626, he received from his eldest son an urgent letter which announced that "one of the Atturnies of the Court of Wards is yesterday dead, so as now that place is void."[4] Winthrop was appointed as a new attorney of the Court of Wards and Liveries, and was frequently obliged to spend Court terms in London away from his beloved Margaret. In London he became more familiar with the interesting parliamentary developments of the late 1620's, and he had personally drafted three bills which may have been introduced but were never passed. In 1628 he was admitted to the Inner Temple.

When Charles I dissolved Parliament on March 10, 1629, Winthrop's growing fears for England and his place in it were undoubtedly confirmed. Just a month later, he wrote his wife a typical Puritan analysis of social problems, and provided later generations with a clue about the fateful decisions he was soon to make. He acknowledged that his own situation was comfortable even though the times were threatening. The Lord would not tolerate England's evil much longer:

> I am veryly persuaded, God will bring some heavye Affliction upon this lande, & that speedylye: but be of good comfort, the hardest that can come shall be a meanes to mortifie this bodye of corruption,

which is a thousand tymes more dangerous to us then any outward tribulation, & to bring us into nearer comunion with our Lord Jesus Christ, & more assurance of his kingdome. If the Lord seeth it wilbe good for us, he will provide a shelter & a hidinge place for us & others.[5]

From that point on, Winthrop's concern for the welfare of his family and the spiritual health of the realm gave him little peace. "I thinke my Office is gone,"[6] he wrote Margaret, and soon after wrote again: "My office is gone, and my chamber, and I shall be a saver in them both."[7] He probably left his office at the Court of Wards and Liveries voluntarily, and it is certain that he was pleased to be quit of London with its odors of sin and despotism.

It is not clear when Winthrop decided to join the Massachusetts Bay Company, which Charles I had incorporated in March. John Endicott was already established at Naumkeag (Salem), and Matthew Cradock was already Governor of the Company. It was essential to Winthrop to understand the migration in terms other than as a utopian quest. It was important to explain the move as a planned attack on this world's pollution, not as a misguided attempt to avoid the necessary evil of the here and now. Should the move be misunderstood, the Puritans could be charged with the naive perfectionism which even they believed characterized the separatist Pilgrims already located at Plymouth. To remake the world by carrying the fight to another battleground was the articulate aim of these westward-looking Puritans.

The decision to leave England was not made under pressure. None of the members of the Company personally had felt religious persecution (Laud did not reach the primacy until 1633). Most of the directors were physically comfortable and some possessed great wealth. They were afraid of the emerging political situation, but it had not yet affected them. The decision was made on the basis of a prediction of a worsening situation. Though they were neither persecuted nor impoverished, they feared that oppression was coming. On the strength of that guess they committed themselves to a hazardous ocean crossing, to abandoning the manicured lawns and rolling hills of manors like Groton in order to face a raw wilderness with its unknown animals and savages. Winthrop thought he saw uncontrovertible hints about the blackness of England's future;

and, after all, it took but one serpent to endanger the entire Garden, and he believed that England would soon be overrun with snakes.

Characteristically, Winthrop worked out an elaborate explanation and justification of his decision to sell Groton and leave England. He found his own participation in the migration relatively easy to explain. He reasoned that he was indispensable to the Company, that God seemed to approve, that his income had been halved now that his sons had come of age, and that his family and friends also approved.

Rationalizing the entire venture was a more serious and difficult problem. Its solution would provide the basic meaning of the migration, its relationship to the fight against sin in England, and, therefore, the basis on which he could himself participate. He listed eight arguments that proved to his own satisfaction that the entire migration was a legitimate affair, that it would constitute service to the Lord. He said that planting a truly reformed church in the wilderness would be a barrier to the kingdom of the Antichrist which the Jesuits were constructing there, and that God provided the New World as a refuge for those who were to be saved from the general desolation of Europe's churches. He argued, thirdly, that England could no longer sustain a general prosperity while, next, he said that it was growing increasingly difficult to keep up with the Joneses: "We are growne to that height of Intemperance in all excesse of Ryot, as no mans estate all most will suffice to keep sayle with his equalls."[8] Ministers and teachers had grown corrupt and, instead of improving children, infected them with their own disease. Sixthly, the Lord gave the entire earth to men, and it was therefore folly to remain in one place when another and fairer land was available. There was no better or more honorable Christian work than to assist a church in its infancy, and the migration would constitute such assistance. And, finally, he suggested that the participation of godly and wealthy men in the severities of the enterprise would inspire others to respect and perhaps themselves join with the Company.

To the charge that the migration would hasten the advent of disaster in England by drawing off so many good men, Winthrop answered that the numbers actually going would be small in comparison with those who remained. He noted the telling objection that men had been for a long time predicting disaster and yet they were still safe. Would it not be wiser to wait and see the actual outcome of events, and leave when and if necessary, than to make a premature and fateful judgment on the relatively slim basis of fear for the future? The answer he gave provides the best single statement of the sense of foreboding doom that was characteristic of the entire Company: "It is like that this consideration made the Churches beyonde the seas . . . to sitt still at home, and not look out for shelter while they might have founde it: but the woefull spectacle of their ruine, may teache us more wisdome, to avoyde the plague when it is foreseene, and not to tarrye, as they did, till it overtake us."[9]

There were further challenges to which he felt it necessary to respond. It was objected that England still continued to be fruitful, and he answered that "our superfluities excepted" it was reasonable to expect like or greater abundance in the New World. But why talk of this? "When we are in our graves it wilbe all one to have lived in plentye or penurye, whither we had dyed in a bedd of downe, or a lock of strawe."[10] He admitted that it was a dangerous undertaking, but "Suche ob[jection] savours to muche of the flesh." Security could not be guaranteed even in England and, in any case, it was all in God's care.

He seems to have been especially concerned about the charge that the Puritans would be stealing land from the Indians. It had been argued that the land belonged to the Indians, "other sonnes of Adam," and with what justification could the Puritans take it? "That which is com[mon] to all is proper to none, these salvadge peoples ramble over muche lande without title or property; 2: there is more then enough for them and us; 3: God hathe consumed the natives with a miraculous plague, whereby a greate parte of the Country is left voyde of Inh[abita]ntes. 4: We shall come in with good leave of the natives."[11] The necessity of resolving the problem of the Indians perhaps blinded Winthrop to the obvious casuistry of his argument.

It was also pointed out that other colonies had failed, and that on the basis of their example it was prudent to expect a similar failure in Massachusetts Bay. But, Winthrop answered, immediate success indicated nothing; in time perhaps even Virginia might prove successful. He thought that other colonies were incomparable to the Puritan enterprise because the purpose of the others "was carnall and not religious; they aymed cheifly at profitt, and not the propagating of Religion. 2: they used unfitt instrumentes, a multitude of Rude and misgoverned persons the verye scomme of the lande. 3: they did not establish a right forme of Gover[n]ment."[12] The example of hardship in Virginia, so far from justifying a prediction of failure, "hathe taught all other plantations to prevent the like occasions."[13]

The extent of his commitment may be assessed on the basis of his willingness to meet quite genuine danger and hardship with open eyes. He recognized that the civilized and protected lives of the stockholders in England had not been designed to produce pioneers. Winthrop knew that living in a wigwam would be a sorry substitute for Groton manor. But, "if we have suffic[ient] to fill the belly and clothe the back, the difference in quality may a little displease us, but it cannot hurt us." The expected trial of the flesh might produce desirable spiritual consequences: "it may be God will by this meanes bringe us to repent of our Intemperance here at home, and so cure us of that disease, which sendes many amongst us to hell. so he carried his people into the wildernesse, and made them forgett the fleshepottes of Egipt which was some pinch to them indeed, but he disposed it to their good, in the ende."[14]

Was not the expectation of success based on an expectation of a miracle, and was that not tempting God? He did not think so because the Company was taking "ordinarye meanes of safety and supplye." Expecting life to be either easy or sure in Europe tempted God just as much. No miracle was expected, but "though miracles be ceased, yet we may expecte a more then ordinarye blessing from God upon all lawfull meanes, where the work is the Lordes, and he is sought in it accordinge to his will: for it is usuall with him to increase the strength of the meanes, or to weaken them as he is pleased, or displeased with the Instrumentes and the Action: and yet bothe without miracle."[15]

The intellectual problems out of the way as far as Winthrop was concerned, there was now nothing left but to complete the other preparations. He signed the Agreement at Cambridge in the late summer of 1629, in which he and the eleven other signers pledged themselves to "be ready in our persons . . . to embarke for the said plantacion by the first of march next . . . to the end to passe the Seas . . . to inhabite and continue in new England."[16] After this commitment Winthrop was more and more absorbed in the affairs of the Company, so that he complained to Margaret: "I am so exceedingly streightened in tyme, as I canot write to thee wth any content."[17]

Unwilling to leave their future to chance, these Puritans exploited what must have been an oversight on the part of those who had drafted the Charter, the unprecedented failure to specify the location of the Company. They decided, as the Agreement at Cambridge said, that they would migrate, "Provided always that before the last of September next the whole governement together with the Patent for the said plantacion bee first by an order of Court legally transferred and established to remayne with us and others which shall inhabite upon the said plantacion."[18]   That decision entailed more than perhaps they knew themselves.   It meant that the Company and its members would remain together; that direct control by English officials would be hindered by three thousand miles of the Atlantic; that the Company, moved to the location of its affairs, would be a relatively autonomous state outside a state, with vast grants of land and power. It meant that the head and body of the corporation would be fused into a body politic, organic, and integral. Now there would be little chance that the Company would fall into unfriendly and impious hands.   That decision meant that these men would be their own masters.

Now, clearly, the officers of the Company would have to decide to sail themselves; since Cradock wanted to remain in England, a new election to the governorship was necessary. Winthrop's steadily growing prestige, along with his success in helping to manage the Company's affairs, made him the likely choice.   He told his wife the news, the heart of which, characteristically, was neutralized in a parenthetical phrase: "So it is that [it] hath pleased the Lorde to call me to a further trust in this businesse of the plantation, then either I expected or finde my selfe fitt for (beinge chosen by the Company to be their Governor) the onely thinge that I have comforte of in it is, that heerby I have assurance that my charge is of the Lorde and that he hath called me to this worke."[19]   The band of brethren was in his hands.

It now remained only to embrace their wives, gather up their provisions, and board the ships.   On April 7, 1630, while the *Arbella* was still riding in Yarmouth waters, the directors fired one final shot in the hope of convincing those who cared that the Massachusetts Bay Company was not guilty of separatism: "wee are not of those that dreame of perfection in this world. . . . wee leave it [England] not therefore, as loathing that milk wherewith we were nourished there, but blessing God for the parentage and education, as members of the same body shall alwayes rejoyce in her good."[20]　When the wind picked up and the *Arbella* moved out, Winthrop was the Governor, not merely of another ordinary trading company, but of a body of people who were to be a body politic, with the wherewithal to defy the Crown and might of England, if need be.　The direction of the Company was in Winthrop's hands, and the intellectual equipment he brought to the task helped to shape the course of things to come.

It is a mistake to think that Winthrop's view of politics was separate from his other views.　His intellectual system was a political theology; its purpose was the Christianization of the state.　The westward-moving Puritans thought that they had a special commission from God to establish a Zion in the wilderness, a commonwealth whose foundation and purpose was Christian.　It was the intention to establish a community made up of persons whose behavior at least would appear to be Christian.　But in order to acknowledge man's inability to tell whether mere behavior reflected the real condition of the soul, persons who acted as Christians were called "visible saints."　Such persons might not be saints in the all-seeing eyes of God, but because men were limited by their senses, they were compelled to acknowledge that no mortal could read the secrets of any soul.　In terms of policy, however, appearance was sufficient.　If men would act as Christians the purposes of the migration would be accomplished.　Visible saints might never sit at God's right hand, but then they also would probably never seriously disturb the peace of Zion.　In order to create a community where law and security would prevail, the visible saints covenanted themselves together so that God's will in civil as well as religious matters would be implemented.　The idea of a unified political organism—a corporation—was the basis of Winthrop's political ideas, as it was also the basis of Congregational church polity.　"It is," he wrote, "of the nature and essence of every society to be knitt together by some Covenant, either expressed or implyed."[21]

While in mid-ocean, on board the *Arbella*, Winthrop composed his single most important statement, "A Modell of Christian Charity," a tract designed to show the unity of the civil state that was to be operative when God had allowed the passengers safe passage, when the business corporation called the Massachusetts Bay Company had become transformed into a political body. In order to prove the organic nature of the state, Winthrop was obliged to defend the various ranks men held in society, a class system. He had to show how political and economic differences among men were centripetal forces tending to the greater cohesion of the political body: "God Almightie in his most holy and wise providence hath soe disposed of the Condicion of mankinde, as in all times some must be rich some poore, some highe and eminent in power and dignitie; others meane and in subjeccion."[22]

There were three basic reasons for this supposedly necessary social stratification.

1. "The variety and difference of the Creatures" conformed to God's creation in general, and testified to His power and glory.

2. The heterogeneity of man's condition gave God "more occasion to manifest the worke of his Spirit: first, upon the wicked in moderateing and restraineing them: soe that the riche and mighty should not eate upp the poore, nor the poore, and dispised rise upp against theire superiours, and shake off theire yoake." The simple existence of the saved and damned gave God a wider canvas on which to labor.

3. The fact of wealth and poverty meant "That every man might have need of other, and from hence they might be all knitt more nearly together in the Bond of brotherly affeccion: from hence it appeares plainely that noe man is made more honourable then another or more wealthy etc. out of any perticuler and singuler respect to himselfe but for the glory of his Creator and the Common good of the Creature, Man; Therefore God still reserves the propperty of these guifts to himselfe."[23]

Variety, meaning economic and social stratification, was decreed by the Lord both for His own purposes and out of His love of man. Those who benefited from the inequality, those who were rich and powerful, as well as those who suffered, must be made to realize that life on earth required masters and servants, that both were creatures of God, and that each had obligations to the other. With such realization, the precondition of an organic community would be met.

Property and power were gifts of God to men, given in order to help them help others in a mutual social covenant. When the community was in danger men must act "with more enlargement towards others and lesse respect towards our selves, and our owne right hence it was that in the primitive Churche they sold all [and] had all things in Common, neither did any man say that that which he possessed was his owne."[24] Since wealth and might were given to individuals for the sake of the political corporation, the needs of the corporation must take precedence over the needs or desires of any individual.

Love was the ligament which held the parts of this political and social body together. "The diffinition which the Scripture gives us of love is this [:] Love is the bond of perfection." Every body consisted of parts, and whatever it was that held the parts together "gives the body its perfeccion, because it makes eache parte soe contiguous to other as thereby they doe mutually participate with eache other."[25] The inequality of men constituted the parts of the body politic, which parts were held together, from man's point of view, by love.

How was it, however, that depraved and sinful men could love their neighbors as themselves? How and why would the sinner turn the other cheek? After the Fall, "Adam Rent in himselfe from his Creator, rent all of his posterity allsoe one from another, whence it comes that every man is borne with this principle in him, to love and seeke himselfe onely and thus a man continueth till Christ comes and takes possession of the soule, and infuseth another principle [:] love to God and our brother." Love of self stood between Adam and Christ, but with regeneration, the conversion of the "old man Adam" to "the new Creature," the Holy Spirit "gathers together the scattered bones or perfect old man Adam and knitts them into one body againe in Christ."[26] Clearly, then, the love which was necessary for the creation and operation of the body politic could come only when that body was made up of the converted. Since the right kind of love was a result of regeneration, it was necessary, from Winthrop's viewpoint, to limit membership in the corporation to the visible saints, since that was as close as mere men could get to actual saints. A sinner in the body inevitably and naturally would tend to endanger the whole.

Winthrop applied this theory of the organic community to the migration in four different categories: persons, work, end, and means. The individual persons had become a single body in their professed membership in Christ. The immigrants as persons were hopefully actual as well as visible saints, members of Augustine's kind of City of God. "In which respect onely though wee were absent from eache other many miles, and had our imploymentes as farre distant, yet wee ought to account our selves knitt together by this bond of love, and live in the exercise of it if wee would have comforte of our being in Christ."[27] The work itself was the seeking of "a place of Cohabitation and Consorteshipp under a due forme of Government both civill and ecclesiasticall." Such a work was based on "a mutual consent through a speciall overruleing providence," and it assumed the primacy of public over private welfare: "In such cases as this the care of the publique must oversway all private respects, by which not only conscience, but meare Civill pollicy doth binde us; for it is a true rule that perticuler estates cannott subsist in the ruine of the publique." The end, or purpose, of the migration was "to serve the Lord and worke out our Salvacion under the power and purity of his holy Ordinances." And, finally, the means necessary for these persons, work, and purpose were extraordinary, because the work itself was. It was not enough to practice Christianity merely as it had been and was practiced in England: "the same must wee doe and more allsoe where wee goe: That which the most in theire Churches maineteine as a truthe in profession onely, wee must bring into familiar and constant practice."[28]

The special commission which God had given to the immigrants obviously implied privileges. But any chosen people also had to face the consequences of their uniqueness, consequences which were awesome. God expected unique behavior from His unique people. He would forgive less because He rightfully expected more. By creating an organic community, Winthrop said, those frail humans could live up to the terms of their divine commission: "wee must be knitt together in this worke as one man . . . our

Community as members of the same body." Only when the persons realized that God had covenanted with the community and that the welfare of each therefore depended on the welfare of the body politic, would each member find it possible to feel that love of neighbor which was the cohesive of the corporation. If the persons could truly covenant with each other in the interest of forming a political body, then men would truly enjoy peace and plenty. In language which was to reverberate throughout American history, Winthrop explained that, as a result of a genuine social covenant, "wee shall finde that the God of Israell is among us, when tenn of us shall be able to resist a thousand of our enemies, when hee shall make us a prayse and glory, that men shall say of succeeding plantacions: the lord make it like that of New England: for wee must Consider that wee shall be as a Citty upon a Hill, the eies of all people are uppon us."[29]

Thus, according to Winthrop, his band of brethren was involved in a mission of cosmic significance. They were not merely fleeing from an anticipated persecution or searching for greener pastures. They were involved in a test case which would determine whether men could live on earth according to the will of the Lord. The Reformation in Europe had started the good work, but everywhere, including England, it had been frustrated. Winthrop believed that it had been given to these immigrants to find out whether they were of sufficient faith to carry that work on, to bring the Reformation to full fruition. Should they succeed, their outpost in the wilderness would "be as a Citty upon a Hill," a moral example to all the world. Should they succeed, their example would help even Europe to begin the work anew, to try to rid itself of the Antichrist. Should they succeed, the place where they planted would become the hub of the universe, whose light and wisdom would radiate out in all directions for the utility and comfort of men and the glory of God.

It is necessary, in order to share their mood, to think of this Great Migration not as some merely human act, undertaken with whatever motives, but to think of it as a necessary step leading to nothing less than the redemption of the entire world. Should they fail, their failure too would radiate outward, and the human race would know that a divine opportunity had been lost, that a chance for progress toward God had been missed. Thus it was that Winthrop thought of this first wave of immigrants not as mere human beings, not as mere colonists of England, but as God's agents, a community with a unique and compelling commission from God to build that city on a hill. Whether they could build properly depended on whether their covenants with each other would be strong enough to support a political order that would be organically whole, a political body which was indeed one body, with one head, and all the member parts in their proper locations, performing their proper functions. Mankind's destiny was at stake.

Merely coming into Massachusetts constituted an implicit acceptance of the covenant, for it was clear that all who entered must obey the laws established by those whose consent had been more explicit. That Winthrop viewed the political corporation as an organic whole, as indissoluble, is proved by his refusal to admit the moral right of men to leave the colony. Of course there were many who left, and Winthrop, displaying an unfortunate and not uncharacteristic excess of righteousness, vindictively recounted the evils which had befallen those who had left and had spoken critically of the Bay saints: "One had a daughter that presently ran mad, and two other of his daughters, being under ten years of age, were discovered to have been often abused by divers lewd persons, and filthiness in his family."[30] Individuals had covenanted themselves and had agreed to migrate because, among other reasons, others had done so too. The Agreement at Cambridge had been such a covenant; it had specified that the signers agreed "that this whole adventure growes upon the joynt confidence we have in each others fidelity and resolucion herein, so as no man of us would have adventured it without assurance of the rest."[31] Each of the signers then pledged himself as a Christian to be ready to sail for the New World at a specified date, provided that the organic unity of the enterprise was protected by the unusual transplantation of the Charter and Company with the migrants. Was not the nature of each man's political covenant altered, and not by his own choice or act, whenever any man left the authority of the nation?

> Much disputation there was about liberty of removing for outward advantages, and all ways were sought for an open door to get out at; but it is to be feared many crept out at a broken wall. For such as come together into a wilderness, where are nothing but wild

beasts and beastlike men, and there confederate together in civil and church estate, whereby they do, implicitly at least, bind themselves to support each other, and all of them that society, whether civil or sacred, whereof they are members, how they can break from this without free consent, is hard to find, so as may satisfy a tender or good conscience in time of trial. Ask thy conscience, if thou wouldst have plucked up thy stakes, and brought thy family 3000 miles, if thou hadst expected that all, or most, would have forsaken thee there.[32]

In the internal affairs of the colony every effort was made to discourage notions about the primacy or independence of the individual, whether in theological, political, social, or economic matters. The law of the colony made it illegal for an individual to live alone; everyone had to be or to become a member of a household or family. The Daniel Boone type was considered as dangerous to the organic community as were mavericks like Roger Williams and mystics like Mistress Anne Hutchinson. The nation was made up of a series of covenants, ascending from the basic and essential covenant between a man and God, to the family, church, and state, and an uncovenanted or otherwise exotic individual would be a threat to the entire structure.

Winthrop's justification of authority in the state was determined by his views of the meaning of liberty. No man in society must be allowed that kind of natural liberty which "is common to man with beasts and other creatures." This kind of liberty was possible only for an individual outside of society, beyond a covenant, and gave that individual "liberty to do what he lists; it is a liberty to evil as well as to good." It was the kind of liberty that Winthrop thought to be "incompatible and inconsistent with authority, and [that] cannot endure the least restraint of the most just authority." The exercise of this natural liberty had to place the individual outside of the properly constituted society, and made of the individual, as Aristotle had said, either more or less than human. God was at liberty, except insofar as He decided to limit Himself to the terms of a covenant, but when a man tried to step outside of the covenant he did not rise to godhood but became "worse than brute beasts."[33]

The kind of liberty that was proper to men was available only in society and under a covenant. Winthrop called this civil, federal, or moral liberty, and said that it "is the proper end and object of authority, and cannot subsist without it; and it is a liberty to that only which is good, just and honest." That kind of liberty was compatible with the dependence of man on man in the Christian corporation, and was consistent with the love necessary to political success. "This liberty is maintained and exercised in a way of subjection to authority; it is of the same kind of liberty wherewith Christ hath made us free."[34] The members of the political body were free to do good, and would do so by obeying lawfully constituted authority. In other words, the individual as an individual could never have moral liberty, while the individual as a member of a body politic could have. As a member, the socialized individual would accept social restraints as necessary to peaceful life on earth: "if you stand for your natural corrupt liberties, and will do what is good in your own eyes, you will not endure the least weight of authority, but will murmur, and oppose, and be always striving to shake off that yoke; but if you will be satisfied to enjoy such civil and lawful liberties, such as Christ allows you, then will you quietly and cheerfully submit unto that authority which is set over you, in all the administrations of it, for your own good."[35]

The lesser members of the political body had the liberty of counsel, and the magistrates had the duty to listen to reason: "If we [magistrates] fail at any time, we hope we shall be willing (by God's assistance) to hearken to good advice from any of you, or in any other way of God."[36] Moral liberty thus could only be maintained so long as the magisterial authority was protected. Both must stand or fall together, and the desire to limit authority was, perhaps unknowingly, a desire also to destroy moral liberty and return to that natural liberty in which welfare and safety were continually jeopardized. In the most extreme terms, Winthrop's argument reads like this: Any individual who attacked properly constituted authority sought a natural liberty whose reward must be danger and death. Thus banishment as punishment for those like Williams, Wheelwright, and Mistress Hutchinson who did not accept the constituted authority of Massachusetts was peculiarly fitting in that it drove them into the untamed wilderness, the most appropriate setting for the exercise of natural liberty.

As men did not have a moral right voluntarily to leave the colony, so Winthrop was convinced that the magistrates had the right to screen applicants for admission into the Bay. Implicit in his argument was the notion that the divisive Antinomian controversy might never have happened if Wheelwright and Mistress Hutchinson had been kept out in the first place, and that in the future such conflict could be avoided by an exercise of such magisterial power. "Antinomian" was the label placed on those who rejected the more legalistic Puritan criteria of sanctification in favor of a more direct and mystical inner light.   The Antinomians, led by Mrs. Hutchinson and Wheelwright and assisted nervously by John Cotton, charged that several of the leading ministers of the Bay had themselves not been converted.   The General Court brought the leaders to trial and maneuvered Mrs. Hutchinson to the point where she confessed to a direct communication from God.   She was banished from the Bay, eventually made her way to New Netherland, and there was killed by Indians.

One of the consequences of the action against Wheelwright was an order of the General Court, in May, 1637, "to keep out all such persons as might be dangerous to the commonwealth, by imposing a penalty upon all such as should retain any [such dangerous persons], etc., above three weeks, which should not be allowed by some of the magistrates."[37]   Those against whom this order was directed protested, and Winthrop wrote a defense of the Court's order.   In so doing he found it necessary to explicate some of his basic political principles:

1. No common weale can be founded but by free consent.
2. The persons so incorporating have a public and relative interest each in other, and in the place of their co-habitation and goods, and laws, etc. and in all the means of their wellfare so as none other can claime priviledge with them but by free consent.
3. The nature of such incorporation tyes every member thereof to seeke out and entertaine all means that may conduce to the wellfare of the bodye, and to keepe off whatsoever doth appeare to tend to theire damage.
4. The wellfare of the whole is [not] to be put to apparent hazard for the advantage of any particular members.[38]

A group of people freely consented to form themselves into a political society "for their mutual safety and welfare."   This consent to subject himself to rule and law was granted by each individual in order that he might be more secure than he could be in that natural state which he shared with beasts and which would make him beastlike. The unified political body that was created by the consent of its citizens had a right to protect itself against the introduction of elements that would subvert the safety and welfare for the realization of which that body had been created in the first place. It was therefore just, according to Winthrop, that the political body of Massachusetts Bay inquire into the beliefs and convictions of all who desired to enter. If some righteous one who should have been admitted was denied entrance, the violation of justice could "not . . . be imputed to the law, but to those who are betrusted with the execution of it."[39] The entire argument was summed up by asserting that the exclusiveness of the Bay was justified by the desire for that political tranquillity which was thought essential for the practice of true reformed religion. In insisting on the authority of the magistrates to screen candidates for admission, Winthrop believed he was doing no more than defending a relatively harmless technique for keeping the Serpent out of the Garden.

To the objection that Massachusetts was a corporation created by the King, and that the colony had no right to exclude any of the King's subjects, Winthrop, probably in August, 1637, answered that "that which the King is pleased to bestow upon us, and we have accepted, is truly our owne."[40] Because the Bay Company accepted the Charter (and transferred it to the New World) the corporation was its own to do with as best suited its own purposes. "The King," Winthrop reasoned, "haveing given all the land within certaine limitts to the patentees and their associates, cannot send others to possesse that which he hath granted before."[41] Had the implications of this position been drawn out at the time, charges of treason against Winthrop and his colony might have been made. Here, Winthrop drew back from logic just at that point where it might do damage to his cause.

Another objection to Winthrop's argument was that the magistrates' power to admit or reject an applicant was unregulated and therefore despotic. Of course he denied the charge, saying that the magistrates were not unregulated because they were church members and bound to live as Christians, because they were freemen and bound by their oath to contribute to the welfare of the state, and because they were also bound by the magisterial oath to do justice and seek the general welfare. The magistrate, in other words, did not have unlimited discretion because of the church covenant and civil oaths which he had taken, and because, as a man of conscience, he would surely honor his pledge. If that conscience proved somewhat deficient, the church or the state, or both, could force him back to the path of righteousness.

The explicit political covenant, or contract, was the instrument by which discrete persons came together and formed themselves into a corporation in order to secure their mutual safety and welfare. But the anterior covenant—that between the individual and God, the covenant of grace—was the necessary antecedent to the formation of a Christian commonwealth, as it was to the creation of individual churches. Government was an institution favored by God to help men live together, if not in absolute brotherhood, then at least without the constant fear of being murdered or, what was worse, being prevented from practicing true reformed religion. God had left the particular form of government for men to determine, because problems varied from time to time and place to place, but the institution itself was of divine origin.

There was no doubt that God stood behind the whole enterprise, or that its success depended upon the fidelity of the citizens to the covenants of grace and of society. Temporal success was the reward to the nation for heeding God's will. It seemed perfectly reasonable to the orthodox Puritans to protect the second covenant by limiting political liberties only to those who were presumably under the first, the covenant of grace. "The way of God," Winthrop wrote, "hath always beene to gather his churches out of the world; now, the world, or civill state, must be raised out of the churches."[42] Church membership became the prerequisite for freemanship, for full political rights and privileges, and since church membership was extended only to those who could demonstrate the validity of their conversion to the satisfaction of the congregation, political liberties could be similarly extended by the General Court. Only the visible saints could be full citizens of the wilderness Zion, though some of those saints chose not to obtain complete citizenship from the Court.

Granting freemanship to church members was not a restriction of the franchise; the Charter had defined a freeman as a stockholder, or one the stockholders themselves thought fit. In a short time there were only eight men who could qualify under this definition, and they were all magistrates. Extending freemanship to those of the visible saints who applied for it thus extended the terms of the Charter in ways probably never dreamed of in England, but in ways which supported Winthrop's ideas about an organic Christian corporation.

Initially Winthrop kept the Charter secret in a special box because, he said, in the beginning of the settlement, there was so much other and more urgent business that there was precious little concern with matters of government. Anyone, he thought, "would easly allowe us pardon of that, or greater errors (which are incident to all Plantations, in their beginninges) especially seeinge our Readinesse to reforme them, and to conforme to the right Rules of our Government."[43]   Extending freemanship to include those of the visible saints approved by the Court conformed nicely to Winthrop's ideas about the political necessity of that kind of love which only the regenerate could feel. But with one foot in the door, the freemen quickly requested—demanded—further rights and privileges. One of the ways they sought to increase their power was to call for a reduction of magisterial authority, and this eventually led to the establishment of a two-house legislature.

The events leading to the creation of America's first bicameral legislature were symptomatic of the growing dissatisfaction of the freemen with their largely passive role in the state. They concluded that power would have to be taken at the expense of the magistrates. The ruling elite, led by Winthrop, tried to resist in a number of different ways. The controversy finally centered around whether or not the magistrates should have a veto power over the actions of the deputies who were the representatives of the freemen. In an extended document that Winthrop wrote in 1643 he argued that the magistrates always had and should continue to have such a negative vote, that any other course would alter the nature of government in the Bay. He began the argument by asserting that the magistrates' right to the negative vote had been authorized by the Charter, and then typically used the occasion further to refine his ideas about the civil state of Massachusetts.

This conflict over the magisterial veto was no small matter, he thought, because it touched the nerve of the Bay's civil polity. The existence of the veto power helped to define the government of Massachusetts, and was therefore considered by Winthrop to be "essentiall and fundamentall." "If the Neg: vo: were taken away," he wrote, "our Government would be a meere Democratie, where as now it is mixt,"[44] a form Calvin had earlier approved. There was general agreement that the deputies represented the democratic part of Massachusetts' government, and to allow them unchecked authority would result in the creation of an unmixed democracy for which, Winthrop argued, "we should have no warrant in scripture . . . : there was no such Government in Israell." To establish a simple democracy would mean, he said, that "we should heerby voluntaryly abase our selves, and deprive our selves of that dignity, which the providence of God hath putt upon us: which is a manifest breach of the 5th Com[mandmen]t for a Democratie is, among most Civill nations, accounted the meanest and worst of all formes of Government: and therefore in writers, and Historyes doe recorde, that it hath been allwayes of least continuance and fullest of troubles."[45] To establish a political system based on notions of human equality would fly in the face of Winthrop's earlier defense of a class system designed by God for His glory and out of His love for mankind. God had made, Winthrop reiterated, "(not the disparitye onely but) even the contrarietye of parts, in many bodyes, to be the meanes of the upholding and usefullness thereof."[46] Such a political system would violate the pattern of authority explicit in the commandment to honor one's father and mother. The transfer of property and power that would be necessary to convert the Bay into a simple democracy would thus, according to Winthrop, be criminal, unnatural, and sinful.

His rejection of simple democracy did not lead Winthrop to reject what he considered to be the rightful democractic powers of the deputies, who, he wrote, "joyned with the magistrates in any generall Court have (together with them) all the power legislative, and the chiefe power Juditiall, of this body Politick."[47] Neither group had any power without the other, and it was simply wrong to assert, as some had, that the deputies were in reality magistrates themselves. The deputies had the same liberties as the body of freemen they represented, and the fact of their having only liberty, not authority, "makes them no otherwise subjecte, then accordinge to their will, and Covenant."[48] A disturbance in the arrangement of the various parts of the body politic would destroy the mutual consent of the parts to accept their disposition in the interest of the health of the organism. To put a foot in place of a head would produce an unsightly, not to say illegitimate, body.

One of the objections to Winthrop's position on the magisterial veto was made on the grounds that "the greatest power is in the people." Winthrop agreed, but changed the terms: "originally and vertually it is: but when they [freemen] have chosen them Judges, etc: their Juditiary power is actually in those to whom they have committed it and those are their magistr[ate]s." The freemen had the right to choose and having chosen had the obligation to obey. This was part of the fundamental law of the organic corporation, and as such could not be altered by the deputies: "thoughe all Lawes, that are superstructive, may be altered by the representative bodye of the Com[mon] w[ealth] yet they have not power to alter any thinge which is fundamentall."[49]   Since he defined fundamental law as that which distinguished one government from another, he was obliged to view those constitutional arrangements which best characterized the mixed aristocracy of the Bay as fundamental. In this connection he believed that the magisterial veto was a necessary defense against the encroachments of the steadily more assertive freemen. Those assertions, if allowed to become policy, would destroy the political theology of the commonwealth by turning from rule by the wise to rule by the most. As Winthrop searched his Bible and his heart and, be it said, his self-interest, he could find no authority for such a transformation.

The oath taken by the specific magistrate, and accepted by those who had called him to office, was the explicit and renewable covenant between rulers and ruled. That oath, as Winthrop understood it, meant "that we shall govern you and judge your causes by the rules of God's laws and our own, according to our best skill."[50]   A magistrate could be called to account for a failure of faith because that would be a violation of his oath; he was not accountable for failures of skill or ability because he was human and thus necessarily deficient, and the electors, knowing this beforehand, still elected him to office. Yet it was the superior skill of the magistrate which, presumably, had led to his election and which justified his authority. When it was clear that the magistrate's will was evil, the electors had the duty to turn him out of office, not even waiting for the annual election meeting of the General Court. Short of this failure of faith and will, the people must suffer his rule because they had chosen him, and once elected he ruled in God's name.   Having exercised their liberty to choose the man, the freemen had given that man the divine authority inherent in the office.   The magistrates, Winthrop announced to the General Court, "have our authority from God, in way of an ordinance, such as hath the image of God eminently stamped upon it, the contempt and violation whereof hath been vindicated with examples of divine vengeance."[51]   He thought that the aristocratic form of government was justified by its existence in the Bible, and by the notion of the divinity of the office of magistracy, if not of each particular magistrate.   That magistrates "are Gods upon earthe,"[52] meant that any resistance to lawful authority which was exercised under a covenant could not be justified and would be punished by God in His heaven and by His magisterial agents on earth.

In 1644, when Winthrop was the Deputy Governor, the deputies once more called for abolition of the magistrates' veto power, and argued that the magistrates had no lawful power when the Court was not in session except that power which the full Court of deputies and magistrates had earlier and explicitly granted. Winthrop accurately viewed this as a revolutionary move designed to transfer authority from the magistrates to the people, a revolution which the deputies disguised by charging the magistrates with arbitrary government.   Even though the church elders sided with the magistrates, Winthrop felt compelled to answer the charge, and he wrote and circulated a "Discourse on Arbitrary Government."   He defined an arbitrary government as one in which the governors assumed powers that properly belonged only to God. "Arbitrary Goverment," he wrote, "is, where a people have men sett over them without their choyce, or allowance: who have power, to Governe them, and Judge their Causes without a Rule." A governor who ruled without either popular consent or a published and known set of laws was not merely a tyrant, but was also a sinner.   The government of Massachusetts, according to Winthrop, was not arbitrary for three reasons: "1: by the foundation of it: 2: by the positive Lawes thereof: 3: by the constant practice."[53]

The royal charter was the foundation of Massachusetts' government.   That charter created a body politic, a corporation, and arranged the "power and Motions" of the various members of the whole body "as might best conduce to the preservation, and good of the wholl bodye." There were two political members created by the charter; the governor "not as a person, but as a State," including the deputy governor and eighteen assistants, and the company or freemen. Authority was granted to the government and liberty was granted to the freemen. "The power of liberty" was "not a bare passive capacitye of freedome or immunity, but such a Libertye, as hath power to Acte upon the chiefe meanes of its owne wellfare."[54] The power of that liberty was made manifest in two ways, election and counsel. The freemen annually elected all governmental officials, and through their deputed agents were required to give their advice and consent to all legislative action.

Such liberties did not allow any intrusion upon the proper authority of the government. Winthrop made clear, immediately following his discussion of the liberties of the freemen, that ". . . if all were Governors, or magistrates, and none lefte, to be an objecte of Government . . . our state should be a meer Democratie." He cited the charter as proof that the authority of "this Government is not Arbitrary in the foundation of it, but Regulated in all the partes of it."[55] The government was, he said, "a mixt Aristocratie,"[56] was not arbitrary, and was regulated in all things.

He thought that the laws passed by the General Court in Massachusetts similarly proved that both the liberty of the freemen and the authority of the government had been respected. Winthrop recalled that in the spring of 1634 the powers of the Court were made explicit by the Court itself. In the annual election, to be held on the last Wednesday of the Easter Term, the freemen could reject any of the officers without showing cause; but any officer could be discharged at any session of the Court if the reasons for discharge were made explicit and proved.

Winthrop's final reason for insisting that the government of Massachusetts was not arbitrary was his opinion that the attempt to bring theory and practice into harmony had been usually successful. Since the Charter and the laws of the colony were just, and since "where any considerable obliquitye hathe been discerned, it hathe been soone brought to the Rule and redressed: for it is not possible in the infancye of a plantation, subjecte to so many and variable occurrents, to holde so exactly to Rules, as when a state is once setled."[57]

Turning then to the basic question of the content of "a Rule to walk by," the content of those laws which restrained or constrained the officers of the government, Winthrop declared that the "Rule is the Worde of God, and such conclusions and deductions, as are, or shalbe regularly drawne from thence."[58] It was of course not possible to legislate for every conceivable situation, but so long as the fundamental law or constitution had been carefully and piously drawn, the later necessary deductions from it might be similarly pious and therefore just. He noted that difficulties in old England were created "because they [English residents] shaped their Course too much by Politike and nationall prudence, and held not strictly to the Rules of Gods worde."[59] Massachusetts could escape the Lord's wrath if it would observe the Lord's word. The rewards of political expedience (which, in Massachusetts Bay, came increasingly to mean excessive religious toleration) seemed to be civil war. The rewards of political piety would surely—hopefully—be temporal success, measured by human standards and desires: peace and plenty and health.

It was clear that God could have outlined all the details of running a political economy had He chosen to do so. Instead of this detail, God "appointed Gov[ernmen]ts upon earthe, to be his vice-gerents."[60] Those governments, following the few but important hints that were included in the Bible, had the obligation to follow the divine precedents, to deduce wisely, with one eye on the Bible and the other on the particular society with which they were concerned. Just as the Lord did not prescribe all the prayers for the ministry, so He did not prescribe all legislation; total prescription in either case would have destroyed the ordinance of the office. "Judges are Gods upon earthe: therefore, in their Administrations, they are to holde forthe the wisdome and mercye of God (which are his Attributes) as well as his Justice: as occasion shall require, either in respecte of the qualitye of the person, or for a more generall good: or evident repentance, in some cases of less publ[ic] consequence, or avoydinge imminent danger to the state, and such like prevalent Considerations."[61]

Let it be clear that Winthrop did not lead governors or magistrates beyond the pale of theology. Puny, vicious, and impotent man could govern well only with divine assistance. Aided only by his natural reason, man would and could only make evil worse. "But . . . when occation required, God promised, to be present

in his owne Ordinance, to improve suche gifts as he should please
to conferre upon suche as he should call to place of Government."[62] The road to divine salvation and political success was the
same road, and each forward step on it could only be taken with
God's help.

Given Winthrop's concept of the organic Christian corporation
based on the consent of the members and limited to only the
visible saints, it followed logically that he should argue that any
man admitted into the corporation implicitly consented to abide
by majority rule, so long, of course, as that rule violated neither
religion nor the objective general welfare. No man who refused to
give implicit or explicit consent could be allowed to walk in the
saints' preserve. None should be allowed natural liberty; all would
be subject to magisterial authority, under which moral liberty could
flourish; and, in cases where numbers were relevant, majority rule
should decide (excepting always the opposition of a majority to the
magistrates). Any variation of these conditions would endanger
the state and therefore the church and therefore the individual
salvation of the saints themselves.

At the center of Winthrop's political thinking was his conviction
that some men were better than others—more pious, moral, and
wise: The best part of a community, he said, "is always the least,
and of the best part the wiser part is always the lesser,"[63] an idea
whose political implications can be traced backward to canon law
and forward throughout most of the colonial period of New England's
history. The first political requirement was to discover who those
wise and pious men were, and the second was to devise ways by
which they could wield sufficient but delimited power. He feared
political decisions reached in passion instead of cool reflection, and
he was convinced that reason and democracy were mutually exclusive, that mass participation in the political process necessarily
elicited the kind of bias that must damage the commonwealth. Even
assuming that one man was merely as good or bad as any other—
an assumption Winthrop could never make—still that man would
be unable to restrain his internal demons in a mass assembly, while
he could do so in a quiet committee meeting: "It is easye to judge,
that 30 or 40 distinct men, chosen out of all the countrye, and by
all reason as free from partialitye or prejudice as any other, may

give a more just sentence in any such cause upon deliberation and quiet discourse than a whole multitude upon the suddaine, when many may be thought not to heare what is proposed, and others not to understand it, and perchance the greater part in a heate and tumult, and when the weakest and worst member of the commonwealth adds as much weight to the sentence as the most godly and judicious."[64] His goal was to devise a government in which wisdom could assert itself over numbers.

Mere men could never do the job, he thought, as the entire history of the world and its calamities proved. It was a mistake to look for wisdom in the governments of the past, a mistake which had led even Nathaniel Ward, who, in 1641, had been selected without the permission of the magistrates to preach at a session of the Court, to separate politics and morality from religion. In his *Journal* Winthrop slapped Ward's wrist: "In his sermon he delivered many useful things, but in a moral and political discourse, grounding his propositions much upon the old Roman and Grecian governments, which sure is an error, for if religion and the word of God makes men wiser than their neighbors, and these times have the advantage of all that have gone before us in experience and observation, it is probable that by all these helps, we may better frame rules of government for ourselves than to receive others upon the bare authority of the wisdom, justice, etc. of those heathen commonwealths."[65] Political vice, like any other kind, came from man's hatred of God. The bloody record of paganism and of the Antichrist would come to an end when the saints in Massachusetts constructed a Christian commonwealth whose essential basis was the word of God, when this new Chosen People legislated and administered God's sovereign will.

In his rejection of Ward's classicism, Winthrop claimed that the secular past was simply irrelevant to Massachusetts Bay, and thus expressed another idea which was to grow and thrive in later America. The entire history of the real world, as read by Winthrop and his fellow Puritans, had been merely the fits and starts leading up to the cosmic climax of Boston's founding. Because the Bay saints were supposedly more deeply and truly pious than any other people in the world's history, they could build a unique society with a unique government. As radically new men they occupied a new world and would fashion their lives on earth in a new way. Their piety had lifted them out of human history, out of time. They argued that they were God's agents and, as such, were freed from the disabilities that had limited the achievements of the past. Only the sovereign will of God could make them creatures of time and subject them to the human failings that had caused the rise and fall of earlier nations.

Sovereignty, for Winthrop, was an attribute of God, and not of men, and most certainly not of the mass of men. If the voice of the people were the voice of God, it would be as a result of God's mysterious will, and not because of inherent qualities in men or society. The function of government, then, was to allow men to rule men through God, to prevent the raising of obstacles between God and man for the sinful and futile purpose of trying to free man from his covenant with God. Men could raise such an obstacle, but it would not keep those godless men from the jurisdiction of the omnipotent and ubiquitous God.

Because political success depended upon the society's adherence to the word of God, it followed that in a Christian corporation the clergy would have an important role. God had revealed part of His will in the Bible, and both the preacher and the politician were enjoined to obey His word. This did not mean that the clergy had or should have control of the state. The political system of Massachusetts has frequently been described as a theocracy, by which the rule of the clergy, not that of God, is meant. From Winthrop's point of view this would be an inaccurate designation because the magistrates had the only authority in the state. The clergy could not hold office, but could and frequently did give advice on political matters. So, in fact, did the freemen and their deputies, but this did not make Massachusetts a democracy. It is true that only church members were eligible for freemanship, and the clergy might try to control the franchise by trying to control church membership, but the whole church controlled admission into its body, not the clergy alone. Whether a given church member would be granted political liberties was determined by the General Court, not by the clergy: not all church members were freemen. In time the General Court could veto the ordination of an objectionable minister, and in the Body of Liberties of 1641 it was said that the government had the authority to supervise church matters, including matters concerning doctrine. Many activities that were supervised by the church in England were directed by the state in Massachusetts Bay, including the disposition of estates, marriage and divorce, recording of vital statistics, superintending of cemeteries, and burial practice (which included no religious ceremony of any kind). No church holidays were observed and the thanksgiving and fast days were regulated by the state. A minister's status continued only while his congregation maintained him in office. Professor E. S. Morgan has concluded that "of all the governments in the Western world at the time, that of early Massachusetts gave the clergy least authority."[66] Winthrop's own concept of a mixed aristocracy is more accurate than the standard concept of a theocracy.

The trial and sentencing of Mistress Hutchinson occasioned much dissatisfaction, and Winthrop heard a rumor that many from the Boston church were trying to persuade their church elders to call him to account. In the interest of preventing a public quarrel, and with the intent of defining the proper relationship between the church and the state, Winthrop wrote an "Essay Against the Power of the Church To Sit In Judgment On the Civil Magistracy." He began with the simple assertion that "The Scripture affords neither Rule nor example of any such power in the Church, but diverse against it." If the church had the authority to try magistrates, the church would become "the supreame Court in the Jurisdiction, and capable of all Appeales, and so in trueth meerly Antichrist, by being exalted above all, that is called God." The church could not act as a judge because it lacked the means to determine the facts of a case; it could not "call in forrein witnesses," examine witnesses under oath, or have access to the records of the General Court. Simply to examine a civil case, even when no penalty or punishment was intended, was forbidden by Christ to His churches.

The crux of the matter was that "Christ [in] his kingdome, cannot Juditially enq[uir]e into affaires of this world." Christ settled this jurisdictional dispute by dividing the authority of His officers between realms as distinct as heaven and earth. As King of Kings and Lord of Lords, Christ "hath sett up another kingdome in this worlde, wherein magistrates are his officers, and they are to be accountable to him, for their miscarriages in the waye and order of this kingdome." Since the magistrate had his authority directly from Christ, he was accountable for his actions as magistrate to Christ, and not to the clergy. There was thought to be a profound difference between the office and its holder. As a man, the magistrate was as much in need of the clergy as any other man, but as an official, because his official actions came from the divine ordinance of his office, he was beyond either the competence or the reach of the church. Should the clergy excommunicate a magistrate, or a magistrate imprison a clergyman, "this would sett Christ against himselfe in his owne Ordinances . . . which cant be."

The true Christian rule was submission "to the highest powers." The church must win the support of kings by meekness, love, and charity. Luther's doctrine of submission to the state was cited, Calvin had for the most part agreed, and the evidence of Job was adduced to prove that "a man may not say to a Kinge, thou art wicked: nor call Princes ungodly."[67] The divinity of the offices of both priest and magistrate could not confront each other because their respective authority was limited to different realms. In temporal matters, including the protection of the organization and doctrine of the church, the magistrate was supreme. The magistrate as a man might not get to heaven, but when he spoke with the power and dignity of his office, he could be challenged by no power lower than God Himself.

An important part of the magistrate's duty was to protect the organization and the purity of the visible church. What was the New England church that the Governor was obliged to defend? It will be recalled that Winthrop had been careful to explain that emigration from England did not constitute a rejection of the Church of England. For a time, at least, one must take the word "Puritan" seriously when applied to Winthrop and his Company. It cannot be doubted that he was aware of the political difficulties that might ensue if complete separation of the churches were allowed, but it seems that his reluctance to separate was more a matter of conscience than of political policy. His early hesitancy even to accept the church autonomy explicit in Congregational church polity is illustrated by his nervousness over procedure; in the late summer of 1630, he reported, "we of the Congregation kept a fast, and chose mr. *wilson* our teacher. . . . we used imposition of handes but with this protestation by all that it was onely as a signe of Election and confirmation, not of any intent that mr.

wilson should renounce his ministrye he received in Englande."[68]

His reluctance to admit that the physical act of separation was in fact also a spiritual separation continued at least through the spring of the next year. When Roger Williams refused to join the congregation at Boston because the members would not repent for having had communion with the Church of England, Winthrop seems to have taken the occasion to write his opinions on "Reformation Without Separation." As a magistrate he had an obligation to be clear about ecclesiastical polity, which it was his duty to uphold. "The corruption of a thinge," he reasoned, "dothe not nullifie a thinge so longe as the thinge hathe a beinge in the same nature, that it had, when it was in the best beinge: so it is with the particular Congregations."[69] The Church of England was corrupt, as Williams had said, but it was a church nonetheless, which Williams denied; it was a church which could be purified, unlike some others where the force of the Papacy and Antichrist had so corrupted the church that its essential nature had been utterly destroyed. The example of the Bay congregations, it was hoped, would encourage that purging in England.

By 1634, when Winthrop's ideas of the nature of the government were already well formulated, he was growing firmer in his defense not of the kinship between the parent church and its offspring in the wilderness, but of the basic differences between them. By then he had accepted Congregationalism, including the absolute theoretical autonomy of the individual congregations. In a letter to England, the Governor showed unmistakable signs of creeping separatism: "For your counsell of Conforminge ourselves to the Ch[urch] of E[ngland] though I doubt not but it proceeds out of your care of our wellfare: yet I dare not thanke you for it; because it is not conformable to Gods will revealed in his worde: what you may doe in E[ngland] where things are otherwise established, I will not dispute, but our case heere is otherwise: being come to clearer light and more Libertye."[70]

Sometime in 1640, Winthrop wrote another letter to a correspondent in England, in which he made clear his commitment to a congregational autonomy so thoroughgoing that only the idea of the invisible church of all true believers could still be thought to bind the Bay congregations to those in England. At least by this time he was willing to insist on the individual church covenants as the very basis of the churches, as the covenant was the foundation of the state. The church covenant, as he reported it, was a dual pledge, including a renunciation of the past and a promise for the future: "I doe renounce all former corruptions and polutions. I doe promise to walke togither with this Church in all the ordinances of Religion according to the rule of the Gospell, and with all the members heerof in brotherly love." He believed that every association required some sort of covenant, even though, as was the case with the churches in England, the covenant was only implicit. "Now to leave it uncertaine, where men have opportuntye to expresse and clear it, were a faylinge (at least)." It was the covenant that gave some permanence to each church, for without it the church would cease to exist when the uncovenanted persons left the assembly. Anyway, the controversy over the covenant was misplaced, because there were so many more weighty matters at hand, or rather in England, as, for example, "communicatinge with all parochiall members, whereof many are no Saints neither by callinge nor profession: submitting themselves to Canonicall obedience."[71]   And what was most important, accepting the covenant was not the process by which one entered a church body in Massachusetts. Being given the opportunity to pledge oneself meant that the individual had already been admitted into the church:

> There is a great mistake in the order of our Covenant, for it passeth for granted everywhere that none can be admitted heere before they enter into this Covenant, whereas in very truth they are tryed and admitted by the vote of the whole Churche before any Covenant be tendered or mentioned to them. Lastly it is sometymes tendered to them as a declaration of their purpose and intention only and not in the words of a Covenant or promise, so willinge are our Churches to please our brethren in all things to our mutuall accord and edification.[72]

Having accepted the covenant that supported congregational autonomy, Winthrop had simply extended his view of the nature of the political body to include also the church body. A number of discrete individuals came together and voluntarily gave their consent to exchange their natural liberty for moral liberty under lawful authority. The process for creating both the state and the visible church was identical, and included the liberty of the members to elect their own officials, either magistrate or minister. Both the state and the church were concerned with salvation, and only active members of the church could be active in the state. The minister's function was spiritual leadership and inspiration. It was the duty of the magistrate to see to it that the minister had a proper congregational body, well organized and obedient in outward behavior, to lead. It was the minister's function to teach, while the magistrate saw to it that the congregation was in attendance and that the lazy or stupid were given the opportunity to meditate on their sinfulness while taking their ease in Boston's stocks.

With congregational autonomy, the relationship between the state and the churches became more complicated. Should the state improperly interfere with a given church, it would violate the rights of the congregation. The clergy could pose small threat to the various churches since each minister held his post by the sufferance of the congregation. The General Court was more dangerous, from the viewpoint of the congregation, and it was usual for the deputies, who represented the towns, also to defend actions of the independent congregations, and all in opposition to magisterial authority.

One such case occurred in 1646 when some of the elders asked the General Court to authorize the calling of a synod. The magistrates complied, Winthrop recorded, but the deputies protested that the state had no proper authority to require the churches to send delegates to a civil convention, and that should the proposed synod agree on uniform church policy either the synod or its master, the state, would be guilty of subverting congregational autonomy.

The answer given to the first objection derived from Winthrop's definition of magistracy: "the civil magistrate had power upon just occasion to require the churches to send their messengers to advise in such ecclesiastical matters either of doctrine or discipline, as the magistrate was bound by God to maintain the churches in purity and truth." The deputies agreed that magistracy could so command the churches. But the threat to Congregationalism required more delicate treatment. Any suggestion of an imposed uniform practice on the churches elicited the fear that the despised Presbyterianism would be raised in Massachusetts Bay out of the wreckage of congregational autonomy. When the magistrates were charged with threatening that autonomy, they had to walk gently: "Whereupon it was ordered, that howsoever the civil magistrate had authority to call a synod when they saw it needful, yet in tender respect of such as were not yet fully satisfied in that point, the ensuing synod should be convened by way of motion only to the churches, and not by any words of command."[73]   The magistrates could not attack the congregational covenant which created the churches without weakening the covenant principle, without endangering the security of their own authority.   Winthrop's own convictions, moreover, led him to defend the covenants of the churches for the same reasons that he bridled at any challenge to magisterial authority, including the rare challenges from the clergy (most of whom, most of the time, sided with the magistrates in the battles with the deputies).   The covenant principle was the very basis of man's relationship with God, and with other men in both the state and church.

Winthrop's ideas about the organic Christian corporation also defined for him the proper relationship between Massachusetts Bay and England.   How was one to reconcile the divinity of the magistracy in the Bay with the supremacy of the English King; how reconcile congregational autonomy with the fact that the King was the head of the Church of England?   What, if any, was the authority of Parliament to direct the ways of God's agents in the wilderness?   Some curious perversions of the theory and law of corporations allowed Winthrop and Massachusetts to wend their way along a very dangerous path.   The consequence of missing a step on that path could be the destruction of Massachusetts and all that it stood for, including even mankind's new chance for redemption.

The traditional theory of the corporation defined it as an unnatural, artificial body which had legal status as a person, fictive but legally real.   Only a sovereign power could create fictions, and the life of a corporation must be a result of a concession from the sovereign.   The fiction theory led to the concession theory.   As one distinguished legal historian put it: "The corporation is, and must be, the creature of the State.   Into its nostrils the State must breathe the breath of a fictitious life, for otherwise it would be no animated body but individualistic dust."   English common law made it a crime for men "to presume to act as a corporation" without the appropriate concession from the state.   "Ignorant men,"

Maitland wrote, "on board the 'Mayflower' may have thought that, in the presence of God and one another, they could covenant and combine themselves together into 'a civil body politic.' "[74]   The Puritans were not as ignorant as the Pilgrims.

The Charter of the Massachusetts Bay Company was a concession by the Crown which had breathed life into that legal fiction. This royal creature was defined as the "Governor and Company of the Mattachusetts Bay in Newe England [which is] one bodie politique and corporate in deede, fact, and name."[75] Massachusetts therefore owed its legal existence to its Charter, and Winthrop never lost sight of that sobering fact.   The Crown giveth and the Crown taketh away.

It was obvious that a creature of the state could not be a state itself, that a corporation could not be an independent sovereign. The Bay held a franchise from the Crown; " 'a Corporation,' Maitland said, 'is a Franchise,' and a franchise is a portion of the State's power in the hands of a subject."[76] Adhering strictly to the theory of the corporation, then, Massachusetts was a subject, a creature, a dependency, and had not the legal right to exercise the kind of sovereignty that had the power to create.   But a community which was covenanted with God as well as with the King, had, to put it gently, a dual allegiance.   Should the wills of the two sovereigns divide, the creature had the alternative of ignoring one and praying for the best, or becoming schizophrenic.   Whenever the first option could be had with relative impunity, Winthrop gladly took it.   The King, after all, was three thousand miles away, while God, it was clear, was immediately present.

In 1639, Massachusetts itself incorporated a military company, and in 1650 it incorporated Harvard College.   Accepting the concession theory to which they owed their existence, the Puritans, in creating corporations themselves, assumed a power in their own body which had the force of denying the sovereignty which had incorporated them.   It might be that the Bay dared to incorporate Harvard only because Charles I and presumably the royal prerogative had already been executed, but the theory of sovereignty could not be changed because of that.   If Massachusetts was a creature of the sovereign of England, she would always be dependent on that sovereign whether King or Parliament.   After the Restoration, Massachusetts was called to account for this and other excesses of authority, on the basis of which a judgment was entered against the colony in 1684 for the cancellation of the Charter.

Very early there was an indication of the drift of the Puritan mind. The oaths required of officials of the Company were first drawn up in England in 1629, and began with the promise that "you shall bear true faith and allegiance to our sovereign Lord King Charles."[77] After the Puritans arrived in America they rewrote the oaths and omitted all reference to the King. A copy of the new oath, in Winthrop's handwriting, has been preserved; it begins: "I, A. B. being by the Almighties most wise disposition, become a member of this body . . . doe freely and sincerely acknowledge that I am justly and lawfully subject to the government of the same."[78] With the substitution of God for King, the Bay saints had, through an exercise of their own will, included God in the concession which had made them into an organic whole. The King had created a trading corporation but God had turned it into a nation. The King, as a magistrate, must provide protection for the fragile colony against Indians and Catholics. For this there would be gratitude. But the saints could afford obedience to the King only when he did not interfere with their divine mission. The saints, in other words, could obey the King only when they were convinced that it would be faithful to their covenant with God to do so. The decision was theirs, as Calvin had earlier concluded it should be.

The institution of magistracy was divine, and its commands had to be obeyed. No one could doubt that the King was a magistrate, but neither could one doubt that magistracy had been established in the Bay. Did the magistrate in Massachusetts owe obedience to the magistrate in England? There was no way for the Puritans, with their intellectual system, to conceive of a hierarchy of magistracy, and it was clear that the primary allegiance of the Bay magistrate was to God, not to King, to the national covenant, not to the Charter. God had created the office of Governor, as He had created that of King, and the theory of the divinity of magistracy led Winthrop to assume an equality of power between one magistrate and another. Governor and King had equal but separate authority, each with his own realm to govern. Politically it was sometimes necessary to express allegiance to the King; functionally, Massachusetts Bay was an autonomous body politic. The Christian corporation was considered to be whole; the umbilical cord had been cut when the *Arbella* weighed anchor in English waters. That the Puritans knew this and the King did not, presented problems of language, not of belief or action.

The growing breach between King and Parliament in England was anxiously and eagerly watched in New England. Early in 1641/2, Winthrop noted in his *Journal* a position which could only mean that he rejected the idea of the permanence or transferability of sovereignty, that the King and not Parliament had incorporated Massachusetts, and that Parliament must be prevented from becoming too interested in the colony. The officials of the Bay decided not to send an agent to plead the case of Massachusetts before Parliament because, as Winthrop phrased it, "if we should put ourselves under the protection of parliament, we must then be subject to all such laws as they should make, or at least such as they might impose upon us; in which course though they should intend our good, yet it might prove very prejudicial to us."[79]

The remonstrance and petition of Robert Child, presented in 1646, was taken very seriously in the Bay as a threat to autonomy. Child, in the interest of driving a Presbyterian wedge into Massachusetts, accused the saints of violating their Charter, and having failed to establish "a setled forme of government accordinge to the lawes of England." Then, in words that anticipated Locke by about fifty years, Child declared: "Neither do we so understand and perceyve our owne lawes or libertyes, or any body of lawes here so established, as that thereby there may be a sure and comfortable enjoyment of our lives, libertyes, and estates, according to our due and naturall rights, as freeborne subjects of the English nation." The Bay government, Child said, was arbitrary, and he petitioned for the introduction of civil liberties based on English citizenship, and not on the kind of piety acceptable to the churches and magistrates of Massachusetts. He wanted freemanship in Massachusetts to be extended to those who were freemen in England "without imposing any oathes or covenant on them, which we suppose cannot be warranted by the letters patent, and seeme not to concur with the oath of allegiance formerly enforced on all." Child's basic charge was that "this place [is] termed rather a free state, than a colonie or corporation of England."[80]

Winthrop, the General Court, and the elders whose opinion was requested, responded to this challenge by announcing that "by our charter we had absolute power of government; for thereby we have power to make laws, to erect all sorts of magistracy, to correct, punish, pardon, govern, and rule the people absolutely." This absolute power implied "a perfection of parts," that all the parts of government had been authorized by the Charter, and also implied "a self-sufficiency . . . and ergo should not need the help of any superior power . . . to complete our government." But, allegiance was due

> 1. because our commonwealth was founded upon the power of that state, and so had been always carried on, 2. in regard to the tenure of our lands, of the manor of East Greenwich, 3. we depended upon them for protection, etc., 4. for advice and counsel, when in great occasions we should crave it, 5. in the continuance of naturalization and free liegeance of ourselves and our posterity.

The subjects owed allegiance, but "we might be still independent in respect of government." The elders, always sensitive to the mood of the magistrates, agreed that "in point of government . . . no appeals or other ways of interrupting our proceedings do lie against us."[81]

Child and the other petitioners admitted that the Bay had some special privileges because it was a corporation, but privileges which were shared by other corporations in England. The magistrates, according to Winthrop, "could not but take this as a scorn and slighting of us . . . allowing us no more than any ordinary corporation." There was an essential difference between corporations "of but not within" England, and those ordinary corporations within England. "Though plantations be bodies corporate . . . yet they are also above the rank of an ordinary corporation." Turning to the example of the past in a way he had earlier rejected, Winthrop said that even the Greeks and Romans had thought of colonies as superior to towns or cities, "for they have been the foundations of great commonwealths."[82] Massachusetts was a corporation, but a special one because of its purpose and location. In this connection, not even Winthrop dared to say how special he thought it was, that God's covenant had to be read alongside the King's Charter.

The charge that the Bay had ignored the laws of England, thereby depriving Englishmen of their lives, liberties, and estates, elicited from Winthrop a sustained argument which best illustrated his view that Massachusetts was a separate and organic political entity:

> they charge us with breach of our charter and of our oaths of allegiance, whereas our allegiance binds us not to the laws of England any longer than while we live in England, for the laws of the parliament of England reach no further, nor do the king's writs under the great seal go any further; what the orders of state may, belongs not in us to determine. And whereas they seem to admit of laws not repugnant, etc., if by repugnant they mean, as the word truly imports, and as by the charter must needs be intended, they have no cause to complain, for we have no laws diametrically opposite to those of England, for then they must be contrary to the law of God and of right reason, which the learned in those laws have anciently and still do hold forth as the fundamental basis of their laws, and that if any thing hath been otherwise established, it was an error, and not a law, being against the intent of the law-makers, however it may bear the form of a law (in regard of the stamp of authority set upon it) until it be revoked.[83]

An English law which was opposed by Massachusetts could not be considered a true law because it would have been "contrary to the law of God." In legislating God's will and law, the Bay could not be accused by any man of true religion of establishing "repugnant" law. The Bible, not Parliament, was the ultimate authority, one which the saints felt qualified to explicate for the benefit of Dr. Child, Parliament, and the King, if need be. The General Court in 1678 entered into its minutes that Massachusetts was not bound by either Parliament or English law, but continued its allegiance to the King. The immediate result of this challenge and accusation was that the Court fined Child fifty pounds, and the others smaller sums, impounded Child's papers to prevent his appealing in England, and put him in jail. These penalties were eventually moderated, but the magistrates had demonstrated their view that the Bay was a largely independent state.

In trying to clarify the imperial relationship, Winthrop and the other magistrates set the substance and tone of a political debate that was to continue until the conclusion of the American Revolution. Their separation of person and office in their own definition of magistracy in the Bay had prepared them to understand the imperial relationship in the way that they did. The colony, they argued, owed allegiance to the person of the King, not to the state. They were using the very old idea of the King's two bodies, the natural body of the King and the political body of the King. The natural King was simply the man who held the throne, while the political body of the King was the political body of the state. The latter King was immortal (so long as the state existed) and infallible. The Puritans remained loyal to the person only, claiming that the political capacity of the King did not extend beyond the political body of England. They did not kill the idea of the King's second body; they did not deny loyalty to the abstraction of the state. They had moved the abstraction to the new world with themselves and their Charter. They had substituted their own political body for the King's second body, and one important intellectual step to revolution had been taken, a step John Adams was later to follow. That the Declaration of Independence referred only to that body of the King which Winthrop and his Company had recognized, referred only to the natural person of the King, may, for now, be taken as evidence of the lasting impact of this concept in later America.

The organic and independent Christian corporation owed its existence to a concession from the natural King, but its meaning to God. The terms of the national covenant had exempted these saints from history, had given them an opportunity to build their exemplary city on a hill. Should they remain faithful to their God, that city would thrive and prosper to the end of time. Should they fail, and there was mounting evidence that they would, the extraordinary blessing of the Lord would turn into an extraordinary curse. In these terms, Winthrop's anguish at seeing the sons of the fathers stray from the path of righteousness he had worked so hard to blaze can be understood. It was becoming painfully clear for those with eyes to see that the cosmic "errand into the wilderness" was failing. The Charter was revoked, and the new Charter of 1691 made property, not piety, the necessary qualification for freemanship. Saints had become Yankees. So terrible was the wrath of the Lord.

SELECT BIBLIOGRAPHY

Champlin Burrage. *The Church Covenant Idea.* Philadelphia, 1904.

Julius Goebel, Jr., "King's Law and Local Custom in Seventeenth Century New England," *Columbia Law Review*, XXXI, 3 (March, 1931), 416–448.

William Haller. *The Rise of Puritanism.* New York, 1938.

George L. Haskins. *Law and Authority in Early Massachusetts.* New York, 1960.

E. H. Kantorowicz. *The King's Two Bodies.* Princeton, 1957.

Charles H. McIlwain, "The Transfer of the Charter to New England and Its Significance in American Constitutional History," *Massachusetts Historical Society, Proceedings*, LXIII (Boston, 1931), 53–64.

Perry Miller. *The New England Mind.* 2 vols., New York, 1939, 1953.

——— *Orthodoxy in Massachusetts.* Cambridge, 1933.

Edmund S. Morgan. *The Puritan Dilemma.* Boston, 1958.

——— *Visible Saints.* New York, 1963.

Samuel E. Morison. *Builders of the Bay Colony.* Cambridge, 1930, 51–104.

——— *The Puritan Pronaos.* New York, 1936.

Albert Peel. *The First Congregational Churches.* Cambridge, Eng., 1920.

Aaron B. Seidman, "Church and State in the Early Years of the Massachusetts Bay Colony," *New England Quarterly*, XVIII, 2 (June 1945), 211–233.

R. H. Tawney. *Religion and the Rise of Capitalism.* New York, 1926.

Horace E. Ware, "Was the Government of the Massachusetts Bay Colony a Theocracy?" Publications of the Colonial Society of Massachusetts, *Transactions*, X (Dec. 1905), 151–180.

II

THEOLOGY ✻ *Jonathan Edwards*

> The earth or this earthly world does by men's persons as it does by their bodies: it devours men and eats them up. As we see this our mother that brought us forth and at whose breasts we are nourished is cruel to us, she is hungry for the flesh of her children.
>
> *Images or Shadows of Divine Things*

With Winthrop's death the single most creative phase of Puritan political life came to a close. The next hundred years of intellectual development in New England displayed a virtually continuous series of crises and failures, of contradictory attempts to reach back to the faith of the fathers and forward toward reformulations that would more easily allow adjustment to changing conditions. With the simple existence of Massachusetts Bay made more secure with each passing year, the inhabitants turned away from the energizing piety which had helped the fathers face the terrors of a wilderness. With growing material success, the inhabitants of the Bay turned their gaze from coffins and the afterlife to coffers in this. Wealth made men impatient with a limiting political theology, with medieval notions of just prices and fair wages, and with the necessity to think of the Lord while making small change. The impressive ecclesiastical and political edifice created by Winthrop and his colleagues began to decay because, in one sense, the Lord had been too bountiful. It was like the Puritan God to tempt His people with an overenthusiastic response to their prayers.   But because His people took from His right hand and turned away from Him, their God crushed them with a series of left-handed blows from which they never recovered.

There had always been something about the House of Puritanism that seemed incomplete or dangerous.   From the very beginning, in the minds of most of the continental reformers and their English and American disciples, the religion of reform seemed to go but part way toward a completed theological system.   Calvin himself, it was clear, had been a man in a hurry, one whose sense of purpose and whose understanding of the enemy were certainly admirable, but whose system raised many questions.   The sense of an only partially constructed theological framework on which the House of Puritanism rested was a challenge and an opportunity to several of the English and American divines—men like William Perkins, William Ames, John Preston, John Cotton, Thomas Shepard, and Thomas Hooker—who carried on the extensive task of closing holes and patching cracks in the foundation of their faith.

There was another worry about this House.   Some parts that were acknowledged to be inherent in the structure were dangerous.   The House was planted firmly in this world, and the possibility, if not probability, of its occupants having their vision directed to the things of the world and its flesh instead of to the things of God and His Spirit was perhaps an inevitable result of the Puritans' insistence on facing evil directly, of refusing to separate from what they considered sin, of accepting the challenge of secularism as if they were equal to the struggle.   They encouraged material success in the belief that its evil effects could be controlled. The architectural theory of this theological House—even then— asserted that form and function were mutually determining.   It was one thing to argue the possible sanctity of a fisherman, and quite another to worship the wealth extracted from New England's codfish.   Success in this world might indicate divine favor, but that favor could be granted only to those who turned their backs on worldly success, who succeeded when they were not looking, as it were.   Protestantism did not discourage a developing capitalism, but capitalism could destroy true religion.   In the century after Winthrop's death, such problems as these simply became more acute in New England.

As the political power of the New England merchants continued to grow, as the new Charter of 1691 replaced piety with wealth as the condition of freemanship, the spiritual life of the city on a hill seemed to many to be mortally wounded. The withering of piety was thought to have been the necessary precondition of the succession of calamities, of which the Puritan community had become only too conscious. The ministers of Massachusetts Bay had an overflowing quantity of catastrophes to recount: The loss of original zeal had presumably resulted in the many evils which flowed from the Restoration through the Dominion of New England, the drought of 1662, the very destructive Indian uprising of King Philip's War, and the disaster of the new Charter, which changed the Bay from a relatively autonomous political corporation into a colony of the King whose governor was made into a royal appointee instead of being elected by the saints. The awful fruits of the decline of piety included also the horror of the witchcraft hysteria, which began in Boston in 1688 and slowly spread its venom to other places in God's country; plague; earthquake; and the certain appearance of the Antichrist.

Almost from the start of their life in the New World, New Englanders had worried about the consequences of failing to live up to the terms of their cosmic mission. They had been entrusted with nothing less than the redemption of the world, but soon there were to be successful fortune tellers, celebrations of Christmas and Easter, and a brothel in Boston. Peter Bulkeley, one of the first ministers in the Bay, had been worried that the saints would abandon their cosmic mission and that God would, in turn, make them mere colonists: "Take heed lest . . . God remove thy candlestick out of the midst of thee; lest being now as a city upon a hill, which many seek unto, thou be left like a beacon upon the top of a mountain, desolate and forsaken."[1]

A nation whose mission depended upon the saintliness of its citizens would of course be destroyed should the unsaintly come to power. And the Lord's wrath would be greater in proportion to the importance of the mission. Since no mission could have more importance than that of the Bay, its inhabitants could expect the worst from a wrathful and vengeful God. Michael Wigglesworth, a minister and verse-maker, had such a God address these backsliding saints in a poem he called "God's Controversy with New England," in which God demanded to know why the citizens of the Bay in 1662 were of a different breed than those who had begun the holy work.

With the development of the theory of the triple covenants of grace, society, and church—the "federal" theology—the New England Puritans had taken a very long step in domesticating Calvin's God. Now God, out of His love for man, had limited His power voluntarily by entering into a contractual relationship with His creatures. The ministers continued to argue that God was essentially incomprehensible, while also teaching that the covenant made it possible for man to sense, if not positively to know, God's future intentions. It was the intention of the Puritan theologians to retain what was then the conventional idea of God's absolute potency and man's absolute depravity. They continued to argue that man could not become justified by God as a result of sanctification, as a result of living a Christian life; they employed the usual reverse order and preached that sanctification was evidence of justification. In cruder terms, the ministers continued to agree with Calvin that men were not saved because they were good, but were good because they had been saved.

The covenant of grace allowed the Puritans to exercise a measure of control over God's mind, since He had limited Himself in His promises to Abraham. Those sacred promises permitted even depraved man to understand the rules by which God would voluntarily play the game of salvation and divine governance. Even while insisting on the perfect arbitrariness of divine sovereignty, the covenant of grace allowed the Puritan to say that God had willingly limited Himself to ideas of justice which men could understand. It was but a small step to argue that, in so doing, God had limited Himself to human justice, and that men could now judge even Him. Thus the possibility of heresy was virtually assured by the language if not the meaning of the covenant of grace, although in taming Calvin's difficult God the ministers evidently did not see where they were going. Thomas Shepard, one of the early leading Puritan divines, put the fundamental departure from the inscrutable God of Calvin in unequivocal language: "For in God's Covenant we see with open face God's secret purpose for time past . . . [and] we see performances for [the] future, as if they were accomplishments at present."[2]

The social covenant was as centrifugal, as potentially contradictory, as the covenant of grace. It was one thing to argue, as
Winthrop had, that the relation between ruler and ruled was
contractual, but quite another to imply, as the deputies did, that
the contract gave the ruler and the ruled equal initiative and
power. Caught in the logic of the social contract, Winthrop was
bound to insist that the purpose of government was the welfare
of the people, but he was also to insist, with equal fervor, that
only the magistrate could be the judge of the people's welfare.
The political implementation of God's Word in Massachusetts Bay
must then result in the security of each man's life, liberty, and
estate, as well as providing the necessary Christian atmosphere for
a faithful observance of a properly reformed religion. A pious
political corporation based on a genuine contract or covenant
would result in the tranquillity of life on this earth and the enjoyment of a religion purged of the iniquities of the old world.
Winthrop insisted that the contract gave liberty to the people and
authority to the magistrates, but this view of the politics of Zion
was a necessary first step toward its self-destruction.

It was Winthrop himself who taught the ordinary citizen of the
Bay that the magistrates were bound to the citizen by a sacred
contract. It was therefore the orthodox political theory of Massachusetts Bay, as it took form in the social covenant, that destroyed
itself. When the deputies understood that Winthrop's defense of
magisterial authority also defended the liberty of the people, the
intellectual groundwork for popular resistance to the magistrates
was laid. As the magistrates attempted to resist the increasing
demands from the deputies for greater power in the affairs of the
Bay by reiterating the social covenant as it had been expressed by
Winthrop, they seemed not to see that their defense of their own
authority was the very heart of the argument that was being used
against them. Covenantal theory was to prove as dangerous to the
magistrates as to the ministers, and both, failing to locate the
essential intellectual source of their growing difficulties, merely
came to stress the self-defeating theory even more in a futile attempt
to frustrate what was becoming a massive impiety and political
assertiveness.

The idea of the covenant was basic to the Puritan system of
social and theological organization. It had been developed in

England and America by middle-class theologians who were also members of a rapidly developing commercial order. The business life of the energetic Puritan nations made its intellectual contribution to the life of the mind by lending its terminology to a view of God. Now, on the basis of a contract between God the seller and man the buyer the quality of the goods and the promise of delivery were supposedly guaranteed.

In Massachusetts Bay the covenant was a great aid to the understanding of the congregations. The ordinary colonist, deeply engaged in or concerned with the commerce of his world, could easily grasp the contractual nature of the relationship between God and man. The ministers could remember that the God they were scrutinizing remained essentially inscrutable, but the congregations, quite naturally, slowly moved toward a vulgarization of the covenant until, in time, the parties to the contract were thought of as approximately equal. Whether man was becoming deified or God was becoming humanized made no difference; either view could only be interpreted by the orthodox as a wicked blow to the heart of the Puritan system. The covenant theory was originally designed to make the awful sovereignty of God understandable and, to a degree, predictable. But if God limited Himself, He was still, after all, limited. Designed as an aid to man, covenantal theory was a herald of the approaching death of Calvin's God.

The relatively slow process of this transformation constituted the Puritan agony. The covenant had been designed to help the Puritan squeeze between the Scylla of Arminianism with its ethical rationalism and the Charybdis of Antinomianism with its anti-rational excesses of piety. In their search for a more comfortable orthodoxy, growing numbers of Bay saints were to crash on both rocks as the frenzy of revivalism passed into the cool aloofness of rationalism and Unitarianism. And yet these two threats were not the gravest dangers to the Puritan Zion. The orthodox Puritan mind itself, seizing the theory of the covenant, had taken hold of a concept whose very vigor was to prove subversive. Some of the ministers saw what was happening even if they did not see why, and they mourned the passing of the chosen people of the Lord. Their sermons, beginning as early as the 1640's, became one long jeremiad, warning the congregations of the wrath of the Lord, of the soul-shattering consequences of continued impiety. And it was the ministers themselves who formulated the necessary compromises with the original church covenant—the third covenant in the system—that made the death of pure Puritanism possible.

From almost the beginning in New England, the Puritans had assumed that the Congregational system of church organization had been divinely decreed. Individual saints coming together would covenant themselves into an association of visible saints and the result would be a true, independent, autonomous church. Only in New England was this view made integral to the system of Puritanism, and an unyielding commitment to Congregationalism marked a Puritan as an American. In a profound sense the churches of Massachusetts Bay were founded on a contract whose legitimacy they thought was assured by Scripture and by the piety of the signatories. That piety was supposedly assured by the demand that each applicant be acceptable to the others, that each must demonstrate by a public profession of faith that he had experimentally known God, an idea that originated in Massachusetts Bay. None but ostensible saints could truly belong to a church because of the heavy burden the members carried: They judged the qualifications of future candidates, elected their own ministers, and in general supervised Christian practice. A sinner in their midst could wreak havoc; he would be a disguised devil whose task of seducing them would be made easier by his inclusion in the brotherhood. Thus, in the original synthesis, the church covenant was based on the anterior covenant of grace, and since freemen were required to be church members, the political covenant was based on the anterior church covenant. The entire hierarchical structure depended upon the ability of the saints to verify the claims of their neighbors. Everything depended on man's ability to penetrate God's most jealously kept secret, to determine who had been truly justified and who not. Every one of the early ministers admitted that no one could do this with positive assurance, but still it was sufficiently practical to form the basis of church and state in the Bay. Mistakes might be made in individual cases, and that was to be regretted, but they believed that the system as a system was the best that men at any time or in any place had ever attempted.

The first major step in the subversion of the church covenant was taken in the early summer of 1657, when thirteen clergymen from the Bay were joined by four from Connecticut for the purpose of reformulating the terms of church membership. An unofficial report, probably written by Richard Mather, was approved by the ministers, and was to become the Half-Way Covenant. This compromise asserted that persons who had been baptized but who had not had an adequate religious experience for them to apply formally for full church membership should be admitted as "half-way" members. These semi-saints would be allowed to present their children for baptism, but they were not considered saints and they were not to partake of the Lord's Supper. The continuation of the churches was supposedly assured because the children of the half-way members, even if of a colder heart than their parents, would have at least one foot in the door and might experience God even if their parents had not. A formal synod affirmed this doctrine in 1662 and soon most Congregational New Englanders were members of a congregation without being true members of a church.

As the language of convenantal theory led men to think of God as having positive contractual obligations to mankind, and as the Half-Way Covenant institutionalized a piety that was becoming evanescent, the stage was set for an even further rejection of the original system. Brushing aside both the Half-Way Covenant and strict congregationalism, Solomon Stoddard of Northampton took the next decisive steps. Stoddard's rejection of the relatively new Half-Way orthodoxy of the Boston ministers, as it was expressed by Increase and Cotton Mather for example, had less to do with theology than with ecclesiastical polity, though there were important theological overtones to his position. He had built an ecclesiastical empire in the Connecticut Valley, and with his status as "pope" of the west he was strong enough to challenge successfully the traditional superiority of Boston. Stoddard accepted both the absolute will of God and the covenant system in which an absolute God agreed to tie His own hands. But the pressures of frontier life led him to conclude that his own heavy hand was necessary to restrain the excesses of his town, and he rejected the Half-Way Covenant. He admitted everyone except the "openly scandalous" into his church. When the howl went up in Boston, Stoddard said what amounted to "why not?" All were given communion in Northampton, and he argued that it could do no one harm and might do some one good. The early dream of an exclusive church made up only of visible saints was finally over.

If Stoddard could now more directly oversee all the inhabitants of Northampton, it was perhaps inevitable for him to ask the next obvious ecclesiastical question: Why only Northampton? The traditional autonomy of the Congregational church stood in his way, but he believed that the founders had been men and not gods, and that future generations must make their own way in the world. He began a movement to conbine the churches of the Valley into a regional association clearly based on a Presbyterian model. The association was to have power to choose ministers and to supervise their conduct. Since he had reorganized the individual church so that it contained people who could not prove their sanctity, it was less important than it once had been to defend the independence of each congregation. The logic of a church made up of visible saints only carried over into the logic of autonomous Congregationalism. As he rejected the first, Stoddard was not constrained to defend the second. Boston, of course, rejected Stoddard's system as he rejected the Half-Way Covenant. The government of Massachusetts Bay, now a royal government, joined Boston, for once, in refusing to permit Stoddard's innovations, and Stoddard, showing something of the spirit of Winthrop, ignored both Boston and the Crown. He established his Hampshire Association, which was now illegal, and through it ruled the churches along his private preserve on both banks of the Connecticut River. The official Saybrook Platform adopted by Connecticut in 1705 legalized Stoddard's idea of regional associations, and the early militant congregationalism of the Bay had matured—or decayed—into semi-Presbyterianism.

Important as Stoddard's revisions were, his greatest, though unintended, act of defiance was yet to come. In 1726, three years before his death, the "pope" selected the man who was to take his place in the powerful Northampton pulpit. The man selected was Jonathan Edwards, Stoddard's grandson, a physically fragile, bewigged, and scholarly graduate of the new Yale College, and the most sophisticated mind Puritan New England was ever to produce. Edwards eventually came to understand that most of what was wrong with the religious life of the Bay was a result of the American contributions to theology. He set about to purge New England of covenantal theory and Stoddardism, and eventually succeeded in leading an astounding religious revival, in getting himself discharged by the town of Northampton, and in producing a theological system of remarkable consistency and power.

A few years after Stoddard's death, Edwards found himself directly responsible for awakening in Northampton a revival of religion at whose intensity even he was surprised. Stoddard had claimed five such "harvests" of souls while he had ruled the Valley, but nothing in the history of New England equaled the emotional explosion that Edwards ignited. He personally was the physician who attended the birth in New England of what has been called the Great Awakening. The phenomenon also spread, with varying degrees of fervor, throughout the Protestant world. Pietism in Germany, Methodism in England, schisms within the Baptist and Presbyterian churches in America, all were characterized by a challenge to the established and rationalistic order. Wesley, after having read Edwards' account of the Awakening in Northampton, was moved to hope that a similar wave might wash England, and, three months later, his auditors began to exhibit some of the symptoms Edwards had described. The frenzied upsurge of faith was sometimes marked with awakening political demands on the part of repressed classes, as was the case, especially, with Methodism. In New England, while Edwards was in control, the passions set loose seem to have been more tightly restricted to the matters of faith, which almost everywhere stood in direct opposition to the rationalism and order of the Enlightenment.

Only in New England did the Great Awakening produce a theological system, and that was a clear result of the nature of the town of Northampton and the history of New England. In time, that town wearied of the religious orgy which Edwards demanded, recalled a less tumultuous past when men could attend more comfortably to the business of making a living, and sent Edwards packing. In his years of exile he had the time and occasion to elevate his vision to a systematic theology. It is a splendid bit of irony that the uncontested leader of New England's greatest hysterical seizure should have built a system whose logic and rationalism would have satisfied St. Thomas. The theological opponents of New England's sternest logician accused him of accepting fervor and even violence as a substitute for sweet reason. Members of his own congregation accused him, rightly, of refusing to accept the ancient order of New England, the ambiguities and compromises of which had made life possible.

In the solitude of his study or in the woods around Northampton, he simply pursued the business of refining a system which would forever ensnare all of the many devils who seduced God's wilderness saints. He was so intent on the matter of purging New England that he quite overlooked the possibility that it would purge itself of him.

The development of Edwards' mind before he struck the spark of revivalism in Northampton was perfectly designed to suit him for intellectual leadership and practical failure. He was born in East Windsor, Connecticut, on October 5, 1703, of Esther Stoddard, daughter of Solomon, and Timothy Edwards, East Windsor's minister. Jonathan, the only boy, was the fifth-born and had ten sisters. When he was about thirteen years old, he wrote his famous little essay "Of Insects," as well as brief essays on the immateriality of the soul, on the rainbow, and on colors; he had already either read or read about Newton's *Opticks*. At about the same time he entered Yale College which was then located in Wethersfield. During his stay there he began his "Notes on the Mind" and "Notes on Natural Science," and he was one of the first in America to read Locke. He finished college in 1720, remained at Yale (by then in New Haven) for two years of additional work, and accepted an invitation to a Scotch Presbyterian church in New York City in the summer of 1722. In September of the following year he took a Master of Arts degree from Yale and became a tutor there in 1724. There was no president of Yale, so that he was practically the head of the college. Learning something about administering a college and teaching its students, he noted in his diary: "I have now, abundant reason to be convinced, of the troublesomeness and vexation of the world and that it never will be another kind of world."[3] In 1726 he was invited to settle in Northampton as Stoddard's heir, and was ordained and married the next year. When Stoddard died in 1729, Edwards assumed the full duties and powers of his grandfather's pulpit.

Late in 1734, after Edwards delivered a number of sermons, the symptoms of a "harvest" of souls began to show themselves. A revival was started when a young woman of rather easy virtue underwent an emotional frenzy that seemed to be the genuine fruits of the Holy Spirit. The passion let loose was to spread throughout his town until he found himself in charge of the most spectacular revival in New England's history.

In a published letter to Rev. Benjamin Colman of Boston, dated November 6, 1736, and entitled *A Faithful Narrative of the Surprising Work of God, in the Conversion of Many Hundred Souls, in Northampton,* Edwards recalled and analyzed this first wave of the Awakening. Renewed faith was from God, of course, but the location of his town helped. Far inland, distant from the sea ports, Northampton was insulated against the evils of this world; its location "has doubtless been one reason why we have not been so much corrupted with vice, as most other parts."[4] Reminiscent of the founders' celebration of the moral superiority made possible by insularity, Edwards was here in a long tradition stretching at least from Plato's *Laws* to the Monroe Doctrine.

In the spring of 1735, as Edwards recalled it, the town was mobilized for God. Throughout much of the year, Edwards' flock continued to grow. He noted that it was extremely difficult to judge, and impossible to know positively, the validity of any single conversion, but he estimated that over three hundred souls had been saved. Some kind of pattern seemed to emerge. The recognition of God's sovereignty and justice seemed to be a first symptom that the Spirit was at work: "Sometimes at the discovery of it, they can scarcely forbear crying out IT IS JUST! IT IS JUST! Some express themselves, that they see the glory of God would shine bright in their own condemnation; and they are ready to think that if they are damned, they could take part with God against themselves, and would glorify his justice therein."[5] As the conviction of absolute human depravity and absolute divine justice spread under Edward's urging, the hideousness of his vision also spread. The conversion of a young woman was described by him: "At a time when her brother was reading in Job, concerning worms feeding on the dead body, she appeared with a pleasant smile: and being asked about it, she said, It was sweet to her to think of her being in such circumstances."[6]

The reaction to this inhumanity was inevitable. Melancholia, understandably, came to characterize this and other awakenings to the Edwardsean God, as individuals shrank before the hell he showed them as their deserved destination. "There is nothing," Edwards reported, "that the devil seems to make so great a handle of, as a melancholy humour."[7]   One Joseph Hawley, sleepless, "meditating terror," "delirious," "despairing," committed suicide by cutting his own throat. Edwards began to worry, as Hawley's death seemed to inspire others to take their own lives: "And many who seemed to be under no melancholy, some pious persons, who had no special darkness or doubts about the goodness of their state— nor were under any special trouble or concern of mind about any thing spiritual or temporal—had it urged upon them as if some- body had spoke to them, Cut your own throat, now is a good opportunity. Now! Now!"[8]   After the suicidal urge subsided, revulsion swept the town and the people deserted Edwards' army. Before the year was out, Northampton settled down to its accus- tomed bickering about the common lands, gossip, occasional but sometimes heroic drinking, and work.   The first phase of the Awakening was over.

In 1740 that first phase looked as if it had been merely a pale rehearsal of the real thing, for then New England took up the business of revivalism with a vengeance.   George Whitefield arrived in Boston in 1740 and sermonized at the top of his mighty lungs for four weeks.   Whitefield, a repulsive creature with a booming voice and a power to reduce masses to agonized weeping, could, it was reported, send an hysterical thrill running through an audience simply by pronouncing the word "Mesopotamia."   One Anglican rector in Boston was outraged because, as he said, Whitefield had caused deep confusion in the town, split families, caused disobedi- ence, set teachers to quarreling, made men neglect their affairs, produced unmentionable transgressions in the dark of the night, and was indirectly responsible for a sharp increase in the number of bastards born along his trail.

After convulsing sweet, staid, reasonable Boston, Whitefield set off across Massachusetts on a triumphal march against sin.   In October he arrived in Northampton, and preached from Edwards' pulpit, while Edwards, his congregation, and especially Whitefield himself wept bittersweet tears.   Edwards was troubled by White- field's evident assurance about the state of others' souls, and was repelled by his condemnation of what Whitefield was pleased to call the "unconverted ministers" of the Bay.   After ranting and braying in towns surrounding Northampton, Whitefield marched off in search of new souls to conquer.   In his wake the second and more virulent Awakening occured, and Edwards preached throughout the entire Valley.

In the summer of 1741, at Enfield, Edwards delivered his most famous sermon, one which has become indelibly associated with his name.   *Sinners in the Hands of an Angry God* is the perfect expression of the revivalistic sermon, though the thought underlying it was left implicit by Edwards.   The terrific fire and brimstone of this classic example of sulphuric sermonizing was meant by Edwards to fulfill the precepts he had learned from Locke. Ideas are formed through the senses; only through experience can knowledge grow.   Digesting Locke's epistemology for the purposes of delivering effective and "sensible" sermons, Edwards attempted to present the meaning of hell to the senses of his auditors.   He did not want to convince his audience through the use of better reasoning or more refined scholarship.   Underlying *Sinners in the Hands of an Angry God* was Edwards' desire to use his words in a way that would actually force his audience to sense hell, to smell the sulphur and feel the fire.   He took his images and allusions from the ordinary experiences of New England farmers, and concentrated his terrible vision in a series of taut and nervous sentences calculated not to distract simple people from the intended horror.   By his own experience, Edwards said, a healthy man knew that any day might be his last: "Unconverted men walk over the pit of hell on a rotten covering."[9]   As the power of his images increased, Edwards tried to force them into the actual experience of his weeping, convulsed congregation: "The bow of God's wrath is bent, and the arrow made ready on the string, and justice bends the arrow at your heart, and strains the bow, and it is nothing but the mere pleasure of God, and that of an angry God, without any promise or obligation at all, that keeps the arrow one moment from being made drunk with your blood."[10]

Not only were his metaphors taken directly from the life of New England so that they would be more deeply felt by the people of the congregation; Edwards also assured them that their long training in covenantal theory was a delusion.   His angry God "without any promise" was sickened at the evil stench of each creature who was screaming for release from Edwards' words:

> The God that holds you over the pit of hell, much as one holds a spider, or some loathsome insect over the fire, abhors you, and is dreadfully provoked: his wrath towards you burns like fire; he looks upon you as worthy of nothing else, but to be cast into the fire; he is of purer eyes than to bear to have you in his sight; you are ten thousand times more abominable in his eyes, than the most hateful venomous serpent is in ours. . . . O sinner! Consider the fearful danger you are in: it is a great furnace of wrath, a wide and bottom-less pit, full of the fire of wrath, that you are held over in the hand of that God, whose wrath is provoked and incensed as much against you, as against many of the damned in hell. You hang by a slender thread, with the flames of divine wrath flashing about it, and every moment to singe it, and burn it asunder; and you have no interest in any Mediator, and nothing to lay hold of to save yourself, nothing to keep off the flames of wrath, nothing of your own, nothing that you ever have done, nothing that you can do, to induce God to spare you one moment. . . . If you cry to God to pity you, he will be so far from pitying you in your doleful case, or showing you the least regard or favour, that instead of that, he will only tread you under foot. And though he will know that you cannot bear the weight of omnipotence treading upon you, yet he will not regard that, but he will crush you under his feet without mercy; he will crush out your blood, and make it fly, and it shall be sprinkled on his garments, so as to stain all his raiment.[11]

At some point the cries of anguish reached such a pitch that Edwards had to wait for relative quiet. He demanded that each individual in the congregation prepare himself to meet the Edwardsean God alone, without benefit of a covenanted and limited God or of any human power of any kind whatsoever. An omnipotent and angry God must, since He was absolute justice, crush each sinner with eternal torture. The image of a blood-spattered God may not be pleasant to contemplate, but it was the image that Edwards lived with, and demanded his congregation to share.

By providing later tub-thumping revivalists with a model of the perfect revivalistic sermon, Edwards did permanent damage to the future social history of America. Though he cannot be held directly responsible for the excesses of his followers, for the mindless reitera-tion of the themes he formulated, still he was the exemplar. The hordes of bombastic revivalists who cawed their way well into the nineteenth century walked a path that led directly back to Edwards' door.

When Edwards addressed Enfield he was part of what had become a general movement. Itinerant preachers appeared in New England, thoroughly upsetting the Congregational notion that a minister was elected by one congregation, and could speak from another pulpit only with the leave of its rightful occupant. Lay exhorting, censoriousness, church schisms, and doctrinal errors were also among the evils which the proper Bostonians laid at the door of the Awakening. Settled ministers were rejected, some forcibly, by their own congregations when the people became convinced that the minister was a cold rationalist who had never experienced God, that the minister was himself unconverted. The paroxysm of revivalism shattered the accustomed patterns of colonial life and the defenders of the older faith were obliged to wait for the orgy to pass before they could counter-attack.

The Great Awakening was most sharply defined in New England. Its definition was a result of the decision by the reverend Charles Chauncy of Boston to challenge Edwards to a theological duel. The actual revival in New England lasted for something less than two full years, and in the calm after the storm, all sides to the controversy reflected on the meaning of the Awakening, and attempted to put their respective cases dispassionately.

Chauncy's position was simply that the Awakening was a revival, not of true religion, but of the old Antinomian spirit that had plagued the churches since their inception. He thundered that not even Catholicism produced more blasphemies, that the Awakening sought to make goods and women communal property. The Edwardsean spirit, according to Chauncy, was based on the notion that an individual could be bathed in the light of God, and, he said, the individual thenceforth would have respect for neither law nor convention. He said that even the Bible was rejected by those in the heat of religious ecstacy, those who were sufficiently deranged to hallucinate that they were prophets, apostles, Christ, or God Himself. The physical manifestations of the new piety disturbed Chauncy and those others of the Boston clergy who had remained aloof. He said that he would no longer tolerate the awful terror which had produced strange physical effects like screaming, swooning, convulsions, and other indecencies he felt obliged to avoid describing.

The Awakening's release of sexual energy, which orthodox Puritanism had never quite encouraged, also disturbed Edwards. In trying to answer Chauncy's charges, Edwards wrote *Some Thoughts Concerning the Present Revival of Religion in New England* (1742). His aim in this work was to defend the revival against Chauncy's charges, as well as to separate the genuine from the fake in his own camp. He had set himself the single most difficult and dangerous task of trying to determine where the Holy Spirit really had been operative, and where not. No man, he believed, could penetrate the inscrutable mystery of God's secret will, but he was convinced that certain signs and probabilities could be fathomed.

The sincere critics of the Awakening, he wrote in his *Thoughts*, had made three errors: 1. they had judged the revival *a priori*, that is, they had rejected the revival because they rejected its supposed causes, instead of concentrating, as they should have done, on its effects. 2. The critics judged the revival with inappropriate tools like philosophy and history instead of placing their exclusive reliance on the Bible. From the Bible, Edwards asserted, one learned to despise passion, not affection, to identify the will with the emotions instead of considering them separate faculties. Most important, men should learn from the Bible that religion was a thing of the spirit, not of the body, and that at least some of the physical peculiarities of the Awakening were therefore not to be admitted as conclusive evidence either for or against the possibility of genuine conversion. 3. The critics' denunciation was too sweeping; they had failed to distinguish between the good and the bad.

Censoriousness, wrote Edwards, was the most noxious weed to sprout in the Awakening. Men should have the prudence to proceed slowly and with great care in the possible presence of the Lord. It was an error to charge the revival with Antinomianism, because those who had undergone probable conversion seemed never to bathe in the white light of mysticism, seemed never to lose sight of either their humanity or their necessary pollution. Those who seemed to be saved did not confuse their infusions of love with the idea that they were perfectly free from sin, a confusion of which the

Methodists, according to Edwards, were guilty. Those who claimed salvation took special delight in contrasting the absolute purity of the Lord with their own infinite corruption.

In his *Thoughts*, Edwards, for the only time in his career, contributed to the national mythology that had been started by the Puritans of the seventeenth century. The idea of America as God's country was not one which he advanced often, but when he did he characteristically was more extreme than any who came before or after. The wonderful movements of the Holy Spirit in the Awakening were a probable prelude to the conversion of the world. One naturally thinks back to Winthrop's notion of the city on a hill whose moral superiority would be a standard and inspiration to the universe.

According to Edwards, it was likely that America would be the scene of the world's rebirth because "it is signified that it shall begin in some very remote part of the world, with which other parts have no communication but by navigation."[12] God had created two worlds on earth, two great habitable continents, one old and one new. The new world was discovered in order "that the new and most glorious state of God's church on earth might commence there; that God might in it begin a new world in a spiritual respect, when he creates the *new heavens* and *new earth*."[13] Unregenerate men in the old world had been given their chance and had failed. So sunk in sin was Europe that God fittingly opened the new world to men in order to have a more appropriate setting for His work. God made men discover America "but little before" the Reformation. The chronology was indicative of the divine plan. When there was a need sufficiently great, the Lord would open a virgin land to the west, whose innocence would inspire men and would form the appropriate setting for the reappearance of Christ: "The other continent hath slain Christ, and has from age to age shed the blood of the saints and martyrs of Jesus, and has often been as it were, deluged with the church's blood.—God has, therefore, probably reserved the honour of building the glorious temple to the daughter that has not shed so much blood."[14]

From the beginning of recorded history men had said that power and happiness moved westward, that somewhere to the west was a happy land of flowers where pleasure would replace misery, where might would replace impotence. Because Providence delighted in balance, Edwards said, the immemorial human thrust to the west would be reversed. The church had been born in the east and moved westward; the rebirth of the church, "in some measure to balance these things," would be in the west and move eastward. "And so it is probable that will come to pass in spirituals, which has taken place in temporals, with respect to America: that whereas, till of late, the world was supplied with its silver, and gold, and earthly treasures from the old continent, now it is supplied chiefly from the new; so the course of things in spiritual respects will be in like manner turned."[15] From Scripture he deduced that it was God's way to begin some new work in a desolate and isolated spot, and New England was desolate and isolated enough to suit anyone's purposes. The reversal of the westward movement of the physical world was most clearly seen by him in the reversal of the sun itself. The physical sun's westward course would be reversed in the movement of the sun of righteousness which would move from the west, America, to the east. The sun of righteousness, he wrote, "shall rise in the west, contrary to the course of things in the old heavens and earth." The spiritual sun "will rise in the west, till it shines through the world like the sun in its meridian brightness."[16]

Now, coming to the crux of the geographical matter, he argued that New England, not all of America, would be the scene of Christ's return, the place out of which the spiritual sun would rise. "I think, if we consider the circumstances of the settlement of New England, it must needs appear the most likely, of all American colonies, to be the place whence this work shall principally take its rise."[17] Thus he hoped that the operations of the Holy Spirit which he saw in the Great Awakening presaged the birth in New England of a spirit which would remake the world, which would bring an end to the long agony of the human race. His chiliastic nationalism was bound to end in what a more modern temper can only call madness. Northampton, Massachusetts, in his view, would be Christ's capitol, and Edwards as one of His lieutenants was already at work preparing His kingdom for His appearance.

In 1746 Edwards published his last word on the Great Awakening, *A Treatise Concerning Religious Affections,* a work which has been called "the most profound exploration of the religious psychology in all American literature."[18] In this work he took the longest step yet in his career toward a systematic theology instead of occupying himself with practical sermons and religious observations. This was the gentlest and most humane work he ever accomplished, one in which the proper Bostonians were virtually ignored in the interest of probing the dynamic of true religious affection. Edwards was here concerned with ridding the Awakening's memory of the cranks and lunatics who had almost made an *opéra bouffe* out of what he considered to be God's work.

Edwards had come to believe that the greatest threat to conversion was not to be found in rationalistic Boston, but in the passionate enthusiasm of his own followers. Underlying his own behavior in the Awakening was a highly refined and rationalistic philosophy of emotional religion; underlying the behavior of men like Whitefield and Davenport seemed to be nothing but a licentiousness which thrived on the odious impact of their bellowing. He stood between the flaming passion of Whitefield and the cool reason of Chauncy; he stood, as it were, between the reasonable man of the Newtonian universe and the Romantic celebration of emotion that was to come in the works of men like Coleridge, Blake, and Nietzsche. Rejecting both the world which was, and the world which was to come, Edwards strove to build one of his own, a world of his own construction that would enclose the best of his own time as well as the best of a future he did not know. Almost nothing in the history of New England could assist him in trying to teach his people the vocabulary of emotion. The legalistic mentality of covenantal theorists had dominated the New England landscape for so long that, though his argument was persuasive, it could not persuade. Edwards had more to fear from his own people than from the worst Boston could offer.

The erosion of Congregational practice from the original requirement that each candidate for sainthood publicly and persuasively profess the reality of God's hand upon him, to the wholesale admission of all who were not "openly scandalous," meant that some new way of determining the truth of conversion was essential. Edwards opened his preface to *Religious Affections* with questions that had always troubled the history of New England: How could God's elect be known? What was the nature of true religion? He made no secret of the fact that he rejected both paths into which New England had stumbled. Exclusive rationality or exclusive emotion was so comprehensive that either or both must lose sight of man's humanity and God's wisdom. Nowhere was Edwards' criticism of New England's intellectual life so powerfully expressed. During the Awakening, emotions were thought to constitute all of religion; in the reaction that followed, all emotion had become suspect. In vacillating from one extreme to the other, his countrymen had demonstrated their own profound intellectual insecurity and the fragility of their faith's foundation. It was his plan to repair the weaknesses of the New England mind.

Underlying the whole of the *Religious Affections* was one of Edwards' most original ideas. Man was regenerated through God's mercy, as Calvin had also said. Nothing that man could do or would do would effect the divine decision that, in each case, had been made before time began. In salvation, God, through the Holy Spirit, would permanently alter the psychology of man so that man would now actually perceive reality in a new way. Edwards had distinguished two different kinds of grace: common and special. By common grace, the Holy Spirit assisted men to do better that which they could do by nature. Even natural man might have a conscience and suffer guilt. Special grace caused men to think and act in ways which were not possible for ordinary human nature; it caused a radical alteration of the human psyche. This basic change in man's nature was called a "new sense," an addition to the five natural senses, through which man, now in a regenerate state, would, for the first time, have the inward and outward vision necessary to a will to love God. This psychological rebirth was a free gift of God to man, and was the necessary precondition of authentic sanctification. The saint with his new sense, still related to unregenerate man, but secure in irresistible grace, found himself more than aware of or believing in God. He presumably found himself in the actual presence of the divine glory.

Because this new sense was a fundamental alteration in human nature, it was necessary for Edwards to inquire, more closely than he had yet done, into the psychology of the human animal. He had learned from Locke that the faculties of emotion, reason, will, and imagination were not separate, not discrete, as the earlier Puritan theologians had assumed, but together formed one whole human personality whose various actions were always a result of the total being. The emotions were not, as Chauncy had taught, a mean principle of human nature which must be always subject to the decrees of reason. Smashing the entire structure of the ancient "faculty" psychology, Edwards argued that will and emotion were identical. When an action resulted from an act of will, it was because the emotion, or affection, inclined the will in that way. The faculties merged into one organic whole every time a thought or an action occurred. As an object or goal of some kind was perceived as good or bad, the will commanded accordingly. If overt action did not result, but only a state of mind, it was called the heart, the disposition, the tendency of the individual. The faculty of the understanding "discerns and views and judges of things."[19]

There has been much confusion because Edwards continued to refer to the faculties—as a result, he said, of the imperfection of language—even while he was rejecting the old view of man. In his private notebook he groaned, "O, how is the world darkened, clouded, distracted, and torn to pieces by those dreadful enemies of mankind called words!"[20] His tendency was always to unify, not separate, and he went so far as to suggest a psychosomatic conception, that the mind-body dualism was also erroneous; there were "laws of . . . union which the Creator has fixed between soul and body."[21] Viewing man as a thoroughly integrated creature, Edwards analyzed the various symptoms of the Awakening in order to decide which symptoms signified true conversion, and which not.

An emotionless piety was inconceivable. Vigorous acts of will and states of mind, or heart, were more important in religion than in anything else. The very vigor was a strong inclination, or motive, which was identical with preference, which was identical with emotion, which was identical with will. The thin Boston piety that was founded on the hegemony of reason overlooked the clear scriptural description of love as the fountainhead from which all religious inclination flowed: "From love arises hatred of those things which are contrary to what we love . . . and from the various exercises of love and hatred . . . arise all those other affections of desire, hope, fear, joy, grief, gratitude, anger, etc."[22]

Even the emotion of love was, by itself, sometimes irrelevant to the reality of conversion. Failure to understand this had led the radical revivalists astray. There were certain signs of affection that were proof neither of the absence nor of the presence of true religion, such as intensity, bodily effects, or religious talk. Similarly inconclusive was the fact that affections "come with texts of Scripture, remarkably brought to the mind,"[23] that the affections appeared to contain love, that many kinds of religious affections came together, "that comforts and joys seem to follow awakenings and convictions of conscience, in a *certain order*,"[24] that there was a zealous observance of the external duties of worship, or the desire of "persons with their mouths to praise and glorify God,"[25] or confidence of grace, or that the truly godly were pleased to hear or witness these affections.

Having now gone so far it was necessary for Edwards to be careful. God's will was, after all, arbitrary, and grace was always unmerited. It was dangerous for man to encroach on the divine prerogative: The Scriptures gave men the rules necessary to their own safety for making a decision about the reality of another's conversion. Such rules, though vague, helped men to avoid false teachers. But God never intended men to be able positively to know who was and who was not among His elect. That was a prerogative God reserved as His own. Edwards then asserted that it was not his intention to so scrutinize the inscrutable mysteries of the Lord. Having made that conventional disclaimer, he proceeded to do what he thought man might do with impunity. The thoroughness of his searching of the religious temper, however, makes his disclaimer seem forced and formal. He went as far as his mind allowed, and was bound by no such doctrinal inhibition as the essential inscrutability of God.

The plan of the *Religious Affections* now shifted to a consideration of those affections which could be construed as evidence of genuine grace. He emerged with twelve signs, the first four of which demanded an intense and personal experience. Looking inward to the shadows of the heart, he now asserted the position which, theoretically, was the basis of Protestantism of whatever flavor. Religion had to do with God and man—no intermediaries, no formalism, no extenuations. Man had the terror and, perhaps, glory of facing his maker alone, as naked as he had been in Eden, as helpless as he had been in the womb. The single bridge between God and man was neither the clergy nor the Bible, because both would be distorted by the unconverted, by natural man, but the

Holy Spirit, which would make man willing to hear and see and feel rightly, would rearrange and add to man's nature. Without grace man could only anticipate every horror of the Enfield sermon, and more. But grace was not a badge to be worn on a checked shirt; it was the birth of a new man in the body of an old one. Introspection—private, honest, and relentless—was the little machine necessary to measuring grace or its absence. In short, Edwards demanded that his people strip themselves bare of convention and conditioned response. He demanded self-knowledge of a people who had been trained to rely on formulas and ritual. He demanded that Americans abandon the intellectual posture that had made their lives possible. A people who accepted enough of the Edwardsean system to faint dead away at his mere description of hell could not truly make his vision their own and continue the business of growing apples. The terrifying Protestant nerve which he exposed could shock almost a whole colony into helpless fright. New Englanders with the idea of the moral superiority of the city on a hill and the early Congregational method of admitting fellow saints to church membership had been trained to judge others, not themselves.

His first distinguishing sign of gracious affection had to do with its origin: "Affections that are truly spiritual and gracious, do arise from those influences and operations on the heart, which are *spiritual, supernatural* and *divine.*"[26] On the basis of a misunderstanding of this Edwards has sometimes been called a mystic. Surely, he admitted, there is mystery in the ways of God, but he proceeded to naturalize the mystery to the point where even Northampton farmers could understand its operation. For though the origin of grace was divine, its manifestations could be compassed by a finite mind.

Another frequent mistake about Edwards is to think of him as a pure Berkeleyean idealist. His second sign should be enough to dispel this almost universal confusion: "The first objective ground of gracious affections, is the transcendentally excellent and amiable nature of divine things, as they are in themselves; and not any conceived relation they bear to self, or self-interest."[27] As the first sign had to do with the origin of grace, this sign was concerned with the relation of man to God's created and real world.

The external world might be an idea in the mind of God, but, for man, a right relation to the factual, external, real world was of the essence. For Edwards, the reality of the external was a product not of man's mind, but a product of itself, of things "as they are in themselves."

The third sign considered man's relation to God: "Those affections that are truly holy, are primarily founded on the loveliness of the moral excellency of divine things."[28] A love of these divine things for their own sake, rather than from fear of the consequences of hatred, was the origin of all truly religious emotion. These divine things were data of experience, to be sensed and not merely thought or imagined, but data that natural man would not know because he lacked the perceptual apparatus for experiencing them. The universe experienced by the saint and sinner was the same universe, but to the former it was beautiful. Without that beauty man must be reduced to simple utilitarianism. Beauty was truth, and truth beauty.

The fourth symptom had to do with man's relation to self: "Gracious affections do arise from the mind's being enlightened, rightly and spiritually to understand or apprehend divine things."[29] Just as Christ had been a second Adam, a new Adam, so the spiritual birth—or rebirth, considering Adam's first nature—made the natural man into a new Adam, a saint. There had been nothing added to the physical universe, nothing to upset Newton's calculations; nothing had been changed in the predestined course of the world, save that the individual would now see unity and purpose and organization where he had earlier, with his decadent inner eye, seen only incoherence. As one historian put it, "Edwards was . . . so much a materialist that he could join hands with Spinoza, and his insistence that the data of experience are extrinsically the same for either the natural or the regenerate man amounts to saying that the grinding of the atoms takes no cognizance of inward fluctuations."[30] The objectivity of nature was in no way affected by the state of man's soul. This new sense was not the flash of inner light of the mystic which illuminated the face of God for the creature to behold. It was an organizing principle that made men understand the relationship between Newton's laws and the decalogue; it allowed man to cooperate with himself in the pursuit of goals which he now desired; it was a sense, an item of intelligence, a knowledge of the truth of the other signs of true religious affection. The effect of this was to keep man in the heart of nature rather than to lift him out of his humanity into a supernatural glow. Man, even in a sanctified state, was subject to the laws governing the motion of bodies, and his new sense would allow him also to understand that fact.

His remaining eight emblems of edifying emotion were more conventional. Gracious affection produced in man's reason and heart a conviction of the reality of divinity, of man's depravity, of man's reflecting the light of the sun of righteousness. Genuine affection led men to the humility, love, and forgiveness of Christ, to a tenderness. Truly pious emotion demanded rigid personal honesty: "if persons appear greatly engaged in social religion, and but little in the religion of the closet, and are often highly affected when with others, and but little moved when they have none but God and Christ to converse with, it looks very darkly upon their religion."[31] Gracious affections also led to a quickening of the appetite for divine things, rather than resting content with its own expression. And finally, of course, was the practice of Christianity itself, which, though not an infallible sign of election, was "as ever is needful to guide them [saints] in their conduct, or for any intent and purpose that needs to be answered in this world."[32]

The tension between Edwards and Northampton could only be aggravated by his developing views of the signs of true piety. Late in 1748 he refused to admit an applicant to his church without the primitive Congregational practice of a public profession of faith. Several months later he announced to the committee of the church that Stoddard's system of rather promiscuous admission was over, that the earlier Half-Way Covenant would be ignored, that more stringent requirements than anything Northampton had ever experienced were now to be put into effect. Naturally the committee balked and naturally Edwards was intransigent. The long-standing feud between Edwards and the Williams clan of Hatfield, whose members were anxious to control the politics of the town and who were angered by the rivalry of Edwards' religious demands, now erupted into serious brawling. In a report to the General Court, Edwards accused the Williams family of dominating the town. His view of the destiny of men who lived on the earth earthly could have endeared him to no American enterpreneur.

Edwards' talents did not extend to protecting himself against the attacks of the rich river gods of the Valley. The quarreling between pew and pulpit raged on into 1750, when finally a council of ministers and delegates of nine churches convened in Edwards' town. By a majority of one vote the council recommended that the connection between Edwards and Northampton be severed, and his church accepted the recommendation.

He was charged, understandably, with claiming to have sufficient insight into the mind of God to enable him to judge accurately the precise condition of men's souls. All of his careful explanation of his own fallibility on this score availed him nothing. As he explained to a colleague: "I have always nauseated the Presumption & folly of such as appeared forward to be quick & preemptory in their decisions concerning the state of mens souls, from a pretended extraordinary skill in the secret methods of the spirits operation."[33] That he was deeply hurt cannot be doubted: "I am so unhappy as to be misunderstood by many notwithstanding all I can say for my self, there appears (as seems to me) a strange disposition to take me wrong, and to entertain uncharitable and injurious Thoughts of my meaning, & also concerning the Principles & dispositions I act from, and the Ends They suppose I secretly aim at."[34] He preached his *Farewell Sermon,* which was not his last, on July 2, 1750, and remained in the town until he could decide his next step.

Offers came to him from Connecticut, Virginia, and Scotland, but he accepted a call from a missionary post at Stockbridge, Massachusetts, where first he and then his vast family—he had eleven children—moved in 1751. There he preached to and instructed the Housatonnuck Indians with one of the tribe, John Wonwanonpequunnonnt, as his interpreter. Perhaps never had a man been quite so unsuited to a place as Edwards was to Stockbridge. His physical frailty and refined intelligence must have been serious disabilities in the frontier community whose filth and barbarism even he, descending for once from his accustomed detachment, was forced to describe. The outbreak of the French and Indian War made life in his outpost even more precarious, and the quartering of troops in his house probably added nothing to the quiet of his study. The Indians proved so insensitive to the exquisite elaborations of his theological system that he usually used old notes and simplified his sermons as far as he was able. He had never been in the mainstream of educated discourse of his day, but his isolation with the Housatonnucks was more extreme than anything he had known. Viewed from Stockbridge, provincial little Northampton must have seemed like a world capital. But the isolation radically threw him back on himself, and he produced his greatest, and most difficult, work.

In 1754, Edwards published his masterpiece. Though he had spent a lifetime thinking about the issues, it probably took him less than five months of actual writing to complete: *A Careful and Strict Enquiry into the Modern Prevailing Notions of that Freedom of Will, which Is Supposed to Be Essential to Moral Agency, Vertue and Vice, Reward and Punishment, Praise and Blame.* He viewed the issue of the nature of man's will as central to the theological crisis that a growing Arminian temper was producing in New England, a temper which he believed was beginning to infect even so staunch a Puritan as Chauncy. Since most Arminians had accepted the necessity of prevenient grace, they argued that the will of God was conditional, that God's mind would be swayed by the conduct and beliefs of men. Men therefore participated directly in the ultimate decision regarding their own eternal destination, and the will of man was free to choose or reject God. The Arminians rejected, categorically, the orthodox Calvinist doctrine of irresistible grace in favor of the doctrine of conditionalism. They went further: Christ's atonement was effective not only for those whom God would save, but theoretically made the salvation of all men possible. So, again, if a man rejected the gift of Christ, he rejected it out of the plenitude of his will, which, in such a case, was freely choosing sin and earning damnation. Supported by the pleasant rationalism of capitalism and the Enlightenment, the relative mildness, ethical rationalism, and ennobling freedom of Arminianism made their way even into the bloodstream of New England's intellectual life. Covenantal theory, by tending to reduce God to human proportions, to obligations and rules which men could know and He must fulfill and obey, helped to fertilize the Bay's stony soil for the tender but prolific plant of Arminianism.

Edwards saw that the issue between orthodoxy and Arminianism was fundamentally a controversy over whether or not man's will was free. His general goal was nothing less than a complete defense of Christianity, and a first step was the destruction of the idea of man's freedom, so that God's freedom could be reasserted. Man and God, Edwards believed, could not both be free. In this he obviously displayed his theological heritage, and admitted that, as he said, "I should not take it at all amiss, to be called a Calvinist, for distinction's sake: though I utterly disclaim a dependence on Calvin, or believing the doctrines which I hold, because he believed and taught them; and cannot justly be charged with believing in everything just as he taught."[35] Regardless of his legitimate qualifications, Edwards was a Calvinist, the most thoroughgoing that New England ever had.

He was a Calvinist, however, with a difference; he had absorbed the liberating spirit of Locke. His artistry was quite necessary to help him try to validate Calvin's basic conclusions with Locke's new vocabulary. His understanding of Locke helped him to go beyond Calvin, to face without blinking some of the issues, and the human will is a good example, which Calvin dealt with rhetorically, not logically. As such, Edwards' system was in large part designed to prove what Calvin had merely felt to be true but had either failed to prove or had mismanaged. Calvin's essential vision was never challenged by Edwards, but much of the earlier evidence and argument was. Because of the similar basic eschatology of the two, it is right to think of Edwards as, at least, an essential Calvinist. As such, Edwards built a theological system that relied not at all on covenants either strict or half-way, and was relatively unconcerned with the ecclesiastical storms that had come to characterize the American Zion. His task was simply to rebuild the entire intellectual framework of the House of Puritanism.

Somewhat wearily Edwards wrote that it would have been unnecessary to define the will "had not philosophers, metaphysicians and polemic divines brought the matter into obscurity by the things they have said of it."[36] For him, an elaborate problem simply did not exist: To will was to choose. "The will (without any metaphysical refining) is plainly, that by which the mind chooses anything."[37] To overrefine the definition of the will was to run the risk of making it too discrete, of making it indeed into a quite separate and autonomous faculty, as he had already asserted in his *Religious Affections*. No progress could be made until it was recognized that a man was a man, and that the intimacy of all of his various faculties must tend toward a holistic, not a divisive, view of his nature.

Even Locke failed to follow his own logic of holism through when he argued that a man's will could contradict his desire as, for instance, when a man felt obliged to speak to another and yet desired that his words should have no effect. A man in this case, Locke had said, willed to speak and desired his own failure. Edwards' Lockean view of man's integrated nature led him to see that Locke had not gone far enough: "A man never, in any instance, wills anything contrary to his desires, or desires anything contrary to his will."[38] Locke's example, so far from proving what Locke had intended, merely showed that even the great Mr. Locke could mismanage an argument. If a man spoke he had willed to speak; if he desired his words to be uninfluential, he desired just that. In Locke's example, as Edwards showed, there were two different issues: speaking and not being heeded. In each separate case the will and desire were in agreement. It was needless to add, Edwards added, that "the will may not agree with the will, nor desire agree with desire, in different things."[39]

Having finished with his lecture to Locke on the utility of more rigorous analysis, Edwards concluded that, in his opinion, everyone would agree that every act of will was also an act of choice. He reasoned that a state of perfect neutrality in regard to some object would make any action in regard to that object impossible. Where there was no preference there was no will; where there was no will an absence of preference could be deduced.

To this point Edwards had shown not much more than that his frame of reference was holistic, that he was a very modern Gestalt psychologist. He now faced the question that had been muddying philosophical waters throughout the history of philosophy: Was the will free or not? He chose not to play the scholar's game of reviewing the history of "that grand inquiry" because "it would be very tedious and unnecessary at present to enumerate and examine all the various opinions, which have been advanced concerning the matter."[40] Rather, he relied on logic and the art of his language to see him through. He simply announced, therefore, that the will was as the apparent good was. The will could not be determined by something that was not apparent to the willing agent, and if what was apparent was perceived as not good the agent would choose to avoid it. Whatever was apparent, and apparent as good, must motivate men to an act of will: "it is that motive, which, as it stands in the view of the mind, is the strongest, that determines the will."[41] Because of his holistic psychology, Edwards defined a motive as the entire complex flow of impressions in the mind that stood behind an act of will. Everything which contributed to an individual's conception of good, everything which constituted choice, was a motive. His argument was tautological: the will was that which was determined by motive, and motive was that which determined the will. The tautology of his argument, though logically unfortunate, reinforced his holistic view of man, and was a consequence of that view.

His argument, thus far, may be summarized as follows: a man wills as a consequence of a motive, which is excited by something that is both apparent and apparently good; motives exist in greater or lesser potency, and that potency is a consequence of the degree of goodness the man perceived. Thus "the will always is as the greatest apparent good is."[42] One notes the identity between the will and the apparent good: One *is* the other. An act which resulted from a will was determined by the apparent good, but the connection between the apparent good and the will itself was too close to speak of determinism. "There is scarcely a plainer and more universal dictate of the sense and experience of mankind, than that, when men act voluntarily, and do what they please, then they do what suits them best, or what is most agreeable to them."[43]

If men wanted to define freedom as the ability to do what one pleased, Edwards would have agreed that men were free. But he showed that men were not free to do anything except what they pleased, or chose, or preferred. Thus that definition of freedom merely begged the question: Why did men please what they pleased? Why did they perceive an apparent good as apparently good? Men, in Edwards' view to this point, were caught and made unfree by their own perception, and that was determined by the entire constitution of the individual.

The usual view of Edwards as a simple idealist is found to be inadequate when his understanding of the good is pursued. He said that there were three conditions that made an apparent object attract or repel. The first was the nature of the object itself, viewed "as it is in itself."[44] Second was the "manner of the view." It makes a difference whether one views a rattlesnake in the hand or behind glass. "The state and circumstances of the mind that views"[45] were the third condition. It is clear that for Edwards there was an exterior and objective reality that intruded itself, as it actually existed, into the mind of the viewer. But this objectivity did not itself suffice to explain reality for any one man. The total relationship between subject and object was the determining fact for Edwards, and neither one nor the other alone would cause the apparent object to be viewed as desirable. A dialectic between the external and factual object and the object as perceived by an individual's total being constituted reality for that person.

The root problem with which Edwards was concerned was how, in a deterministic universe, men could be held responsible for their actions. If a man is not free, the usual Arminian argument went, he does the bidding of his master, and the master must be guilty when man goes astray. Given this view, the Arminian not infrequently charged that, in the orthodox Calvinist scheme of things, God was made the author of sin, and man was a simple puppet who could not justifiably be called to account for his actions, since he could not control them. The concept of free will, according to the Arminians, was essential if man was to receive rewards and punishments; without freedom there could be no accountability. The three terms in the debate were freedom, responsibility, and determinism. In order to meet the Arminian objections, Edwards was obliged to eliminate one of those terms, to show that either freedom or responsibility was consistent with determinism, or else to abandon determinism altogether.

The issue was fairly drawn when Edwards announced that he intended "to prove that necessity is not inconsistent with liberty."[46] He was willing to grant the proposition that liberty was essential to responsibility, and he assumed the other burden of reconciling determinism and liberty, as St. Augustine and Calvin had also tried to do. Determinism, or necessity, he said, "is really nothing else than the full and fixed connection between the things signified by the subject and predicate of a proposition, which affirms something to be true."[47] His need to avoid the concept of an efficient cause if he were to rescue liberty resulted in his use of the concept of a "full and fixed connection" between antecedent and consequent.

The "connection" of the things referred to by the subject and predicate of a statement might be a full and fixed and certain connection in three different ways. (1) The "connection" might be inherent in the terms themselves "because it may imply a contradiction, or gross absurdity, to suppose them not connected."[48] One could not deny, for instance, the existence of being in general, because the mind must fail before the concept of the positive existence of absolute and universal nonexistence. There were, in short, a number of propositions whose truth was self-evident. (2) The "connection" between antecedent and consequent was certainly fixed in the case of events which had already happened. "Thus the existence of whatever is already come to pass, is now become necessary; 'tis become impossible it should be otherwise than true, that such a thing has been."[49] (3) There was also a future necessity in the "connection" between the subject and predicate of a proposition which affirmed something to be true in the future, but in this case the necessity must be a consequence of the category of either inherent or past necessity. Future necessity, he wrote, "is either fully and thoroughly connected with that which is absolutely necessary in its own nature, or with something which has already received and made sure of its existence."[50] Future necessity could not be inherently true because, if so, it would always have existed, and the future obviously could not have the necessity of that which had already come into being. "This [future] necessity lies in, or may be explained by the connection of two or more propositions one with another."[51] His view of future necessity was clearly true of past necessity before the past came to be. All necessity therefore was either intrinsic or past, or a consequence of those two.

In human terms Edwards distinguished two general categories of necessity: moral and natural. Both categories were equally compelling, and their difference arose from the difference in the nature of their respective causes. Moral necessity arose in a man himself, in the manifold nature of his total personality. Natural necessity, on the other hand, surrounded man from outside of himself, and was unaffected by the personality of the creature. By this category a wounded man would necessarily feel pain. At rather great length, Edwards argued that the degree of compulsion in these two categories was equal, and that the basic difference had only to do with the nature of the terms being connected: Moral causes would produce moral consequences as necessarily as natural causes would produce natural consequences.

Viewed in such a light, it was in "the nature of things" that moral necessity was as compelling as natural necessity. Choice, therefore, was not, as commonly supposed, a principle opposed to nature, but an integral part of nature itself. As a principle in a Newtonian world of nature, choice became for Edwards a principle of motion and action that was related to objects in the external world: "Choice often interposes, interrupts and alters the chain of events in these external objects, and causes 'em to proceed otherwise than they would do, if let alone, and left to go on according to the laws of motion among themselves."[52] Through their laws of motion, the planets swung in their orbits; as a law of motion, human choice, within the limits of human power, also contributed to the behavior of nature. Choice now became an ingredient in the physical universe.

Man's various *in*abilities limited the field over which his choice could operate. No man's choice to grow wings and fly could be implemented, because of a natural inability. "We are said to be *naturally* unable to do a thing, when we can't do it if we will."[53] Moral inability consisted of the absence of the will to do, or the strength of a contrary willing: "A woman of great honor and chastity may have a moral inability to prostitute herself to her slave."[54] Because the act of the will was a result of the strongest motive, the will was always unable to act any way other than it acted. If a man failed to act in some moral category, therefore, it was always inaccurate to say of him that he was unable to do the thing. He was, rather, unwilling, even though he had the power or ability to perform the act in question. In the case of a failure to perform some moral act, everything necessary to that act was present except the will. An individual who was not restrained by natural inability and who did not act in a certain way was restrained by moral inability: He would not, though he could.

Freedom for Edwards, and here he was in unlikely agreement with Hobbes, Spinoza, and Hume, consisted in man's doing as he pleased, in acting as he willed to act. "And the contrary to liberty, whatever name we call that by, is a person's being hindered or unable to conduct as he will, or being necessitated to do otherwise."[55]   If a man desired to act he was not limited by moral inability, and if he was not limited by natural inability he was perfectly free to act as he willed. He would always will as he pleased, or as the greatest good for him was apparent to him. Nothing, in Edwards' system, could stand in the way of an implementation of the will except natural inability or the absence of the will itself. Constraint, or force, might of course compel an individual to act contrary to his will, but that was largely irrelevant to the personal psychology of willing. In this sense, all action was obviously a result of will, and all men were free to act as they willed, though they were not free to will otherwise.

Edwards now faced three other Arminian arguments: The will itself was free or self-determining or uncaused; the mind before the act of willing was morally neutral or in equilibrium; contingency in the sense of denying all necessity was of the essence of freedom.

He destroyed the Arminian position with a *reductio ad absurdum.* If the will was thought to be self-determining, an assumption was made that an act of the will must have caused the first such act. But if there was a first act of the will, that first act could not have been preceded by an earlier act. Given the hypothesis of a first act of will, that act must have been preceded by something outside of the will. If the first act of will was not free because no act of will could have preceded the first act, none of the subsequent acts, caused by or based on that first act, could be free. The contradictions in the Arminian argument were patent.

If the Arminians argued that the will was neutral before the act of will, they were caught again, because, if freedom consisted in the will being determined by the will itself, they destroyed themselves by arguing that something other than the will moved a neutral will out of its equilibrium. The argument of contingency was also self-contradictory, because a will that was determined by nothing at all was not determined by itself. Contingency also contradicted the absolute foreknowledge of God that both Edwards and the Arminians assumed to be true. The Arminian concept of contingency therefore implicitly but necessarily denied one of the essential attributes of the godhead.

A system of morality, so far from being destroyed by the Calvinist system of strict determinism, was destroyed by the Arminian concepts of neutrality and contingency in the will. It was clear, Edwards thought, that moral law could not regulate accident, and the contingency argument must make any directing or restraining law whatsoever inconsistent with the nature of man's will. Since the purpose of law was to "*bind to one side;* and the end of commands is to turn the will one way,"[56] the concept of a neutral will was similarly inconsistent with the efficacy of moral government, or, indeed, government of any kind.

Edwards had argued that every act of the will was caused by some motive. The will, in any specific case, was determined by the necessity of the connection between antecedent and subsequent, by the motive or choice which called the will to exertion. If there were no motive, the will could have no goal in view, and the will would then will to realize nothing, another absurdity. An act of will was the effect of a motive and was necessarily such an effect. "Thus it is manifest, that volition is necessary, and is not from any self-determining power in the will: the volition which is caused by previous motive and inducement, is not caused by the will exercising a sovereign power over itself."[57] Because of his holistic view of human nature, Edwards, it will be remembered, defined motive as the complete and intricate composition of a personality which led to a preference of one thing to another. His argument may be translated into these terms: Man's total being determines the degree of goodness he perceives in any apparent thing; that degree of perceived goodness constitutes choice, which constitutes will; man's total being therefore determines will. With will there was moral ability and, assuming a natural ability, man then would and could act. Man was quite free to do as he willed, though his will was itself determined.

Now Edwards was ready to turn to the question of freedom and moral responsibility. The Arminians had argued that no mere puppet could be called to account for dancing the dance of the puppeteer. Only if man's will was free, they had argued, could he be justly rewarded or punished for his actions. They had maintained that God would be unjust to demand from man actions which he could not perform, that man was unable to give perfect obedience, and that Christ died so that God would accept imperfect in the place of perfect obedience. Displaying the internal contradictions of this piece of the Arminian system, Edwards began to suggest some of the more important theological conclusions to which he was coming.

According to Edwards, the Arminian position amounted to a conviction that God had abolished the original law which had demanded perfect obedience from men, that, because of Adam's fall, God had introduced a milder law that required only imperfect obedience from men made infirm by original sin.   There were, Edwards showed, problems with such a formulation. If a milder law existed, the imperfections of man's obedience were not a breach of the law and were not sins. If they were not sins, why did Christ die to atone for them?   Since Arminians argued that it would be unjust of God to require perfect obedience, they must conclude that it would be unjust of God to punish man for the imperfections of his nature.   Again, if it would be unjust of God to punish man for a failure to live up to a law which had now been abolished, why did Christ die? "What need of Christ's dying to make way for God's accepting such an obedience, as it would be unjust in him not to accept?"[58] If the Arminians argued that Christ died to satisfy the old and more rigorous law in order that the new and more mild law could be introduced, they argued that Christ died in order to compel God to replace one law with another when, by their very argument, it would have been unjust of God to do anything else, whether Christ died or not.

The Arminian conception of grace was similarly tongue-tied. If, as some said, men could achieve pardon for sin only by grace, and if it would be unjust and cruel of God to demand from men actions which men could not perform, then God's grace to men was not His free gift, but was a positive debt He owed to men. As such it was not grace at all.

According to Edwards' understanding, it was perfectly just of God to demand from men behavior which they could but *would* not perform. God never required men to transcend their natural inabilities, and it would be unjust if He demanded from men behavior which they *could* not perform. Because moral inability was simply the absence of will, or the presence of a contrary and stronger will, it was not properly termed an inability at all, but was simply a disinclination. "If merely that [moral] inability will excuse disobedience, which is implied in the opposition or defect of inclination, remaining after the command is exhibited, then wickedness always carries that in it which excuses it."[59] Of course, he admitted, natural necessity made praise or blame irrelevant. Only when a man's choice was involved in his actions was he justifiably held to account. And in every act of man's that was not dictated by either duress or natural law, his will absolutely determined his actions. Every man was free to do as he willed, and no man was free to do otherwise.

All men, therefore, out of the rottenness of their whole beings, committed evil because they willed to commit evil. They were able to do good though they would not. Since they were absolutely free to do as they willed to do, it was just that they should be condemned by God. The original law which had applied to Adam applied still to his descendants. Adam's will to evil, as one link in the chain of the human story, helped to fashion the wills that came after Adam. Depravity was universal and all men willed sin. Only those would be saved, therefore, whom God chose to save, not as a result of man's actions, but as a perfectly free and unmerited gift of God. Those whom God saved were necessarily reborn. The whole frame of their beings was altered so that they would now perceive and therefore will differently. Now, with the grace of God, men would will the goodness which, in their unregenerate condition, they had despised. So justification preceded sanctification, not the reverse, as so many splinters of Christianity had maintained. The freedom of the elect was in no way lessened by the fact that they were necessarily sanctified, just as God's necessary holiness did not diminish His freedom, the freedom to do as one pleased.

Still, the Arminians demanded to know, if unregenerate men would not will good, and if only unmerited and free grace could alter the human character, why should men go to church, heed their ministers, or use other means to encourage piety? This is the question that was then and is now usually asked of or about Calvinists. If a man's destiny is already determined, why should he not live a life of pleasure? If he is damned already it cannot make any difference how much he enjoys himself, and if he is already saved he cannot alter that decision either. Edwards answered with two arguments.

It was conceivable, he wrote, that in the long series of antecedents and consequents which made up the world's activity, the means used to elicit piety probably were among the antecedents "which are connected with the consequents we aim at, in the established course of things."[60] Either from observation of nature or from divine revelation, men assumed that the accepted means of piety would be connected with divine favor. If an individual willed to heed his minister, was that not some slight sign that—perhaps—he had been justified? Since the will itself was the only place to look for signs of regeneration, the existence of a will to employ the means of piety was of major importance.

The second argument was stronger. A man might say to himself, since the Calvinist world is determined and I cannot effect the future by what I do or fail to do, why should I do anything but that which adds to pleasure and happiness? "Such a man," Edwards reasoned, "contradicts himself: he says, the measure of his future happiness and misery is already fixed, and he won't try to diminish the one, nor add to the other: but yet in his very conclusion, he contradicts this; for he takes up this conclusion, *to add to his future happiness*, by the ease and comfort of his negligence; and to diminish his future trouble and misery, by saving himself the trouble of using means and taking pains."[61] If determinism was true, a man could not decide to seek pleasure because determinism was true. A man could not have decided to avoid the hard pew of the church if he had gone to church. Whatever was, had to be. If he did not go to church he willed not to go, and was not free to will otherwise. And what might that indicate of the state of that poor soul?

Edwards' God was the governor as well as the creator of the universe. All that happened was foreknown and predestined. The final Arminian charge against the Calvinists was, understandably, that Calvin's God was the author and cause of sin. God, said Edwards, did in fact permit sin, and did in fact so arrange the condition of things that sin inevitably and necessarily followed. "If this be all that is meant, by being the author of sin, I don't deny that God is the author of sin (though I dislike and reject the phrase, as that which by use and custom is apt to carry another sense), it is no reproach for the most High to be thus the author of sin."[62] Though God permitted and even arranged for the existence of sin, He was not Himself the actor of sin. It was clear to

Edwards that God "for excellent, holy, gracious and glorious ends, ordered the fact which they committed, who were concerned in Christ's death; and that therein they did but fulfill God's designs."[63] Nonetheless, as he had already argued, men, in fulfilling God's purpose, even to the extent of crucifying Christ, were themselves accountable for their act because they had themselves willed it. God willed the existence of evil for good purposes; men willed evil out of their love of it. God caused sin the way the sun caused darkness, which, Edwards hopefully said, was no cause at all. God had a secret will that was unrevealed in Scripture, and sin was a part of that mysterious aspect of the Lord.

As God had decreed, so the world was. As the Holy Spirit, as an emanation of God, touched the human heart, so man would be reborn to see the meaning of the Lord. Redemption by Christ was a necessary chapter in the history of the world, but a chapter that neither eliminated sin nor guaranteed universal salvation. After the atonement, as before, men willed evil. Only the breath of the Father into the nostrils of the creature was sufficient to call forth a new life.

Humanity did not inherit the sin of Adam through any vague system of transmission. In *The Great Christian Doctrine of Original Sin Defended* (1758), Edwards clarified his position that God had dealt with Adam not as an individual but as the representative of the species. The essential unity of the human race made each member directly and personally responsible for the act of its representative. Original sin was, therefore, not the sin of the father visited upon the sons, but the actual commission of the sin by the father and sons as one unit. It was true that Adam's will was freer than that of his posterity because his "reason and judgment never was held down by the inferior inclinations,"[64] but because of Adam's representativeness his abuse of relative freedom was the direct crime of the human race. Every man was present in Adam, and Adam continued to be present in every man; every man was therefore justly condemned for the sin in Eden. Edwards' logic finally failed, and he asserted the essential mystery of original sin. God allowed Adam to transgress, but the allowance was an efficient cause of the transgression. Why innocence would fail its test of freedom was never, and could never, be made clear by Edwards, or any one else for that matter. Edwards' grand retreat deserves quotation:

the first arising or existing of that evil disposition in the heart of Adam was by God's *permission;* who could have prevented it, if he had pleased, by *giving* such influences of his spirit as would have been absolutely effectual to hinder it; which it is plain in fact he did *withhold:* And whatever mystery may be supposed in the affair, yet no christian will presume to say, it was not in perfect consistence with God's *holiness* and *righteousness,* notwithstanding Adam had been guilty of no offence before. So root and branches being one . . . the case in fact is, that by virtue of oneness answerable changes or effects through all the *branches* coexist with the changes in the *root;* consequently an evil disposition exists in the hearts of Adam's posterity, equivalent to that which was exerted in his own heart when he eat the forbidden fruit. Which God has no hand in any otherwise, than in not exerting such an influence as might be effectual to prevent it.[65]

Before Edwards' defense of *Original Sin* was published he received from the trustees of Princeton a letter offering him the presidency of the college. He answered that he was too weak, inadequately educated, and pressed for time by his writing. The trustees persisted, and Edwards left his decision to a council of ministers from surrounding towns. They decided that the offer from Princeton might also be an offer from God, and on their recommendation, Edwards tearfully accepted. He arrived in Princeton in February of 1758 in the midst of a smallpox epidemic. A lifelong defender of advanced science, he could not turn his back on medical discovery now, so he was inoculated on February 13; from the effects of the inoculation he died five weeks later.

His understanding of the Christian scheme of things led Edwards to emphasize the sovereignty of God over all of His other attributes. The arbitrary rulership of the Father took precedence over the humanity and mercifulness of the Son. There was no room in his most masculine theological cosmos for the tender attributes of feminine mercy or concern with the fleshy flesh of the children. Edwards' most male God turned away from representation of Himself in images, and even the Incarnation was barely tolerable. Nowhere in Edwards' system does the Mother appear. Mercy was admitted, but as the darkest mystery, the one attribute of God that He most jealously kept from men.

Abstraction, not flesh or personification, was the stuff of this Protestant God; justice, not mercy, was the usual divine attitude.

Even the flesh of the Son was abstract, for "The Son Himself is the idea of the Father,"[66] and the Holy Spirit was God's love of Himself radiating out into the cosmos, as St. Augustine had also believed.   Edwards' definition of the trinity shows perfectly this hypertrophy of abstraction: "we shall never be able to make more than these three, God, the idea of God, and delight in God,"[67] that is, the Father, the Son, and the Holy Ghost.

The Puritan mind, as one of the radical wings of Protestantism, had always been committed to abstraction and fearful of personification.   That Christ's birth and death were not only deemphasized but, in a sense, rejected, is shown by the Puritans' elimination of Christmas and Easter.   The idea of Mary filled them with loathing as a purely Catholic idea.   In political terms, their abstraction took the form of opposition to King and loyalty to the state, and the idea of loyalty to the person of the King was a way to weaken, not strengthen, the tie to England.   Winthrop's alteration of the King's two bodies and Edwards' understanding of theology both represented the extreme Protestant recoil at any suggestion of personification. In politics and theology they were committed to the Word, the idea, and shunned what they were pleased to call the golden calves of Catholicism and monarchy.   Their distrust of personification led them to construct intellectual systems that raised abstraction to ascending levels of rarification.   It led them to reject Mary, Pope, and King because each violated abstraction by giving particular flesh to the higher idea.   It further led to a literalism that supported their hatred of beauty in a Gothic cathedral, courtly pomp, or an elaborate literary style.   They built their plain white meeting houses with no steeple and no crucifix, and developed a literary technique called the "plain style."   In their fear and hatred of person and their commitment to abstraction, these Puritans helped to set both the tone and substance of much of America's future intellectual history.

Edwards was the quintessential Protestant mind.   All other intellectual growths from the Reformation are deviations from the necessary logic of his works.   His vision, as should be clear by now, was neither pretty nor comfortable.   "Edwards' system," said Oliver Wendell Holmes, "seems, in the light of to-day, to the last degree barbaric, mechanical, materialistic, pessimistic."[68]   So it must have seemed to the nineteenth century in America which had learned to do without the inexorable kind of logic Edwards had brought to his task. A world that could listen to Emerson could not hear Edwards.

Coming close to a complete theological system, Edwards himself virtually assured that his own life would ring with irony and tragedy. He should have been born in London instead of the intellectual and emotional desert of colonial America, though his intellectual lineage went directly back to the Boston of Winthrop. His radical Protestantism might have been diluted anywhere but in New England, and the world would have lost its paradigm of the utter Protestant mind. He should have had closer contacts with better minds. He should have known that the cramped and narrow world in which he spent his days would send him out into a literal wilderness. But, to do him the honor of following his own logic, it is fair to say that he himself willed his own course in a world of forces he could not control. He was free to do as he willed, and he remains responsible for the path he chose to travel.

SELECT BIBLIOGRAPHY

Bernard Bailyn. *The New England Merchants in the Seventeenth Century.* Cambridge, 1955.

Loren Baritz, "The Idea of the West," *American Historical Review,* LXVI, 3 (April 1961), 618–640.

Norman O. Brown. *Life against Death.* Middletown, Conn., 1959. Ch. XIV.

Edwin S. Gausted. *The Great Awakening in New England.* New York, 1957.

Joseph Haroutunian. *Piety versus Moralism.* New York, 1932.

Perry Miller. *Jonathan Edwards.* N.P., 1949.

———— *The New England Mind: The Seventeenth Century.* Cambridge, 1939.

Edmund S. Morgan. *Visible Saints.* New York, 1963.

K. B. Murdock. *Literature and Theology in Colonial New England.* Cambridge, 1949.

Paul Ramsey. "Introduction," in Jonathan Edwards, *Freedom of the Will.* P R ed. New Haven, 1957.

Herbert W. Schneider. *The Puritan Mind.* New York, 1930.

John E. Smith. "Introduction," in Jonathan Edwards, *A Treatise Concerning Religious Affections.* J E S ed. New Haven, 1959.

Ola E. Winslow. *Jonathan Edwards.* New York, 1940.

III

POLITICAL THEORY * *John Adams*

> In short, philosophers, ancient and modern,
> appear to me as mad as Hindoos, Mahometans,
> and Christians. No doubt they would all think
> me mad, and for any thing I know, this globe
> may be the Bedlam . . . of the universe.
>
> *1814*

The dominant mode of intellectual life in colonial America had been theological; and from the generation of Winthrop to Jonathan Edwards the development of religious thought had been considered the most pressing task. When Edwards died the colonies were involved in the French and Indian War, some of whose consequences were to force Americans to embark on a relatively new intellectual quest. In driving the French from North America, England unwittingly removed one major cause of colonial dependence on the mother country, for the colonies had on occasion looked to England for protection against the Catholic French in the New World. When that need was eliminated by England's costly victory, the colonists were freer of England than they had ever been before. They were free to begin a political education whose completion was made urgent by continuing policies of the Crown. Under the press of events, thinking Americans turned from a consideration of the nature of God and men's relationship to Him, to a consideration of the nature of the King and Americans' relationship to him.

As an immediate consequence of the French and Indian War, British policy was significantly changed from what it had been before the war. England attempted to make the frontiers more secure against the Indians by prohibiting further colonial migrations to the west, and, through the Stamp Act, intended to raise a revenue that would ease the war debt by taxing the colonists. The conflict between England and America that resulted from these departures generated a momentum which led to further attempts to modernize imperial policy. As news of each step toward that goal was received in colonial America, Americans were forced to assess what they thought would be the probable consequences.

Although Americans were forced to turn to political theory by the politics of the empire, they were not entering an entirely new intellectual mode. It had been necessary for the very first colonists to clarify their understanding of the imperial relationship. They had been obliged to create and administer governments. But the first colonists had the luxury of building their states in relative isolation, and, in New England, they had been equipped with an elaborate theology that constituted a firm foundation for their political decisions. The revolutionary generation of Americans became political once more, not in the provincial calm of Winthrop's Boston, but in a crisis that could have deep personal meaning, at least in a financial sense, and usually meaning in wider terms.

The God of Winthrop had grown steadily weaker as a result of His rigid demands. Men, even Americans, indeed even New Englanders, were unable to satisfy that Puritan God because of their unwillingness to abandon the consuming business of making a living in order to think more steadily on divine things. There were moments of doubt and guilt about this desertion from the God of the fathers, and the Great Awakening was such a moment. But Edwards, out of the wreckage of the Awakening, made that God even more difficult and jealous. In trying to purge the American compromises from theology, Edwards had unintentionally directed men away from the church, back to their farms and ships.

The French and Indian War somewhat upset farming and fishing. The peace threatened to alter permanently the accustomed "salutory neglect" England had long permitted the colonists to enjoy. The revolutionary generation had to make its political way in an emergency and without the security of theology. But Americans had American experience and, in turning to that, they turned to the works that had been built on the faith of their fathers. In turning to their own immediate past, Americans of the century of alleged enlightenment turned to a tradition radically different from those accessible to European *philosophes.*

The so-called American *philosophes* were anxious to conserve the wisdom of their American fathers, and saw local tradition as right and helpful and worthy of honor. They fought a revolution in order to conserve that tradition, in order to conserve the already mature commitment to freedom. The freedom they meant was the freedom to allow the continued emergence and development of the ideas of the seventeenth century. But those ideas, in order to be acceptable and effective, had sometimes to be changed. Even with such changes, however, American thought of the eighteenth century remained largely autochthonous, and it therefore diverged significantly from Enlightenment thought in Europe.

American ideas about America, time, and nature account for most of the divergence between the thought of the age on the two sides of the Atlantic. Of course there were internal differences within both Europe and America, but dominant climates of thought may be suggested. Underlying many of the peculiarities of American thought, and contributing to an extension of that thought, were the substance and implications of the idea of the west.

Always to the west of civilized America lay the forest, the French, the Indians, and, later, the British. The colonists climbed over each of these obstacles in their westering. Through pioneering and victory in a war and in a revolution, the continent was made more open. The observable facts of politics and expansion in the eighteenth century thus became a buttress to the earlier American ideas of the west. As seventeenth-century Americans had Christianized the idea of the west by relating it to the kingdom of God, eighteenth-century Americans secularized it by recalling the west of empire. As the idea of the holy west persisted, and the idea of the imperial west was added to it, the idea of America came to include grandeur and power linked to godliness and innocence. The idea of the west was an inextricable part of the American idea of progress. As Americans defined progress in terms of their providential nation, rather than in terms of the species, they diverged from usual eighteenth-century ideas of progress.

The imperial idea of the west became one basis of the hope that America would one day be great in power. In 1726, Bishop Berkeley, using an ancient theme, applied the imperial west to America:

> Westward the course of empire takes its way;
> The four first Acts already past,
> A fifth shall close the Drama with the Day;
> Time's noblest offspring is the last.[1]

Joel Barlow, the poet of republican virtue, who also identified the apocalypse with America, agreed:

> Earth's blood-stain'd empires, with their
>   Guide the Sun
> From Orient climes their gradual progress run;
> And circling far, reach every western shore,
> 'Til earth-born empires rise and fall no more.[2]

The historical law that had condemned earlier nations to eventual decline was presumably abrogated for or by America, as Winthrop had earlier thought. Just past midcentury, the popular almanack-maker, Nathaniel Ames, took a less political view when he argued that the course of literature would inevitably move westward. Benjamin Franklin agreed. By 1775, John Witherspoon, preaching at Princeton, could combine every one of these ideas when he articulated what was to become the usual American formula: "some have observed that true religion, and in her train, dominion, riches, literature, and art, have taken their course in a slow and gradual manner from East to West, since the earth was settled after the flood: and from thence forebode the future glory of America."[3]

The idea of the west seems to have been acknowledged by growing numbers of Americans. A traveler in the middle colonies reported that during the French and Indian War, "An idea, strange as it is visionary, has entered into the minds of the generality of mankind, that empire is travelling westward; and every one is looking forward with eager and impatient expectation to that destined moment, when America is to give law to the rest of the world."[4] From Rome itself, the seat of the first idea of the imperial west, America was assured of the validity of her new role; an American traveling in Rome inspired a poet to an extemporaneous paean:

> But all things of heavenly origin, like the glorious sun, move Westward; and Truth and Art have their periods of shining, and of might. Rejoice then, O venerable Rome, in thy divine destiny, for though darkness overshadow thy seats, and though thy mitred head must descend into the dust . . . thy spirit, immortal and undecayed, already spreads towards a new world, where, like the soul of man in Paradise, it will be perfected in virtue and beauty more and more.[5]

The journey west within America was, like the westering of all ages, a rebuke to organized society. Thus for the pioneer engaged in the actual journey the west meant, among other things, freedom from an already organized America. For the contented American who accepted civilization if it was American, the west meant that power and virtue would soon be American, that a civilized America was to be free of an east which was Europe. Whether the mythological west was located in the American forest or along the Atlantic seaboard depended on whether the rejected society was thought to be civilized America or Europe. In either case, a rejection of a civilized past was a central aspect of the American idea of the west.

In eastern America, ideas of the west provided one major intellectual support of the more general eighteenth-century idea of progress. Whether the conception was cyclical or linear, a growing number of Americans were becoming adherents of a peculiar version of geographical or national promise and destiny. Even Americans who believed that there was an inevitable cycle in human affairs, that a fall from power and goodness could not be avoided, usually argued that America was in the infancy of her career, that the heights their country would achieve justified sometimes unlimited optimism. It might be true that some day a fall from those heights would mortify Americans, but that day was usually put far enough into the future to have but little effect.

The idea of progress rested not only on intellectual and mythological bases; concrete developments were also employed. For many, the richness of American soil and the rapid growth of population and wealth were incontrovertible facts in the argument that defended the idea of progress in America. Also utilizing the more common faith of the Puritan tradition and of Enlightenment thought, some Americans argued that the development and implementation of reason would assure American progress, as would a presumably growing secularism and religious toleration.

A benign optimism seemed to settle over many articulate and established Americans as they witnessed and perhaps aided the revolutionary effort. That the young and avowedly frail republic could bring the English lion to heel seemed more than ample proof that the new nation was to rise to heights that would make sober men giddy. Contemplation of the prospect of war with England led some to worry that a revolution might damage America's prospects for success, but once the war came such doubts were effectively laid to rest. During the course of the war, leaders of thought deduced from the anticipated victory the facts necessary for deifying or sanctifying the nation. By now the reflex in mythology was virtually conditioned to seek the Hebraic analogy. The nation at war became "our Israel,"[6] the battle dead "of GOD's American Israel," became "*beauties of Israel*," and Washington was an "American *Joshua*."[7] If the people of the new nation would take proper care, "it will be true of them as it was of the people of the Jews, that *in them all the families of the earth shall be blessed*."[8]

With the coming of peace, the idea of progress assumed its most extreme and most American form. The new nation, reported the *Massachusetts Centinel*, in a paraphrase of Joel Barlow, was "reserved to be the last and greatest theater for the improvement of mankind."[9] The Revolution, said one, was a "principal link" in "a grand chain of Providence," a link which was necessary to the arrival of the *"Millenial State."*[10] Another went further: "What great things has the God of Providence done for our race! By the revolution we this day celebrate, he has provided an asylum for the oppressed . . . and in due time, the universal establishment of the Messiah's kingdom."[11] From England, the sympathetic Richard Price announced: "Perhaps I do not go too far when I say that, next to the introduction of Christianity among mankind, the American revolution may prove the most important step in the progressive course of human improvement."[12]

The outcome of the war was obviously important to Americans; it was presumably of equal importance to God, who had ordained an American victory in order that His kingdom might at last be erected on earth. To some it was clear that Washington's puny army could succeed only with divine aid; that it did succeed was therefore proof of that aid. Even the English Thomas Pownall, frequent governor of American colonies, conceded to Benjamin Franklin that the "revolution . . . has stronger marks of divine interposition, superseding the ordinary course of human affairs, than any other event, which this world has experienced."[13]   By the military victory and the establishment of the federal government, the perfection of man would presumably be attainable.

Out of the political theology of the eighteenth century, out of the faiths and assumptions underlying the ideas of the west, the idea of progress, and the epiphanic conception of the war, an intellectual *cul de sac* was created. As a geographical and, later, national eschatology was elaborated, a number of Americans asked about the immediate consequences of the proliferating mythology. Was this then what God's kingdom looked like? Was this the behavior of the new race of men who were to save the world? Was this the flavor of freedom? The American mythos began to strain. Despair began to assume an American accent as the almost necessary antithesis to the concepts of God's country.

Because of the nature of the goals and of the significance attached to the Revolution, because this struggle was invested with cosmic and universal meaning, the postwar recoil was assured. Instead of felicity there was growing anger. Shays' Rebellion and the Society of the Cincinnati expressed the poles of the discontent that resulted from a growing awareness that the individual was not given a new birth of freedom and equality, that the aims of the war had aborted. The war opened the western safety valve, and the search for a new happy land began again as citizens of the new nation began the westward movement in an attempt to escape the burdens of a society that failed to live up to its promise, a society increasingly reminiscent of the eternal east which had earlier and still was driving men to the west. At the end of the war, a significant number of Americans decided that the organized society of the Atlantic coast was not the west, and that the Cumberland Gap was the new gateway to Eden.

Because the Revolution brought in its train neither the Lord nor the diffusion of universal joy, it was once more necessary to enquire into the meaning of the nation. Were Massachusetts, Virginia, and Kentucky all in the west, or had earlier Americans evolved a mythology that had now been superannuated?

From the beginning the American Puritans had argued the uniqueness of their commonwealth, their peculiar piety, and their consequent holy mission. Out of their theology the Bay saints had deduced the function of their new commonwealth to be an example to the world, an example which, if followed, would result in the eventual salvation of the race. To succeeding generations of Americans, descended from the saints or not, the idea that the destiny of mankind depended on America was neither new nor strange. The idea that America could reform the world, not by direct intervention (since that required power which America did not have), but by example, grew from the root deep in New England's earliest history. Thus, even before the Revolution presumably provided additional evidence, men of the eighteenth century had argued that America was unique, that her people were morally superior to all others, who were either deformed by barbarism or seduced by decadent civilization.

It was the war and the peace which followed that turned the idea of American exemplary morality and mission into a necessary ingredient in the national mythology. In *Common Sense*, Thomas Paine had set the tone: "We have it in our power to begin the world again. A situation, similar to the present, hath not happened since the days of Noah until now. The birthday of a new world is at hand."[14] Jefferson, late in his life, summed up his consistent attitude by describing his nation as "destined to be the primitive and precious model of what is to change the condition of man over the globe."[15] Joel Barlow thought that the hope of Europe was in "the example of political wisdom and felicity here to be displayed [which] will excite emulation through the kingdoms of the earth, and meliorate the conditions of the human race."[16] A growing number of Europeans agreed that the new political "errand into the wilderness" was valid, that America, as Turgot said, was the hope of and could be the model for the world. Voltaire wrote that the remedy for Europe's sickness could be found in America.

Because of their presumed virtue, God had presumably blessed Americans and had presumably intervened in their behalf. Now, in order partially to deserve His mercies, Americans had to remain models of virtue. According to Samuel Adams and others, the soul of a true republic was virtue. Without its soul the government would perish; should the government succeed, its success would prove the existence of its soul. Thus Americans could show their gratitude for the Lord's help by building and maintaining republican government.

How could Americans either remain or become virtuous? Were they not men and subject to the weaknesses of the species? In what way were Americans different from other humans? Were vice and stupidity irreconcilable with the idea of the new nation? Would the assumed law of the eventual decline of all earthly power be truly nullified for the United States?

Answers to those questions came from many sources, but most depended upon the idea that Americans as individuals were in fact human and therefore suspect, but politically, as a federated nation, Americans could build better than they were themselves. One of the central ingredients in the earlier national mythology was now applied. Time was abolished for God's country. Lifted out of history, free from a limiting past, Americans were presumably more self-determining than any other national people had ever been. Fighting against the old world, they believed that they were fighting against old age, decrepitude, and decadence. The idea of the west contributed its share to the notion that Americans swung free in seemingly limitless space unhampered by the dead and deadening hand of the past. Jefferson, for instance, late in his life, conceived of mankind's immemorial struggle with nature and the eternal westward course of civilization as physically present in America, where time had been changed into space:

> Let a philosophic observer commence a journey from the savages of the Rocky Mountains, eastwardly towards our sea-coast. These [savages] he would observe in the earliest stage of association, living under no law but that of nature, subscribing [sic] and covering themselves with the flesh and skin of wild beasts. He would next find those on our frontiers in the pastoral state, raising domestic animals to supply the defects of hunting. Then succeed our own semi-barbarous citizens, the pioneers of the advance of civilization, and so in his progress he would meet the gradual shades of improving man until he would reach his, as yet, most improved state in our seaport towns. This, in fact, is equivalent to a survey, in time, of the progress of man from the infancy of creation to the present day.[17]

American concepts of nature were different from those of most Europeans, and contributed to the sense that individual Americans were less trustworthy than Americans in the body politic. Those few who knew Rousseau's glorification of the savage found it laughable. When the pioneer meditated on the Indian, wrath rather than rapture was likely to ensue. From the most potent of their intellectual and emotional solutions, Americans had concluded that the untamed, unspoiled, nonhuman universe was dangerous, that the state of nature was fearful, that the natural man stank in the nostrils of God and was a threat to the lives of socialized men. Indian wars led the colonists in America to conclude that there were differences between a conceptualized and an experienced nature. Puritans and Virginians continued, however, to talk of the benignity of God's nature while they desperately fought to clear and maintain the land, and to push the Indian out of mind, if possible, or at least out of sight. The orthodox Puritan view of the necessary goodness of the universe became a compartmentalized creed that did not withstand the subversion of experience.

The American attitude about nature usually assumed that men had to transform the wilderness into a garden if the rudiments of a settled life were to be possible. To permit a continued hegemony of the forest would have direct human consequences: The European would become of the forest, a white Indian, with sensibilities and customs equal to or lower than the natural savage. There was no need for Americans to speculate about man in a state of nature. One merely had to walk west and view the life of the furthermost pioneers, as Jefferson had suggested. Crèvecoeur explained that such pathfinders disgusted him: "There, remote from the power of example and check of shame, many families exhibit the most hideous parts of our society."[18]

For the American, nature in its purest and therefore most dangerous state was the central enemy whose defeat was usually thought to be essential to godliness, prosperity, and progress. Only with the domestication of the forest did Americans also smilingly talk of nature and nature's God; only when the forest and the Indian became remote did Americans attempt to ennoble the savage and glorify the virgin land.

The fear of the forest led to a virtual apotheosis of the farmer, who would destroy the enemy and give birth to the garden. In

America the farmer was the essential instrument of humanization, and as such occupied a central position in the thought of the age. As American myth-making continued, most of the earlier ideas and many of the emerging ones began to coalesce around the farmer whose symbolic voice now began to resonate in almost all categories of thought. He was *the* American, the savior of the nation that was to be savior of the world. Recognizing the importance of the farmer, the men of the eighteenth century made his significance explicit.

The American farmer now emerged as the hero who was peculiarly blessed in his land, who was unique in his innocence and virtue, who held in his calloused hand the fate of the race. The political economy adequate to this man would be an example to all the world, "a beacon on a hill," as the Puritans had said of their own mission. From a model of piety America grew into a model of life. A republic of virtue was to be the result, and virtue in America came from the soil. Americans, wrote Crèvecoeur, were purified by "the simple cultivation of the earth . . . [and] are the western pilgrims . . . [who] will one day cause great changes in the world."[19]

American thought of the eighteenth century, strengthened by the conviction of America's continuing uniqueness and mission, rejected the remote past of America and the entire past of Europe, rejected unregulated nature as well as advanced civilization. It rejected the economy of Europe with its cities, luxury and poverty, and decadent politics. It rejected the American wilderness and the bestiality, as the Puritans had said, of untamed nature. Americans could praise neither nature nor human nature until both had been tamed, until they distinguished between the forest and the garden, between the savage and the farmer.

The threat to American virtue thus came from both directions. Barbarism and civilization were the fatal extremes to be avoided, and the resulting solution endowed the farmer with the essential attributes of heroism. He had learned from both pasts and had become a natural European, maimed neither by the lawlessness of the forest nor the decadence of civilization. Fearing the anarchy of the wilderness as well as the oppression of Europe, the American farmer was thought to be a new species of man who alone could afford never to look back while constructing the New Jerusalem, the republic of virtue, the city on a hill.

The alternative to the extreme into which Europe had fallen was thought to be a society of independent yeomen who knew with their own muscle the bounty of the new land. Americans now argued that great wealth was dangerous, that virtue was the first and major consequence of the farmer's moderate prosperity. In arguing this, the earlier Puritan attitude was completely reversed, since the saints had said that prosperity was the result, not the cause, of virtue. With the apotheosis of the farmer, however, virtue was thought to be the result of the magical effect of the land, and this virtue was an adequate safeguard against the vices that hitherto had been feared as a consequence of wealth.

The abstract farmer had thus become the rock on which the entire political economy rested, even though individual farmers were still mere men who were as depraved as the rest of mankind. As individuals, men were evil; and, as always, a view of man's inherent evil led away from democracy. From the Puritans through the eighteenth century, Americans who abhorred nature sought a restraining authority in government. Americans had experienced the savage and the forest and were convinced of the enmity of nature. Unwittingly, of course, the savage and the forest contributed to the fundamental politics of the new nation. Afraid of the natural forces a revolution might unleash, Gouverneur Morris noted, with a significant natural analogy, that "the mob begins to think and reason. Poor reptiles! it is with them a vernal morning; they are struggling to cast off their winter's slough, they bask in the sunshine, and ere noon they will bite."[20]

When the time came to write a constitution, the eighteenth-century fear of man was an essential premise for further thought. Several scholars have shown that the spirit of the Massachusetts saints breathed in that document, that fear of power in the hands of men led to the acceptance of the doctrine of the separation of powers and checks and balances. The social contract, "taught by over sixty Calvinists, and successfully practised by Calvinists in six countries before Locke popularized it,"[21] was a congenial idea to men long exposed to the covenant theology of New England. The federalism of the Congregational New Englanders also aided the deliberations that made a nation. The influence of Locke is obvious, but he was acceptable to Americans because he had articulated well the politics implicit in Calvinism, if not in Calvin. The founding fathers took ideas where they could be found. Aside from Montesquieu, whom even Jefferson distrusted, the political theory of the French Enlightenment was not widely known. Americans derived their ideas from classical sources, from seventeenth-century England, but mostly from life in America.

An understanding of the thought of John Adams, because he so fully illustrated the development of American thought in the eighteenth century, shows how that development both paralleled and diverged from the Enlightenment in Europe. Adams was thoroughly an eighteenth-century American who, both in part of his career and in his thought, summed up the spirit of the time and place. He did not always or even usually agree with other leaders of thought, but his verbal battles with his colleagues were often more a matter of personality than of position; his monumental distrust, almost paranoia, led him to quarrel with many whose abstract thought he might otherwise have found acceptable. Though he was always a personal maverick, his intellectual system was in the mainstream of the American intellectual tradition. Even in his constant muttering and growling he was completely American, at least during the Revolution and the immediate peace that followed; a man who often said that he preferred the simple life of his Quincy farm to the excitement and glamor of political power.

Adams was born in Braintree, Massachusetts, on October 30, 1735, the year in which Jonathan Edwards was leading Northampton to the first flash of the Great Awakening. After having received an M.A. from Harvard in 1758, Adams began his career as an obscure provincial lawyer. He lost his first case, was admitted to the Suffolk bar, and began a legal practice that was to last until the onset of the revolutionary temper. He inherited the Braintree estate when his father died in 1761, and married Abigail Smith three years later.

One of the traditions developed by the seventeenth-century Puritans was the keeping of a diary as an aid to more systematic introspection, as a balance sheet of the spirit that would record an individual's daily struggles with the Evil One. It took an earthquake in New England to shake John Adams into the proper work of keeping a diary, and once started it seemed to rumble on of its own accord. The diary is the major source of his revealing early self-doubts, and of his consciousness of having failed to live up to some ideal virtue or other. Partially out of his understanding of himself, he began to gather the material that would later provide one important basis for his political system.

During his twenties he began to record some of his weaknesses and desires. He longed to study, he told his diary, but he had no opportunity; he had, he said, "no Books, no Time, no Friends. I must therefore be contented to live and die an ignorant, obscure fellow."[22] Ignorance and obscurity were the twin worries of this period of his life, and he seems to have been convinced that should he suffer those personal horrors it would be a result of his failure to work sufficiently hard, to allow the spiritually unprofitable diversions of this world to seduce him from a diligence that would have been rewarded. If he could practice those virtues he had learned from his Puritan fathers, his dessert, which would be just in any case, would also be pleasant. Remaining anxious about the station in life he would eventually occupy, passionately wanting to distinguish himself in some honorable and useful work, he continued privately to berate himself for character flaws which a just providence must punish with a hateful anonymity.

Demanding the truth about himself from himself, he reiterated the positive abhorrence he had of blending into the crowd. He seemed to sense some special talents which, if properly exploited, would carry him into the admiration of others. When he was twenty-three years old, he had already concluded that he would have to think his way to fame, and he worried that he might not have the necessary intelligence or originality to capture the attention he needed: "Why Have I not Genius to start some new Thought. Some thing that will surprize the World. New, grand, wild, yet regular Thought that may raise me at once to fame."[23]

By this time Adams had already learned enough about himself to know that there were whole categories of thought for which he was unsuited. He found the more speculative subjects unsatisfactory and uncongenial. He later recalled an interview he had had in 1758 with one of the leading lawyers of Boston, who examined him in metaphysical subjects which, Adams wrote, "neither of Us understood, and which I have long been convinced, will never be intelligible to human understanding."[24]

The political situation that was developing between Britain and the colonies in the 1760's provided Adams with the most appropriate stage for the exercise of his talents. The growing crisis changed his outlook by changing his life. The industrious and morose provincial lawyer found that he had been preparing himself, without knowing it, to act the role of a revolutionary, and he discovered that political thought, unlike what he was pleased to call "metaphysical speculation," suited him perfectly. The emerging Revolution helped him to find himself.

Successfully defending John Hancock against charges of smuggling, Adams was becoming one of the leaders of Massachusetts Bay, who were beginning to assert America's claim to a different kind of justice from that envisaged in Parliament. With typical courage and commitment to the law, he successfully defended the commanding officer in charge of the British troops who had been involved in the so-called Boston Massacre. In the same year he was elected to the Massachusetts General Court as a representative from Boston, where he served until 1771.

In a series of articles published in the *Boston Gazette* in 1763, Adams began to articulate some of his political ideas. He made clear what was later to become a characteristic feature of his thought: that politics was a science, and a proper political system must be founded upon an accurate and full knowledge of man. The echo of Puritanism continued to sound in his ears and informed his view of human nature. "Self-love or self-preservation," he wrote, "is the only spring that moves" natural man.[25] Civilization was distinguished from savagery by the agreement of individuals to resign their private judgment to courts of law. Though an intelligent, humane, and impartial legal system could restrain the worst excesses of men, it could never alter fundamentally the essential and original evil of all men. He concluded "by advising all men to look into their own hearts, which they will find to be deceitful above all things and desperately wicked."[26] A bad legal system or the growth of party spirit would unleash rather than contain man's essential evil. With a bitterness and an evaluation that was prophetic of his own political future, Adams denounced partisanship:

Many of the ablest tongues and pens have, in every age, been employed in the foolish, deluded, and pernicious flattery of one set of
partisans, and in furious, prostitute invectives against another; but
such kinds of oratory never had any charms for me; and if I must
do one or the other, I would quarrel with both parties and with
every individual of each, before I would subjugate my understanding, or prostitute my tongue or pen to either.[27]

In the summer of 1765, again in a series of articles in the *Boston
Gazette* (later published in England under the title of *A Dissertation
on the Canon and Feudal Law*), Adams elaborated his notion of
the consequences of an inadequate legal system. He argued that
popular intelligence and arbitrary government had always been
antagonistic to each other. The love of power in a prince resulted
in slavery for the people; but the same desire for power in the
people was the cause of freedom. The systems of canon and
feudal law had been designed by the mighty to prevent the growth
of popular intelligence and to repress the popular love of power.
Canon law reduced men to ignorance, and feudal law kept them
in bondage. There arose a partnership between the beneficiaries of
the two systems that was even worse: "It seems to have been even
stipulated between them, that the temporal grandees should contribute every thing in their power to maintain the ascendency of
the priesthood, and that the spiritual grandees in their turn, should
employ their ascendency over the consciences of the people, in
impressing on their minds a blind, implicit obedience to civil
magistracy."[28]

The Reformation began the process that opposed this domina-
tion of man's mind by canon law, and his flesh by feudal law.
With Protestantism came more general popular education, especially in England. The struggle against the twin engines of oppression, according to Adams, was the same struggle that resulted in
the settlement of America. The resolution to oppose that

infernal confederacy . . . was a resolution formed by a sensible
people, —I mean the Puritans, —almost in despair. They had
become intelligent in general. . . . After their arrival here, they
began their settlement, and formed their plan, both of ecclesiastical
and civil government, in direct opposition to the canon and feudal
systems.[29]

Thus it was that he wrote in an early draft of the *Dissertation*, but omitted from the finished version, "I always consider the settlement of America with reverence and wonder, as the opening of a grand scene and design in Providence for the illumination of the ignorant, and the emancipation of the slavish part of mankind all over the earth."[30]

In Adams' view, Winthrop and his company had not merely fled from persecution, but had been central figures in the heroic stand against the corrupt legal system which had been based on ignorance and fear. Winthrop's Boston was, as Winthrop himself had said, a city on a hill, one that had been destined, not as Winthrop had said, to serve mankind as a model of piety and sanctity, but as a model of the ways by which men could achieve political maturity and human freedom. But Boston, for Adams as it had been for Winthrop, remained the model destined by Providence to be some kind of example for the human race, and for both men the significance of their city was that in rejecting the past, it sought to chart the future. It was in this connection that Adams, later in his life, admitted that the peculiar American idea of the west had been his steady companion: "There is nothing, in my little reading, more ancient in my memory than the observation that arts, sciences, and empire had travelled westward; and in conversation it was always added since I was a child, that their next leap would be over the Atlantic into America."[31] The past against which Winthrop had protested was still the same past which Adams rejected. Adams was still a full participant in the national mythology.

No legislators in the history of the world, Adams wrote, had been superior to those of the original Christian corporation of Massachusetts Bay. They had remained obedient to the Crown, he thought, but had insisted on placing their own power as a check on the powers of the King and the priest. Those Puritans built their churches upon the Bible, and their state upon human dignity: "They saw clearly, that of all the nonsense and delusion which had ever passed through the mind of man, none had ever been more extravagant than the notions of absolutions, indelible characters, uninterrupted successions, and the rest of those fantastical ideas, derived from the canon law, which had thrown such a glare of mystery, sanctity, reverence, and right reverend eminence and holiness, around the idea of a priest, as no mortal could deserve, and as always must . . . be dangerous in society."[32] According to him, the Bay saints had rejected the "dark ribaldry of . . . the Lord's annointed" and the mysteries in which the priesthood had shrouded the feudal monarch. The Puritans "knew that government was a plain, simple, intelligible thing, founded in nature and reason, and quite comprehensible by common sense."[33] Their recognition that ignorance was an indispensable condition of oppression led them to establish their college and local grammar schools almost from the start. The consequence was, Adams said, that in the America of 1765, the year of the Stamp Act, there was a higher level of general education than had ever before been true in the history of any nation.

The Stamp Act was a violation of British liberties, he argued, because those liberties had not been granted by the state and could not therefore be withdrawn by the state. When Adams wrote his *Dissertation* he already knew Rousseau's *Social Contract*, and he used a primitive form of contractual political theory to justify his notion of British liberties, a form not significantly different from the older Puritan covenantal theory of the state. The Puritan fathers, not Rousseau and not Locke, were the primary source of his contractual theory. Those British liberties were "original rights, conditions of original contracts, coequal with prerogative, and coeval with government." They were anterior to Parliament and were founded on truth, liberty, justice, and benevolence. Should those bases "be removed, the superstructure is overthrown of course."[34] That is, should the state destroy, or seek to destroy, the fundamental rights of the citizen, which the citizen had never and could never resign or delegate to the state, a revolution would be instituted by the state against its citizens, against which the citizens had a perfect right to protect themselves. Because he saw the Stamp Act as a device to tax education and the press, he worried that the secret motive of that act was a desire to reimpose that kind of public ignorance which had supported the canon and feudal systems, systems which still had sufficient vigor in England to endanger the liberty of Americans.

The Stamp Act crisis thoroughly upset his own career, and though at the time he saw the disruption he did not see the opportunities opened to him. Though the crisis was eliciting a common spirit of resistance throughout the colonies, he thought it was likely to destroy his legal career:

> So sudden an Interruption in my Career, is very unfortunate for me. I was but just getting into my Geers, just getting under Sail, and an embargo is laid upon the Ship. Thirty Years of my Life are passed in Preparation for Business. I have had Poverty to struggle with—Envy and Jealousy and Malice of Enemies to encounter—no Friends, or but few to assist me, so that I have groped in dark Obscurity, till of late, and had but just become known, and gained a small degree of Reputation, when this execrable Project was set on foot for my Ruin as well as that of America in General, and of Great Britain.[35]

In September, 1765, Adams was asked to compose the instructions from the town of Braintree to its representative in the General Court. In that public document, he denounced the Act and argued that Parliament had no lawful authority to tax the colonies without their consent. In the privacy of his diary he elaborated these early ideas about the limited powers of Parliament. The Puritans had been driven by oppression from the realm, "till at last they offered to make a Contract with the Nation, or the Crown, and to become subject to the Crown [and not to Parliament, as Winthrop had also argued] upon certain Conditions."[36] The right to tax themselves had been one of those essential conditions. The Pilgrims, he said, had come from Leyden, not England, and all of the colonies were then considered allies, not subjects of England. No part of the first colonization had been an act of the English nation, because neither the crown nor the collective people had shared in any part of the expense of the voyages of Raleigh or of the Cabots, or of the Plymouth Council. Colonization had been a private act.

As Adams continued to think about the Stamp Act and its consequences, he discovered support for the idea that his America continued to have a version of the Puritan concept of an "errand into the wilderness." From instruction in piety, America had grown into instruction in freedom:

> They [Americans] think that the Liberties of Mankind and the Glory of human Nature is in their Keeping. They know that Liberty has been skulking about in Corners from the Creation, and has been hunted and persecuted, in all Countries, by cruel Power. But they flatter themselves that America was designed by Providence

for the Theatre, on which Man was to make his true figure, on which science, Virtue, Liberty, Happiness and Glory were to exist in Peace.[37]

About one month later, this time in public print, Adams continued this line of thought, one which was to lead him onto dangerous ground. Americans, he wrote, calling himself the Earl of Clarendon, "have the most habitual, radical sense of liberty . . .; they are descended from a race of heroes."[38] In language and thought that anticipated the Declaration of Independence by a decade, he wrote that because of the habitual virtue of these sons of the Puritan fathers, Americans would defend the true British constitution, based on natural law and natural rights, against any usurpation "with their lives and fortunes." He took as a commonplace that "all men are born equal,"[39] an assumption that, along with the laws of nature and contractual theory, with its necessary right of revolution, led him to respond to the Stamp Act crisis with a system which, though crude, was moving rapidly toward greater sophistication, high treason, and independence.

As he continued to hold minor public offices and to build his law practice he, like others of the revolutionary generation, began to form some idea of "the people." His personality was such that some abrasion was probably inevitable, as it probably was not, say, for Jefferson. Growling about the ingratitude of the public in his diary, Adams noted that he would be well advised to concentrate his efforts more in his own career, to turn his back on those who had accepted his services with what he thought was contempt. He resolved to abandon his unappreciated political activities in the interest of minding his own legal business and attending to his farm.

Out of his need for acclaim and because of his commitment to principle, Adams was incapable of honoring his resolution, of rejecting an invitation to appear in or serve the public. At its annual town meeting in 1772, Braintree voted to ask him to give a speech about the rights of the people. In his fragmentary notes for that speech he demonstrated that his conception of politics was growing firmer. Even though he postulated man's equality, Adams was not led to a more sanguine view of human nature than the one he had earlier expressed. "The Love of Power," he continued to insist, "is insatiable and uncontroulable."[40] At least one element of human equality, as he saw it, was the equal threat each man posed to the welfare of his neighbors: "There is Danger from all Men. The only Maxim of a free Government, ought to be to trust no Man living, with Power to endanger the public Liberty."[41] He intimated that some system ought to be devised to allow all men liberty, and to prevent all men from satisfying the universal thirst for power.

The foundation of liberty was in the character of the people who composed the society. "The People can never be enslaved but by their own Tameness, Pusillanimity, Sloth or Corruption."[42] The ambitious few in every society were always aware that the success of their designs depended upon popular moral or intellectual decay, and therefore usually began their rise to power with an attack on the virtue or education of their society. English policy constituted such an attack, especially the revenue laws and the maintenance of a standing army in America. By now Adams was convinced that the Crown was attempting to corrupt the Americans in order to encourage them to accept their own enslavement. Wherever and whenever freedom had been lost in the history of Europe, the mechanism had always been the same: the ignorance and weakness of the people had always allowed and even encouraged their own oppression. Americans, he told his Braintree audience, would be responsible themselves should England's policy of oppression succeed.

Perhaps because of Adams' opposition to England's policies from the conclusion of the French and Indian War, he was sent by Massachusetts to the first Continental Congress. Though he suggested to his diary from time to time that he would much prefer the pleasures of his study, office, and farm to the temptations of public life, it still seems reasonably clear that he so enjoyed the notoriety and excitement of public office that he welcomed the opportunity the Congress offered him. That he had mixed feelings about leaving his home is certainly true, and that he encountered at least some of the frustrations that he had predicted and feared is equally true. He discovered in Congress the common fate of all committee members:

> In Congress, nibbling and quibbling—as usual. There is no greater Mortification than to sit with half a dozen Witts, deliberating upon a Petition, Address, or Memorial. These great Witts, these subtle

> Criticks, these refined Genius's, these learned Lawyers, these wise Statesmen, are so fond of shewing their Parts and Powers, as to make their Consultations very tedius.[43]

While he was in attendance in Congress, America declared her independence. His role in bringing the Revolution about was indispensable but not spectacular. He could not catch the public fancy or speak to the heart with the success of James Otis, Samuel Adams, Thomas Paine, or Patrick Henry. He was a solid worker for the cause rather than a source of inspiration. His large view of the issues often led him to qualify his position in a way that might have seemed timid and often sounded bookish. In 1774 he feared a break with England, for instance, because he believed the chances of failure were equal to those of success. His typical caution did not result in popular applause.

His characteristic contribution to the emergence of revolutionary zeal took the form of reasoned analyses of the law, of the diverging constitutional theories of England and America. In 1774, again in the columns of the *Boston Gazette*, he published a series of articles later collected in book form under the title of *Novanglus: Or A History of the Dispute with America*. Written in answer to a series of essays by Daniel Leonard, who wrote under the pseudonym of "Massachusettensis," Adams showed that his understanding of the issues was continuing to grow.

In his *Novanglus* papers Adams said that there were only two kinds of men in the world, freemen and slaves, and that consent to law was the only difference between them. He reasoned, again in a vein that Winthrop had explored, that Parliament had no authority of any kind to legislate for America, and that if such authority were claimed, violence would be the result. The greatest danger to American liberty would come from allowing Parliament to exercise authority over American affairs, without some American representation in that body. Almost as dangerous would be some arrangement that would allow for American representation in Parliament, an idea, he said, which was simply impracticable. The only safe path to follow was that which had already been traveled, by "going on as we began, and fared well for one hundred and fifty years, by letting parliament regulate trade, and our own assemblies all other matters."[44] Only if the colonists were adequately represented in their own assemblies, as had been the custom throughout the life of the colonies until the end of the French and

Indian War, would American liberty be relatively secure; unless that system were revitalized, he flatly announced, "Great Britain will lose her colonies."[45]

Turning now to the crux of the *Novanglus* papers, Adams urged that the history of the colonies, and particularly that of Massachusetts Bay, supported the principle that Americans who were deprived of the power to assent to or dissent from law would be forced to violence in order to recapture the original sense of colonization. When one of the King's subjects left England with the King's permission (and if the collective people remained silent, with the permission of the people also), that subject "carried with him, as a man, all the rights of nature."[46] Such a subject still owed allegiance to the King, and the King therefore still owed him protection. New Englanders derived their authority from their rights as men and from the social contract of the colonial charters. Leaving the realm, the colonists left the reach of Parliament, but did not thereby abandon their rights as Englishmen. They still retained the right to be governed as they saw fit, and no power on earth could rightfully or legally impair that right. "So that our ancestors, when they emigrated, having obtained permission of the king to come here, and being never commanded to return into the realm, had a clear right to have erected in this wilderness a British constitution, or a perfect democracy, or any other form of government they saw fit."[47]

"Massachusettensis" had argued that the original charters would be forfeited should the colonists fail to fulfill what he thought to be the terms and conditions of those charters, and that the charter governments would then revert to "absolute monarchy." Adams was unconvinced that the original charters could be legally forfeited, but even if they could, the consequences would be "that the king would have no power over them at all."[48] The system of allegiance and protection would be utterly destroyed, and there would then be no tie between the colonies and England. The charter of London once had been declared incapable of forfeiture (after it had earlier been forfeited) by Parliament itself. Several American charters had also been declared forfeited, including the original charter of Massachusetts Bay:

> The Massachusetts alone were tame enough to give it up. But no American charter will ever be decreed forfeited again; or if any should, the decree will be regarded no more than a vote of the

lower house of the Robinhood society. . . . The passivity of this
colony in receiving the present charter in lieu of the first, is, in the
opinion of some, the deepest stain upon its character. There is less
to be said in excuse for it than the witchcraft, or hanging the
Quakers.[49]

Because he thought that Americans still owed some kind of allegiance to the King, it was necessary for him to explain the precise
nature of the relationship. In order to do so he turned for his ideas,
in a curious way, to feudal law. After his scornful rejection of
feudal law in his *Dissertation,* he now invoked the feudal concept
of the King's two bodies in order to explain the nature of allegiance,
and to help pave at least the intellectual way for revolution. For
centuries English lawyers had been laboring to separate the person
and office of the King, legally to separate the King's natural body
from the body politic. The latter—the Crown—was immortal and
infallible, but the natural King, the warm human body of the King,
as opposed to the abstraction of his political body, would live and
die and make mistakes. The lawyers finally succeeded in divesting
the natural King of the powers once claimed, and investing the
King's political body with glory and law that commanded allegiance. In elevating the office at the expense of the person, the
lawyers argued that they were elevating law and restraining
human whim.

Adams followed Winthrop in reversing what had become the
usual legal argument: "The fealty and allegiance of Americans
. . . is undoubtedly due to the person of King George III. . . . It is
due to him in his natural person, as that natural person is intituled
to the crown, the kingly office, the royal dignity of the realm of
England."[50]   In their charters and implied contracts with the
various human Kings, Americans had agreed to give allegiance only
"to the natural person of that prince, who shall rightfully hold the
kingly office in England."[51] The significant point was that Americans
were subject to the King but not to the Crown. Failing to understand this, "Massachusettensis" accused Adams of dredging up
archaic and superannuated feudal law that was irrelevant. The
genuine relevance of Adams' juggling of the King's two bodies
was clarified when he explained that allegiance only to the person
meant that Americans were not subject of the Crown and therefore
not subjects of Parliament. English lawyers had believed that the

elevation of the royal office was a way to control the royal person; Adams implied that, for colonists, the formula was more powerful in reverse: Liberty in America was more securely grounded if the tie to England was made as tenuous and personal as possible. One could more easily legitimize a break with the person of the King than a break with the abstraction of the state. Because America was outside the realm of England, the hoary doctrine of two bodies took on revolutionary significance. Feudal law was being used to justify modern revolution by the man who had utterly rejected feudal law as a system which oppressed the natural rights of man.

The original charter of Massachusetts Bay was interpreted by Adams as corroborating his view. Charles I himself, according to Adams, thought that the colonists were bound to his person but neither to Parliament nor to the body politic because Charles had dissolved Parliament before the charter was issued, and because he was at the time determined never to call another Parliament. Adams believed that it was wrong to think that the colonists had been granted their lands by the political body of England—Crown and Parliament—because "lands are holden according to the original notices of feuds, of the natural person of the lord."[52] Following the standard opinion of Sir Edward Coke, he argued that the relation between lord and tenant was legally always personal:

> And therefore no homage, fealty, or other services, can ever be rendered to the body politic, the political capacity, which is not corporated, but only a frame in the mind, an idea. No lands here, or in England, are held of the crown, meaning by it the political capacity; they are all held of the royal person, the natural person of the king.[53]

The transfer of the original charter to Massachusetts Bay by Winthrop and his company was the basis of Adams' interpretation of the relationship between the colonies and the mother country. It was of course true that the charter had been issued under England's great seal, "but this seal runneth not out of the realm."[54] The original intention was for the charter to remain in England, and for the corporation of the Massachusetts Bay Company also to remain, where it would be an ordinary corporation. With the transfer of the charter the great seal "lost all its legal force."[55] Adams believed (with what evidence it is impossible to say) that "all parties" had agreed to the transfer of the charter, and that therefore the force of the charter was that of a free contract, and did not come from its royal source or from the seal. Had the charter and company remained in England it was clear that the agents of the company who went to the New World would have been subject to the body politic of England. With the removal of the charter, the colonists "got out of the English realm, dominions, state, empire, call it by what name you will, and out of the legal jurisdiction of parliament." Because of their free consent in the contract, Americans chose to continue their allegiance to the natural person of the King who could "have commanded them to return; but he did not."[56] The severance of the tie to the King was, in his mind, facilitated because the original relationship was contractual and personal. The tie therefore could be broken should the fallible royal person violate his contractual obligations to honor the natural rights of Englishmen in America. Americans had nothing to do with common or statute law, or with Parliament, except as they freely chose to adopt whatever best pleased them. In thus weakening the tie to England in his own mind, Adams was preparing himself to think through to the next step, and to neutralize the effect of revolution by making it relatively insignificant, by interpreting it as nothing more than a rejection of continued allegiance to that natural King who had already rejected his contractual obligations.

The outbreak of violence at Lexington brought the *Novanglus* series to an end and made the work of the Congress more vital. Adams was repeatedly returned by Massachusetts to Congress where he submitted the name of Washington as commander-in-chief, was instrumental in the foundation of an American navy (which he continued to advocate throughout his life), supported the establishment of state governments, made the major address defending the Declaration of Independence, and presided over the important Board of War and Ordinance, among almost countless other activities and duties. Finally, exhausted, he left Congress in November, 1777, and returned to Braintree.

The work and tedium of Congress sweetened his disposition not one bit. He described himself at Philadelphia as over-worked and lonely, as "a morose philosopher and a surly politician."[57] He was growing increasingly restive as a result of his fears of the social and political consequences of revolution. One incident that he later recalled that should have produced laughter, he said, "struck me into a profound Reverie, if not a fit of Melancholly." He had met a horse jockey who had frequently been involved in law suits, sometimes as Adams' client. He saluted Adams with gratitude for helping to close the courts and with the hope that they would never reopen. In response all of Adams' worst fears were rekindled:

> Is this the Object for which I have been contending? said I to myself, for I rode along without any Answer to this Wretch. Are these the Sentiments of such People? And how many of them are there in the Country? Half the Nation for what I know: for half the Nation are Debtors if not more, and these have been in all Countries, the Sentiments of Debtors. If the Power of the Country should get into such hands, and there is great danger that it will, to what purpose have We sacrificed our Time, health and every Thing else?[58]

At least in part as a result of his fears about the possible consequences of revolution, and also because of the nature of his now obvious talents and preferences. Adams turned to the business of designing government, a task which delighted and occupied him for the next half century. At the age of forty he had found his calling. "I embraced with Joy," he remembered, "the opportunity of harranguing . . . on a general recommendation to all the States to call conventions and institute regular Governments."[59] The personal solicitation which always nourished him was now also forthcoming. Members of Congress began to listen to him with more patience than he was accustomed to, and, he happily noted, "some began to ask me civil questions."[60] It was generally recognized that he was equipped to help with the difficult task of creating revolutionary but orderly governments.

He relied on American, and especially Massachusetts, political experience rather than on innovation. He was then less committed to theory than to practice, and the revolution, as he viewed it, became a search for the method by which there would be as little change as possible. His reliance on reason, therefore, meant stability, a celebration of the American past, as contrasted with the sometimes revolutionary use of reason in the French Enlightenment. In this Adams ostensibly placed himself in the camp of the English Enlightenment, but his toughest roots reached back to Winthrop's Bay colony.

In January, 1776, George Wythe of Virginia asked Adams for a plan on how to establish state governments in the revolutionary situation. In the same month the legislature of North Carolina instructed its delegates in Congress to get Adams' opinion on the same subject, and New Jersey made a similar request. In response Adams immediately published *Thoughts on Government: Applicable to the Present State of the American Colonies.* He later said that the crudities and weaknesses of Paine's *Common Sense* had also moved him to put his own political theories into circulation. *Thoughts on Government* was his first extended plan of government and was widely circulated; it was approved by the leaders in Virginia, especially by Patrick Henry.

In terms of his own intellectual development, the most important aspect of his *Thoughts on Government* was the emphasis on the importance of political form. He was now prepared to abandon the Puritan idea of the acceptability of many different forms of government, an idea he had supported four years earlier. This time he disparagingly quoted Alexander Pope's couplet:

> For forms of government let fools contest,
> That which is best administered is best.

Now Adams believed that nothing could be more wrong, but what could one expect from poets who "read history to collect flowers, not fruits"? From his changing understanding of history and human nature Adams now argued "that some forms of government are better fitted for being well administered than others."[61] This stress on the formal qualities of government, which in time was to grow into something like an obsession, is an important clue that Adams was growing into the eighteenth century and away from the seventeenth, was moving toward an acceptance of mechanism that seemed to harmonize with Newtonian science and away from Winthrop's reliance on the piety and virtue of the governors. Never truly abandoning the Puritans' ideas about the depravity of individuals, Adams sought a system that would exploit human weakness for the benefit of society. If the right political laws could be discovered, and the right form of government established on the basis of those laws, men would be governed for the first time in human history in their own interests.

Convinced that "the divine science of politics is the science of social happiness, and [that] the blessings of society depend entirely on the constitutions of government," Adams said that the happiness of society was both the purpose and test of government. The best form of government would give happiness to the most. Every government was founded on some principle or passion, and fear had been the basis of most. But fear was "so sordid and brutal a passion, and renders men in whose breasts it predominates so stupid and miserable, that Americans will not be likely to approve of any political institution which is founded on it."[62] If some form of government that was based on virtue could be discovered, it would better promote public happiness. He implied, but did not yet say explicitly, that virtue in individuals, without the proper political form, would be inadequate.

Only a republic, which he defined simply as a government of law and not of men, could serve the public interest. There was an infinite variety of republics because the precise distribution of power in society was perhaps infinitely various. Because he thought that law was the essence of good government, he found it necessary to begin his consideration of some of the details of good government with a discussion of the best method for producing law. With a large population in an extensive country direct democracy was impracticable. "The first necessary step, then, is to depute power from the many to a few of the most wise and good."[63] He hurried over the problems of selecting the representatives, and turned to the ideal result. The representative assembly "should be in miniature an exact portrait of the people at large. It should think, feel, reason, and act like them."[64] Because the assembly by its size would be unable to keep secrets and would be too cumbersome for speed, it was unsuited to exercise the executive power. Again because of its necessary size and slowness, and, in this case, lack of knowledge, it was also unfit to have the judicial power. A separation of powers between the legislature, executive, and judiciary was therefore essential.

Corrupt elections could destroy the most wisely designed government, but he thought that a specification of the proper rules of election could wait for the emergency to subside. He was already convinced that annual elections were necessary in order to teach the politically powerful men of the society the desirable lessons of personal insecurity, to teach them "the great political virtues of humility, patience, and moderation, without which every man in

power becomes a ravenous beast of prey."[65] At the confused and
revolutionary moment it would be most prudent to rely on habit,
to change as little as possible, to use colonial experience and institutions shorn of all monarchical vestiges. Despite the potential danger
and actual confusion of the moment, it was a time of unique opportunity, "a time when the greatest lawgivers of antiquity would have
wished to live."[66] In no other period of human history had three
million people a chance to choose their government, to reach for
the as yet unknown limits of political wisdom, and to institute their
governments on what he hoped would be the exclusive basis of
reason.

He was in search of a system of government whose design would
guarantee success. Newton had seemed to prove that the motion
of the physical universe was regulated by immutable law. If similar
laws of politics could be discovered, government would be able
to function as mechanically as the orbiting planets. A correct
knowledge of man's nature would lead to the desired science of
politics, a science whose principles he thought to be as fixed as those
of mechanics.

At this stage of his intellectual development, he was committed
to James Harrington's first law of action and reaction in politics
as it had been formulated in *The Commonwealth of Oceana:* "power
always follows property."[67] The distribution of property in land
was always reflected in the distribution of political power. The
only way, therefore, to support popular power was to support an
easy acquisition of property for every member of the society. The
relationship between property and power were the two first meshed
gears in his clockwork of government.

The formal Declaration of Independence suspended his sustained
political writing. He finally welcomed the revolutionary war as an
unprecedented opportunity for Americans to be politically wise,
even though he was not convinced that his countrymen would
exploit their opportunity. "It is very true," he wrote from Congress,
"that no people ever had a finer opportunity to settle things upon
the best foundations. But yet I fear that human nature will be found
to be the same in America as it has been in Europe, and that the
true principles of liberty will not be sufficiently attended to."[68]

The early Puritans had also argued that Americans had had a unique opportunity, but they had believed that the American saints were made of better stuff than Europeans, a belief that had been basic to Winthrop's Bay. Adams thoroughly rejected the ideas about the uniqueness of Americans as men while he retained the idea about the special opportunity an American nation provided for quite ordinary people. Whether individuals would seize the opportunity, therefore, for the time, simply remained a question.

That some evidence of the stupidity or corruption of Americans was already available, Adams had no doubt. A popular distrust of men of learning was depriving the states of the best counsel. Granting to each state an equal power in Congress was unfair to the more populous and wealthier states, like Massachusetts. Thus the people themselves, without the dominion of vile masters, were beginning to destroy their own opportunity for freedom. The war with England could be won, but what then? Unless Americans proved wise enough to institute a proper political mechanism, they would find themselves in no better situation after the war than before. In a private letter he wrote that "there is one enemy, who to me is more formidable than famine, pestilence, and the sword; I mean the corruption which is prevalent in so many American hearts, a depravity that is more inconsistent with our republican governments than light is with darkness."[69] A popular understanding of the need for a system of government, a science of politics, was not yet to be found in America.

Part of his difficulty in Congress was his discovery that not all Americans were Yankees. In his diary he described the gentlemen from Maryland, but he meant those from the entire slave-holding South: "The Lands are cultivated, and all Sorts of Trades are exercised by Negroes, or by transported Convicts, which has occasioned the Planters and Farmers to assume the Title of Gentlemen, and they hold their Negroes and Convicts, that is all labouring People and Tradesmen, in such Contempt, that they think themselves a distinct order of Beings." Because of their disdain of labor, the planters raised their sons "in Idleness or what is worse in Horse Racing, Cock fighting, and Card Playing."[70] Though Adams did not elaborate this discovery his worry is perfectly clear: Would the slave owners of the South desire, and support free republican government?

In the same year Adams' angle of vision was to change as a result of his growing prestige in Congress. In November, 1777, he was notified that he had been elected by Congress a joint commissioner to France. He arrived at the French court in the spring of the next year, and took his place with Benjamin Franklin and Arthur Lee. Just after he first arrived in France Adams' enthusiasm and excitement was properly recorded in his diary: "Europe thou great Theatre of Arts, Sciences, Commerce, War, am I at last permitted to visit thy Territories. —May the Design of my Voyage be answered."[71]

As an innocent abroad, he had to make his peace with Parisian society. Though he was repelled by what he took to be the luxury, dissipation, and effeminacy of all Europe, he admired the temperance of the French. Soon after his arrival, he wrote to his wife that he had "found nothing to disgust me, or in any manner disturb me, in the French nation."[72] His talent for worrying did not, however, leave him. Paris offered everything "that can inform the understanding or refine the taste, and indeed, one would think, that could purify the heart. Yet it must be remembered, there is every thing here, too, which can seduce, betray, deceive, deprave, corrupt and debauch it."[73] Paris, in other words, offered intelligence and taste, and Adams offered innocent virtue. He was not convinced that innocence could confront experience and remain pure. He brooded in his diary: "Innocence is not Proof against the Arts of Paris. Simplicity is a Prey—and Virtue is melted away, by Wine and Artifice."[74]

The ladies of France gave him particular trouble—intellectually, that is. Time and again he was shocked by their boldness and by what he took to be their un-Bostonian immodesty. To his wife he admitted: "I admire the ladies here. Don't be jealous. They are handsome, and very well educated."[75] On one occasion he tried to participate in the wicked conversation of French society, but the heavy Yankee hand inevitably smothered the talk and recorded the details in the diary: "Some hints about Language, and glances about Women, produced this Observation, that there were two ways of learning french commonly recommended—take a Mistress and go to the Commedie [sic]." Adams' retort clearly demonstrated Yankee ingenuity: "the Language is no where better spoken than at the Comedie."[76] The ladies finally fell into perspective when

Adams later understood their political significance. In the section of his *Autobiography* that deals with his first Parisian period, he concluded "that the manners of Women were the most infallible Barometer, to ascertain the degree of Morality and Virtue in a Nation." The way the ladies conducted themselves was the most certain criterion by which to judge whether republicanism would succeed. He thought that all the great republics of the past failed when their women lost their modesty and domesticity. Innocent and republican America would go the way of eastern flesh should officials "be appointed by Harlots for Money, and their Judgments, Decrees and decisions be sold to repay themselves, or perhaps to procure the smiles of profligate Females."[77] Children could not learn the habits of virtue on which republicanism rested if they were trained to infidelity by the examples of their parents.

He thought that the innocence of most American ministers at European courts was more than merely personally significant. The differences in European and American tempers might jeopardize the missions of American diplomats. He noted in his diary that "the Subtilty, the Invention, the profound Secrecy, the Absolute Silence of these European Courts, will be too much for our hot, rash, fiery Ministers, and for our indolent, inattentive ones, tho as silent as they."[78] Only an intensification of Americanism—reason and virtue, as he defined it—would help American diplomats resist the intrigues of the more experienced and sophisticated Europeans. As Adams tried to explain to the Count de Vergennes, "the dignity of North America does not consist in diplomatic ceremonials or any of the subtleties of etiquette; it consists solely in reason, justice, truth, the rights of mankind, and the interests of the nations of Europe, all of which, well understood, are clearly in her favor."[79]

Benjamin Franklin could play the game of European diplomacy with what Adams called European techniques. Adams had never been persuaded that Franklin's virtue was pure enough to represent America, and Franklin's favor with Vergennes was simply additional evidence that Franklin was not the innocent that Adams was. Adams never forgave him. Franklin did have a charming way, but "it is the most silly and ridiculous Way imaginable, in the Sight of an American, but it succeeds, to admiration, fullsome and sickish as it is, in Europe."[80]

After a year in France, Congress relieved Adams of his commission and he returned home, arriving in the summer of 1779. Three days after he arrived he was elected by Braintree to the state constitutional convention, which appointed him to the subcommittee charged with producing a first draft. He was principally responsible for the finished product, though several important amendments were made both by the committee and by the convention. He was generally delighted with the Massachusetts Constitution of 1780, believing that never before had a people so jealously guarded their liberties, and that no previous government had ever been made to rest as squarely on ideas of equality and right. This document, he said, "is Locke, Sidney, and Rousseau and De Mably reduced to practice, in the first instance."[81]

His design of the Massachusetts Constitution was among the most influential actions of his career, since that organic law was later used as an important model by the founding fathers. In no other state constitution was the idea of the necessary separation of powers made as explicit. Nowhere else was the principle of popular sovereignty justified better in theory or implemented as thoroughly as in the Massachusetts ratifying conventions. The later federal convention approved of the distribution of relative power between the executive and the legislature, especially of that section dealing with the executive veto, and followed his lead almost word for word.

Another original part of the Massachusetts Constitution was entitled *The Encouragement of Literature, & c,* and was written by Adams. This section made it the positive obligation of the state "to cherish the interests of literature and the sciences, and all the seminaries of them," to reward the advancement of theoretical and applied knowledge, and to encourage and teach "the principles of humanity and general benevolence . . . sincerity, good humor, and all social affections and generous sentiments among the people."[82] The novelty of this section consisted not in its substance but in its inclusion in the organic law of a state. Many, of course, had held similar sentiments before Adams did, but he was the first to make them a constitutional requirement.

In September, 1779, Adams was again elected by Congress to represent the United States in Europe, this time as the sole commissioner to negotiate treaties of peace and commerce with Great

Britain. After he returned to Paris he was also commissioned by
Congress to arrange a loan with the Dutch, in which he succeeded
after two full years of difficult negotiation. In 1781 the terms of
the commission were again changed, and Adams was named first of
five commissioners charged with negotiating peace. The definitive
treaty bringing the Revolution to a close was signed by Adams,
Franklin, and John Jay in Paris in 1783.

When Adams returned to France for the second time, he had
already refined his ideas about his relationship with the more
sophisticated Europeans. He still remained the innocent at court,
but now he was taking more pride in the fact. Europeans excelled
in matters with which he could not allow himself to be concerned.
He wrote to his wife that he at least had learned to put first things
first, and that meant exclusive concentration on the matters of
politics and war. Nothing else should concern a new nation fighting
for its life. There would come a time when America's security
would be sufficiently firm to allow its citizens to pursue elegance
and the arts, but that time would come only if Adams and his
generation constructed a lasting political foundation. In words
which turned out to be an uncanny prophecy of the future history
of his own family, Adams said that

> I could fill volumes with descriptions of temples and palaces, paint-
> ings, sculptures, tapestry, porcelain, etc., etc., etc., if I could have
> time; but I could not do this without neglecting my duty. The
> science of government, it is my duty to study, more than all other
> sciences; the arts of legislation and administration and negotiation,
> ought to take place of, indeed to exclude, in a manner, all other
> arts. I must study politics and war that my sons may have liberty to
> study mathematics and philosophy. My sons ought to study mathe-
> matics and philosophy, geography, natural history and naval archi-
> tecture, navigation, commerce and agriculture, in order to give their
> children a right to study painting, poetry, music, architecture, statu-
> ary, tapestry, and porcelain.[83]

The elaborate ritual of European diplomatic protocol no longer
intimidated him. Indeed, the longer he lived with it, and as he began to succeed with his missions, the more scornful he grew. After
the French ambassador gave a dinner for the entire diplomatic
corps at the Hague, Adams wrote to the secretary of Congress that
"etiquette, when it becomes too glaring by affectation, imposes no
longer either upon the populace or upon the courtiers, but becomes

ridiculous to all."[84]   That not all Americans could remain pure in the face of Europe's manners was proved for Adams by the case of Franklin. It was not merely that a Europeanized American became somewhat foppish and ridiculous; it was that the change in manners produced a dangerous change in convictions. Congress had not been told the truth, and was in danger of becoming a mere pawn of French policy.

Adams often tried to teach Congress what he thought to be the essential differences between the courts of Europe and America. Fearful of Franklin's prestige, Adams' lectures to Congress usually concluded with the admonition to that body to rely on itself, to remain independent of European influence, even the influence of its friends, especially France. He always worried that the greater experience of French diplomats would awe Americans and impair their judgment. Americans would have to learn to analyze international relations with more objectivity. Most, if not all, of the European powers approved of the American Revolution, not out of an attachment to its principles, but out of their own self-interest, out of a desire to see England's power reduced. But not one European power, not even France or Spain, wished to see America grow strong. Americans therefore should abandon their ideas of the generosity of European courts. Americans would have to learn to look to their own self-interest.

Exploiting a theme which was as old as the Puritan concept of the city on a hill and which was to become a central doctrine in later American foreign policy, Adams wrote to the president of Congress: "Let us, above all things, avoid as much as possible entangling ourselves with their [European] wars or politics."[85] To England's peace commissioner, with whom he was negotiating, Adams said that it was obvious that every nation of Europe would be "continually maneuvring with Us, to work us into their real or imaginary Ballances of Power."[86]   Though America's power was limited, it was enough, he thought, to tip the European scales one way or the other. But it would be a dangerous enterprise from which his country would be well advised to withdraw entirely. America's proper relationship to Europe was commercial, not political. It was time, he thought, for his country to disengage herself from the intricacy and intrigue of European diplomacy, to abandon the sorry posture of a puppet.

America's republican virtues were perfectly apparent to Adams, but he was far from believing that his countrymen or any other men for that matter were perfect. He had earlier concluded that Americans were human and thus weak and often base. In 1784 the English reverend Richard Price published some letters that Turgot, the French reform minister of finance, had earlier written about America. The letters moved Adams to fill the margins of the book with his responses to Turgot. Turgot was convinced that America's immediate future was already clear, that independence was certain. He wondered whether the new nation would be free and happy, and Adams wrote a laconic "yes" in the margin. Turgot asked whether Americans would be equal to the opportunity of writing an ideal constitution. Displaying again his omnipresent puritanical rejection of ideas about perfection on earth, Adams answered: "The new Jerusalem, the Kingdom of the Just, if it is to exist upon earth, is not yet to be built. Knowledge and virtue must become more general . . . even in America, before this ravishing scene can be realized or exist anywhere but in imagination."[87] When Turgot asked whether Americans could permanently guard against corruption and decay, Adams simply noted "no." Adams expressed his gratitude to Dr. Price for the book, and commented that it was important for writers on politics to explain that there was nothing mysterious or divine about government, that it was a science compassable by mortal minds. Should this explanation ever prevail, genuine social improvements would follow. Still believing that politics could be reduced to a science, Adams had not yet clearly formulated his own systematic version of that science.

In 1785, Congress once more changed Adams' commission, appointing him the first American minister to the Court of St. James. He remained in London through what was for him the most interesting period in America, the years when the federal Constitution was framed. It seems a reasonable guess to say that if he were in America during the time he would have participated in the Constitutional Convention. Separated from the great event for which his life seemed to have prepared him, he came to feel increasingly isolated and homesick after a decade in Europe. Frustrations with his mission in England aggravated his unhappiness with his European career. Early in 1787 he announced his intention of returning to America in the following year. He hoped that Congress would authorize his return, but even if he had to disobey he would return, and he did in June, 1788.

While he still occupied his English vantage point, Adams began to worry about the government of the Articles of Confederation. He was concerned lest the alleged disunity of the states reduce America's prestige in the eyes of Europe. Reports that circulated in Europe about the constant creation of new states were taken as evidence of American instability. He therefore received the news that a new constitution was being created favorably, but with his accustomed caution. He wrote to Jefferson, who was then stationed in Paris, that "the project of a new constitution has objections against it, to which I find it difficult to reconcile myself."[88] More important than his fear of the consequences of a new constitution was his unhappiness with crucial parts of the organic law itself. Unlike Jefferson, Adams was unafraid of executive power but feared aristocracy. He thought that the presidency had been made too weak and the senate too strong. At the time of his letter to Jefferson, Adams was only weeks away from completing his major work on the theory of government, a work which was, at least for him, the beginning of an answer to his own plea for a scientific analysis of government, and a work which was to make clear why he feared the senate in America's new constitution.

The first volume of *A Defence of the Constitutions of Government of the United States of America, against the Attack of M. Turgot, In His Letter to Dr. Price* was published in London in 1787. The book was a polemic designed to clarify the principles of some of the state constitutions of America. Immediately after it appeared it was printed in Boston, New York, and Philadelphia, and, according to Adams' editor, "was much circulated in the [federal constitutional] convention, and undoubtedly contributed somewhat to give a direction to the opinions of the members."[89] With the favorable reception of this volume, Adams was encouraged to finish the work the next year, when he completed two additional volumes. All of the volumes were hastily written and both repetition and clumsiness marred the entire work. But Adams was writing to an immediate situation which he hoped to influence, and he felt that he could not take the time necessary to complete a more polished book. Because mistaken and therefore dangerous works like Paine's

Common Sense were causing Americans to be "running wild," he did not take "more time to digest and connect it." But the result, which he thought had a despised air of pedantry, was effective, "more effectual then if I had contrived it with more art to promote my own reputation."[90] The proof of its effectiveness was that the new constitution was formed, at least in part, on its principles.

It is true that the *Defence* is almost an anthology of political opinion instead of Adams' own work. Direct quotations, almost always without quotation marks, from over fifty other authors constitute three-quarters of the first volume, nine-tenths of the second, and the first half of the third. He connected those extended quotations with his own sometimes quite brief commentary, so that the finished product, as he understood it, was more a compendium of the world's political wisdom than his own contribution. But, almost buried under the weight of other opinion, Adams did make his own position clear.

Turgot was the target of the three volumes of the *Defence,* and the illumination of a natural and therefore perfect political system was the goal. Turgot had written to Price that the majority of state constitutions in America were mere imitations of the English government. "Instead of bringing all the authorities into one, that of the nation, they [the states] have established different bodies, a house of representatives, a council, a governor, because England has a house of commons, a house of lords, and a king."[91] Americans had sought to create a political balance between those institutions, a balance which had been necessary in England because of the "enormous preponderance of royalty." A republic based on political equality, according to Turgot, in creating orders created a source of division. In trying to prevent imaginary dangers, the American states had created real ones. The diversity of the several states, Turgot believed, would continue to prevent the creation of a truly unified political body.

The idea that republics had no need to balance the various powers of society was the height of political folly, according to Adams. That the idea still flourished was proof that knowledge about free governments had progressed not at all for at least two thousand years. The mindless reiteration of political theory had characterized the works of the so-called masters, from Plato through Machiavelli to Locke.

The idea underlying the three volumes of the *Defence* was that every society in the history of the world had been composed of rich and poor. There was nothing any legislator could do to change that fact. Political wisdom consisted in the recognition of the inevitability of economic inequality, and of the need for a system which would alleviate the evil effects of the contention between the classes. "All nations," Adams said, anticipating Madison's celebrated tenth number of the *Federalist Papers,* "under all governments, must have parties; the great secret is to control them."[92] As Winthrop had argued in his *Arbella* statement, Adams was convinced that the effects of economic inequality need not be an unmixed curse. He made himself clear on the title page of the first volume; he chose Pope's aphorism as his motto: "All Nature's difference keeps all Nature's Peace." A way must be found to turn class war into a system of social stability. Anticipating but inverting what was to become a part of Marxism, Adams designed the *Defence* to demonstrate the universality of the class struggle, and to try to provide a political solution for that economic fact of life.

He believed that some kind of political arrangement that distributed power equally between the rich and poor must result in a stalemate in the universal attempt of the classes to devour each other. Thucydides had said that class war was a result of human nature and must therefore always characterize human society. Adams answered: "But if this nervous historian had known a balance of three powers, he would not have pronounced the distemper so incurable, but would have added—*so long as parties in cities remain unbalanced.*"[93] Without the introduction of some third force to negotiate between the demands of the rich and the poor, no balance of power could be achieved. The political history of the ancient world showed Adams that the only effective balance against Kings, who always had degenerated into despots, was the nobility, which abolished kingship and established an aristocracy that became an oligarchy; against the oligarchy, a democratic power was set in motion and mob rule resulted, which gave birth, in time, to kingship again. Apparently agreeing with Polybius about the inevitable cycle of unmixed political forms, Adams said that the pendulum of power in society composed of only two orders must continually be swinging, with each arc culminating in revolution. Stability would be the prize of a proper allocation of power between the one, the few, and the many—between the monarchic, aristocratic, and democratic elements that exist in every society.

Though the rich constituted one of the great social classes, its spokesmen need not be rich themselves. Any man of exceptional talent or influence would naturally gravitate to the side of the rich in order to reap the benefits which that class could offer:

> Monarchies and aristocracies are in possession of the voice and influence of every university and academy in Europe. Democracy, simple democracy, never had a patron among men of letters . . . [who] must have a great deal of praise, and some of the necessaries, conveniences, and ornaments of life. Monarchies and aristocracies pay well and applaud liberally. The people have almost always expected to be served gratis, and to be paid for the honor of serving them.[94]

The simple honesty of the mass of plain people would usually be inadequate protection against the power, hypocrisy, and talent of the rich and the able whom the rich always commanded. America had an opportunity, for once in the world's history, to provide a firm and durable foundation under the political power of the democratic element. Echoing the Puritan jeremiads about the betrayed "errand into the wilderness," Adams feared that the grand chance would be missed: "The people in America have now the best opportunity and the greatest trust in their hands, that Providence ever committed to so small a number, since the transgression of the first pair; if they betray their trust, their guilt will merit even greater punishment than other nations have suffered, and the indignation of Heaven."[95] For him, the exploitation of that opportunity meant that Americans would put the three-pronged political system into practice.

Adams was convinced, of course, that the extraordinarily able and influential members of any society should be used for the benefit of the whole. But because the plain virtue and honesty of the masses could always be corrupted by the talented and powerful, it was necessary to check the natural power of the rich, able, reputable, beautiful, or any others who for one reason or another stood out from the mass. Power and talent should be put at the service of the society while not allowed to command it. Those with the greatest power or talent, should, therefore, "be separated from the

mass, and placed by themselves in a senate; this is, to all honest
and useful intents, an ostracism."[96] The most illustrious individuals
should be locked up in a senate where their wisdom would be
available to the people, but where their collective voice could be
nullified should the people so desire. The man of great wealth or
transcendent talent would have less chance to do harm in a senate
than he would have as a member of the popular branch of the
legislature where, through bribery or cleverness, he could seduce
the simpler people into consenting to be eaten alive. Enclosed in
a senate, with popular representatives guarding one exit and an
independent executive guarding the other, the voice of the rich and
able would be forced either to serve the state or to be silent. He
expected that the powerful and talented would aspire to the senate
because that body would best satisfy their passion to be noticed.

Because the differences between the one, the few, and the many
were natural differences, the political system that adequately considered them would also be natural. Adams had found what he
took to be Newton's law of political motion, and his rejection of
political ideas of divine right was complete. The men who had
drafted America's state constitutions were ordinary mortals (as he
may have known from his own experience in writing the Constitution of Massachusetts) whose extraordinary accomplishment was a
result of their exclusive reliance on experience and reason. Building
their constitutions on natural principles, the Americans had implemented a true science of politics. "It will never be pretended that
any persons employed in that service had interviews with the gods,
or were in any degree under the inspiration of Heaven."[97] The
state constitutions of America had supposedly put an end to political theology and had inaugurated a practicable political science.
"Unembarrassed by attachments to noble families, hereditary lines
and successions, or any considerations of royal blood, even the
pious mystery of holy oil had no more influence than that other one
of holy water."[98]

Now Winthrop's Holy Commonwealth had been brought down
to earth, though its relocation did not transform all of its substance.
Rejecting Calvinist theology, Adams retained the essentials of the
politics of Calvinism. He accepted the *Shorte Treatise of Politicke
Power* that the Calvinist John Ponet had written in 1556, which

contained, as he said, "all the essential principles of liberty, which were afterwards dilated on by Sidney and Locke."[99]   Calvin's Geneva itself was worthy of honor for what Adams thought to be its contribution to religious liberty.   The Puritan institutions of governor, magistrates, and deputies might be purged of their divine secrets, but they constituted a good part of the experience on which he and the other constitution builders had relied.   "It was not," Adams explained, "so much because the legislature in England consisted of three branches, that such a division of power was adopted by the states, as because their own assemblies had ever been so constituted."[100]

The durability of the tripartite system of politics proved either the scientific knowledge of the Puritans or the continued piety of Adams.   In either case, Adams' relatively new vocabulary should not obscure his debt to New England's seventeenth century, a debt which included his passionate hatred for the Catholic rituals of coronation.   He did not seem to know it, but his enemy in this connection was not political theology in general, but Catholic and monarchcial political mysticism.   Insisting that his own political trinitarianism was thoroughly secular, Adams dipped his quill in an inkstand that would have been strange to Winthrop, but he elaborated a system that the Puritans would have recognized easily. What had been the Puritan plain style had become republican simplicity, covenantal theory became contractual theory, and Congregational federalism became political federalism.

Agreeing with Winthrop that a simple democracy would produce nothing but chaos, Adams also agreed that a mixed constitution was essential.   Agreeing also that an inequality of condition was an immutable fact of life, Adams used the three volumes of the *Defence* to show the wisdom of Americans in conserving the practice of their colonial forebears.   The experience of Europe would be useful to prove to Americans the urgency of avoiding the mistakes of that continent, mistakes for which the mass of the people always had paid.   To protect the people against themselves it was necessary to limit their power also.

Man, in short, whatever his station or influence, could not be trusted with power.   Adams was not, as is sometimes charged, a defender of the upper class.   He trusted no man with power, thus extending the idea of the corruptibility of men even further than

Winthrop had. Puritanism's politics was mitigated by the faith that
God would assist His chosen; Adams was left with human weakness
and had no mitigation of any kind. "It is weakness rather than
wickedness," he wrote, "which renders men unfit to be trusted
with unlimited power."[101] He replaced the Edwardsean concept
of universal depravity with one of universal frailty. He asserted
that the human passions were naturally limitless, and merely
increased in strength when exercised. The three "aristocratical
passions" of wealth, praise, and ambition, if their demands were
heeded, would not rest until both the reason and the conscience of
the individual were made wholly responsive to their insatiability.
Only if the passions were balanced with equally powerful faculties
of reason and conscience could man escape the tyranny of his own
lusts.

Men naturally were political or social animals, "but they know
each other's imbecility so well, that they ought never to lead one
another into temptation."[102] Should the plum of political power
be made available to those who were ambitious to pluck it, society
must then be made subservient to those who would be drunk on
power. "The passion that is long indulged and continually gratified
becomes mad; it is a species of delirium; it should not be called
guilt, but insanity."[103] Increasing the number of lunatics in an
assembly would provide no greater security for the nation. Jealous
men must be made to watch jealous men; each man's mad lust to
tyrannize must be exploited to prevent the creation of tyranny.

Because man's weaknesses were natural, they were universal,
characterizing Kings and peasants alike. The simple American
farmer was as likely to tyrannize in a mob as either an aristocrat
in the senate or a president upon his throne. Faustian restlessness
was everywhere and always the same, and could never be eradi-
cated. Man's relentless compulsion to distinguish himself from his
peers could be directed, but only by force. Adams agreed with
Paine and Jefferson that if the golden rule were observed there
would be no need for government. The golden rule was not
observed, however, because the iron rule of man's passionate hunger
for distinction would not allow it. To appeal to men to behave
themselves in contradiction to their nature could cause no change:
"how long will republicans be the dupes of their own simplicity!

how long will they depend upon sermons, prayers, orations, declamations, in honor of brotherly love, and against discords, when they know that, without human means, it is but tempting and insulting Providence, to depend upon them for the happiness of life, or the liberty of society."[104]   It was useless either to plead or to reason with men: "Something more efficacious . . . than moral song, ingenious fable, philosophic precept, or Christian ordinance, with reverence be it spoken, must be employed in society, or dissensions will still ravage and desolate the world."[105]   Men would have to be compelled to sublimate their ineradicable drives into socially useful activity or, at least, would have to be blocked in their more antisocial instincts.   Nothing short of force would change or direct human behavior.

He conceded that generosity and benevolence also formed part of human nature, but selfishness was almost always stronger.   Even if all men had some concern for and love of the public, probably none would put the public interest above their own.   "We are not, indeed, commanded to love our neighbor better than ourselves."[106] In order to govern men it was essential to remember that "although reason ought always to govern individuals, it certainly never did since the Fall, and never will, till the Millennium; and human nature must be taken as it is, as it has been, and will be."[107] Should a legislator take man for what he naturally was, a system of government could be devised that would protect liberty because its basic maxim would be recognized: *"trust not to human nature, without a control, the conduct of my cause."*[108]

It followed from his view of human nature that social disasters resulted from political ignorance, not from evil.   Since government could direct or control men, uncontrolled human passion always meant that the government had not been adequate to the task. Adams asserted that because the raw human material was always constant, variations in behavior were always caused by variations in government.   All customs and behavior were a result of "the form of government, not . . . [of] the temper of the people, the latter being but the natural and necessary effect of the former."[109] Human passion, when not compelled to seek gratification in acceptable ways, would always explode into socially destructive selfishness. Only government could force the necessary sublimation.

An unbalance constitution not only allowed but encouraged man's instinctive egotism to disrupt society; a balanced constitution would rely on one man's selfishness to check another's. Thus a proper constitution would exploit man's weakness in the interest of social strength. A frame of government that failed to take human nature for what it was, that assumed a more optimistic view of man, must end in disaster because it would refuse to use man's frailty, the greatest of all weapons useful for social tranquillity and order.

Because man was reasonable as well as weak, he could be taught to see the need for a balanced constitution. Properly educated men, sensitive to their own self-interest, could accept an organic law that would restrain each man's neighbors. The amount of necessary self-restraint in a balanced constitution would be individually justifiable because of the inhibitions placed on everyone else. The argument may be summarized: All men intelligent enough to know their own lusts can be reasonable enough to accept a measure of self-restraint in order to inhibit all others who are similarly lustful. Without checking weakness with weakness, society must degenerate into a Hobbesian state of perpetual warfare of all against all.

Adams supposed that the choice about the form of government was free. Even under a government whose lack of balance necessarily caused immorality, men could use their reason to see the precariousness of their own perhaps exalted position. Nothing prevented men from creating the political conditions necessary to peace on earth. Thinking perhaps of Montesquieu whose ideas about geographical conditioning had become widely accepted, Adams asserted that policy and education always took precedence over every natural situation. Because there was no necessity in political stupidity, men could build as they chose. Whether they would ever choose wisdom was a question already answered in the balanced state constitutions of America.

Even in America, however, there was already an infant but menacing aristocracy. In every state there were a few distinguished families who, in time, might "be able to divide the state into two parties, one generally at the head of the gentlemen, the other of the simplemen, [who would] tear one another to pieces."[110] Should that happen, it will not be the fault of these individuals or families; they will not be able to avoid it, let their talents or virtues be what they may; their friends, connections, and dependents, will stimulate and urge them forward, by every provocation of flattery, ridicule, and menaces, until they plunge them into an abyss, out of which they can never rise. It will be entirely the fault of the constitution, and of the people who will not now adopt a good one; it will be the misfortune of those individuals and families as much as of the public; for what consolation can it be to a man, to think that his whole life, and that of his son and grandson, must be spent in unceasing misery and warfare, for the sake only of a possibility that his great grandson may become a despot![111]

The creation of the Society of the Cincinnati convinced Adams "that the disposition to artificial distinctions, to titles, and ribbons, and to the hereditary descent of them, is ardent in America."[112]

Though it is true that Adams trusted no man with power, he was most concerned about the dangers to a republic of its aristocratic members, and he therefore wished that the new federal constitution had given more power to the president and less to the senate. The world's history had taught him that the combined force of the people and of an independent executive was necessary to restrain the rich and the talented. Indeed, neither the people (as a political body) nor the King or first magistrate could long exist without the other; the aristocrats would always be able to destroy the people or the executive should one or the other be either too weak or altogether absent. It was not even possible to exclude the rich or its agents from any share in political power. Their natural social influence was such that even if completely barred from political office, they could still control the conduct of others. Even though the executive was the natural ally of the people in the struggle against aristocratic encroachment, the mass of men had an unfortunate jealousy of the executive power. Because of that jealousy it was easy for aristocrats, out of their hatred of both executive and popular power, to encourage the people to resist the executive, and thus to destroy themselves by handing their liberty over to the most ambitious few.

Adams saw a westward progression of political wisdom from Sparta to Rome to England to America. Each step forward was a recognition of the need to balance power. The English constitu-

tion was, in theory, almost perfect, and the corruption of political
life in England was merely a result of departing from the theory.
The achievement of the Americans was the implementation of the
wisdom of the English theory, was improving that wisdom and
putting it to work. The House of Commons should have but did
not represent the democratic element in English life. In America,
as a result of the almost universal ownership of some parcel of
land, the abolition of hereditary offices of all kinds, and of a recognition of the need to balance the three powers, the people's rights
were secured more firmly than at any other time or in any other
place. The experience of the houses of representatives in the several colonies demonstrated that the American people had learned
their political lessons well, and had had the sense and virtue to
practice what they had learned. It was true that "there is no
special providence for Americans, and their nature is the same
with that of others."[113] But they were on that account to be congratulated all the more for achieving more balanced constitutions
than any other people.

The mass of citizens in Periclean Athens had less real authority
than the people of the several states in America. Precisely because
the Americans occupied so vast a land and could not therefore
meet in one assembly, they enjoyed more tranquillity than was ever
known in the Athens of the golden age. Property requirements in
America were so modest that almost any man could aspire to
office and power. The system of balanced power might even eliminate intrigue and corruption. The American states, therefore, not
Athens, should be considered the fairest test of whether a government committed to representing the will of the people could endure. "If it can," Adams thought, "there is reason to hope for all
the equality, all the liberty, and every other good fruit of an
Athenian democracy, without any of its ingratitude, levity, convulsions, or factions."[114]

The widespread ownership of property was the basis of any democratic claim to political power. Adams rejected ideas favoring
universal manhood suffrage, as did virtually all of his contemporaries
in America, France, and England. Though he argued that the
rights of property were inviolable, his insistence on a property
qualification was no mere celebration of the wealthy, whom he
trusted, it must be emphasized, no more than the poor. Property,

for him, meant an independence of mind that the propertyless who depended on some master for daily bread could never know. A modest property qualification in a country where property was widely held was therefore justified as a device that would *reduce* the political power of the rich.

Man's moral equality and his right to equal opportunity—ideas Adams held—were, in his system, lessened not at all by his insistence on a property qualification. The fact of an inequality of condition did not mean either an inequality in worth as a man or that opportunity for advancement should be denied to anyone. It was true, he believed, that farmers, merchants, and artisans were usually ignorant of public affairs, and that the most sober and industrious among them were of course the most ignorant. But even the most ignorant was able to decide which of his neighbors he would prefer as a representative. Through frequent elections to a popular and representative assembly, the simpler people could be given their equal rights as citizens. Because there would always be men of genius hidden among the people, elections would give those men an opportunity to rise in power and influence. Any man who believed with Aristotle that inequality of condition reflected a moral inequality was simply wrong. A modest property qualification coupled with frequent elections would show that the people could sustain a virtuous and democratic share of the government.

Elections, for Adams, constituted the great school of political knowledge. Simple folk without political sophistication, in choosing a representative from several contending for their favor, would find their own political acuity increased. The fundamental questions of political succession in the states of America had been answered as well as was humanly possible. The annual election of governors, senators, and representatives was the best possible system of political opportunity and education for the mass of men, and was the surest means of making the people's political agents responsive to the people's collective will. Unlike his idea about the automatic workings of a balance of power was his doubt that the form of elections guaranteed their proper function. Corruption could distort and destroy a perfectly designed election system. "Mankind have universally discovered that chance was preferable to a corrupt choice, and have trusted Providence rather than themselves."[115]

The fear of corrupted elections remained with Adams for the rest of his life, constituting part of the disturbing questions that brooded behind his approval of the American constitutional system. The other part of his concern for the future was that, because the congress could override a presidential veto, the president would not be equal in a genuine struggle for power, although he had earlier supported this provision for the Massachusetts Constitution. He worried that an aristocracy of wealth would someday dominate the politics of the United States, converting it from a republic to an oligarchy, precipitating the cyclical convulsions of unmixed political forms. In time, his fear of the inordinate power of the Senate grew to the point where his faith in the Constitution was shaken. His own congenital gloom coupled with his political theory allowed him to make a flat prediction: "from the constitution of human nature, and the constant course of human affairs, it is certain that our constitution will be subverted, if not amended, and that in a very short time, merely for want of a decisive negative [veto] in the executive."[116]

During his own life and since, Adams has been accused of being a monarchist at heart. An understanding of his *Defence* should suffice to lay the charge to rest—finally. His categorical rejection of hereditary offices, and his argument that executive power was necessary to protect the people from the aristocracy, reflected his profound republicanism. He refused to participate in national narcissism, in the belief that America's political system was the best for all the world's nations. It followed logically from his political theory that a relatively advanced social and economic condition was needed before republicanism would be practicable, and he did therefore accept kingship for nations still threatened by potential oligarchs or still impeded by monopolization of land. That government and society were both the cause and the effect of each other meant that an ignorance of one side of the equation would lead to a self-defeating solution. His tolerance of royalty, celebration of executive power, and personal *hauteur* caused his undeserved reputation as a monarchist. So unblemished a republican as Jefferson hailed the *Defence*, with a minor reservation about the nature of the congress under the Articles, and hoped that it would become a classic for all American politicians, though Jefferson was later to agree that Adams was guilty of monarchism.

None of Adams' contemporaries were more committed to republicanism than he was, but none had his somewhat complicated reasons for the commitment.

Agonizing over what he considered the stupidity of democrats on both sides of the Atlantic, Adams began a new series of papers on April 27, 1790, under the general title of *Discourses on Davila*, in the columns of the Federalist *Gazette of the United States* of New York. In order to understand the background of the French Revolution Adams turned to the account of the revolutions in France in the later sixteenth century in Enrico Caterino Davila's *Historia delle guerre civili di Francia*. Nothing Adams ever wrote was better designed than his *Discourses on Davila* to do himself serious and permanent damage, and when even he recognized that he was supplying his enemies, including Jefferson, with their best ammunition, he discontinued the papers before he had finished with the subject.

The lesson he drew from Davila was a foregone conclusion: An unbalanced French government had produced disaster in the sixteenth as it must do in the eighteenth century. A demand for excessive democratic power had created a condition favorable to the reestablishment of despotism in the sixteenth century, a result that must come finally as a perhaps unintended consequence of the French Revolution of his own day. Napoleon's career was later taken by Adams as the final and full proof of the immutable truth of his political theory.

Both the method and substance of the *Discourses on Davila* were extensions of his *Defence*, and the *Discourses* were a sequel to that work. More than two-thirds of the papers were almost literal translations, again without quotation marks, of Davila. But Adams slipped in a series of papers on human nature that best expressed his most mature view of that subject, a view taken almost entirely from the chapter called "The Origin of Ambition and the Distinction of Ranks" in Adam Smith's *Theory of Moral Sentiments*.[117] Though the psychology was Smith's, its political application was Adams', and it was always with the politics of human nature that Adams was most concerned.

Because the view of man in the *Discourses* was merely an elaboration of earlier statements of Adams', it can be reconstructed with relative brevity. Men, he said again, were naturally gregarious, and were almost always motivated by an unquenchable thirst to be noticed. That desire remained the most compelling human drive to either vice or virtue. A fulfillment of the desire for reputation was nature's reward for men who served the public, as contempt was the punishment for unregulated selfishness. Beneficence was thus one result of the passion for distinction, and public service a result of private needs. Regulation but not eradication of that passion was the principle goal of government, since the existence of the passion was the principle means whereby government could accomplish its goal. Men could distinguish themselves by either remarkable virtue or remarkable vice, and it was government's task to encourage the one rather than the other.

Wealth was pursued by men neither for its own sake nor for utility, but because it was applauded by the world. A man of small property was always more content than the rich, Adams believed, but the rich could nourish themselves on the attention of their peers. Thus, though some poor individual might have a good conscience, he was ashamed because he was neglected: "He is not disapproved, censured, or reproached; *he is only not seen.*"[118] The invisibility resulting from poverty, not the mere lack of creature comforts, was the true curse of poverty.

Rome had understood and applied this need for attention better than any other nation. Signs of distinction were granted for public service. The senatorial purple, golden ring, ivory chairs, rods and axes, and crowns of laurel, among other things, all served as goads to those who aspired to the esteem of the world. Through pomp and symbols of authority, power, and merit Rome hoped to attract men of genuine merit to serve the state and thereby earn the purple. Other nations had vainly sought to improve on Rome's example, and no device for selecting men to office was more educational but more dangerous than an exclusive reliance on popular elections.

Europe's superiority to Asia and Africa resulted from the unification of lands, offices, and families, and the hereditary descent of all three. (In 1812, Adams finally saw how easily that argument could be misinterpreted as a justification for nobility, and he noted in the margin of his copy of the *Discourses* that such had not been his intention; by that time, of course, it was too late either to avoid or to rectify the political damage he had already suffered.) He tried to explain himself to Samuel Adams but one suspects to no avail: "By nobles, I mean not peculiarly an hereditary nobility . . . but the natural and actual aristocracy among mankind."[119] Hereditary office was preferable to corrupt elections; when corruption flourished the state was always and necessarily directed by men of guile, which, for him, was the worst conceivable situation. Nevertheless, he did feel that corruption was perhaps not an avoidable condition.

For all their accomplishments in literature and philosophy, the French had failed to learn that their essential humanity precluded the possibility that they could build heaven on earth. The assumption underlying and crippling the French Revolution, Adams thought, was that in the age of Enlightenment human perfectibility would finally be realized. That dazzling assumption, blinding men to the limits of their powers, would be a swamp instead of a rock on which to build a state:

> FRENCHMEN! Act and think like yourselves! confessing human nature, be magnanimous and wise. Acknowledging and boasting yourselves to be men, avow the feelings of men. The affectation of being exempted from passions is inhuman. The grave pretension to such singularity is solemn hypocrisy. Both are unworthy of your frank and generous natures. Consider that government is intended to set bounds to passions which nature has not limited; and to assist reason, conscience, justice, and truth, in controlling interests, which, without it, would be as unjust as uncontrollable.[120]

Americans should reject the promised utopia of the French dreamers in favor of a reality based on the federal constitution, a frame of government that both acknowledged and exploited the weaknesses of men for the benefit of man.

Within a few months after his arrival in America, he was elected first Vice-President of the United States, and was reelected in 1792. He described the office to his wife as "the most insignificant office that ever the invention of man contrived or his imagination conceived."[121] In December of 1796 he was elected to the presidency, and assumed the office in the following March. Defeated in his second presidential campaign by both Jefferson and Aaron Burr, he finally left major public office in March, 1801, and spent the rest of his life in writing, remembering, corresponding, reading, and watching the rise of his son, John Quincy Adams, to national leadership.

As Vice-President and president of the Senate of the new United States, Adams had a good opportunity to observe American politicians at closer range than had been possible for the previous decade when he had been in Europe.   And they had a similar opportunity to take his measure.   Observers on both sides of Adams' desk frequently did not like what they saw.   Party lines were stiffening in the new nation, and Adams was clearly not a man of the people.   Democratic senators found him tedious, overbearing, and politically suspect.   William Maclay, a democratic senator from Pennsylvania, thought Adams an impossible wretch, and recorded his opinions in a free-swinging diary.   Maclay was especially offended by Adams' fussing about the proper forms of address, about the titles to be given to the various officers of the new government. For his protracted attention to the matters of titles, Adams earned one of his own from the democratic senators who dubbed him His *"Rotundity."*   Maclay received the news of the abolition of nobility in the French Revolution with a prayer for the continued success of the Revolution, and thinking that Adams wanted to introduce nobility in America, the senator sputtered: "Ye gods, with what indignation do I review the late attempt of some creatures among us to revive the vile machinery [of nobility]!   O Adams, Adams, what a wretch art thou!"   The trouble with Adams, from Maclay's viewpoint, was that he had spent too long in Europe and had been seduced away from American innocence.   The earlier suspicions of Adams about Franklin were now turned against him, and with prose as acidic as his own: "Guardian goddess of America, canst thou not order it so, that when thy sons cross the Atlantic they may return with something else besides European forms and follies?" And, of course, Adams' obsession with checks and balances merely convinced Maclay that Adams was either an enemy of the people or crazy, or both:

> He [Adams] got on the subject of checks to government and the balances of power.   His tale was long.   He seemed to expect some answer.   I caught at the last word, and said undoubtedly without a balance there could be no equilibrium, and so left him hanging in geometry.[122]

Adams' presidential administration was marked by tension with France, and by his own independence of Hamilton and the Federalists at home. The French Directory's refusal to receive an American minister and the lurid XYZ Affair gave the Federalists, and especially Hamilton, whose military ambitions were boundless, grounds for demanding a declaration of war against France. Though Adams insisted on continued peaceful negotiation he authorized military preparations of a defensive nature, and an undeclared naval war with France proceeded. The Convention of 1800 brought peace to the two nations and war to the Federalist party. Realizing finally that his Cabinet was largely in Hamilton's control, Adams dismissed two secretaries and found himself opposed now by both Federalists and Republicans. The unfortunate Alien and Sedition Acts of 1798, which Adams continued to defend even though he came to believe they had been unnecessary, had confirmed Republicans in their fear of him. His defection from Federalist orthodoxy was finally made complete when he later took as strong a stand against banks as John Taylor of Caroline, the most inflexible Republican of them all. In time, Adams was to repudiate capitalism and Hamilton's entire fiscal policy, but his own political theory kept him out of the camp of Republicanism, which never forgave his "midnight appointment" of Federalist judges at virtually the last minute of his administration. It seems appropriate that his political independence should have turned almost all organized support away from him, and that Hamilton's hatred, which Adams returned with real pleasure, should have given the election of 1800 to Jefferson and the Republicans.

For his part, Adams reciprocated the kind of contempt exhibited by Senator Maclay with exquisite scorn. Retaining, of course, the political ideas he had articulated in England, Adams viewed the democratic movements in America and France as necessarily self-defeating. From his point of view, the Republicans in America and the revolutionaries in France, in demanding either a preponderance of or complete power for the democratic element in society, would destroy the balance of power on which a durable democracy naturally rested. Republican or revolutionary opposition to the one and the few, to a first magistrate and the aristocracy, would make a stable share of democratic authority impossible. Politically ignorant democrats, he thought, were the people's worst enemy.

Political ignorance was a certain symptom of an anterior ignorance about human nature:

> The revolution in France could not . . . be indifferent to me; but I have learned by awful experience to rejoice with trembling. . . . I know not what to make of a republic of thirty million atheists. . . . Too many Frenchmen, after the example of too many Americans, pant for equality of persons and property. The impracticability of this, God Almighty has decreed, and the advocates for liberty, who attempt it, will surely suffer for it.[123]

Though he was usually pessimistic, rejected ideas about the perfectability of man, had no faith in nonpolitical reform movements, and viewed nature as a source of both strength and weakness, though he lacked the felicity of phrase and wit of the *philosophe,* Adams was a true man of the eighteenth century. The mechanical nature of his political system, his reliance on what he called reason and experience, and his environmentalism, show his debt to Newton and Locke. But the Enlightenment came to Adams through the filter of American experience, especially through the highly charged Protestant atmosphere of Winthrop's city on a hill. Reason, for Adams, was not a lever of revolution; it was a device, as it had been for the pre-Edwardsean Puritans, for helping man try to overcome himself. Precisely in his celebration of America, in his conservatism, Adams was a figure of the Enlightenment in America, for he read the American past as the revolutionary history of the utility of applied reason. According to this view, the revolutionary generation of Americans was trying to conserve the revolutionary nature of colonial America. He viewed what he thought was the French *philosophes'* revolutionary use of reason as a violation both of experience and of the logic of his political mechanism. Rousseau's arguments from a state of nature were misleading because Rousseau was merely speculating, actually ignorant of actual nature, and motivated simply by a desire, not to find truth, but to destroy Christianity and monarchy.

The nature of the American Enlightenment can best be seen in Adams' opposition to the French. No less committed to the rights of man and the laws of nature than Rousseau or Jefferson, Adams insisted that both ideas must be tested by and accommodated to American history if they were to avoid being merely impracticable utopian speculation. Optimism was his *bête noire.* From wherever they came, assumptions about the universal goodness or perfectibility of men contradicted his experience, violated his intellectual system, and drove him wild:

> I am willing you should call this the Age of Frivolity . . . and would not object if you had named it the Age of Folly, Vice, Frenzy, Fury, Brutality, Daemons, Buonaparte, Tom Paine, or the age of the burning Brand from the bottomless Pit: or anything but the Age of Reason. I know not whether any man in the world has had more influence on its inhabitants or affairs for the last thirty years than Tom Paine. There can be no severer satire on the age. For such a mongrel between pigs and puppy, begotten by a wild boar on a bitch wolf, never before in any age of the world was suffered by the poltroonery of mankind to run through such a career of mischief. Call it then the Age of Paine.[124]

A simple trust in man's allegedly natural goodness became harmful, according to Adams, only when it was used as a justification for tampering with the natural laws of politics that he had described. The political implication of a faith in man was an unbalanced democracy, a self-defeating political form. Condorcet's *Outline of an Historical View of the Progress of the Human Mind* was perfectly suited, among other things, to elicit Adams' automatic and violent response. Condorcet wrote, for instance, that progress could never be completely reversed, and Adams dissented in the margin of his copy of the *Outline.* Rejecting what he thought to be French atheism, Adams disagreed with Condorcet's assertion that the Greeks had done the most for mankind with the counter-assertion that the Jews had the best claim on the world's gratitude. "In spite of Bolingbroke and Voltaire," he wrote in a private letter, "I will insist that the Hebrews have done more to civilize men than any other nation. . . . The Jews . . . preserve[d] and propagate[d] to all mankind the doctrine of a supreme, intelligent, wise, almighty sovereign of the universe, which I believe to be the great essential principle of all morality, and consequently of all civilization."[125]

When Condorcet criticized the American Revolution for not going far enough, for stopping with mere independence instead of attempting a thorough social reformation as the French Revolution had, Adams became convinced that Condorcet was a fool. Viewing Condorcet's trust in unbalanced democracy with the knowledge of

Napoleon's power in 1811, Adams could dismiss the *philosophe* as a dangerous *naif*. The refusal or inability to admit that the necessary inequality of fortune or fame demanded that government should balance what would otherwise be unequal parties led virtually all the political philosophers of the world to take positions as pleasing to the mass of men as they were inaccurate:

> Nothing seizes the attention of the staring animal so surely as paradox, riddle, mystery, invention, discovery, wonder, temerity. Plato, and his disciples from the fourth century Christians to Rousseau and Tom Paine, have been fully sensible of this weakness in mankind, and have too successfully grounded upon it their pretensions to fame. I might, indeed, have mentioned Bolingbroke, Hume, Gibbon, Voltaire, Turgot, Helvetius, Diderot, Condorcet, Buffon, De la Lande, and fifty others, all a little cracked.[126]

Adams' alienation from the growing democratic mood led to interesting debates by correspondence with both Jefferson and John Taylor of Caroline, the two high priests of republicanism in America. To both men Adams repeatedly urged, indeed fairly shrieked, that he did not favor an aristocracy, if by the term was meant a special class of men whose privileges were created and protected by law. He was apparently growing weary of defending himself against charges of monarchism and aristocracy, and he complained to Taylor that the *Defence* was "a book that has been misunderstood, misrepresented, and abused, more than any other except the Bible."[127]   And to Jefferson he promised, as he put it, to "forfeit my life, if you can find one sentiment in my Defence of the Constitutions, or the Discourses on Davila, which, by a fair construction, can favor the introduction of hereditary monarchy or aristocracy in America."[128]   For Taylor, Adams tried to clarify the troublesome term:

> By *natural aristocracy*, in general may be understood those superiorities of influence in society which grow out of the constitution of human nature. By *artificial aristocracy*, those inequalities in weight and superiorities of influence which are created and established by civil laws. . . . By aristocracy, I understand all those men who can command, influence, or procure more than an average of votes; by an aristocrat, every man who can and will influence one man to vote besides himself.[129]

He insisted, as he had done in both the *Defence* and the *Discourses,* that men were not, had never been, and never would be equal in condition, although they were equal in worth. He tried to convince Taylor that he had "through life asserted the moral equality of all mankind," arguing that his political system "was calculated and framed for the express purpose of securing to all men equal laws and equal rights."[130] But moral equality did not mean equality in condition. The "five pillars of aristocracy" were beauty, wealth, birth, genius, and virtue, and the first three would always take precedence over the last two. There was, he said nothing either pleasant or desirable about this; it was merely a fact which the Republicans would do well to consider.

Taylor insisted that an aristocracy of wealth was not natural because it was always created by the favors of corrupted government, and Adams replied that whether the rich were so naturally or actually made little difference, that their influence must be countered in either case. Adams joined Taylor in condemning capitalism as "the madness of the many for the profit of the few."[131] But Adams demanded to know what to do about it "when the few are craving and the many mad for the same thing?" When all men sought to corrupt government for their own profit, only a system that exploited, rather than hid from, that universal hunger could survive.

Again and again Adams tried to show that his insistence that a natural aristocracy did in fact exist in no way moderated his attachment to republicanism, and he fired a shot at Taylor that should have been felt by all of the Virginia Republicans:

> You had the honor and felicity to marry the only child of my honest and sincere friend, the honorable John Penn, of North Carolina. From this marriage, you derived, with an amiable consort, a handsome fortune. . . . I will be bolder still, Mr. Taylor. Would Washington have ever been commander of the revolutionary army or president of the United States, if he had not married the rich widow of Mr. Custis? Would Jefferson ever have been president of the United States if he had not married the daughter of Mr. Wales?[132]

Taylor himself was, Adams informed him, "the most eminent aristocrat of them all."[133]

Failing to understand human nature, the Republicans, according to Adams, too often found themselves defending the proposition that the United States was based on some novel political or moral principles. The only unique characteristic of the nation was the actual application of quite ancient ideas, Adams said. To argue that America was God's country and that Americans were His chosen people was both pleasant and totally false. Americans did have an opportunity—the fairest in man's history—to build wisely, and they might do so if they would learn to assess their own and therefore their neighbor's madness more accurately. The several actual and near rebellions of both rich and poor, from Shays' to the Hartford Convention, convinced Adams that not even Americans were willing to accept the necessary restraint. He asked Taylor: "Must you and I humble ourselves in dust and ashes to acknowledge that the United States have had more rebellions and *quasi rebellions* in thirty years than England has had in one hundred and twenty?"[134] Human nature was always and everywhere the same. Adams was willing to grant "that the first want of man is his dinner, and the second his girl,"[135] but the Republicans in wanting to portray men as angels were running the risk of turning them into devils.

The Jeffersonian faith that education would change the world was yet another piece of unexamined piety, according to Adams. "Has the art of printing increased democracy?" Knowledge was always a weapon of the dominant class, and the greater its increase the more effective the weapon:

> Depend upon it, unless you give a share in the sovereignty to the democrats, the more you increase knowledge in the nation, the more you will grind and gripe the democrats, till you reduce them to the calculations concerning West India negroes, Scottish and English coal-heavers, Dutch turf-lifters, and the street-walking girls of the night in Paris and London. For knowledge will forever be monopolized by the aristocracy.[136]

It was no more realistic to favor a community of knowledge than it was a community of wives or property. Adams hoped for an improvement in education and the widest possible dissemination of knowledge because "humanity will be improved and ameliorated" through the process. "But," he asked Taylor, "after all, did you ever see a rose without a briar . . . a good without an evil, in this mingled world?"[137] Knowledge could be put to bad as well as good purposes, and there was every guarantee that knowledge without the sense to fight power with power would usually be exploited in the interest of the rich and always against the interests of the people. With a quite profound understanding of academic life, Adams concluded: "You may read the history of all the universities, academies, monasteries of the world, and see whether learning extinguishes passions or corrects human vices."[138]   Jefferson's University of Virginia would be polluted if European professors were employed, because they were necessarily tainted with false political and social ideas. Nature alone was the great schoolteacher, but she was so profligate with her charms that any man, however evil, who wanted the power she could give would get what he wanted. Society could as easily suffer as benefit from vigorous educational improvement.

The farthest that Adams could go toward some commitment to an idea of progress was a hope that things might get somewhat better rather than a good deal worse. Positively rejecting all ideas about human perfectibility, Adams announced to Jefferson that he was "a believer in the probable improvability and improvement, the ameliorability and amelioration in human affairs."[139] But yet at about the same time he could tell James Madison that "this nation must be purified in the furnace of affliction."[140] There was no contradiction, because man's capacity to lighten his burden was no guarantee that he would do so. Should the fires of affliction come, and should man pass through, he would emerge tougher than before the trial. As Adams vacillated between gloom and semigloom in response to the changing conditions of his nation, he finally came to the point where some hope was possible. "We shall leave the world with many consolations. It is better than we found it."[141] Man, though not perfectible, was improvable, and improvements had been made. If government could continue to suspend or mitigate the class struggle, further progress could be made—not to heaven on earth, but to a life whose security would not be daily threatened by starving cannibals.

With advancing age, Adams began to think more about his own religion. In his youth he had flirted with though never completely accepted Deism, but the leisure for and the occasion to meditate produced in Adams one of the first, if always tentative, Unitarians.

As with other issues, the political implications of religion weighed heavily in his scales. Without God, human equality, which for him was moral equality, could not exist. "There is no right or wrong in the universe without the supposition of a moral government and an intellectual and moral governor."[142]

In a famous correspondence renewed with Jefferson when he too was an elder statesman, Adams especially tried to communicate his religious ideas. To Jefferson, Adams said that Christian theologians believed that God "created this speck of dirt and the human species for his glory; and with the deliberate design of making nine tenths of our species miserable for ever for his glory." Such a God was a "Wretch!"

> What is his glory? Is he ambitious? Does he want promotion? Is he vain, tickled with adulation, exulting and triumphing in his power and the sweetness of his vengeance? Pardon me, my Maker, for these awful questions. My answer to them is always ready. I believe no such things. My adoration of the author of the universe is too profound and too sincere. The love of God and his creation . . . are my religion. Howl, snarl, bite, ye Calvinistic, ye Athanasian divines, if you will; ye will say I am no Christian; I say ye are no Christians, and there the account is balanced. Yet I believe all the honest men among you are Christians, in my sense of the word.[143]

Of course this son of Edwards' Massachusetts would argue that evil was an essential part of life. Nothing that men could do could change that unlovely fact. But, through submission and resignation, they could learn to live with it, and perhaps adjust to it so that their individual portions of misery might be borne more easily. Resignation, perhaps coupled with a sigh, was the best that men could do in a universe that was far less malleable than the *philosophes* dreamed. In his moments of deepest gloom he sometimes seemed to reach out for Edwards' hand, as when he described life for Jefferson's instruction as "a vapor, a fog, a dew, a cloud, a blossom, a flower, a rose, a blade of grass, a glass bubble, a tale told by an idiot, a *boule de savon*, vanity of vanities, an eternal succession of which would terrify me almost as much as annihilation."[144]

Adams rejected the Calvinist idea of universal human depravity, replacing it, as has been shown, with his idea of universal human weakness. He saw the collective species paralyzed by the fear of pain and death and especially by life after death. The spectacle of man's frailties and fears overcoming his reason and conscience, Adams said, "has sickened my very soul, and almost reconciled me to Swift's travels among the Yahoos."[145]   He could not become a misanthrope in good standing because, as he put it, "I must hate myself before I can hate my fellow-men, and that I cannot and will not do."[146]   He pitied them instead.   His compassion for a human race that was usually disgusting did not, however, incline him to a more favorable reading of his own religious tradition:

> I must be a very unnatural son to entertain any prejudices against the Calvinists, or Calvinism, . . . for my father and mother, my uncles and aunts, and all my predecessors, from our common ancestor, who landed in this country two hundred years ago . . . were of that persuasion.   Indeed, I have never known any better people than the Calvinists.   Nevertheless, I must acknowledge that I cannot class myself under that denomination.[147]

Thinking of himself as a simple Christian, he represented the next stage of the Puritan urge to divest religion from centuries of human and therefore evil accretion, thereby making possible a return to a purified and primitive faith.   For Adams, who belonged to no organized religious movement or institution, a life of virtue, in the last analysis, was the best test of any religion's validity.   He had no more patience at the end of his life than he had had as a young man with highly refined theology or with what he thought to be excessive mysticism.   Because of either wickedness or ignorance, men had spun abstruse and obtuse speculations about the inscrutable merely in order to dupe more simple souls.   Man's reason was best suited for politics, not religion:

> Mr. Adams leaves to Homer and Virgil, to Tacitus and Quintillian, to Mahomet and Calvin, to Edwards and Priestly, or, if you will, to Milton's angels reasoning high in pandemonium, all their acute speculations about fate, destiny, foreknowledge absolute, necessity, and predestination.   He thinks it problematical, whether there is, or ever will be, more than one Being capable of understanding this vast subject.   In his principles of legislation, he has nothing to do with these interminable controversies.   He considers men as free, moral, and accountable agents; and he takes men as God has made them.[148]

Man's responsibility to a moral law and his accountability to an eternal lawgiver were meaningful only if man himself were free, intelligent, and able to discriminate between good and evil.   All men were naturally possessed of those necessary attributes, and Adams had no sympathy with deterministic intellectual systems that tried to deny human freedom, intelligence, or an ingrained moral sense.

Throughout his life, Adams had wrestled with the Puritan ghost that roamed New England. Although he succeeded in freeing himself from its more formal demands, he found it difficult to escape its restraining hand; although he rejected the Puritan theological system, his vision remained colored by what he abhorred. Adams, that Enlightenment man, remained convinced of the essential validity of Puritanism's view of human nature and rested his political system on it. The result was that his thought was more similar to than different from Winthrop's political theology.

The roots of the American Enlightenment were mostly embedded in seventeenth-century Boston, rather than in seventeenth-century London or eighteenth-century Paris. The easy acceptance of Locke by the American revolutionaries proved that the politics of Calvinism and of Locke generally had been mutually congenial, if not identical. Locke, in approving the political thought and accomplishments of the Puritans in England and America, proved to be equally acceptable to them, including Jonathan Edwards, the most orthodox of them all. One perceptive historian said of Locke that "it rather looks as though he was more influenced by the facts and events in America . . . than the founders were influenced by his *Treatises of Civil Government.*"[149] English whiggery, in short, had become useful to Americans because it had itself come from the common Puritan parent who had sired both Locke and the Zion in the wilderness. No matter how hard John Adams tried, he could never completely escape the intellectual air he breathed and did not like.

After ninety full years Adams died, appropriately and with a fine sense of the dramatic, on the Fourth of July, 1826, the fiftieth anniversary of the Declaration of Independence, just hours after Jefferson (whom Adams had mentioned with his last words) died at Monticello. The two patron saints of their nation had quarreled because Jefferson had misunderstood Adams. But then Adams was easily misunderstood because of his own intellectual rigor and personal obstinacy. John Adams (and all the most creative members of his family of the next three generations) seems to have been born stubborn, incapable of adjusting to change. His fall from the favor he had known during and immediately after the Revolution to the isolation of the last quarter of his life came not because he had changed, but because he had not, while his nation was growing. As the nation made material progress and adjusted its thought to meet new conditions, he came increasingly to seem anachronistic, a raspy voice out of a dead past. That he had contributed in an essential way to the bringing about of the very conditions which made him seem hugely irrelevant, is an irony that seems fitting in the light of his own attitudes about the inevitability of public ingratitude.

The central tragedy of his life was that he had become isolated almost immediately after the federal Constitution was adopted, before he had been elected to the highest offices the government offered, and because of his own efforts to support the new government. Elected, it seems, because of his past achievements, he found himself an unwanted national leader. His genius had to do with devising governments, not with administering them. When he became President he already was, as one of his great-grandsons, Brooks Adams, later called himself, an "unusable man," but one whose utility had been thoroughly exploited in the fight for independence and the establishment of a new nation. His own recognition that the sand was shifting under his feet was a demon that gnawed at him constantly throughout his long life.

Despite his extraordinarily crowded career, Adams managed to produce the best body of writing of the time and place. Typically, he wrote his most ambitious books at those periods of his life when the duties of office were most pressing. Throughout his entire active career he tried to develop a consistent system of political thought that would, he hoped, show the way to active political wisdom, to both national and personal success, and to acclaim. He succeeded in his thought and in his career, at least until his final return to America. Unable to moderate his vision, he was finally and almost completely rejected by a nation at whose birth he had been instrumental; and that rejection seems to have flowed easily from the political lessons he had spent a lifetime trying to teach the American electorate. He knew that the future would misunderstand him, just as his contemporaries had. He complained that the history of the revolutionary period would be one enormous lie, that future generations would be convinced that Benjamin Franklin sent an electric charge into the earth and summoned up George Washington. It finally turned out that his political vision was too rigorous, too demanding, too dependent on that kind of public virtue for which John Winthrop had also called, to suit a nation that was beginning to turn to expansion, capitalism, and democracy. In rejecting the future, John Adams was consigned to the past, an unhappy fate he had himself predicted.

SELECT BIBLIOGRAPHY

Randolph G. Adams. *The Political Ideas of the American Revolution.* Durham, 1922.

Hannah Arendt. *On Revolution.* New York, 1963.

Carl Becker. *Declaration of Independence.* New York, 1922.

Ernst Cassirer. *The Philosophy of the Enlightenment.* Princeton, 1951.

Gilbert Chinard. *Thomas Jefferson.* Boston, 1929.

Zoltán Haraszti. *John Adams and the Prophets of Progress.* Cambridge, 1952.

Leon Howard. *The Connecticut Wits.* Chicago, 1942.

Merrill Jensen. *The Articles of Confederation.* Madison, 1940.

Howard Mumford Jones. *America and French Culture.* Chapel Hill, 1927.

Adrienne Koch. *Jefferson and Madison.* New York, 1950.

A. C. McLaughlin. *Foundations of American Constitutionalism.* New York, 1932.

R. R. Palmer. *The Age of the Democratic Revolution.* Princeton, 1959.

Ralph Barton Perry. *Puritanism and Democracy.* New York, 1944.

Page Smith. *John Adams.* 2 vols. New York, 1962.

Moses Coit Tyler. *Literary History of the American Revolution.* 2 vols. New York, 1879.

IV

AGRARIANISM ✶ *John Taylor of Caroline*

> The cottager has no historian to commemorate
> his misery, and the historian of the prince is
> bribed to hide it.
>
> *1814*

Once there was a time when an American nation existed. It was a time when at least the most articulate citizens of the republic had a sense of identity that had not existed before and was not to exist later. It was the time when the American Constitution was written.

The Constitution was a national document. It was a cement of union; and it accurately reflected a unique and temporary consensus—the sense of one nation that had been partly elicited by the victorious conclusion of the American Revolution. That victory had convinced many that something properly called one nation had in fact been called into being.

It was possible for Americans to agree during the period when the Constitution was framed and ratified because the uneven social and political development of the most important areas of the country had temporarily come together. It was a time when the North and South could agree because the two sections had at that moment reached a meeting point in their respective histories; the Northern sense of community had dissolved and the Southern sense of community had not yet been born. It was thus the time when men could compromise, could will to cooperate, could write and ratify a single frame of government. In order to succeed at Philadelphia it was necessary for the founding fathers to view their colleagues as men who could be understood and even trusted. That trust was impossible before, and was to become impossible later. Any sense of genuine community would militate against the nationalism that was a necessary anterior condition to the good will at and success of the Constitutional Convention.

In at least one sense the history of New England and the history of the South moved in exactly opposite directions. New England began with a corporate sense at a time when the South was committed to individualism and mobility, and each section slowly evolved until each took the other's original position. The Revolution was won and the Constitution was written at the juncture of their separate histories, but their histories continued, of course, and the eventual exchange of positions compelled the South, in time, to condemn the compromises that earlier Southerners had made.

Colonial New Englanders had been and ante-bellum Southerners were to be at least partly energized by their sense of the distinctiveness of their respective ways of life, by their feelings that each belonged to an organic, exclusive, and local community. The New Englanders began with a sense of their special mission, their distinctiveness, believing that they were a new Chosen People of the Lord when Southerners took pride not in their distinctiveness but in their similarities to English society. While Southerners were trying to recreate the style of the English gentry and were building straggling settlements along their rivers, the men in the North built compact towns. When Southerners were committed to individualism, Northerners were participants in community. When the Northerners were committed to a total and organic way of life which John Cotton called the New England Way, Southerners were hard at work cultivating their separate gardens.

While piety, which was the organizing principle of the New England community, had become evanescent, slavery, which was the organizing principle of the Southern sense of uniqueness, was growing. But slavery was not defended by the South until the 1820's. The founding fathers from the South did not defend slavery as a positive good; they predicted and applauded the eventual death of their peculiar institution. The South did not become a community until after the Constitution had been written and ratified.

In a sense the North was moving away from feudalism while the South was moving toward it, the North becoming more and the South less bourgeois. It was only after the Southern community had been created that a relatively rigid and accepted social hierarchy was created. Dueling, the unique Southern mansions, the honor system in colleges, full-dress balls, the idealization of the Southern woman, and even jousts were created at the time when New England had already turned to manufacturing and majority rule. The descendants of the individualistic Southerners who had accepted the Constitution took up the pennant of knight errantry, celebrated leisure and condemned labor, and eventually fought a Civil War in order to prove, among other things, that their way was sufficiently distinctive so that one supreme law of the land that suited Yankees could not by definition suit them too.

"We the people" meant majority rule, and the majority came to be defined as a majority of the nation. Society, as an organic and corporate entity, was wounded by America's supreme law when that law raised person above group, when it created national power strong enough to establish a number of centrifugal forces. The government of the Constitution was empowered to create an army strong enough to implement genocidal policy against the Indians, and to obtain western lands. The success of both policies encouraged Americans, especially New Englanders, to move, and mobility struck the final blow at the already moribund body of the earlier community.

Mobility, however, was not enough. The organic community requires some principle of self, something by which it can define itself and simultaneously define others by their difference. As the blood-spattered and angry God of the Puritans stalked through the Bay, He gave those visible saints the principle of exclusiveness necessary to their communitarian concept of the city on a hill. As the original piety declined, individuals began to spin away from the old static center. The phrase "We the people" in the state constitution of Massachusetts and the Constitution of the United States merely recognized that anterior fragmentation of the city on a hill, the dissolution of the new Israel.

The Nation was born when individuals were loose in the land, when the only forms of association, the states, were political, when those political bodies did not reflect an underlying social reality. It was born at a time when America was more universally bourgeois

than at any other time before the Civil War.   But as Southern
society grew increasingly real, as it became increasingly isolated
and alienated from the rest of the world, the result was the existence of an American nation in the North and a community in the
South.

In the South's intense period of transition after the Constitution
and before the Missouri Compromise, legends of magnolias and
chivalry seem almost true. It was a time when at least a few men,
Virginians mostly, stretched themselves toward a Renaissance
ideal of omnicompetence. These men spoke with a haughty republicanism, and they seem to have relished being what and where
they were with an enthusiasm that would have been inconceivable
in New England. They had a grand style, and yet believed in trying to live simply, as, they said, was befitting a republican. Freedom was more central in their rhetoric than slavery, though both
were present. Usually when they spoke of slavery they condemned
it. And under all was the Southern earth that nourished them,
that sustained a way of life, and whose protection demanded their
full effort. In order to live their lives they raised plantations; in
order to guard their land they entered politics; in order to legislate
well they turned to scholarship.

Because the South was then moving from nation to community,
from individual to group, representatives from the South spoke
for a wide range of attitudes. Jefferson and Madison illustrated
Southern nationalism while John Taylor of Caroline, as he was
called, was already beginning to feel his way toward an understanding of the South as a conscious community. Indeed, virtually
alone among the members of Southern leadership in the period of
transition, Taylor carried the ideals of the group to an almost
perfect extreme.

Taylor was born in Virginia in 1753, and, because of the early
death of his parents, was raised by his uncle, Edmund Pendleton.
After a brief stay at the College of William and Mary, he read law
in Pendleton's office, and received his license to practice in 1774.
He fought in the Revolution, became a major, and resigned in
1779. He was then elected to the Virginia House of Delegates,
where he served several terms. He practiced law for ten years and
retired with property said to be worth nearly $100,000. He had

also invested in land, and after six years of law practice he was among the one hundred richest planters in the state. In a short time, and with help from his father-in-law, he had acquired three Virginia plantations: Hazelwood where he lived, Hayfield, and Mill Hill, along with other tracts of land in Virginia, Kentucky, and Ohio. In 1783 he owned nine slaves, to whom he added 136 more by 1810, at which time he was the largest slaveholder in Caroline County.

He served in the national Senate as a replacement three different times, but he grew increasingly fond of Hazelwood and dissatisfied with active politics. Fearful of and repulsed by the corruption of public life, Taylor repeatedly left the public scene for the substantial pleasures of his lush acres along the Rappahannock. During what was for Taylor the loathsome administration of John Adams, he said that if the Republicans failed to eliminate the enemies of the Constitution, he would leave politics permanently in order to concentrate on raising, as he said, his cabbages and potatoes. He was already convinced that the power of public office could damage moral character, and he was eager simply to pursue the regenerative life of his plantation. James Madison, for one, regretted Taylor's aversion to public life, and reported that Taylor's retirement should be regarded as a national calamity.

The peculiar flavor of simplicity, political engagement, and affluence was caught by a visitor of 1814:

> I found an old grey-headed gentleman in an old fashion'd dress plain in his manners full of politics and fond of conversational debate. . . . He lives . . . on the finest farm I have ever seen. In front of his door he has 800 acres in Clover, 300 acres in Corn, 2 or 300 in wheat and rye all in a perfect plain. . . . The Soil here on the banks of the Rappahanoc [*sic*] is very fertile and [the] rich luxuriant appearance of the Country is delightful.[1]

In his day Taylor was known as one of the most successful farmers in Virginia, and as the most consistent political theorist of the Jeffersonian Republicans. He admitted to Jefferson that "there is a spice of fanaticism in my nature upon two subjects— agriculture and republicanism, which all who set it in motion, are sure to suffer by."[2] His works on political economy convinced his enemies that he was trying to obstruct national progress, and his friends that he understood how to purge American life of the evils

which had befallen it. For those like Jefferson and Monroe who
were most closely associated with his political system, but whose
public responsibilities made his nice consistency either uncomfortable or impossible, Taylor's voice was the voice of conscience.
Jefferson recognized Taylor's intellectual strength, and, late in both
of their lives, wrote that, as far as he knew, the two men had never
differed in any important principle or action. Jefferson may have
failed to understand that Taylor's political consistency made him
a bad party member; and he was ignoring the fact that Taylor
often, and sometimes loudly, took issue both with Jefferson and the
Republicans.

In the election of 1808 Taylor joined with other dissident
Southern Republicans in opposing the nomination of Madison,
Jefferson's choice. Taylor, with John Randolph of Roanoke and
Nathaniel Macon of North Carolina—they called themselves the
Tertium Quids—favored Monroe, whose republicanism was less
suspicious than that of Madison, remembered as one of the authors
of the *Federalist Papers*. They also opposed the War of 1812 and
the tariff of 1816. It became characteristic of the Quids to think
of Jefferson himself as a fallen angel, though Taylor was always reluctant to reject or dismiss him.

Taylor's system of political economy was essentially destructive.
Convinced that the United States had achieved during the period
of the Articles of Confederation something close to political perfection, he believed that change since that time had been change
for the worse. Toward the end of his life he came to believe that
national consolidation in violation of states' rights, and capitalism
in what he thought was a violation of private property, had reinvigorated conditions against which a wiser generation had fought
the Revolution. In time he became a Southern Jeremiah, weeping
over the tragedy of virtue wilfully becoming vice, of America deliberately remaking herself in the image of England.

Taylor developed his system of political economy in several
pamphlets and five books: *Arator* (1813)—made up of a series of
essays that first appeared in a newspaper in 1803, *An Inquiry into
the Principles and Policy of the Government of the United States*
(1814), *Construction Construed, and Constitutions Vindicated*
(1820), *Tyranny Unmasked* (1822), and *New Views of the Con-*

stitution of the United States (1823). Taken together, his work constituted a system of agrarian politics, and was the prototype of the South's defense of itself. Except for his literary style, which even he admitted was "wild, careless, and desultory,"[3] he would probably be more widely known today.

He sought to understand human nature as the basis of his system. In searching out what was for him the heart of the matter, he arrived at a single generalization that supported virtually everything else he had to say: "Virtue and vice are naturally and unavoidably co-existent in the moral world, as beauty and deformity are in the animal; one is the only mirror in which the other can be seen, and therefore in the present state of man, one cannot be destroyed without the other."[4] Man was both good and evil, he would be neither if he were not both, and all the works of which he was author would be so, too. It could be that it would be difficult to determine in advance the intrinsic goodness or badness of a given event, but since every political or social policy would excite either good or bad qualities in men, the moral effect, if not the moral essence, could be perceived.

In spite of man's polarized moral nature, he had an instinct for the right. Natural man was a free agent who might, and given the opportunity would, commit evil. But in so doing he would recognize his crime, because he knew the difference between virtue and vice. Taylor thought that men were preponderantly virtuous, but that was no safeguard against the commission of evil. Because man's most compelling instinct was self-preservation and improvement, he was led "to do evil to others, for the sake of doing good to himself."[5] Out of a natural and morally neutral impulse, Taylor, unlike Adam Smith, derived social evil. From instinctual self-love, he also derived the desirability of self-government, assuming, as Adam Smith had, that each man would know best what constituted his own good. Out of the social evil that resulted from self-love, Taylor eventually derived ideas about the need for public responsibility of public officials. He concluded that they should have only severely limited powers, as John Adams had also said.

The polarized nature of man, the opportunity to commit evil, and the power to do so meant that governors were dangerous to those who were governed. Individuals or minorities had more to gain from plundering societies, than societies had from robbing them. History as well as theory showed that individuals or minorities, because of the greater profit to be made, were infinitely more likely to oppress nations, than the other way around. Because social evil was a result of the extent of gain for the plundering individual, monarchy was the worst form of government, and aristocracy was only somewhat better.

These general assumptions supported Taylor's deductions about man, society, and government. Though universally applicable, their manifestations varied in time and place. Locale conditioned the way in which any man would respond to a situation, and the mark of a man's birthplace on his thinking was indelible: "the geography of human nature sticks to a man like his skin, or travels with him like his shadow."[6] Rejecting John Adams' analogies between cultures and epochs, Taylor asserted that men in different societies were made different by the determining quality of their total environment, even though their essential natures, in general and therefore less significant terms, were more alike than not.

Taylor found two ideas of man's nature especially disabling. Deterministic theories of either materialism or human depravity deprived men of the hope necessary to political will:

> Horrible or impious, as the atomical philosophy may be, it cannot be more so, than the idea of a natural depravity in man, rendering him unfit for self government. One doctrine assails the existence of a God; the other, his power or goodness. If man, the noblest creature of this world; if mind, the noblest attribute of this creature; are both incorrigibly imperfect; the inference that the world itself is a bad work, is unavoidable. Man's case is hopeless. If he is the creature of malignity or imbecility, and doomed to be governed by fiends, naturally as bad, and artificially made worse than himself, where is his refuge? Shall he fly to the hereditary system, which teaches him to dispair; or adhere to one, which inspires him with hope?[7]

In a world rotten with force and fraud, self-government was the only hope for free men. From Taylor's ideas about human nature, he developed his ideas about the nature of society.

Following the formula which, by his day, had become conventional, he argued that free individuals in a state of nature voluntarily came together to form an association. He rejected the explicit language of a social contract, because he understood by that concept a version used only to justify absolutism. When societies attempted to secure liberty by extracting concessions from governments, they placed themselves in the dangerous and foolish position of accepting grants that might be revoked at the pleasure of the grantor. Genuine and secure liberty had to be based on inalienable natural rights, not on contracts or charters.

Man had two basic natural rights, one to his conscience and the other to his labor. The purpose of creating a civil society was to protect those rights. In political terms men, as a result of free consent, created a collective and indivisible society. In Taylor's vocabulary this indivisible association was either a society or a nation, between which he refused to distinguish: "by the magick of avarice and ambition, the word society is severed from a nation, and converted into a metaphysical spectre, auspicious only to the tyrants of society."[8]

The society (or nation) was an abstract body designed to protect natural rights. But it was necessary for each participant to give up part of his natural rights to the association, especially part of the right to his own labor and property, in order to sustain essential public institutions. A part of a man's property or money had to be transferred to his government, which, if it were a good one, would provide each man with security to compensate for the loss. Every individual must renounce part of his natural rights in order to protect the residue. The individuals who made up this society, because they retained most of their rights to conscience and labor, retained more political will and power than they relinquished.

The individual, as a member of society, was the creator of institutions necessary to social life: government and law. The nation or society created a constitution which, in turn, created government, which makes law:

> Society is paramount to law; law, therefore, cannot transfer social or national rights from its creator, society, to its creature, hereditary orders. An exclusive right to form or alter a government is annexed to society, in every moment of its existence; and therefore a direct or indirect exercise of it by a government, a combination or an individual, is a badge of usurpation, and a harbinger of despotism.[9]

His understanding of human nature led Taylor to reject the idea that individual virtue would lead to social or political virtue. Each man's quest for private welfare would, more likely than not, create public havoc. The extent to which a nation relied on the supposed goodness of its leaders to protect liberty was the extent to which that nation was in danger of becoming enslaved. "By expecting publick good from private virtue, we expose ourselves to publick evil from private vices."[10] From the beginning of time, the uncontrolled passions of individuals had brought slavery to the world. It was indispensable to liberty to control those who were given some share of power; that control was called political law; that law was the constitution which created and delimited government.

In his discussion of government, Taylor also sought some basic moral principles from and by which deductions and observations could be made. In so doing, he was obliged to clear his path of some ancient and very widely accepted ideas. In thinking about government he felt hampered by ideological underbrush; most of it, in his view, was inapplicable to the American scene and useless to an American mind.

He rejected the idea of a government constructed of a mixture of monarchy, aristocracy, and democracy, an idea that had the authority of Plato, Aristotle, Polybius, and Cicero, among others of antiquity, and had become a virtual reflex in contemporary political theory. Using an analogy drawn from the thought of ancient Greece, he hoped to refute the Greek conception of mixed government:

> Unity, harmony and proportion, are as necessary in politicks, as in the drama, musick or architecture. A tragicomical government, a Corinthian capital over a Doric column, jarring dissonances mingled with soft notes, an aristocratick democracy or a monarchick aristocracy, destroy sympathies, proportions and melody. It is consistency which produces perfection in arts and sciences.[11]

He argued that the presence of each of the three forms of political organization in a single government, so far from nullifying the evil effects of each, would produce continual tension between them as each struggled to achieve supremacy over the others. His reading of history convinced him that internal tranquillity was usually a result of an unmixed constitution which allowed and even encouraged one interest to repress its competitors. Unless a government was founded on sound moral principles, individual happiness and welfare could not result, but the single forms of political organization, at least, usually avoided civil war because the parties not represented in government were too weak even to protest. Pure political repression had led to calm, if not to justice. A mixed constitution, such as he thought had existed in Greece, Rome, the Italian city-states, and England, invariably had bred contending and powerful factions which could and therefore had made war on each other.

Taylor's usual method of argument led him to emphasize effects and consequences and to try to avoid definitions of essence. The national or social consequences of any form of political organization were, for him, the meaning of that form. On this point he was occasionally explicit:

> I see no infallible criterion for defining the nature of a government, except its acts. If the acts of a monarchy, aristocracy and democracy are the same, these forms of government are to a nation essentially the same also. To contend for forms only, is to fight for shadows.[12]

He found the question of political form somewhat troublesome. He argued that form and administration might be contradictory, that even a bad form might be wisely and virtuously administered. But certain forms might preclude certain consequences: "All that man can accomplish, is to adopt a form, most likely to produce liberty, and containing the best precautions against the introduction of tyranny."[13] In any case, he was evidently convinced that the first step to an actual tyranny was a formal tyranny built into the structure of government, though it was not inevitable that any form would actually determine function.

Because man was what he was, self-government was essential to the protection of his natural rights to conscience and property, which included natural rights to life and liberty. Taylor considered the idea of the social contract, so often used by political theorists, and self-government to be mutually exclusive. "No contractor," he wrote, "with the right of self-government, can exist."[14] A presumed contract that brought discrete individuals into an association for the purpose of creating a government must dissolve, he thought, when its purpose was accomplished. Under the terms of such a contract, government became the creator and master of society. Instead of being the parent, society then would be the child of government, and would owe it due obedience. Taylor argued that his conception of natural rights must destroy the idea of the contract, because under such rights society was anterior to government, was the author of government, and remained its eternal master.

The fundamental human community was formed to secure right, and government was instituted only to further that end. The idea of a contract between societies and their governments had been enough to corrupt them, because the active government could always construe the contract virtually as it chose, thereby tyrannizing over the necessarily more passive society. To justify governmental power on the basis of a contract was to misunderstand what he claimed to be the omnipotence of society. Sovereignty, which he defined as the will and power to act, always remained in society, and, if rights were to be secured, could never be transferred to a government.

With the passage of time and the increasing complexity of life, especially resulting from an increase in wealth and commerce, the problems of government became more difficult. Civilization, he said, multiplied the vices, virtues, passions, and interests of men, and government must respond accordingly. Government was thought to be, as John Adams had said, a moral agent whose essential function was to make men better than they were. Though individuals were vicious they could create a moral government. Civilization increased man's vices, in Taylor's view, and men in cities were more dependent on the moral character of the government they created than others. Civilization put the greatest possible burden on government.

All governments were founded only on one of two essential principles—virtue, which was reason, or vice, which was fraud and force. The principle implemented would partly determine the character of the citizens. Evil or good government would tend to elicit evil or good in men. Government must recognize the polarity of human nature, repress the evil, and encourage the virtue. All nations had agreed with part of this by legislating what Taylor called municipal law, whose purpose was the restraint of private or individual crimes. Beyond such law, however, was the need for what he called political law to restrain public crime: "By publick vices and political law, I mean, injuries committed by governments against nations, and regulations to prevent or punish them."[15] As societies or nations grew ever more wealthy and complicated, the temptations to commit public or political crime grew apace. In response to the growing criminal opportunities of civilization, either the political law or fraud would correspondingly grow. As the magnitude of plunder was a greater temptation for the commission of political rather than private crime, so the need to legislate political law was greater than that of municipal law.

Governmental poverty and public virtue seemed, in Taylor's understanding of history, to go hand in hand, because the poverty would result in a relative absence of temptation. As their wealth increased, nations had usually multiplied municipal law and ignored political law, with the result that "for private vices, they have provided the prison and the gallows; for publick vices, wealth and power."[16]

Unlike Paine and Jefferson, Taylor thought that government was not necessarily an evil, though it usually had been. It could be the single most effective instrument for both social and individual virtue and welfare. A utilitarian test was the way by which the quality of a government could be detected: Good government produced the happiness of a society, and happiness was understood as the enjoyment of the natural rights of conscience and property, including the right of self-government.

Any government that had been founded on evil moral principles must produce tyranny, and an evil foundation had always subverted any political form. "Cupidity, avarice or monopoly, both in the savage and civilized state, is the quality of human nature, always requiring control, and always striving to break down the restraints imposed upon it." Unless this quality of the human animal was curbed, all political theory, all political forms, must produce evil. "The fallacy of form," and a fallacy of which Adams had been especially guilty, was the assumption that ingenuity could produce virtue without confronting the essential human cause of vice. Taylor believed that "instead of amusing ourselves with these new forms, not to be confided in, it behooves us to search for a remedy, able to remove or control the cause itself."[17]

Virtually every government in human history had aggravated this evil, for whose control they had all been established. Distributing property by law, instead of allowing each man to reap the rewards of his own labor, constituted the great crime of all forms of government, and drove them all, whether monarchies, aristocracies, or democracies, "into a circle of forms, through which they have perpetually returned to the oppression they intended to escape."[18]   Had men abandoned their concern with the structure of government, and thought more about essentials, "they would have discovered, that a power of distributing property, according to its pleasure, has made governments of the best forms, bad."[19]   Republics generally had been worse than monarchies because in republics there were simply more thieving sovereigns to pillage the society. The fewer the tyrants, the more tolerable was life. For those who governed, however, monarchy and aristocracy were the most corrupting forms, because the greater profit for fewer thieves was more tempting and because they had the power to rob with relative impunity. These two forms, he said, since he had also said that forms were not quite determining, were evil because of the inhuman strain they put on the governors' self-restraint.

He argued that good government must be based on the absence of a tyrant, and a tyrant was defined as one who had power over another's property. "In defining a tyrant, it is not necessary to prove that he is a cannibal."[20]   When a government grew wealthy, its wealth was an unmistakable symptom of tyranny, because more of the nation's property was being transferred to the government than was essential for national or social preservation. "It is a species of political irrigation," he wrote in one of his magnificently turgid sentences, "which exsiccates a nation to overflow a government and exclusive privileges."[21]   Frugality in government was always an indication that the individual's natural rights were being properly guarded. The happiness of the Swiss and the poverty of their treasuries, coupled with the misery of the French and the opulence of theirs, were sufficient proof of this hypothesis for Taylor.

Perhaps his most basic assumption about government was the idea that men in society and under government must retain the freedom of political will they had before they entered into first social and then political association. Because men had intelligence and will they could understand and control government; the existence of tyranny indicated either a failure of intelligence or will, or both. He flatly rejected the relevance to politics of metaphysical questions about whether the will was free, as John Adams had also done. It was enough, according to Taylor, simply to assert that some events could be controlled by men. Since men were good or evil and since they created governments, those governments would also be either good or evil. If they were evil, men had the power to make them good even though they chose not to. Political crime was therefore a symptom either of a private failure of will or of stupidity, or both.

Among the causes of the bad principles by which societies created evil governments was the failure to see the intimate relationship between politics and wealth. Perhaps a majority of the founding fathers understood this relationship, but Taylor went further than most. He argued that the nature of tyranny had changed as the world had become civilized, as the lust for blood in the savage tyrant became avarice and ambition in the civilized tyrant. Ambition, if fed with power, would rob with impunity; avarice, because it too yearned to rob, sought the political power necessary to legal theft. "Enormous political power," Taylor wrote, "invariably accumulates enormous wealth, and enormous wealth invariably accumulates enormous political power."[22] Excessive wealth or power each signalized a tyranny, because each would seek to deprive a society or nation of liberty to gratify ambition, and deprive it of property to gratify avarice. Since both appetites were insatiable, an absolute deprivation of natural rights would be the result of a society's failure to understand the nature of the political economy. "Money," he had said, "governs the world. Is a corporate despotism over the money or currency of a nation no political power? That which is able to do good or harm to nations, is power."[23]

The techniques used by governments to plunder societies had developed along with an advancing civilization. His own age, Taylor believed, had devised a capitalistic system whose operation would guarantee a transfer of property from those who had earned it to those who held political favor or power. Capitalism, as he understood it, was a modern technique by which politically powerful individuals could steal from the society or nation. The government must grant special privileges to capitalists in the form of, for example, a tariff or a banking system, and the government therefore created robbers whose power allowed them to dominate the nation. Instead of remaining the creature of society, government under capitalism created monsters who would pervert both the society and the government out of their desire for limitless and unearned wealth.

He accepted a version of Locke's labor theory of property—which helps to distinguish Taylor from the physiocrats—in which private property was defined as that in which the owner had "mixed" his own labor. Wealth without labor, for Taylor, must necessarily be unnatural, a result of fraud, probably on the part of individuals and governments. He strained to make clear that he did not condemn all capitalists. Those who used their surplus capital in improving the face of the earth were obviously desirable. The other variety of capitalists, those whose wealth was derived from exclusive privileges granted by their allies in government, the artificially created monopolists, were, without exception, thought to be parasites who would bleed the nation white. Taylor thought that there had never been a single instance of this second type of capitalist returning anything to the society upon whose life-blood he had fattened.

Democracies generally had employed force in gratifying their lust for pillage; aristocracies had used fraud. The only difference was that fraud usually created more permanent afflictions. Though both forms of aggression had the same ends, they became opponents in their scramble for the wealth of others. Unless a political economy was designed to frustrate the goal of either violent or legalized theft, the natural rights of man would inevitably be destroyed, and the purpose of his political association would be violated.

Taylor thought that it was within man's capabilities to devise a protective political economy. One of man's first needs was a proper understanding of the nature of money. Currency and hard money, he said, had two distinct natures, that of exchanging and that of transferring property. Under exchange, which was its good nature, he included the intercourse between individuals; by transfer, which was its bad nature, he meant all payments made without the receipt of an equivalent. These "two souls" of money must struggle for supremacy, and the one that was allowed or encouraged to succeed would determine the political economy of the nation. When government granted special and perhaps exclusive rights to one or a few individuals, it was encouraging money to reveal its whorish aspect rather than its virginal one; and as a whore money would pollute the political body of the nation. It was because of such activity that government had been called an evil, because of a misunderstanding about the essential but minimal amount of property all governments must transfer. It became evil when it transferred more property than was absolutely necessary to accomplish the desires of the society which had created it.

The two faces of money resulted in a similarly bifurcated political economy. It could either diffuse or restrict comfort and happiness, and, since these were the only satisfactions allowed to men on this side of heaven, the judgment about which aspect a given political economy had adopted was always clear, as clear as the differences between privations and gratifications. He continued to deny that there was any difficulty or mystery in assessing the good or evil of any system. Concrete knowledge was the instrument by which the judgment was made. "The mind has full evidence in the experience of nations, upon which to decide between the species of political economy which breeds monopolies, enriches capitalists, and deprives the people of comforts; and that which leaves to individuals the free use of their earnings."[24] Knowledge of political economy would allow free men to penetrate the rhetoric designed by capitalists to obfuscate the problems:

> It is constantly repeated (an old story in Europe) that the capitalists will produce a home market, and compensate all other interests by purchasing their labours with their own money. If the argument is a good one, there can be no such thing as a pecuniary tyranny. Aristocracies of all sorts are not pecuniary frauds because they eat. Hierarchies, bishops, and monks, are blessings, as they eat also.[25]

That rhetoric was the argument used by thieves to convince the victim that the loss would benefit both parties, but especially the loser.

Taylor designed his general system of political economy to aid in understanding the course of events in his own country. In applying his general system to the United States, he believed that he had a sound basis for making concrete historical judgments. It was the clash between his theory and his view of the policies adopted by America that led him to write, to attempt to avoid active politics, and to become increasingly pessimistic in his prognosis of the nation's health. He began to write only when he saw

America's developing political economy show symptoms of artificiality and civilization, that is, symptoms of both fraud and force. And how else could it be? He thought he knew the road to national wealth and happiness, and through corruption and treason small men with big lusts were detouring the nation from the path it had once correctly chosen for itself. The nation always had the power to protect itself, but it chose instead, out of the plentitude of its political will, to destroy itself. Given Taylor's sense of the nation's wrongheadedness and his own consequent isolation, it is not surprising to find Jefferson describing Taylor's voice as "the voice of one crying in the wilderness."[26] The pain of Taylor's intellectual isolation was merely heightened by his conviction that he was right. The intellectual consistency of his work leads to the conclusion that his conviction was not shaken by the contrary history of which he was a part.

Taylor's point of departure in the application of his theory was his view that the United States was an absolutely unique phenomenon. It had long been conventional in political theory, often identified by Americans as having derived from Montesquieu, to hold that republicanism and a large territory were irreconcilable, that size and political centralization must grow together. Madison had already denied this in the tenth paper of the *Federalist*. Now Taylor argued that the territory of the United States, in its great extent and peculiar situation, provided a singular geographical foundation for liberty. The extent of territory presumably insulated the majority of the nation from war and from the designs of any one special and private interest group or class, and therefore provided that majority with the security necessary for reflection and the exercise of reason. Small nations were exposed to continuing conflict because shared borders conduced to that end. "The pledge for a free government arising from the extent and situation of our territory is so transcendant," Taylor wrote in 1814, "that the enemies of a republican form of government craftly inculcate an opinion, that this form is not adapted for an extensive territory; for the purpose of producing territorial divisions to discredit republican systems."[27]

The territory was something, but the spirit and manners of the people were more important. A genuine republic, founded on the national interest, would receive national affection for justice dispensed, and that affection would be a cement sufficiently adhesive to hold together even a vast and perhaps loose-jointed territory. When he contemplated the geographical isolation of the United States, the growing population, the increasing number of religious sects, and the division of the territory into states, Taylor thought that he beheld a miracle designed by God to save human liberty in at least one corner of the earth. But that political errand into the wilderness placed an awful responsibility on the American people. In his version of the national mythology, Americans were still playing the leading role in a drama whose climax would decide the fate of the race:

> They [Americans] seem to have been selected to evince the capacity of man for sustaining a fair and free government; and if by their failure, with such pre-eminent advantages, they shall renounce the favours of heaven, and consign a whole world of endless generations to the tyranny of expensive governments, they will be reprobated as another infatuated and rebellious people, who have rejected benefactions visibly flowing from an Almighty source.[28]

In Taylor's view, as it had been in some sense for Winthrop, Edwards, and Adams, Americans were God's political guinea pigs, and the United States was the hope of the world, for its destiny was nothing less than to test whether human nature could maintain a free society. "No other people ever were, or ever will be in so good a situation to settle this question affirmatively; and their practical testimony will therefore be considered as conclusive."[29] With her Revolution, America entered a new epoch in the history of nations, an epoch which was to decide, once and for all, whether men either deserved to or could be free. That Revolution, and the principles underlying it, taught the supposedly novel idea that personal conscience was an inadequate defense against the universal injustices of governments to nations. John Adams wrote to Taylor that such an idea was flattering but wrong because Americans had developed no novel political ideas, that they had merely the sense to implement what the world had long known but could not or did not put into practice. Taylor was not convinced by Adams and continued to insist that "out of the complete discovery then made, arose our political laws for assisting the consciences of governours; and if they can emancipate themselves from restraint by civil laws, sowing cancerous seeds in the body politick, the discovery will probably be lost forever."[30]

Americans had moved from the Puritans' concept of a moral example to Adams' and Taylor's concept of a political example to all the world. But since they both explicitly included morality in politics, perhaps Americans had not moved very far at that. In any case, as with the Puritans, the penalties that would accompany failure to honor the terms of the vastly significant errand on which Americans had been sent were almost too heavy to contemplate. Given the greatest opportunity to build wisely, Americans would pay a correspondingly high price for failure.

The elucidation of American political theory required of him, as Taylor saw it, explication, not invention. The largest part of his writings was concerned with finding the cohesive, perhaps implicit, principles whose implementation had resulted in a dramatic, if temporary, example of political perfection in America of the revolutionary period. Almost alone among the major visions of the American intellectual tradition, Taylor's included a golden age when life had been better. In defining even a very brief segment of the past in this way, Taylor departed from the usual utopianism of American thought, and, in so doing, began to develop a peculiarly Southern mentality. In turning to the past instead of the future, Taylor added an Edenic dimension to a tradition that had and would characteristically reject the past as irrelevant to the unique phenomenon of God's country.

The most radical principle that had been adopted by the Americans who planned the nation was, according to Taylor, the idea that public welfare was dependent upon the public's control of its officials, that the government was the creature of the society. Americans had presumably discovered that the society was responsible for political law and the government for municipal law. The society, in that view, established in convention the fundamental law of the land beyond which governors might not go. The government of the states, limited by the law of the society, became the executive of municipal law in order to avenge private violations of duty.

Self-government was defined as social or national control of the governors. It meant locating sovereignty in the nation or society and not in the government. He mistakenly said that it had not been recognized before the American Revolution that self-government and sovereignty in government were contradictory ideas. He asserted that because the collective people were sovereign, government was the people's trustee and its actions were limited by what it was told to do. Undelegated power remained with the people who were the source of power. The crush of events had led the founding fathers foolishly to accept dangerous bills of rights:

> In the hurry of a revolution, before this subject had been well considered, and in imitation of the English practice of receiving franchises from kings, a bill of rights was annexed to several of the state constitutions; but it was soon discovered, that this was both superfluous and dangerous; superfluous, as according to the right of self-government, powers not bestowed, remained with the people; dangerous, as it seemed to imply that the people, as in England, derived their rights from the government.[31]

The people, according to Taylor's reading of American political practice, had two hats to wear: political and civil. Under the first they became associated and were empowered by themselves to act as a society with such rights, for example, as those of creating and controlling governments. With the civil power the people became discrete individuals in command of individual rights and responsible for individual duties. Individuals might judge the society as the society judged the state, though the individual's authority was less than that of the society to which he had surrendered his sovereignty. These two aspects created a mutual power of restraint on the part of the people, or society, and the government; the first by exercising political law, and the second by exercising civil law.

Where to locate sovereignty was for Taylor, as for most of his contemporaries, a major problem. Using his vocabulary, the problem was how to define and locate "the people." Politically speaking, the people was always an association or society. The problem of locating the society in America was compounded by federalism. Most of his efforts in this regard were directed toward proving that there had never been "an American nation," that the various individuals who owed allegiance to the federal government did not constitute a nation or society, that the people and therefore sovereignty resided elsewhere.

Taylor had reinvigorated the constitutional theory of the Articles of Confederation. His idea of "the people" was one of the first statements of what was later to become a dominant conviction in the South when the South abandoned majority rule and nationalism in favor of corporatism. Taylor's definition of "the people" was useful to those who were in search of a way to protect minorities from majorities or, what amounts to the same thing, to find an alternative to majority rule.

Taylor believed that the basic principles of union on which the federal Constitution had been based were defined in the Declaration of Independence, which had said that the several states were both "united" and "free and independent states." The fact of union was thus not incompatible with the idea of state sovereignty. The political history of the revolutionary period, as he knew it, confirmed the idea that sovereignty had not been given to the federal government. The Articles of Confederation clearly had been based on the Declaration, and the Constitution, because it had intended to create "a more perfect union," not to invent a new union, had the same basis.

The constitutional phrase "We the people" had been construed by some of Taylor's contemporaries to mean that an American nation made up of all American citizens did in fact exist. He answered that an association of people had obviously existed before the creation of the federal government, since the state governments had been created first. That the several states possessed political power antecedent to the Constitution was also proved by the explicit constitutional reservation of power by the states. His point was that the legitimacy of the federal government depended upon the admission that society was anterior to government, and that sovereignty remained in society, never in government. What the people created, they could destroy.

Because sovereignty resided with the people, because politically "the people" designated an association, and because in America the only act of political association had been the separate agreements of the peoples of the several states to form themselves into state-nations, it followed that sovereignty in America resided in the collective people of each independent state:

> Common consent is necessary to constitute a people, and no such consent, expressly or impliedly, can be shewn, by which all the

inhabitants of the United States have ever constituted themselves into one people. This could not have been effected without destroying every people constituted within each state, as one political being called a people cannot exist within another.[32]

The people in their political and not in their natural capacities were the creators of government, and therefore government was their creature.

This argument further invalidated the concept of a social contract between nations and governments, according to Taylor. The several peoples in America had created their state governments and limited the powers conferred. Those several peoples then also created a federal government with even more limited powers. If there had been contracts between the state governments and the several peoples, those contracts would have been violated with the creation of the federal government, some of whose powers were taken from the state governments. "The state governments did not surrender, but the people transferred a portion of power, without their consent, from them to the general government."[33] Neither could there have been a universal agreement between the citizens of the United States to create this new federal government, because no such association of citizens had ever existed.

The explicit language of the Constitution, as Taylor understood it, corroborated this view. He added italics to and condensed the first clause of the Constitution to read: "The people of the *United States* to provide for the common defence and promote the general welfare establish this constitution *for the United States of America.*" "United States" referred not to an organic entity, but to a group of states which had agreed to unite while maintaining their separate identity. The Constitution was applicable only to the several states, not to the individuals living in the United States. Those individuals did not form a political body because they had never consented to do so. The Constitution referred only to the political bodies of the states and was barred from extending the meaning of the words "common" and "general" to include private persons. Given that argument, any act of the federal government that enriched either private persons or one state at the expense of another was clearly unconstitutional. Congress had no legitimate power over persons and things of a local or personal nature, whose defense and general welfare were left to the states. Especially, it had no power to legislate for the benefit of "political fungi."[34]

The accepted processes of constitutional ratification and amendment was also used by Taylor to locate sovereignty and to define the nature of the union. Ratification of the Articles of Confederation had required the unanimous consent of the several states. Though the ratification of the Constitution required not unanimity but a majority of states, he thought that the principle was unchanged: "The [constitutional] contract derives its force, not from a consent of a majority of states, but from the separate consent of each."[35] Individuals were irrelevant to both ratifying actions, except in so far as they made up the voice of the people of the state-nation of which they were members, because men in their natural capacity of single and discrete human bodies had no political existence, as Winthrop and others had earlier argued.

When a majority of states ratified the Constitution, their decision was not binding on the other states. Ratification was the consent of distinct sovereignties, and a majority could not bind a minority. Within each separate state, however, majority rule did obtain, because the majority represented the total society, which each individual had consented to form. The absence of that consent among the inhabitants of the United States meant that there was no American nation even though the thirteen separate nations had created an American government. The creation of the American government proved the prior existence of the sovereign nation-states, and the existence of the sovereign states proved the prior existence of the thirteen associated peoples.

The founding fathers had agreed that no general American nation existed, Taylor believed, because of the procedure they had devised for amending the Constitution. Since the state-nations had created the federal government, of course the right to alter it was reserved to them. Because the states, and not the people as individuals, had the right of amendment, the states, and not the people as individuals, had the rights of construing the Constitution. That document was the "supreme Law of the Land," and the inalienable power of interpreting both that law and actions in relation to it was reserved to the states. In cases where the Constitution was silent, the issue was similarly clear: powers not explicitly transferred to the federal government by the states were retained by them. In a characteristically maddening example of his style, Taylor expressed these ideas: "The constitution was not intended to be an alembick, fraught with heterogeneous principles, to condense the tortuosities of construction, and distil from taciturnity a supreme power of construction, and consequently a negative upon state legislation."[36]

A strict adherence to federalism was for Taylor, as it had sometimes been for Madison, the only security available to a republican form of government if it possessed a large territory. Every large nation had been subject to monarchy. Size had destroyed republicanism in Rome and again in post-revolutionary France. With the discovery of federalism by the United States, the antidote had finally supposedly been found. Any theft of power from the states would water the antidote and raise the danger of monarchy even in the new world. The tendency toward political consolidation of any kind was a tendency toward tyranny.

The ugliest dragon in Taylor's landscape was the hoary concept of checks and balances, most vigorously advanced in America by John Adams. Taylor's *Inquiry* was an explicit attack on Adams and that concept. Adams, according to Taylor, had misunderstood the American political genius by confusing it with the English, and by assuming that monarchy, aristocracy, and democracy, or some combination of the three, exhausted the possibilities among forms of government. The authors of the *Federalist,* as well as Adams, "had paid too much respect to political skeletons, constructed with fragments torn from monarchy, aristocracy and democracy." They had paid too much respect to "numerical analysis; and too little to the ethereal moral principles, alone able to bind governments to the interest of nations."[37] His own analysis of the political principles of the United States led him to believe that he had escaped from the illogic of the numbers game and that he had discovered the root morality without which freedom would continue to remain elusive.

The three pure governmental forms, according to Taylor, did in fact usually excite conflict and offer rewards to evil passions. It had been assumed that every form of government must have supreme power, and that the age-old contest between the pure forms was a mere struggle for that power. But he thought that the United States discovered the idea that government had no right to supreme power, and in federalism had implemented that discovery. Federalism rested on what Taylor believed to be the eternally true proposition that people know their own self-interest and local condition better than anyone or anything else. It therefore left the regulation of persons to the local political association of the individual nation-states, and created a national government whose power was rigidly and severely limited. Nothing should be allowed to interfere with the federal distribution of power, and interference with each local and associated people "by a majority of states, or by decisions of the supreme court, are only metaphysical satraps, despatched by despotism into provinces, for the usual purpose of gathering money."[38]

It was federalism, with the local freedom it meant to Taylor, rather than Adams' checks and balances within the national government, that constituted the American political discovery. Adams had included federalism as another check and balance, but he failed to convince Taylor of that. Taylor began his *Inquiry* with the sentence: "Mr. Adams's political system, deduces government from a natural fate; the policy of the United States deduces it from moral liberty."[39] Taylor meant physical or deterministic by "natural," and intellectual or free by "moral." The differences between Adams and Taylor, according to Taylor, stemmed from Adams' political determinism and Taylor's political free will. It was an appropriate disagreement for Taylor to have with one raised in New England Congregationalism, even though Adams denied the validity of the entire argument.

Adams, said Taylor, thought that a given form of government could be deduced from certain principles, and that the resulting form would be natural. Taylor argued that human nature had been able to corrupt or subvert every form of government yet invented, and that every form had been capable of improvement. "That he [Adams] must resign his political predestination, and all its consequences, I shall attempt to prove, by shewing, that aristocracies, both ancient and modern, have been variable and artificial; that they have all proceeded from moral, not from natural causes; and that they are evitable and not inevitable."[40] Taylor said that Adams had argued that knowledge, virtue, and wealth constituted something Adams had called a natural aristocracy. Printing, Taylor answered, had diffused knowledge and virtue throughout society, as wealth had been diffused by commerce and alienation. Thus the early justification of aristocracy had become the modern justification of republicanism. By asserting the naturalness of aristocracy, Adams had supposedly allied himself with Filmer and the concept of the divine right of Kings, even though Adams had been severely critical of Filmer.

Because the political axioms of the United States had not been founded on the existence of social orders or classes, Adams' theories of balancing class against class were irrelevant to the United States, according to Taylor. Indeed, the entire system of checks and balances was considered both irrelevant to and subversive of the unique achievement of the founding fathers, among whom Taylor included Adams. To create a political department invested with power, and attempt to limit that power by creating another but competitive department was "something like weakening alcohol with alcohol."[41]

The idea of a separation of powers and checks and balances between those powers was created by men who were either unable to comprehend essential republicanism, or unwilling to permit its implementation. The policy of the United States rested on the principle that power could not be balanced. "Instead of balancing power, we divide it and make it responsible."[42] Power was to be divided between the political departments which the sovereign nation-states had established through their Constitution, not divided between factions or classes within the larger whole:

> Mr. Adams's system is bottomed upon a classification of men; our constitutions, upon an application of moral principles to human nature. He arranges men into the one, the few and the many, and bestows on the one and the few, more power than he gives to the many, to counter-balance numerical or physical strength; our constitutions divide power with a view to the responsibility of the agent, and jealous of the danger of accumulating great power in the hands of one or a few, because all history proves that this species of condensation begets tyranny, bestow most power on their most numerous functionary.[43]

If orders were truly balanced, they would exercise no control over each other and would be free of the restraint supposedly designed by the nation for self-protection. With true equilibrium, the goal sought by Adams and his followers, the nation would be enslaved. If power were truly checked, the competitors for power could not be balanced. If a check were successful, that alone would constitute proof that one department or order or class was more powerful than the others, and thus would be a threat to the freedom of the nation. But the essence of America's political invention was the realization that only when the nation-states checked the government, could those states be secure.

The power of election, by itself, was no assurance that the will of the electorate would be protected, as Adams and even Winthrop had also tried to make clear. Many of the world's despots had been elected. Only with the American Revolution was the right of election understood as an inherent natural right instead of as a gratuitous donation by a superior power. Supposedly, America had taught the world that it was necessary to divide power in order to prevent the elected governor from abusing national trust. After the division of power, the associated people retained the same sovereignty as King Lear did when he had given a share of his kingdom to each of his daughters.

No power was actually transferred either by election or by representation, because transfer could be achieved only in a constitution and with the assent of the sovereign people in society. Representation and election were simply means for selecting persons to execute the powers of the office, means by which the actual magistrate would be selected to occupy the office of magistracy, in the language of the idea of the King's two bodies. The terminology had now been altered to suit republicanism, but its meaning continued to inform American political theory. The government was subject to the Constitution, which in turn was subject to the state-nations. The Constitution created offices, not personal privilege.

Taylor had vigorously opposed ratification of the Constitution in Virginia, because he thought that it did not protect the nation-states and their people, and yet he came to assert that its strictest observance was the only hope for the nations of the United States. His opposition led one of his relatives to say that Taylor thought he knew more about government than "all the rest of the world put together."[44] When the Constitution was proposed Taylor had worried that it might establish a central government, which in time would equal and perhaps surpass the energy of England's government. This energy would have to be expended to the hurt of the states and therefore people. It was Taylor who introduced and most vigorously supported the famous Virginia resolution which asserted the right of a state to nullify an obnoxious or illegal federal action.

The single most corrosive element actually written into the Constitution, according to Taylor, was the powers of the presidency. That office had been made too strong, strong enough to endanger the virtue of its holder and the safety of the people, and on this point he genuinely disagreed with Adams. The growing complexity of civilized life had forced tyrants to learn new schemes of victimizing societies. "If knowledge has taught tyranny new devices, without suggesting to liberty new defences, mankind will have to regret the loss of an ignorance, which cheapened the price and diminished the weight of their chains."[45] Divided power was the modern answer of nations to tyrants. Under the Articles of Confederation the nations of the United States had known that a strong executive was a threat to the division of power between the states and the union. The plural executive that existed then successfully guided the war for independence, and secured the benefits for whose realization the government had been created in the first place. With the coming of peace, Americans

> were dazzled by the prospect of permanent union. The sponsors for liberty, were forgotten in the general joy; and a president of the United States was invested with far greater powers than sufficed to Caesar for enslaving his country. Patronage, negociation, a negative upon laws, and a paper system, render some of those talents which Caesar possessed, unnecessary to enable a president to perform what Caesar effected.[46]

Because the President was empowered to appoint justices of the Supreme Court, the much-vaunted separation of powers had been violated, as it would have been had justices appointed the President. The patronage controlled by the President would corrupt the legislature. With the power to control the judiciary and corrupt the Congress, the President, so far from securing national welfare, was the single greatest threat to it.

Taylor reminded his readers that Adams and many other theorists had said that monarchical powers could be checked only by an aristocracy. He wondered whether such powers had been given to the President in order to provide an excuse for the creation of an aristocracy. In any case, the nations of the United States should have sufficient wit to see the necessity of reducing such power by amendment. If a covert and nascent aristocracy had engineered the creation of a monster President so that it could come out of hiding in the guise of a defender of the weak, the nation could best protect itself against it by attacking the presidency. In the case of this office, the Constitution was more of a threat than a safeguard: "The presidency, gilded with kingly powers, has been tossed into the constitution, against the publick sentiment, and gravely bound in didactick [i.e., theoretical] fetters, like those which in England and France have become political old junk."[47]   Between the powers of the presidency and the preservation of natural rights there could only be total war and, eventually, unconditional surrender.

The presidency was dangerous, but certain policies and forces let loose by the first five administrations were unequivocal indications of the impending and final end of liberty and union in the United States and hope in the world.   Governmental grants of privilege, especially that to the Bank of the United States (in raising which issue Taylor antedated Jackson) and those to private interests in the form of tariff policy (in which he anticipated Calhoun), and the usurpation of power by the Supreme Court in its policy of judicial review, seemed to prove that the government was being controlled by men who were eager to destroy America's chance for political success.   By a too free interpretation of the Constitution, America's public enemies—presidents, secretaries, congressmen, judges—had gone far toward the goal of changing a federal into a national government, a change which would fill their own pockets and a goal which was, in a word, treasonable.   The means claimed as necessary to accomplish the ends specified in the Constitution had been stealthily designed to alter the substance of the government.   The power of taxation had been interpreted to mean that banks could be incorporated; the power to make roads had been deduced from the war power, and giving money away supposedly had been implied in the power to appropriate it; the power to regulate trade had been twisted to justify granting monopolies, as the power to admit new states was used to prescribe state constitutions.   Loose construction was the magic wand which turned good men into traitors.

The proponents of a strong national government had failed to win their point in the Constitutional Convention, but after the establishment of the government they succeeded in implementing the plans which the convention had rejected.   Behind the protective coloration of a hypocritical federalism the centralists were quietly making a revolution.   The Constitution, by assuring the people that significant change could not occur without the public amendment process, was itself a narcotic, and induced a national stupor sufficiently heavy to prevent self-protection.

The Supreme Court's action in reviewing state and federal legislation under John Marshall's leadership was a major threat to federalism and thus to freedom.   Taylor believed that the status of the federal judiciary in the United States was unique in that it was independent of the sovereign.   Even the despised political system of England made the judiciary immediately responsive to the sovereign will.   The state-nations of the United States had built more wisely than the federal model by making their local judiciaries responsible either to the people or their agents.   The federal court was also unique because it chose to act on agencies of government instead of exclusively on individuals.   In so doing it was deciding political law, which was solely the people's right, instead of concentrating on municipal law, which had been the intention of the Constitution.   By concerning himself with political law, Marshall was usurping the rights belonging to the people when they were organized into constitutional conventions.   Because the founding fathers had feared this, there had been no mention of the powers of judicial review in the Constitution, and "the appellate jurisdiction given by law to the Supreme Court, was deduced by Congress from the Federalist [Papers], and by its elegant authors, from their personal opinions."[48]   Jefferson agreed with Taylor's view of the federal judiciary, and he thought that Taylor's *Construction Construed* was "the most effectual retraction of our government to its original principles which has ever yet been sent by heaven to our aid. Every State in the Union should give a copy to every member they elect, as a standing instruction, and ours [Virginia] should set the example."[49]

Because men could be governed by wealth or force as well as by fraud, the national powers to create a debt and raise armies also threatened the American nation-states. A ready local militia was security against standing armies. Excluding any person from the legislature who would profit from any financial decision of the government would be a check against the other power. The nations of the United States had taken steps to guard against federal force, but pecuniary fraud had been allowed to spread its venom to the point where "it has made matter for another Paradise Lost."[50]

On the question of the debt Taylor was weak. He assumed that a large national debt was burdensome to the living and an irrevocable curse to posterity. Hamilton's program, however, had resulted in a debt that, so far from being irrevocable, was being liquidated during Taylor's own lifetime and was completely retired by 1835. Though Taylor was wrong about the endurance of the debt, he had been right about its politics.

The free commerce of the United States had supposedly raised it to the point of power required to win the Revolution. Under free trade the nation had enjoyed that same unprecedented growth, at least until the federal government under Hamilton's supervision began to intervene in the economy in the interest of enriching private persons or special classes. A revival of laissez faire would revive prosperity. "Our commerce, both before and since the revolution, increased the national prosperity, with undeviating progress, and we are exchanging its solid benefits for restrictions, bounties, exclusive privileges, and monopolies, recommended by recondite and intricate speculations about the balance of trade."[51]

Hamilton's financial program had been a very large step in the direction of destroying republicanism, because its basic strategy had been to use the government as the instrument by which wealth could be transferred from one individual or class to another. By speculation and manipulation, some men had grown enormously rich as a result of Hamilton's system, and the majority of the nation had paid the bill. Exerting himself in opposition to Hamilton's policies Taylor had enough local success to cause Edmund

Randolph to tell George Washington that "Fredericksburg is in-
flamed by the doctrines and representations of Col. Taylor of
Caroline. . . . It would astonish you, sir, to learn the success which
has attended his efforts to rouse the cool and substantial planters."[52]
Taylor's attitude was expressed in a question: What could one think
"of the politicians who have bloated up a capitalist interest to a
pecuniary plethora, by starving down the other members of the
body politick, to a pecuniary famine?"[53] In his view, the ensuing
conflict between the capitalistic minority and the agrarian majority
had been the origin of political parties in the United States.

The postwar funding system had been designed to transfer, not
exchange, property. That system caused revolutionary certificates
to appreciate, Taylor said, to more than twenty times the original
price, and had resulted in

> a transfer of property by law, of about one hundred millions from
> the publick to a few fortunate speculators. The local residence of
> congress, the local expenditures of the war, and the local ingenuity
> of those who formed the funding project, had amassed these certifi-
> cates in the north, and their conversion into national debt . . . sud-
> denly created a great property-transferring capital or currency.
> In this acquisition, the majority in no state participated; it was
> bestowed on the initiated few, skilled in the secrets of legislation,
> and able to manage its stratagems for their own emolument. The
> effects of the transferring currency being thus tasted by a capitalist
> junto, and its wealth having invested it with legislative power, it of
> course adverted to banking as another item of the property-transfer-
> ring policy.[54]

When the group enriched by funding turned to the creation of
the Bank of the United States, it was merely following the logic of
its treason. The power to create corporations was an attribute of
sovereignty, and the federal government by incorporating the
Bank had usurped that power from the sovereign people. He
thought that the silence of the Constitution about any power to
create civil corporations was an express prohibition. The Bank was
not merely illegal, however; it was also the second step on the path
capitalists wanted to tread in their search for unearned profit, a
search which would transform a federated nation into a plutocracy.
Capitalism was not merely unwise or undesirable; it was treason.

The next step was the protective tariff. This was a tax on the
consumers of the nation, and since the poor class was the most

numerous, it included the majority of consumers. The tariff, then, according to Taylor, was a tax on the poor for the benefit of the rich. In a defence of Jefferson's administration, written in 1804, Taylor had argued that a gradual encouragement of manufacturing was necessary to national prosperity, and that tariffs operating for this end should be recommended. Whether this was simply political propaganda, or whether he had been convinced of this position then, cannot now be verified. The fact is that within the next ten years he completely rejected the tariff as pernicious class legislation.

His objections to the protective tariff system were sweeping. That system was "unconstitutional, injurious to morals, and productive of pauperism; improper to be extended; a tax on the many, and a bounty to the few; a restrictive system; a destroyer of revenue; ruinous to commerce, and destructive to agriculture."[55] Because the hard facts of geography meant that the Southern states could best employ their wealth and labor in agriculture, the tariff system was invidious sectional as well as class legislation. The farmer, as one of the majority of consumers who made up the poorer class, and as a Southerner, would have to pay a bounty to manufacturers in order to encourage, in the day's language, "infant industries." "How long," Taylor asked, "will the world be persuaded that it is an infant, and ought to be scourged into knowledge?"[56] This scourge in the United States had placed free farmers in the position of factory workers; both groups were compelled to turn their profit over to the factory owners. "In fact the whole United States are, by the protecting-duty laws, turned into one great factory, and all the people are placed upon the factory regimen as to profits." The result was the creation, by governmental fiat, of a "vast pecuniary aristocracy."[57] The tariff, as a device calculated to transfer property from farmer to capitalist, from South to North, was a violation of the natural right to property, of federalism, of state sovereignty, and, of course, of the Constitution.

One of the more serious consequences of capitalism and its tariffs was the creation of factions or sub-societies in the larger and theoretically indivisible state-nations. Taylor argued that factions or parties were not inevitable consequences of popular government, and cited the tranquil history of Connecticut over two centuries as proof. All men who labored honestly, including manufacturers, deserved equal treatment from government, if freedom were to be preserved. Partiality to one group or class of laborers was the mark of irresponsibility, which in turn was the mark of tyranny. Should factions once become firmly established in the United States, the uniqueness of the American political system would be abandoned in favor of a European model in which the power and right to distribute property had been deduced from the false idea of sovereignty in government. This acceptance of the substance of monarchy inevitably would convert the United States into a real monarchy, even if a republican façade were maintained. The advocates of capitalism and protection, and thus also of faction, had abandoned the American idea of federalism by arguing that the tariff would benefit "the American nation," whose existence Taylor had denied.

The system of political parties that had emerged in the United States was no help. The "two senseless standards," Federalist and Republican, merely encouraged prejudice and blind confidence at a time when intelligence and perception were required. Both parties had accused each other of passing unconstitutional laws. Neither party had repealed the legislation of the other once it entered office. The apostasy of the Republicans under Jefferson had led to a revival of substantial Federalism in the guise of "national interest": "Federalism," Taylor explained to Monroe, "indeed having been defeated, has gained a new footing, by being taken into partnership with republicanism."[58] The labels had lost meaning because the substance had: "If a man had successively married two wives, one called Lucretia, and the other Penelope; and should believe in their chastity, after having seen both in bed with several gallants of the worst characters, should we call him a blind cully, or an acute observer."[59] Farmers and laborers, whose honest labor should unite them into a political alliance, were deafened by the rhetoric of party politics and blinded by the glitter of gold which capitalists had promised to pay at some future date:

> We farmers and mechanics have been political slaves in all countries, because we are political fools. We know how to convert a wilderness into a paradise, and a forest into palaces and elegant furniture; but we have been taught by those whose object is to monopolize the sweets of life, which we sweat for, that politics are without our province, and in us [are] a ridiculous affectation.[60]

Political knowledge and sophistication were indispensable attributes for a majority interested in protecting itself from being plundered by a minority. James Madison had argued that the republican principle of majority rule would guarantee self-determination to a majority, and he had given much thought to the problem of protecting minorities in a republican system. Taylor reversed this by denying the automatic protection a majority ostensibly enjoyed under republicanism, and especially in the United States. Elections were ineffectual for an uninformed majority, he said. Minor interests were cunning and wise and, throughout the history of the world, had led majorities to vote against themselves, as Adams had also argued. A minority always administered governments and legislated. A minority never had taken wealth from itself to give to the nation, and almost always had taken wealth from the nation for its own enrichment. Where plunder was involved it was always the majority, and never the minority, which was endangered. As with elections, a reliance on virtue was no substitute for wisdom. But even wisdom was not completely adequate. The general will could only be expressed in conventions or in political laws. Without those levers the people, however wise, would still be helpless.

In America in general, and Virginia in particular, the majority was made up of those who labored, especially farmers. The government's policy of granting special favors could not benefit the farmers, because government had not the power to do so: "The utmost favour which it is possible for a government to do for us farmers and mechanics, is neither to help nor hurt us. The first it cannot do."[61] Nature could help the farmer if law did not get in the way. Law could hurt him whenever it chose. The farmer could help himself by protecting the laws of God from defilement by the laws of men. Because of this negative quality, farmers generally had not taken the interest in government that others had. Those who would subvert American republicanism by using the government for their selfish purposes had become, out of self-interest, experts in government, while the farmers, because they knew that government could not benefit them, had remained dangerously naïve. But since ignorance was the necessary precondition to slavery, the politically innocent farmers in America were in danger of becoming the creatures of an artificially created and potent capitalistic aristocracy. The class of capitalists could not rest until its logic of greed and treason had been satisfied, until a civil war would bury the hope of the world in the same graves that held the dead Americans:

> The great pecuniary favor granted by Congress to the certificate-holders [during the funding plan], begat banking; banking begat bounties to manufacturing capitalists; bounties to manufacturing capitalists begat an oppressive pension list; these partialities united to beget the Missouri [Compromise] project; that project begat the idea of using slavery as an instrument for creating a balance of power; when it is put in operation, it will beget new usurpations of internal powers over persons and property, and these will beget dissolution of the union.[62]

Because of the peculiarities of geography in America, class interests had also become sectional interests, and sectionalism would be the weapon which would destroy the union. Taylor had warned about the dangers of sectionalism as early as 1781, and was one of the first to do so. For him, sectionalism was not a direct result of geography, but of special legislation—funding, tariffs, banking—that favored a class that lived in the North. Sectionalism was therefore a result of boundaries drawn by legal fraud, and that kind of dividing line always had produced more hatred than natural or geographical borders. These were the terms in which he understood and opposed the Missouri Compromise. That debate, he said, was not about slavery, but was concerned with achieving a balance of power between the sections. That kind of a balance of power had always bred hostility and, finally, war. Congress' role in such a balance would be that of a convention whose purpose would be to negotiate between the contending sections, while each section would seek supremacy over the other. Should that contention occur, the Constitution and the union would be destroyed.

He thought that the entire system of federalism had been motivated by the fear of the centrifugal force of sectionalism. Had the sovereignty of the several states not been impaired, that localized power might have prevented an association of some of the states, and could have protected itself against such an illegal association should one have been formed. The emergence of sectional passion was therefore a symptom of consolidation, a sign that federalism had been or was being subverted. The advocates of a national,

instead of a federal, government during the constitutional convention had been fortunate in their failure, because a national government would have violated the basic local rights of the state-nations,
and such a violation would have remained as an unbearable irritant:
"If the national government proposed in the convention had succeeded, it could not have oblitered [*sic*] the local interests established by nature; and these would have remained as a pledge for a
revolution."[63] The prerequisites for that revolution had been kept
out of the Constitution, but the politicians who had managed the
government since that time had put them into practice. The form
of the government had been wise, but the practice had been
vicious; and that vice, more than any other, would bring about
death where life should have been.

The growth of sectional animosity would not only destroy the
happy solution of federalism; it would also impair the symbiosis
legislated by nature. The division of labor resulting from the various natural resources of the different sections had created mutual
markets that had benefited all concerned. If the North taxed the
South with one form or another of Hamilton's system, the purchas-
ing power of the South must be reduced, and the North would
surely join in the general suffering "as a punishment for their having endeavored to make a better scheme for themselves, than that
formed by the Creator of the universe."[64]

One of the proofs that capitalism had set out to mulct agriculture was its growing reluctance to invest its money in farming.
Even under the special disadvantages of the colonial situation,
Americans had then found agriculture a rewarding investment. By
the early nineteenth century, however, capitalists showed their
wisdom in avoiding agriculture: "Capital, like rats, deserts a falling
house; and who can so well discover that the dwelling is ruinous,
as those who are gnawing it down."[65] Agriculture, he said, had
in fact become a bad business, because of the transferring policies
of the federal government. The solution lay with political retrench-
ment, and until that was accomplished, any sane man would do
well to find some other field for investment.

The problem of agriculture arose because the United States could
not sensibly abandon it. Only when the United States could provide manufactured goods at a competitive world price would it be

profitable to turn from farming to manufacturing. The nature of the economy in the first decades of the nineteenth century, however, meant that farm surpluses should remain the country's most competitive export item for the foreseeable future.

Taylor argued that the existence of virgin land virtually demanded an expanding farm economy, because its availability, fertility, and low cost would operate continually as a lure to bring factory workers out of the cities. The worker "will compare the beneficence of the Deity with the beneficence of a capitalist; and consider whether it is better to work himself for another, than to have the best labourer in the world, the earth itself, to work for him."[66] So long as land remained cheap and labor expensive the United States would naturally turn to agricultural exports for world trade. To try to replace cheap farm products with the naturally less efficient and more expensive manufactured goods would be to enter into a forced and artificial situation. The point of the contrived capitalism of the United States was precisely the desire to substitute the wiles of men for the laws of nature.

> Had the man who foolishly killed the goose that laid the golden eggs, spared her life, and only persuaded her that she did not lay such eggs at all whilst he was daily taking them away, it would have been a case fitting both the capitalist and agricultural interest. The facts are stated to be "that agriculture has ceased to lay golden eggs; that factories will lay them in abundance; and that, when laid, the capitalists will give them to the agriculturalists." I shall not presume to say which of the parties would represent the goose.[67]

The existence of unoccupied land was not an unmixed blessing. Oppression in Europe, and especially in England, tended to force farmers into a more efficient use of the soil, because they had no place to which to escape. In America, oppression had the opposite consequence, because the farmer might always flee westward to fresh land in order to increase his profit. The result was wasteful farm habits and a rapid exhaustion of the soil. That exhaustion, coupled with the ignorance of American farmers, contributed to the farmer's growing inability to meet the increasing taxation forced on him by the capitalists of the North.

The final result of the artificial political economy being imposed on the United States could only be the death of agriculture. The tragedy, for Taylor, was that agriculture, because it combined a "thorough knowledge of the real affairs of life, with a necessity for investigating the arcana of nature, and the strongest invitations to the practice of morality, . . . becomes the best architect of a complete man."[68] Agriculture in America was "the sponsor for knowledge, for good manners, for liberty and for national power."[69] An attack on it inevitably would subvert all of its blessings. In the *Arator*, which even John Adams had praised, he went as far as human imagination could go in extolling agriculture:

> At the awful day of judgment, the discrimination of the good from the wicked, is not made by the criterion of sects or of dogmas, but by one which constitutes the daily employment and the great end of agriculture. The judge upon this occasion has by anticipation pronounced, that to feed the hungry, clothe the naked, and give drink to the thirsty, are the passports to future happiness; and the divine intelligence which selected an agricultural state as a paradise for its first favourites, has here again prescribed the agricultural virtues as the means for the admission of their posterity into heaven.[70]

The rape of America's farms in the interest of her factories was thus not merely a crime, but was a sin. Never adopting the full system of physiocracy, Taylor nevertheless believed that land was the only or the most enduring source of wealth. To destroy agriculture was to exchange the known for the unknown, the natural for the artificial, the virtuous for the vicious. The South's entire way of life was at stake, and since that section would eventually be compelled to defend itself, the union itself was endangered by the traitors who ran the government and the fools on the farms who had elected them.

Taylor recognized that the issue of slavery was the most divisive of all. He argued that slavery was a misfortune to agriculture. The condition of the slave could be improved, but slavery could not be abolished. Southern slave owners were innocent of the original guilt of slavery, for it was not they who had brought the slaves from Africa, but their fellow Americans who lived in the North. "The fact is," he wrote, "that negro slavery is an evil which the United States must look in the face. To whine over it, is cowardly; to aggravate it, criminal; and to forbear to alleviate it, because it cannot be wholly cured, foolish."[71]

It was the politics surrounding slavery, rather than anything intrinsic in the system, that made the problem as frightening to him as it was. He believed that slavery, as practiced in the South, had something to recommend it. Personal slavery was preferable, he said several times, to class slavery. The Southern Negro was supposedly treated more humanely than either the poor of Europe or the factory worker—the wage slave—in the North. The personal investment of the owner in his slave as well as the owner's concern with his own reputation would presumably moderate his treatment of his slaves. He said that no such moderation could be expected by those who were slaves to a depersonalized system like capitalism, thereby anticipating much of the pro-slavery argument that was to come, especially that of Calhoun and George Fitzhugh. In the *Arator*, he explicitly took issue with Jefferson's view that slavery would cause a decay of Southern morality and character, though he admitted that some scheme to reexport Negroes to Africa might be at least a partial answer to the problem.

More characteristic of his thought, as he continued to think about slavery, and as pressure began to build, was the view that free Negroes must be moved out of the South, where they acted as a stimulant to rebellion; that federalism properly understood meant that the North should mind its own business. Should Northern abolitionists continue to foment slave uprisings, the South would be driven into an even more intransigent position, and the disaster that would certainly ensue could not be laid at the door of the South. Men of good sense and sound morality could not fail to agree, he thought. But the momentum of the political economy of capitalism had created a blind sense and a depraved morality; although men had the power to be wise, they had, out of avarice and ambition, wilfully elected to crusade against slavery, and thus against the Constitution and the union. Out of an insatiable appetite men had decided to be fools.

Taylor was not a secessionist. Though his arguments were later used by Southerners in search of a way out of the union, he remained a committed federalist to the end of his life. Federalism meant a union that secured the sovereignty of the state-nations. That he predicted failure did not mean that he favored it. As early as May, 1794, for example, after Taylor had announced to the

Senate his intention to resign, two Northern Federalist Senators—Rufus King and Oliver Ellsworth—closeted themselves with Taylor in order to discuss what they called a very important subject. The Northerners believed that the North and the South could no longer live under the same roof, "that it was utterly impossible for the union to continue," and that peaceful separation then "was preferable to a certainty of the same thing, in a less desirable mode." Taylor answered that he was not convinced that the union could not survive, and added that the problem was the existence of the two political parties created by the national debt. In his remarks on this discussion to Madison, Taylor said that King and Ellsworth had the "mistaken opinion, that he [Taylor] was secretly an enemy to the union."[72]

His support of the union, however, was on his own terms. Sound principles, as he defined them, commanded his allegiance. He had periodic and acute attacks of pessimism, as expressed in a letter written to Jefferson, who was then the Vice President: "But I give up all for lost. The malady of all governments is monopoly. This is creeping and creeping into ours."[73] At least once, Monroe tried to tell Taylor not to worry so much about domestic dangers (while Monroe admitted that he was too worried about foreign problems). It was to no avail.

If Taylor was any one thing, he was a critic. In the single most revealing letter he ever wrote he told Monroe to be assured of his support for Monroe's bid for the presidency, and his criticism after Monroe was in office:

> If indeed you should get the presidency as I hope you will one day or other, it would probably be an irreparable breach with the republican minority [the Tertium Quids], should any such party then exist; because you must in some measure suffer yourself to be taken in tow by an administration party; and I do not recollect in the history of mankind a single instance of such a party being republican. Should I live to see that day, I hereby give you notice, that you are not to infer from my espousing your election, that I will join a party yell in favor of your administration; No, no, the moment you are elected, though by my casting vote, carried an hundred miles in a snow storm, my confidence in you would be most confoundedly deminished, [sic] and I would instantly join again the republican minority.[74]

John Taylor became a bitter critic of American life through his understanding of American history, through his sense that the promises of America had been broken by corrupt individuals, a stupid citizenry, and a government bribed and cajoled into treason. American life, as he understood it, had promised an Arcadia but had been made to deliver an individualistic capitalism; it had promised simplicity and tranquillity and had been made to deliver complexity and turmoil; it had promised to secure the individual's rights in a local community and had been made to deliver a highly centralized system that exploited the individual in the interest of a privileged class. America had held out the possibility that men could live close to nature and would thereby grow increasingly virtuous and politically dependable, and had placed a series of intolerable burdens on the innocent farmers of the nations of the United States.

America, for Taylor, had meant rural simplicity and had degenerated into civilization. It was the imposition of civilization that constituted the great betrayal of America's promises. Remaining committed to the old national mythology which defined the nation in terms of moral superiority, Taylor had abandoned the Puritans' allegiance to the *city* on a hill. He had redefined the national self-consciousness as the garden on the hillside. The cultivation of that garden, however, was not accomplished by moral or political anarchs. He understood that the nation-states of the union were a result of a series of anterior local communities made up of like-minded men who knew and trusted each other, whose sense of purpose was equally shared, and who understood and could therefore implement the general will of the homogeneous community. Civilization meant mobility, diversity, and the almost irresistible temptations of the flesh and the pocket. Arcadia and capitalism were mutually exclusive.

There had been one moment in America's history when the national promise had been honored. The few years of revolution had contained the world's first and last example of a thoroughly natural, and hence virtuous, social organization. That arcadia did not result in weakness was proved, he thought, by the fact that the simple and inexperienced American yeomen won their war with England. Virtue was strength.

Despairing of the future and celebrating one golden moment of the past, Taylor, and the Southern mentality he illustrated, departed from one of the central myths that had sustained American thought. He denied the timelessness of the new, had a burning sense of history, and asserted that his nation, through willful avarice, had forced itself into time, process, and decay. America had had a chance to become the garden of the world—in political, moral, and intellectual senses—and had forfeited its claim through self-induced corruption. Time and decay began with money, as Benjamin Franklin may have sensed but did not understand.

Capitalism was civilization, and it necessarily destroyed the homogeneous and idyllic local community. Winthrop's Christian corporation had become Taylor's agrarian corporation, and that had been transformed into a centralized and illegitimate nation of discrete individuals who defined a corporation as a form of business enterprise. Individualism required a new political theory which opposed a rule of the national majority to the hegemony of the states. A money economy demanded that America abandon nature, the community, and the Constitution. It demanded that the person be elevated above the group, that a centrifugal force be generated of insatiable individuals who would make Taylor's land simply another among the world's nations.

It remained for Ralph Waldo Emerson to salvage the national mythology from the attrition of Southern dissent. It was Emerson's task to reconcile Taylor's commitment to nature with a celebration of the individual, to rescue the sense of the new while yet maintaining an allegiance to pastoralism. In order to succeed, Emerson was compelled to deny the validity of Taylor's kind of attachment to community. Emerson's task, in short, was to reconcile American experience with American aspiration, promise, and myth. In rejecting American experience, Taylor rejected the hope that the dream could yet become the reality. Emerson began where Taylor stopped.

To the end of his life, Taylor remained either opposed or blind to the main drift of the political economy of the United States. Yearning for a return to Eden, he was swept forward toward what he believed would be a cataclysm. As an increasing number of Southerners came to stand in his shadow, his tenacity became a sectional mood, a mood which itself was no small contribution to the disaster he had feared. He had wept over Virginia for over a quarter of a century; when he died, in 1824, it was Virginia's turn to weep over him. Though this Southern Jeremiah was dead, his echo lived on to help ensure that his doleful prophecies would come to pass.

SELECT BIBLIOGRAPHY

T. P. Abernethy. *The South in the New Nation, 1789–1819.* Baton Rouge, 1961.

Charles A. Beard. *Economic Origins of Jeffersonian Democracy.* New York, 1915.

Daniel Boorstin. *The Lost World of Thomas Jefferson.* New York, 1948.

Jesse T. Carpenter. *The South as a Conscious Minority.* New York, 1930.

Wilbur J. Cash. *The Mind of the South.* New York, 1941.

Stanley M. Elkins. *Slavery.* New York, 1963.

Eugene T. Mudge. *The Social Philosophy of John Taylor of Caroline.* New York, 1939.

R. G. Osterweis. *Romanticism and Nationalism in the Old South.* New Haven, 1949.

Arthur M. Schlesinger, Jr. *The Age of Jackson.* Boston, 1946. Chs. 2–4.

Henry Nash Smith. *Virgin Land.* Cambridge, 1950.

C. S. Sydnor. *The Development of Southern Sectionalism, 1819–1848.* Baton Rouge, 1948.

William R. Taylor. *Cavalier & Yankee.* New York, 1961.

C. Vann Woodward. *The Burden of Southern History.* New York, 1961.

V

TRANSCENDENCE ❉ *Ralph Waldo Emerson*

> Standing on the bare ground,—my head bathed by the blithe air and uplifted into infinite space,—all mean egotism vanishes. I become a transparent eyeball; I am nothing; I see all; the currents of the Universal Being circulate through me; I am part or parcel of God.
>
> *1836*

Before the Civil War split the nation and the century, America had grown and prospered to an extent that gratified even the most demanding. The bald eagle could screech with pleasure over the expansion of the nation, over the continued westward thrust of its people into lands paid for with lives and gold to England, France, Spain, and Mexico. The "manifest destiny" at whose altar Americans worshipped seemed to unfold before the eyes of the world. A national hymn of thanksgiving was sung by a people grateful to the providence which had marked out a continent for their pleasure, and which had actually put the proverbial pot of gold at the proverbial westernmost end of the rainbow in the hills of California.

The material success of nineteenth-century America helped to close the political phase of America's intellectual history. The revolutionary generation had done its work well, as the expanding borders, wealth, and sense of national security testified. A concern with politics did not absolutely die, of course, for the Civil War was a gigantic political moment. But, in the period following the deaths of John Adams and John Taylor of Caroline, the most vital part of the American mind turned from statecraft to literature. When the question of America's survival as a nation seemed answered by its apparently continuous progress, a few men began to question the significance of material progress, to assert—or, rather, to reassert—the primacy of spirit over matter, and to demand that a reluctant America follow their lead into the unfamiliar world of beauty.

In another sense, the political stage of the American intellectual tradition ended, not because the founding fathers built well but because, in demonstrating the limits to which political thought and action could go, they unwittingly showed the narrowness of political solutions. The revolutionary generation had assumed that politics was central, had believed that politics would show the way to secure life, liberty, and even the pursuit of happiness. That generation had sometimes confused independence with liberty. Winning the Revolution and framing the Constitution did not produce heaven on earth; indeed, it did not, for some, even result in the creation of a tolerable condition of life. Even the magnitude of America's material growth was evidence for some of its very irrelevance. Neither ingenious politics nor relative abundance was an adequate answer to the questions that antedated the war for independence, questions that continued to engage the minds of at least a few sensitive Americans when the new nation seemed secure.

The fact that political independence from England was merely a step towards freedom, and was not itself that freedom, was widely recognized. Much of the impetus behind the active cultural nationalism of the early nineteenth century was the desire to create a culture along with a nation. Politics could accomplish only the second goal. But in order to create a culture independent of England and Europe, it was necessary for Americans to change the intellectual mode, to move away from politics, whose work was completed and whose achievement left an entire world of problems still unanswered.

There are several reasons why the new intellectual mode was literature. Theology was dead, politics exhausted, and philosophy inaccessible because of a relative lack of facilities and training. Creative Americans were largely forced back on their own individual resources in the antebellum period by virtue of their being Americans. Even a country as culturally arid as young America could nor prevent a few of the citizens from contemplating their perhaps battered egos. Supported by the celebration of the self they discovered in the contemporary Romantic movement in Europe, the best of American writers turned inward to find their material and inspiration. The very absence of cultural resources helped to turn American authors to Romantic literature.

The Americans who became concerned with literature in the generation before the Civil War knew that there was little in the American tradition to assist them. To what extent their own national history was usable for their purposes was a question they all asked, and they turned inward and to each other rather than to the past for inspiration. The belief that the past was not usable was sustained by more than its supposed cultural aridity. Many aspects of the national mythology had already rejected age, the past, time, and perhaps even death. The millennial idea of the west, the deep sense of newness in the New World, and, most important, the belief in the uniqueness of America's alleged moral superiority had all contributed to the American discomfort with time. The self-reliance which the demands of survival forced on the pioneers carried with it a presumed sense of the past's irrelevance to the vital business at hand. A rejection of both tradition and form was an inevitable consequence of the presentism that, according to de Tocqueville, equality encouraged. As the past had been identified with evil by the Puritans, and with intrigue and duplicity by the revolutionaries, so the most creative members of the pre-Civil War generation viewed time and its contents as the great millstone that could grind them to dust. Few, if any, European Romantics viewed the past as Americans did.

Preoccupied with the corrosive qualities of time, Nathaniel Hawthorne elevated the popular rejection of the past to a fine art. The moral of *The House of the Seven Gables* he said in 1851 was "the truth . . . that the wrong-doing of one generation lives into the successive ones, and, divesting itself of every temporary advantage, becomes a pure and uncontrollable mischief."[1] Holgrave, the photographer and reformer in *The House of the Seven Gables,* cried the American cry: "Shall we never, never get rid of this Past? It lies upon the present like a giant's dead body!"

Feeling choked by the weight of that corpse, the creative men of Hawthorne's period sought either to portray the corpse in its detail or else to shake it off altogether. Which course each chose was a matter of temperament and inclination. Hawthorne and Poe were drawn to an examination of decay; Thoreau, Emerson, and Whitman could breathe only in the open air of the present and future. Emerson simply announced that "Whatever is old corrupts, and the past turns to snakes."[2] European Romanticism almost always looked backward; American Romanticism almost always looked inward.

The search for an escape from the past, either through outlining its pathogenesis or through a steadfast concentration on the future, contributed to a remarkable literary achievement. The cluster of works appearing in the six years from 1850 to 1855 included Emerson's *Representative Men,* Hawthorne's *The Scarlet Letter* and *The House of the Seven Gables,* Melville's *Moby Dick* and *Pierre,* Thoreau's *Walden,* and Whitman's *Leaves of Grass.*

The American literary mentality, at least as it was represented by those five authors, had committed itself to finding new answers to old questions. Becoming convinced, at some point of their own development, that the foul air of the past was polluting the present, each sought to refresh the older atmosphere. That old dank air continued, however, to sustain them all.

The Puritan synthesis was the primary threat to intellectual and artistic progress, according to those authors of America's literary renaissance. Step by step they said "no" to most of the major Puritan affirmations, but in limiting themselves to the Puritan categories they gave to the creative writing of their time the peculiar metaphysical and theological flavor that only the particular intellectual enemy they shared could give. Their major intellectual task was to answer a series of questions with their contemporary voice: What is the nature of God and man? What is man's proper relation to society? What is the nature of good and evil?

A second strand holding the work of the renaissance together was a rejection of material America in favor of an ideal America. They were determined to integrate appearance and reality, and it was therefore inevitable that they should rely on symbols. Their desire to make the word one with the thing was a consequence of the anterior desire to destroy the gulf between the ideal and actual.

The poet came to occupy for them the station of prophet and hero, because the poet could know the problem and could have the necessary equipment for its solution. The poet could see the fact as symbol and the symbol as fact. He alone could negotiate between the two worlds, and his eye could see the path all men must walk. But the poet should walk with men. All of the renaissance authors insisted on the organic nature of art in society; they all explored the possibilities of art in democracy and the need for a cultural equivalent to political independence and progress.

Committed to unity between art and life, between fact and appearance, they created a world of symbols that could bridge the gap. Their symbols were often smoothed to suit the conventions of their day, but beneath the surface the peculiar metaphysical agony of American creative writing of the time quietly raged. D. H. Lawrence understood first: "You *must* look through the surface of American art, and see the inner diabolism of the symbolic meaning. Otherwise it is all mere childishness. That blue-eyed darling Nathaniel knew disagreeable things in his inner soul. He was careful to send them out in disguise."[3] The diabolism of the best creative writing of the pre-Civil War period was a result of the power of Puritanism to force men to continue to ask its questions. Creative Americans still believed that a man must face himself and his God alone, and they were faced with only three alternatives: to collapse under the sovereignty of God and return to the old fold; to clasp God's sweet hand in companionship and a sense of man's own towering divinity; to find and use the weapon that could pierce the heart of God, whose death would be man's first true birth.

These alternatives all derived from the vision that Jonathan Edwards had had, and the unwillingness of men to accept his answers. But Edwards' God still lived to inspire through hate, although not through the justice or love that once had been paramount. To move through the early renaissance to Ahab is to move increasingly close to the death of God, until finally men could see, in Melville's nightmare, that terror came from within as well as without, and that the Puritan God of righteousness and wrath seemed still comfortable out of his usual heaven and in the separate souls of his American victims.

The path to Ahab was first of all the path from Edwards. And

Ralph Waldo Emerson took the major step from the rejected past
to the agonized present. Emerson was the intellectual father of
the renaissance, and the spiritual son of Edwards. Ahab sprang
from the desire to kill God that sprang from Emerson's vision of
the divinity of men. From Luther's "priesthood of all believers" to
Emerson's discovery of man's divinity, to Melville's search for a
way to murder God to Nietzsche's announcement that God was
dead—the path proceeded in a straight and orderly fashion. Emerson's contribution was essential.

Emerson was born in Boston in 1803, one hundred years after
the birth of Edwards. His paternal ancestral line ran back through
a series of ministers to Peter Bulkeley, who had been the first minister of Concord, Massachusetts, a friend of John Winthrop's, and
an architect of the original city on a hill. Emerson's childhood was
difficult as a result of the early death of his father and the hardships
his mother faced in raising the family. An aunt, Mary Moody
Emerson, who still breathed the spirit of the Great Awakening
Edwards had led, was an important educational force in the life of
the young Emerson. He entered Harvard when he was fifteen and
distinguished himself in no way during his four years there, although
he was named class poet.

The force of family tradition seemed to make the choice of the
ministry inevitable for Emerson, though he had already begun to
think seriously of literature as a career. After suffering as a teacher
in a girls' school in Boston, he took the almost automatic step and
entered Harvard's Divinity School in 1825. He completed the usual
course with an unspectacular record. Illness, especially trouble
with his eyes, began to afflict him, and he was forced to delay his
acceptance of a regular post while he went south in search of
health.

He had started to keep a journal, the time-honored practice of
the New England Puritans. Pursued by the same Fury as the young
John Adams, Emerson began to complain while he was a senior at
college both of his seeming incapacities and of the threatened success of his fellows. He was afflicted with a sense of a dreary future
which he would deserve because of his unwillingness to improve
himself in the present. The language of his lament seems to be an
accurate reflection of his deepening dissatisfactions:

Too tired and too indolent to travel up the mountain path which leads to good learning, to wisdom & to fame, I must be satisfied with beholding with an envious eye the laborious journey & final success of my fellows, remaining stationary myself, until my inferiors & juniors have reached & outgone me. . . . Look next from the history of my intellect to the history of my heart. A blank, my lord. I have not the kind affections of a pigeon. Ungenerous & selfish, cautious & cold, I yet wish to be romantic.[4]

As he craved distinction and as his self-knowledge began to deepen, he concluded that the ministry offered him the best chance to use those talents he did have. He had already discovered that his powers of analysis were not as strong as he could wish, and that his social presence was often awkward. Both medicine and law required more poise than he had. His formality of speech and love of eloquence seemed to fit him for the ministry, and he believed that he had certain powers to direct the reason and emotions of masses.

Throughout the 1820's, Emerson was developing an abstraction of person that seemed to make him transparent. He lived his real life in books and in his journals. That he came to loathe his own laughter is perhaps an indication of his increasing and self-induced disembodiment. His marriage to Ellen Tucker, who died seventeen months after the wedding, also seemed to anchor him no more firmly on earth. Even his physical suffering was characteristically put to literary use. He found the ancient doctrine of compensated evil a satisfying explanation of his own illness, as well as a way to abolish evil altogether. He wrote that every pain had a reward, that every evil contained a larger good. He was coming to understand evil as Jonathan Edwards understood it, simply as a stage of good becoming itself. But he was later to say that "He has seen but half the Universe who never has been shown the house of Pain. Pleasure and Peace are but indifferent teachers of what it is life to know."[5] The utility of pain and corruption became, through his idea of compensation, the proper appreciation of the relation of the parts to the whole, for evil was always particular while good was always universal.

The young Emerson was showing signs of a willed saintliness that threatened to vaporize him entirely. Success, as that was defined by his milieu, seemed an unattainable goal, and his personal disposition made worldly struggle distasteful if not impossible. He longed to find a serenity and perhaps a security located nowhere on earth, and withdrawal into self seemed a satisfactory alternative to a competition he felt he would lose: "To forget for a season the world & its concerns, & to separate the soul for sublime contemplation till it has lost the sense of circumstance & is decking itself in plumage drawn out from the gay wardrobe of Fancy"[6] became an aspiration of his when he was eighteen years old and remained with him for the rest of his life. His expatriation from the City of Men was to be more or less complete, and the sweetest peace he knew was to come to him in isolation and in communion with the immaterial world of eternal spirits.

The Puritan theological synthesis that Emerson inherited had always threatened to fall apart into its precariously balanced halves. The rationalism and the piety Edwards had succeeded in juggling became mutually repulsive. Demanding both the most rigorous logic and the total warmth of emotion, the old Puritanism perhaps inevitably gave rise to disparate religious reactions. It was easy for Puritanism to explode into the frenzy of revivalism, and easy for it to become a cold and rational Unitarianism. Emerson never understood or sympathized with the fervor of the awakenings or revivals, but the mysteries of the pietistic side of Puritanism attracted him. On the other hand, the freedom and dignity offered by the Unitarians was equally attractive. Characteristically he was to find himself involved in a double rejection; the violence of emotional Puritanism and the abstraction of rational Puritanism were both repellent: "Calvinism stands . . . by pride and ignorance; and Unitarianism, as a sect, stands by the opposition of Calvinism. It is cold and cheerless, the mere creature of the understanding, until controversy makes it warm with fire got from below."[7] He was in search of a way to protect both the mystery of piety and the intellectual freedom of Unitarianism. It was not a comfortable search for a proper minister.

Complicating Emerson's search was his positive admiration of the spirit of the old Puritan faith. In his view Puritanism even without theology meant morality. He could look around him, no farther than Aunt Mary, to see out of what admirable stuff the modern saints were made. He had no doubts about the contribution of

Puritanism. It had inspired improvements in the British Constitution, settled America, and contributed sense and practicality to America that made the nation what it was. The energy and purpose of the Bay saints had been equal to the task of making a civilization in a forest. Lesser men, more timorous men, even less fanatical men would have failed.

The Puritan heroes, as Emerson saw them, tempered their steel with love. He believed that the conflicts between Winthrop and the deputies of the Bay were girlish misunderstandings that resulted in loving forgiveness. The Puritan sense of love was duty to their God and to their fellows, and resulted in a masculine sense of community:

> What a debt is ours to that old religion which, in the childhood of most of us, still dwelt like a sabbath morning in the country of New England, teaching privation, self-denial and sorrow! A man was born not for prosperity, but to suffer for the benefit of others. . . . Not praise, not men's acceptance of our doing, but the spirit's holy errand through us absorbed the thought. How dignified was this! How all that is called talents and success, in our noisy capitals, becomes buzz and din before this man-worthiness![8]

The formal Puritan theological system had contributed to the creation of heroes, but that system was unacceptable to Emerson, despite his adoration of its adherents: "Great, grim, earnest men, I belong by natural affinity to other thoughts and schools than yours, but my affection hovers respectfully about your retiring footprints, your unpainted churches, strict platforms, and sad offices; the iron-gray deacon and the wearisome prayer rich with the diction of ages. Well, the new is only the seed of the old."[9] The new was to be precisely the seed of the old, and though the new to which Emerson made a significant contribution was to pride itself on modernity it betrayed its lineage at almost every step.

Emerson began his formal religious liberation by rejecting the pale negations of Unitarianism, and by discovering a secret deep in the folds of the old faith. The eye of Jonathan Edwards had been dazzled by a gilded emanation of the Holy Ghost. Mysticism, pure and simple, had always been a heresy contained within Puritan pietism, as the case of Anne Hutchinson had demonstrated. And as Emerson felt the spirit rise in him, he found nourishment in part of the spirit, though not the form, of the old piety:

> And what is to replace for us the piety of that race? We cannot
> have theirs; it glides away from us day by day; but we also can
> bask in the great morning which rises forever out of the eastern sea,
> and be ourselves the children of the light. I stand here to say, Let
> us worship the mighty and transcendent Soul.[10]

Before he could call up that Soul he had to free himself of all
institutional restraint, to shed altogether the husk of the old formal-
ized theology. In order to give his spirit room in which to soar, he
needed to free himself from convention and orthodoxy of all kinds.
In order to develop heresy, he needed to separate from the duties
and obligations of a minister.

Soon after the death of his first wife he began to acknowledge
his dislike of the church. "Official goodness" interfered with authentic goodness. The institutionalized creed he was obliged to preach
was irrelevant to a questing mind; it was the voice of the past and
dead to the present. The entire ministerial profession was anti-
quated. In changing times religion had remained authoritarian and
repugnant to reason. He thought that even paganism would be
better than an effete and superannuated Christianity.

He had decided to break with the church altogether, and he
made his discomfort with the administration of the Lord's Supper
the issue. He told his congregation that changes in the rite would
have to be made or he would leave the church, and a committee of the church politely said that the ordinance was satisfactory the way it was. Emerson insisted that the Last Supper created
confusion, that it transferred worship from God to Christ. For the
Unitarian, he said, worship was due to God and commemoration
due to Christ. The Puritans had prepared the way for this, too,
in rejecting the celebration of Christmas as pagan, and in generally
placing overwhelming emphasis on God the Father's attribute of
sovereignty.

Emerson's heresy had been born in the old church. The effect
of the ordinance, according to Emerson, was to invest Jesus with
a distracting and illegitimate authority. There was one God
only; Christ was a man who was an instructor to other men, teaching them how to become godlike. The rite was not suitable to
Emerson, he said, and even if it had been enjoined by Christ as a

permanent mode, Emerson would not adopt it but would choose his own form of worship which, since it would be more effective for him, Christ would approve.

The more genuine issue was that Emerson was already aware that there were new spiritual currents at work in the world, and he was touched more deeply by them than by formal religion. He had just discovered Schiller and Goethe in translations by Carlyle, and knew the work of Fénelon and George Fox, along with that of Coleridge, Wordsworth, and Carlyle. The precise impact of this body of thought on Emerson is of course impossible to assess, but he must have felt some sense of an expanding intellectual horizon, a smashing of inhibiting formalism, and a joy in finding others who knew something of the magnitude of the human soul along with its thirst for freedom. He was preparing to turn from theology to literature in order to find philosophy, but he disguised his new sense to his parishioners in his intramural quarrel over the Last Supper. The church finally accepted his resignation and he was free to follow wherever the spirit would lead.

The spirit led inward for the rest of his life. The theological nature of the issue he raised was central to his future direction: Men were as divine as Christ; there was thus no essential difference between worshipping oneself and worshipping God. Luther's elevation of all men to the priesthood was now taken to its next logical step: All men were elevated to divinity. Thus self-reliance became now not merely one of Benjamin Franklin's prudent maxims but also a sacred duty.

Finding the Holy Ghost in his own being, Emerson was discovering that he sympathized with the ancient company of mystics, those inspired souls who could directly communicate with their God without an intermediary of any kind, who felt that perfect union with the godhead was possible. From Plotinus to Jacob Boehme, the Quakers, and Swedenborg, the mystical tradition was available to Emerson, and he began to feed on it wherever he could. The result was the elaboration of Emerson's mature and simple religious sense: God was the moral law; the world was an emanation from God; man shared in divinity and therefore should rely on self; true religion spoke not of authority but of vitalizing spirit. He found some of the vitality symptomatic of religious health in the Quakers and Swedenborgians of his time, but his developing liturgy of individualism was to keep him outside of any institutionalized church from then on. Though he could admire the inner light of the Quakers as well as the Swedenborgian insistence on the primacy of the spirit, Emerson was now sufficiently convinced of the uniqueness of the separate ego to foreswear the churches altogether.

Late in 1832 he sailed for Europe in order to find health and intellectual nourishment. He met Coleridge, Carlyle, and Wordsworth, among others, and was reinforced in his own spiritual and intellectual liberation. Returning home he moved to Concord, with his mother; he married Lydia Jackson in 1835.

The next year Emerson took his first major positive step toward announcing the self he was coming to know when he published *Nature,* his first book. It was a slim volume put together from his notes, journals, letters, and sermons. But the finished product was a new departure for him in its intensity and its concentration of ideas. It was clearly the work of one of a group that in New England was being called the Transcendentalists.

The definition of Transcendentalism is Emerson, especially his *Nature.* Transcendentalism was an unorganized antiformalism, a radical idealism, an opposition to the world that could be seen or heard or touched. Emerson later explained that Transcendentalism was not new, but was simply idealism made modern. The war of materialism and idealism had been waged through all time. Materialism had always been founded on experience, and idealism on consciousness; the former always trusted the data of the senses and the latter believed only the mind. Transcendentalism was "the Saturnalia or excess of Faith," an ancient human response whose specific content varied as situations changed. That response raised Stoics out of Rome, patriots out of despotism, prophets out of superstition, protestants out of papacy, Puritans out of prelacy, and idealists out of commercialism and Unitarianism. The belief in the absolute superiority of mind over matter led the latter-day idealists called Transcendentalists away from empiricism and science toward either rationalism or mysticism and art, especially poetry. One contemporary caught the Transcendental temper and excitement this way:

> The Transcendentalist was satisfied with nothing so long as it did not correspond to the ideal in the enlightened soul; and in the soul

recognized the power to make all things new. Nothing will content him short of the absolute right, the eternally true, the unconditioned excellence. He prays for the kingdom of Heaven, lives in expectation of it; would not be surprised at its coming any day.[11]

There was no organized Transcendental movement or party, though a group of like-minded individuals did begin meeting in an informal way. The voices of Transcendentalism were not, as is usually said, simply an American variant of the Romantic movement in Europe. The American Transcendentalists were Platonists made Christian, and that some of them were also Romantics did not make Transcendentalism entirely Romantic. The Romanticism of some of the Transcendentalists was implicit in their version of idealism, but there was no necessary connection between Romanticism and idealism. The Transcendentalists were deeply involved with the American intellectual tradition, they were essentially idealists, and some also became Romantics. Emerson's own development clarifies the relationships between American thought, idealism, and Romanticism.

At the foundation of *Nature* was a radical idealism, a conviction that the created universe was strictly a metaphor of the human mind. The natural world was "the great apparition"—"shadows of divine things" Jonathan Edwards had called it—whose secrets were the secrets of human nature. Man could be understood by understanding nature, because the latter was the former writ green. Emerson later put it cogently: "That which once existed in intellect as pure law, has now taken body as Nature. It existed already in the mind in solution; now, it has been precipitated, and the bright sediment is the world."[12]

In *Nature*, Emerson looked for answers to several problems. How could idealism be proved? Could an ideal unity be found? And what was the concrete relationship between man and nature?

The quest for unity is intrinsic in idealism which must deny the reality of the disparate incarnations or embodiments of idea. Because of his own share in that quest, Emerson believed that occultism—phrenology, astrology, alchemy—would be more fruitful than the more respectable sciences because it tried to find human meaning in the physical universe. The world as idea must have its various bits and pieces of material stuff unified to idea, else the one would disintegrate into the many. To protect the unified whole from such disintegration was the major burden of *Nature*.

The adhesive of the heterogeneous material world was a universal spirit which Emerson later called the Oversoul. Beauty was, as Edwards had also said, the recognition of unity, the realization of relationships ascending into universal harmony. Emerson rendered that very old idea with economy: "Nothing is quite beautiful alone; nothing but is beautiful in the whole."[13] To find the whole in the parts, the one in the many, was the task of the free spirit.

The proper relationship of man to nature would free him from particularity, would allow him to merge with the Universal Spirit in a liberating apotheosis. The sense of Emerson's now-famous language is found in that denial of the particular and in that ecstasy of unity that could occur in nature:

> Standing on the bare ground—my head bathed by the blithe air and uplifted into infinite space,—all mean egotism vanishes. I become a transparent eyeball; I am nothing; I see all; the currents of the Universal Being circulate through me; I am part or parcel of God.[14]

The Egyptian mysticism of Plotinus had been transferred to the woods of Concord, and Emerson could feel his ego dissolving into transcendence, into God. As the universal spirit liberated his soul from actual time and space, Emerson became one with God.

Jonathan Edwards had argued that the good which each man perceived was radically different before and after regeneration. With grace, he had said, a new sense of the unity and beauty of the world would strike men and lift their hearts to a sweet love of God. The human faculties had been in perfect harmony before the Fall, but sin had pitted the human organism against itself. For Edwards, the glory of man's innocence could be detected even in the ruins of the decadent present. In *Nature* Emerson applied every detail of that aspect of Edwards' system to his own purposes, showing, among other things, the persistence of the theological question in New England's best thought. Edwards could have approved each aspect of Emerson's statement:

> The problem of restoring to the world original and eternal beauty is solved by the redemption of the soul. The ruin or the blank that we see when we look at nature, is in our own eye. . . . The reason why the world lacks unity . . . is because man is disunited with himself.[15]

Of course, the use to which Emerson put his sense of unity and nature would have been condemned by Edwards, who would, however, have understood the Emersonian ecstasy.   Edwards would have thundered against Emerson's idea of liberation, and would have been aghast at the notion of apotheosis.

The superiority that Emerson ascribed to mind over matter, to symbol over fact, meant that the use of nature must be human. He thought that a passive or morally neutral nature was a premise of materialism, which denied God altogether. For Emerson nature existed for man's benefit and was itself a reflection of man's conscience, of a universal moral sense.   Nature, as matter or fact, had to be interpreted as idea or symbol in order to discover its secret. Emerson worshipped the domesticated or humanized nature that had already become characteristic of American thought; he never rhapsodized the wilderness, but he was made giddy from the fragrances of a conceptualized garden.

Nature was incorruptible and served as a criterion of man's own progress toward divinity. He later wrote that "the beauty of nature must always seem unreal and mocking, until the landscape has human figures that are as good as itself."[16] When men were equal to nature's goodness, they would "shame the brook." If man served nature instead of using it, he became a slave by overlooking "the fact that the world is only his teacher, and the nature of sun and moon, plant and animal only means of arousing his interior activity."[17]   Natural perfection was a rebuke to human failings which could be eliminated under nature's own inspiration.

The merging of the particular into the universal spirit could never be achieved so long as men responded to nature with their minds alone. It was indispensable for men to confront the universe in a primary and original way. Inspiration, not tradition, was the way of and to the spirit, and men who had sacrificed the unconscious to the conscious must walk through life as cripples, as cold Unitarians. An unreasoned, instinctive yielding to the spirit of the forest would release the soul from its bondage to particularity, and allow it to glide among the eternal shades with which it found the purest distillation of disembodied love. "As the power or genius of nature is ecstatic," he later tried to explain, "so must its science or the description of it be. The poet must be a rhapsodist; his inspiration a sort of bright casualty; his will in it only the surrender of will to the Universal Power."[18]

Emerson's idealism was more extreme than Kant's and more inclusive than Coleridge's. Kant argued that the "thing in itself" had an objective existence even though it was unknowable; Coleridge limited the scope of intuition to religion and morality. Emerson denied all objectivity, and argued that the self was also idea, thereby approximating Fichte's idealism; Emerson did not distinguish between immediate intuition and poetic imagination. The pleasures of the spiritual orgy justified the petty material sacrifices that must be made along the way, and the discovery of God in the ego was worth a world of mere stuff. Emerson was now free to soar in air too thin to sustain flesh.

It was evidently important to Emerson to clarify his new status, to explain and perhaps to justify the role of the intellectual in American life. He lectured at Harvard on "The American Scholar," and elevated the intellectual to an ideal realm where any American nervousness or guilt about the impracticality of the life of the mind would be alleviated or eliminated. There was a natural division of labor, he asserted, which required intellectual specialization. The true scholar was not merely some one particular individual, but was the intellectual representative of the race, a delegated mind. Both the scholar and his function were ideal essences emptied of all particularity. As the soul could merge and become one with the universal spirit in nature, so the authentic mind would raise itself and become lost in universal mind. Just how the particular human mind prepared itself for its leap to universality, and what it should do when it got there, was the burden of Emerson's address.

Primarily the scholar must learn from nature properly seen. The individual who could read the human heart in flowers and birds was prepared to ascend from detail to master plan. He must also learn from the past, from books, but again, properly seen. Emerson appreciated the definition of the past in the earlier American intellectual tradition and now put it to work for him. The past was dead. The purpose of books, as that of nature, was inspiration, not imitation. Books should either release the self or be ignored. The only utility of the past was its relevance to the mind in the present. Any veneration of tradition for its own sake would turn Man Thinking into a mere actual bookworm. Should genius develop in the present, it would have to guard against the geniuses of the past: The disciple was a slave at a time when freedom was needed.

The final teacher of the scholar was his own experience, especially those aspects of life which forced the scholar to think on the vanity of life and the particularity of evil.

Prepared by a careful attendance on nature, by a selected past, and by the self, the scholar was ready to perform his task. Man Thinking was an office designed to be a guide to fact amidst appearances. Only the scholar knew the world, knew that reality was never what it seemed to be. As an idealist the scholar did not need romance; the commonplace became colorful and exciting when it was understood as symbolic. Idealism, therefore, allowed the scholar to stay home—perhaps in Concord—while his mind was lifted to eternity through contemplation of—say—milk turning sour.

Through his version of idealism, Emerson was able to see the all in the each, the whole in the part, and that vision made the each and the part sufficiently inspirational for him to reject the exoticism that had become characteristic of the Romantic movement in Europe. His need for intellectual and emotional excitement could be satisfied by contemplating and idealizing a pine tree, a focus that was, after all, just as well, since Americans had no gothic cathedrals to celebrate. But simultaneously he subscribed to a yet more significant Romantic preoccupation, one that had suggested itself to him in *Nature* and earlier. An understanding of the separate self was among the scholar's sacred functions. The scholar must aspire to the office of universal Man Thinking, a universality that could be achieved only by nourishing the particularity of each discrete ego.

The quest for unity is basic to any system of idealism, as the quest for diversity is to virtually all varieties of Romanticism. A system of Romantic idealism, therefore, must develop internal tensions as a result of a desire to discover unity and disunity simultaneously. Emerson lived with the tension by asserting that the road to unity was passable only by separate and isolated selves: "Every thing that tends to insulate the individual . . . tends to true union as well as greatness."[19] Though the centrifugal forces within a system of Romantic idealism continued to generate problems for the rest of Emerson's intellectual life, he usually prevented an impossible contradiction through the flat assertion that unity could come only from disunity, that a merging with universality could result only from reliance on self.

An opportunity for applying the ideas of *Nature* and of "The American Scholar" to theology was given him in the summer of 1838, when he was asked to address the senior class in the divinity school at Harvard. No one seems to have expected the mild, sweet author of *Nature* to explode an intellectual bomb that would, among other things, make him unwelcome at Harvard for almost thirty years.

The crux of his new conviction, and one that shocked even the most liberal clergymen in the audience, was put boldly. He declared that when a man became just he became God. Only Christ had properly estimated man's greatness, and Christ, as a man, was true to the best that was in every man. Christ was a true prophet who understood that God was incarnate in all men. All men, not Christ alone, were thus the Word made flesh, and all men were true Sons of the Father. He argued that the fallacy of historical Christianity was its emphasis on the person of Jesus, whereas the true and eternal soul recognized no particular individual, because it was everywhere aloft in the universe.

In denying the divinity of the person of Jesus, Emerson was again in agreement with a central idea in the American intellectual tradition. The rejection of personification had already taken the form of a rejection of Mary, a Puritan nervousness about the person of Christ, a rejection of the pope, and a rejection of monarchy. Steadily elevating law, system, and some fundamental word—the Bible or the United States Constitution—above any person, American thinkers had characteristically sought ways by which to return to a Hebraic God who was pure idea, pure "I AM," and who had told the prophet Samuel to tell the Jews to beware of Kings. Americans had characteristically sought to purge the flesh and personification from their world views, and in so doing they rejected the continuity of the generations of men. The American discomfort with continuity and time was a reflex related to the rejection of person, and growth, and decay. Emerson's predecessors had prepared the way for his next logical step. In describing Christ as divinity in office but not in person, Emerson was rendering Christ acceptable to republican political theory, to the then conventional version of the King's two bodies. The radical abstraction of American thought, its utter Protestant qualities, led easily from one depersonification to another, starting with Mary and ending with Christ, and all the while on the political level committed to a government, as was said, of law and not of men.

Emerson's declaration that all men were divine was, in one sense, a mere extension of the Puritan concept of the elect to all of mankind. Now, if each man would be true to his own divinity each would attain the kingdom of the just. As Emerson followed the implications to the end, introspection became prayer. Virtue was an intuition that could not be received from another. "Truly speaking, it is not instruction, but provocation, that I can receive from another soul. What he announces, I must find true in me, or reject; and on his word, or as his second, be he who he may, I can accept nothing."[20] When men lost their own integrity and authenticity they lost their virtue and became victims of "this perversion, that the divine nature is attributed to one or two persons, and denied to all the rest, and denied with fury."[21] When men became blind to their own divinity they would attribute their own lost glory to Christ, and the holy life would exist only as ancient history.

To discover self was to discover truth, and inspiration was the only way into self. The man inspired by his own internal angels could speak truth, unlike those who learned to speak from books, synods, or society. In hiding behind the authority of the past, Christianity had become an exercise of memory instead of an exercise of the soul. With that scholasticism, piety would decay and genius would leave the church for the senate or the market. Only if a new breed of preachers could be found would religion become real again. Demanding total obedience to self, Emerson asked the young clergymen to dedicate themselves to those mystical flashes of insight that would result in no church whatsoever, but a living together of pious poets each praying to that self whose secrets promised everything.

Emerson was accused of encouraging a religion of the ego. People of all shades of religious conviction were either dismayed or outraged, and there was indignation that he had been asked to speak in the first place. Aunt Mary wished the speech consigned to oblivion as an inspiration "of some malign demon,"[22] and a Presbyterian journal discovered signs in the lecture of evil German idealism, Oriental philosophy, Carlyle, and Cousin, and concluded that Emerson was an infidel. Emerson remained composed and relentless throughout, and years later wrote the poem "Uriel" as his own account of his angelic vantage point that allowed him his unobstructed vision in a world beset with blindness.

The divinity school address was the most revealing public statement Emerson ever made. He could declare and win his independence from creed and church. He could not turn from what he understood to be the spirit of Christian morality. His version of inspirational and mystical religion formed the source of all of his other ideas about philosophy, literature, and politics. The rest of his intellectual career was an exercise in the application of the ideas of the divinity school address to other categories of thought. Three implications of that address were to be developed in particular: The view of the created universe as an emanation of God led to the rhapsody of nature; the worship of the eternal and universal spirit and rejection of form disposed him to a more formal idealism; the celebration of the ego and instinct led him to give credence to the contemporary Romantic movement in Europe.

No longer searching for his particular voice, he was now ready to pronounce an unqualified hallelujah to the Ghost of all time and all space. His essay on the Oversoul was the most characteristic statement of idealism in New England and thus of the Transcendental impulse in America. The heavy moral cadence of that essay betrays its particular place of origin, as well as its author's continuing struggle to free himself from a past whose mark on him was indelible.

As the Puritans had attempted to scrutinize the inscrutable essence of God through the concept of divine attributes, so Emerson was faced with the problem of how to put the ineffable into words. The extreme rationalism of the Puritans had allowed them to deduce what they could not know directly. Emerson had the more difficult task of relying on rhetoric to describe the unutterable. He hoped to communicate in words his own wordless ecstasy to an audience that would respond in kind; he hoped to penetrate into subverbal regions where his words would ignite a spark of recognition of truth men felt but did not know. At the heart of his technique was his fundamental assumption that the truth he wrote was already in the unconscious of every reader or listener; he had to release rather than instill truth. Words could start a fire that words could not describe.

The transcendent unity of the ostensibly heterogeneous universe was the Oversoul. God and man, flowers and rocks, all merged into that eternal ideal and became indistinguishable from each other:

> We live in succession, in division, in parts, in particles. Meantime within man is the soul of the whole; the wise silence; the universal beauty, to which every part and particle is equally related; the eternal ONE. And this deep power in which we exist and whose beatitude is all accessible to us, is not only self-sufficing and perfect in every hour, but the act of seeing and the thing seen, the seer and the spectacle, the subject and the object, are one.[23]

Refusing to be blinded by separate trees, men could view the sacred forest whose voice would sing of transcendent unity. The aeolian harp he kept in his study window was activated by the breath of God.

The merely apparent physical existence of particularities was unreal, while the spirit which they contained was all. Fleshly men were mere canisters for the universal soul. When the illumination fell on man's mind it became genius; when on his will, virtue; and when on his affections, love.

Men could distinguish the real from the apparent, truth from seeming, instinctively. Man's soul, not his mind, perceived and revealed truth, and men knew the soul's voice from the cacophony of mind or will as they knew when they were awake that they were awake. The soul's revelation of truth always elicited feelings of the sublime because truth was the result of man merging with divinity. A reliance on mere intellect resulted in man's drowning in words. Language itself was a sign of deception. Truth was supraverbal and unconscious, and its presence was often marked by the soul's mute worship of itself. Rationality, custom, an unwillingness to face the divine flame in his own breast—these were the obstacles to the soul's freedom.

Using rhetoric against itself, Emerson hoped that his words would release the wordless truth in his readers, none of whom, he counseled, should take truth second-hand from anyone. If there was an authentic release, the audience would know truth not because of Emerson's authority, but because of each man's original experience of the things of his own soul as it lifted itself to the heaven of transcendent unity and became God.

Time as well as space was a merely apparent limitation, though the blind called that idea insane. History was the record of the one mind of all men. Since each particular mind was the one universal mind also, it was true that all of history was contained in the experience of each individual. Each actual man therefore was also the living record of the total race; introspection and historical research would find the same answers to the same questions. Looking inward or backward men would discover the transcendent. "All history becomes subjective; in other words there is properly no history, only biography."[24] The fundamental unity of mind, and nature as the correlative of that mind, were the ideal solvents in which time and space would dissolve by making the each and the all indistinguishable.

Evil might tend to disappear in a universe that mounted to transcendence. Since the particular rose to become unified with all, the evil of the particular would, as Emerson earlier believed, not merely become good, but was an essential part of good. It was not, as has frequently been said of him, that Emerson ignored evil; he justified it. It was not that he simply turned away from the less attractive world of men and things to the lovelier ideal world; he had the facility to look hard at the actual world, to see its pain and misery, and to pronounce all good as necessary links in the chain that ascended to heaven. The elder Henry James, while in hot pursuit of Swedenborg, knew that there was something diabolical in Emerson's seeming sweetness, that there was more than an empty optimism blowing from the direction of Concord. James saw enough to conclude that Emerson "had no conscience, in fact, and lived by perception, which is an altogether lower or less spiritual faculty." Emerson was therefore "fundamentally treacherous to civilization, without being at all aware himself of the fact."[25]

Yeats was wrong when he declared that Emerson lacked a vision of evil. Emerson's vision was acute, and though he preferred to look upward, he knew what the world below was made of, and continued to believe that the lower world was also right. He saw disease and called it health. But he did not merely look at evil and see good; he saw evil as evil and called that good. He was no more blind to the world's evil than any loyal son of Puritan fathers could be. The undercurrent of diabolism in Emerson's ostensible optimism showed Baudelaire, Nietzsche, and Gide that there was something more to be found in Carlyle's "angel" or James' "unfallen friend" than was immediately apparent.

The key to Emerson's idea of good and evil is to be found in the radical dualism of experience and idea. He labored throughout his intellectual life to achieve an ideal unity, but his experience in the world was also a brute fact from which he could not altogether hide. The divergence of faith and experience contained the unintended diabolism in his will to sweetness. His faith was forced on him by what Emerson had himself called "the ghastly reality of things." His life was made possible through continued assertions of the reality of ideal and the unreality of daily experience.

Idealism allowed him to continue to subscribe to the idea of compensation he had held from his youth. Evil was actual and therefore real only as a symbol of an absolutely benign ideal reality: "All loss, all pain, is particular; the universe remains to the heart unhurt."[26] As the actual became real only when it was raised to an ideal realm, the unidealized actual supposedly did not exist: "Good is positive. Evil is merely privative, not absolute: it is like cold, which is the privation of heat. All evil is so much death or nonentity."[27] Such affirmation was Emerson's characteristic response to the question of evil, but the idea of compensation held a secret he perhaps hid from himself.

His more mature thoughts about the idea of compensation were not significantly different from the theory he announced when his eyes first became diseased. But the concentration of mood was new, and the vision of evil was more radically controlled. Evil might be understood as it was raised to harmonize with the universal spirit, but did it thereby altogether cease to afflict particular men in the particular present? Could not properly spiritual men drink their fill from God's sweet cup? "There is a crack in every thing God has made. . . . In nature nothing can be given, all things are sold."[28] There was a value to evil and a price on good. His theory of compensation contained an implicit recognition of the stark authenticity of evil which, through faith, one could come to understand, not abolish. The dialectic between good and evil as equal forces was buried under his rhetoric of faith, but his prayer for ideal light in which to see evil did not make the actual evil he described any less actual.   Actuality, as it began to emerge in his writings, was a close approximation of the horror of Edwards' lament over sinners in the hands of an angry God.

There seems to be an obvious difference between Edwards and Emerson on evil.   For Edwards, evil was an integral part of a determined universe and a necessary expression of man's inherent depravity.   Emerson, as the spokesman of universal deification and of absolute self-reliance, knew that the idea of determinism was the central intellectual obstacle he had to overcome if he was to free himself from the past.   The relationship between determinism and evil was one he was obliged to explore.   One of the peculiarities of American thought at the time was its felt need to contend with the Puritan mind, to alter or destroy the intellectual synthesis of the Christian corporation.   As Emerson thought on the problem of evil he turned to the question of freedom.   In so doing he had to stand up to the ghost of Jonathan Edwards.

Unable or perhaps unwilling to attack the Edwardsean logic frontally, Emerson chose the characteristic path of rhetoric.   He recognized that the extent of man's freedom depended on the resolution of conflict between fate and power.   The Oversoul allowed no man to violate its law and prosper.   The higher law regulated events, and man became powerful only when he acted in accordance with its decrees.   Because each man was a particular embodiment of the Oversoul, each man when true to his own deepest nature was, to that degree, true also to God.   Men could make the world by knowing and trusting themselves.   With faith in the interior divinity, man's power was equal to the creation of self and the universe.   Man was free to exercise virtue.   But he was equally free to be stupid, to become lost in detail, particularity, and privacy.

The power of character was one side of the equation; the other was fate, the law of the world.   Emerson knew that free will and fate were mutually exclusive, but he refused to allow the contradiction to oppress him.   No sane man could deny the terrible forces and powers in the world which limited man's freedom.   But it was necessary to health to concentrate on freedom rather than on force: "it is wholesome to man to look not at Fate, but the other way: the practical view is the other."[29] An emphasis on the limits of freedom could produce meanness, and might produce the very darkness feared by those who were too broken in spirit to turn to the light.

Emerson could not decide which way to look. There was health in facing freedom, but wisdom in facing fate. Accuracy demanded cognizance of evil, which, in turn, produced a tragic sense. What he called the American tendency to boast and brag betrayed a surface view of reality; great men and great nations had learned to see and resist terror. The Puritans, he said, had the dignity that came from that sense.

In the temple of nature, man might feel the rapture of ideal harmony, but that was of no concern to nature. The natural world was neutral so man had to put nature to his purposes; it would not voluntarily serve men. "The world is rough and surly, and will not mind drowning a man," he said in a Melvillean vein. The absolute tyranny of nature set limits to human freedom beyond which no man might trespass. Human power was restricted by race, temperament, sex, and climate. Man's will was everywhere limited by the unconcerned force of nature and of his own total self. He could act in one way and not in another: "Nature is what you may do. There is much you may not." He admitted that "once we thought positive power was all. Now we learn that negative power, or circumstance, is half."[30] True; but half was not all.

There was, he believed, a limitation to limits, a circle enclosing the iron ring of necessity. Fate was natural history, but natural history was not all of history. Fate had its lord in man. "For though Fate is immense, so is Power, which is the other fact in the dual world, immense. If Fate follows and limits Power, Power attends and antagonizes Fate."[31] Undaunted by the blatant contradiction in his position, Emerson made the bald statement that "freedom is necessary." The ghost of Edwards may have been scandalized by such logic, but perhaps it was also, in its pride, gratified that the old syllogisms were still unchallenged.

Man, according to Emerson, could turn his disabilities to advantage, could put nature and its tyranny to work for his own purposes. Thought freed men to do what they had to do, Emerson concluded with Edwards. Men were free to obey, not now the Jehovah of Northampton, but the spirit in and out of man. In language that Edwards might have used, Emerson said that "with the perception of truth is joined the desire that it shall prevail; that affection is essential to will."[32] To perceive nature's truth was to desire to act truly. For Edwards the will had been identical with the good which was perceived. And so now with Emerson. If men were caught in the slough of the actual, it was a result of their faulty perception. But could men correct their faulty perception, or was that too a result of natural forces over which they had no control and for which they could not be held responsible?

> All men, in the abstract, are just and good; what hinders them in the particular is the momentary predominance of the finite and individual over the general truth. The condition of our incarnation in a private self seems to be a perpetual tendency to prefer the private law, to obey the private impulse, to the exclusion of the law of universal being.[33]

Personification encouraged particularity, and both were obstructions to truth.

To be struck with the divine fire of the Oversoul was to perceive rightly, a belief akin to the Puritan idea that regeneration altered perception. To perceive was to do, and perception came and went with the spirit in the woods. Thus the question of responsibility for acts committed in the absence of the spirit was still unanswered. It was one thing to say that the spirit saved, and quite another to damn those who had not been visited by that spirit. Edwards had reasoned to that conclusion, but Emerson could not. Emerson's hero was made by the spirit, as Edwards' saint had been. Neither the hero nor the saint could will his own salvation, as each had to pray for a divine visitation. Bathed in the light of the ideal, Emerson's man would be forced to be free, to be true to the self that had been raised to universality through no act of its own.

In the Emersonian dialectic between force and freedom, nature and thought, it became increasingly clear that freedom and thought could come only in obedience to the laws of the Oversoul or in obedience to force and nature. From that eternal dialectic he asserted the reality of man's free will; from the same dialectic Edwards had deduced an absence of freedom. Because Emerson was not blind to an evil he could not bear to look at, he answered an intolerable experience with the rhetoric of faith.

That faith had a dark side to which he may have been blind. It came from his inability to see evil in evil, from the implicit cruelty of his optimism. Emerson announced that a belief in universal depravity was the uttermost profanity, that it was one basis for atheism, and would lead to mass suicide should it ever be widely accepted. Replacing universal depravity with universal deification, Emerson became a mystical gentleman who was led either to aloofness or to justification of crime, either to the usual renunciation of the mystic or to the usual acceptance of society of the gentleman. He intended to do neither and denied both, but the fiend hiding in his apparent magnanimity is there, whether Emerson liked it or not.

His response to the death of his son shows the aloofness of his optimism. Experienced misfortune drove him to hide on his ideal hilltop:

> In the death of my son . . . I seem to have lost a beautiful estate, —no more. I cannot get it nearer to me. . . . This calamity . . . does not touch me; something which I fancied was a part of me, which could not be torn away without tearing me nor enlarged without enriching me, falls off from me and leaves no scar. It was caducous. I grieve that grief can teach me nothing, nor carry me one step into real nature.[34]

The icy detachment of Emerson's renunciation of humanity drew a rebuke from Carlyle, who asked Emerson to stop soliloquizing on the eternal mountain tops: "It is cold and vacant up there; nothing paintable but rainbows and emotions; come down and you shall do life-pictures, passions, facts, —which *transcend* all thought, and leave it stuttering and stammering." Emerson answered that he heard the same charges in America, and he did not understand: "If I can at any time express the law and the ideal right, that should satisfy me without measuring the divergence from it of the last act of Congress." He did speak to actuality on occasion, he said, but always felt these occasions to be an intrusion "into another sphere, and so much loss of virtue in my own."[35] If the price of tracking the Oversoul was an intellectual renunciation of actuality, he was glad to pay. Lovers of mankind, reformers, he explained elsewhere, "inquire whether Transcendentalism does not mean sloth: they had as lief hear that their friend is dead, as that he is a Transcendentalist; for then he is paralyzed, and can never do anything for humanity."[36] But men usually loved mankind badly, reformed trifles, and ignored the essential. "Paltry matters" like the abolition of slavery "have a certain air of quackery"[37] and were too particular and too actual to divert the Transcendentalist from his affairs with the cosmos.

When experience was ugly, one could either withdraw or one could justify the ugliness. Even the horror of the slave trade could dissolve in the callousness of optimism:

> A tender American girl doubts of Divine Providence whilst she reads the horrors of 'the middle passage;' and they are bad enough at the mildest; but to such as she these crucifixions do not come; they come to the obtuse and barbarous, to whom they are not horrid, but only a little worse than the old sufferings. They exchange a cannibal war for the stench of the hold. They have gratifications which would be none to the civilized girl.[38]

He thought tragedy to be a result of terror which, in turn, was a result of the belief that the universe was governed by some particular whim. He proclaimed that the idea of whimsical destiny must recede before the reason and faith of civilization, even though the law of the universe would always frustrate ignorant individuals who failed to understand the particularity and unreality of suffering and evil. Only an uninstructed or uninspired person could be thwarted by particular and definite evil because "tragedy is in the eye of the observer, and not in the heart of the sufferer."[39] Because all passion, including melancholy, belonged to the exterior life, suffering from particular causes was always merely superficial, a result of ignorance:

> The intellect is a consoler, which delights in detaching or putting an interval between a man and his fortune, and so converts the sufferer into a spectator and his pain into poetry. It yields the joys of conversation, of letters and of science. Hence also the torments of life become tuneful tragedy, solemn and soft with music, and garnished with rich dark pictures. But higher still than the activities of art, the intellect in its purity and the moral sense in its purity are not distinguished from each other, and both ravish us into a region whereunto these passionate clouds of sorrow cannot rise.[40]

The intellect could teach the beauty of evil, could transform a victim into a spectator of life, could, in short, raise man to that level where in his splendid solitude he could not be hurt in the ways he was always hurt on earth. Mind could save men from experience, and thus Emerson's idealism was central to his optimism. The spirit saves, other Protestants had said.

Emerson still had to face the problem of the man to whom the spirit was a stranger. Men had to wait and to open their minds; they could not do more. The one thing certain was that men could not be self-reliant; they were as much creatures of the active spirit as the Puritan saints had been creatures of the Holy Ghost. Yet, for Emerson, each man was himself the spirit for which he waited, and his salvation was therefore his own doing. Man, as power, could create the world by creating himself. Emerson never did resolve the diverging tendencies of these conclusions, but he remained true to his belief that it was healthier to stand erect as the lord of creation than to cringe out of fear that the spirit might be engaged elsewhere. His optimism was therefore not an inference from his thought but a willed response to a problem he could not and did not want to solve. His optimism was not a conclusion; it was a faith necessary to prevent suicide, as he put it, from depopulating the planet. "I cannot myself use that systematic form which is reckoned essential in treating the science of the mind,"[41] he admitted.

Emerson joined hands with Romanticism partly because of his inability to rationalize the conflict between force and freedom. With scores of other Romantics he condemned the life of reason as inadequate to a truth that could not be encompassed by reason alone. He was reacting against what he thought to be the frigidity of rational Unitarianism, rather than against the infidelities of Voltaire or the coldness of Diderot. Because the American Romantics were not rebelling against the French Enlightenment but against the decay of piety in America, their Romanticism was almost always Christian. They usually thought of instinct not only as power but piety, and usually they were more restrained than their European counterparts by their desire to rediscover a freedom consistent with scripture. The differences between European and American Romanticism were partly differences in mood and degree, and partly a result of the Americans' participation in their own national intellectual tradition.

The demand for freedom characteristic of Romanticism, wherever it flourished, generally included the demand to be free from systems of any kind, including intellectual systems. That Emerson could not meet Edwards on Edwards' own ground was simply irrelevant to Emerson. Intellect without poetry gave a living death:

> The analytic process is cold and bereaving and, shall I say it? somewhat mean, as spying. There is something surgical in metaphysics as we treat it. Were not an ode a better form? The poet sees wholes and avoids analysis; the metaphysician, dealing as it were with the mathematics of the mind, puts himself out of the way of the inspiration; loses that which is the miracle and creates the worship. I think that philosophy is still rude and elementary. It will one day be taught by poets. The poet is in the natural attitude; he is believing; the philosopher, after some struggle, having only reasons for believing.[42]

The mind he condemned as a Romantic was not the mind he affirmed as an idealist. The former was sheer logic or pure reason, while the latter was the incarnation in the particular form of the universal spirit. He thought that the former was restraining and the latter was liberating. As individual freedom was a consistent Romantic goal, that form of mind that sought to enclose the cosmos in system was seen as an enemy of the human spirit. Not comprehending the nature of man, formal thinkers had supposedly deluded themselves into thinking that their own geometric systems described a reality, into confusing their own cleverness with nature. The organic quality of man was necessarily missed by those who elevated reason to an unwarranted position. The nonrational, the instinctive springs of human behavior, were precisely the most precious and the most human. Any other view was mere mechanism, not dynamism; system, not life. Thus it was that "a foolish consistency is the hobgoblin of little minds, adored by little statesmen and philosophers and divines. With consistency a great soul has simply nothing to do."[43] A great soul sought transcendent truth, not intellectual nicety; a great soul sought man in the fullness of his essence, not in the single clarity of his reason.

As Emerson himself understood, his idealism was the source of much of his Romanticism. That the individual should stand alone was a conclusion of the supposed incarnation of the all in the each. Man was God and needed no one and nothing for his spirit. Emerson's dedication to the integrity and radical autonomy of the individual was related to that of the Faust he knew, but had as its goal the freedom from the restraints of self and society that would make religion more vital. He touched but did not embrace the more demonic Romanticism of, say, Goethe, Blake, or Byron. Emerson too had an internal seething creature demanding release; but his creature lived on religious ecstasy, rather than on pure ego. Yet the self was all for Emerson. The difference between him and the representative Europeans was that the ego he worshipped was a smiling power of vast sublimity, while theirs could be an insatiable rage to do and to be and to wreck the universe if need be. Emerson sought to be rather than to do, and he did not find wrecking the universe a congenial pastime. He did seek to wreck the Christian corporation of the seventeenth-century Puritans that had made the individual a mere member of a superior body. He persistently placed the self, with whose freedom nothing should be allowed to interfere, at the center and circumference of the universe.

Obedience to the full particularity of each man's internal voices was the way to freedom and manhood. The self rather than the world should be the teacher of the man. In his essay on "Self-Reliance" Emerson put it well: "A man should learn to detect and watch for that gleam of light which flashes across his mind from within, more than the lustre of the firmament of bards and sages."[44] The explicit presentism of the American intellectual tradition was given additional support by Emerson's conviction that the self was truer than the past, that the true self, in fact, was the past.

The actual and particular self was pressed on one side by the authority of the past, and on the other by the social demands of the present. Authority had to be sloughed off, and society had to be put in its place. It was necessary to pit the self against the world because the self was real, that is, ideal, and the world was merely apparent. The self was sacred and on the way to godhead. Society was the din of material gratification and had absolutely nothing to offer but the interference that meant the soul's death. The struggle to protect the self from the other, the I from the

Thou, had been eternal, because society never progressed. Social change sometimes meant the acquisition of new arts, but old instincts were lost. "The civilized man has built a coach, but has lost the use of his feet."[45] Freedom would come with the realization that the spirit needed no coach in order to roam the world.

In order to understand the centrality of the ego it was necessary to see that social evil and crime were truly irrelevant. The misfortunes of others should not distract a man from the meditation on self. Emerson's idea of compensated evil coupled with his ego worship allowed him to condemn reform and to ignore the pain of others:

> Do not tell me . . . of my obligation to put all poor men in good situations. Are they *my* poor? I tell thee, thou foolish philanthropist, that I grudge the dollar, the dime, the cent I give to such men as do not belong to me and to whom I do not belong. There is a class of persons to whom by all spiritual affinity I am bought and sold; for them I will go to prison if need be; but your miscellaneous popular charities; the education at college of fools; the building of meeting-houses to the vain end to which many now stand; alms to sots, and the thousand-fold Relief Societies; —though I confess with shame I sometimes succumb and give the dollar, it is a wicked dollar, which by and by I shall have the manhood to withhold.[46]

The man with the courage to heed his own genius in a society gone mad with materialism would be Emerson's Man Thinking. The authentic individual with the vision of glory could follow his ego up to greatness by rejecting "emphatic trifles" such as friends, children, and charity. The self was the all, and the rest was therefore nothing. Though cold reason might demand a mitigation of ego worship, "heroism feels and never reasons, and therefore is always right." Though Christianity might demand more compassion, what would it serve for man to turn from God to men, from self to the low state of the particular? A hero could emerge from the crowd of little men if he would will his own obedience to his inward self. If he allowed interference with his religious ceremony in the woods he would fall from greatness to mere humanity, and Emerson's Romanticism demanded more than that.

He drew the portrait of the hero in *Representative Men*, which he gave as a series of lectures in Boston in 1845–1846, repeated in

England in 1847, and published on the first day of 1850. He drew the faces of the hero, as Carlyle said, "in the line manner," without depth. But he was not interested in the lights and shadows of his subjects' lives because his own eye was on the movement of the Oversoul in time. His subjects were heroes because each had understood the source of human power, each had represented the race of lesser men who had been diverted from greatness by blindness. Emerson drew Plato as the philosopher, Swedenborg as the mystic, Montaigne as skeptic, Shakespeare as the poet, Napoleon as the man of the world, and Goethe as the writer. Most concerned with the meaning of greatness, he made ghosts of his subjects in order to keep the Universal Spirit flowing through their words and deeds.

In mid-nineteenth-century America the emphasis on practical success was supposedly smothering man's innate dream of greatness. The typical American was a boring small drudge. Enclosed in a bank or in a senate, potential giants shrank to mediocrity and lost the opportunity to become Man Thinking. Men were choosing creature comfort instead of greatness, and the shock to manhood was enormous. The race of men lived off the credit of the hero. Societies without the vision of heroism were abhorrent: "enormous populations, if they be beggars, are disgusting, like moving cheese, like hills of ants or of fleas, —the more, the worse."[47]

Each of Emerson's heroes had found a truth which could help others to become free of a spiritually inhibited self. Plato taught all the philosophy in the world, released the idea of the human spirit, and gave men intellectual room in which to grow. Swedenborg found that spirit and made it both more human and more divine. Montaigne understood that every fact wore two faces, one of sensation and one of spirit. He showed the intimate relationship of the two, and his skepticism, standing between idealism and materialism, was manly. Shakespeare found beauty not because he was original but because of his range, because his pulse was that of his time and place. Napoleon was the other hero, the man whose greatness came from pushing a command of sensible material to its limit, the man of practical power. But he too owed his stature to the representative quality of his deeds. Because Napoleon's goal was mere actual wealth of one kind or another, he was the hero who would inevitably fail, but, nevertheless, the world was indebted to him for a picture of the enormous reach of man. Napoleon represented the external life of the nineteenth century. Goethe was its internal life, the most modern reincarnation of the universal spirit, and alone rescued the era from the dreary monotony of an otherwise unheroic moment. Emerson's depiction of the peculiar genius of each individual was an extension of the Puritan concept of the calling. Each man had a divinely appointed task which, if discovered and honored, would lead to success.

Sharing the worship of the individual with the Romantics, Emerson shared too in their conviction that the individual truth was hidden in nonverbal, nonrational corners of the psyche, that the instinctive and unconscious life was true in a way that consciousness could never be. Nature was the wordless analogy of the human mind, and its truths would not yield to the power of words. The wordlessness of truth and beauty required silent faith about which only the poet could sing. Unconscious vision was required to see where words could not go: "the path of science and letters is not the way into nature. The idiot, the Indian, the child and unschooled farmer's boy stand nearer to the light by which nature is to be read, than the dissector or the antiquary."[48] Instinct, rather than mind, was the way to truth, and on this level Nietzsche found Emerson a source of inspiration.

Dependence on self was an aesthetic as well as an ethical theory. The creation of beauty was a consequence of giving expression to the absolutely unutterable but raging spirit. To put a spark from the unconscious fire into words was poetry; into form, painting and sculpture; and into action, morality. But the transformation of that spark necessarily changed it from its own holy essence into something baser: "For poetry was all written before time was, and whenever we are so finely organized that we can penetrate into that region where the air is music, we hear those primal warblings and attempt to write them down, but we lose ever and anon a word or a verse and substitute something of our own, and thus miswrite the poem."[49] The artist could only suggest, not complete, as virtually every nineteenth-century Romantic agreed. The inexpressible was at the heart of Romantic expression; as Keats said,

> Heard melodies are sweet, but those unheard
> Are sweeter.

And Emerson with less grace but equal conviction: "A beauty not explicable is dearer than a beauty which we can see to the end of."[50] There was an "unknown country" which was the source of beauty and truth, and men could only try to map a terrain they could not see. The result was always puny compared to the glory of the unseen, but the result was all of the best in the human story. He put it well: "Consciousness is but a taper in the great night; but the taper at which all the illumination of human arts and sciences was kindled."[51]

The artist gave form to the formless beauty of the universal spirit in his unconscious, and he was a passive instrument of a transcendent power. Emerson's irresolution about free will and fate continued to trouble him, and he was compelled to conclude that self-reliance was wholly irrelevant to the creation of timeless beauty. "The muse may be defined," he said, as *"Supervoluntary ends effected by supervoluntary means."*[52] When the Oversoul bestired itself in a man, he could reach to beauty; when it slumbered, the man could merely wait passively for the interior shock, whose appearance he could not cause.

His Romanticism affirmed an individuality that was rejected by his idealism. His Romantic demand for heroes inclined him to place the individual against the world, while his idealism converted the individual into the world. Either way, creativity came from some expressive silence in the artist which was called variously, depending on which direction Emerson was leaning, the universal spirit or the unconscious. The former led to ideal unity, and the latter led to an affirmation of differences. In neither case, however, was the artist's own will or consciousness the source of his strength. The philosopher of self-reliance almost always abandoned the self to a divine fire which raged only when it pleased. And when it raged it melted the individuality of the artist so that he flowed into the eternal stream of beauty and truth. The same mind that created nature created art, and the individual was the instrument through which that mind asserted part of itself. Man was the mind of God which man could not command. But men had nothing and no one to turn to but themselves, and thus, taking their own silent counsel, they had to wait for their own inner fire to be lighted. They could wait in readiness, no more.

The illuminated mind would provoke other minds to seek their own light away from the confusion of society, away from the actual. The solitary individual, on his knees but with his soul erect, praying to the God within for inspiration, was the unit and body of the enduring world. The other world of things and flesh, the world of conflict and politics, was a mere distraction whose power, however, was strong enough to kill the God in men. In order for the individual to become the world in idealism, he had to shun the world as a Romantic.

Actual political and social involvement meant death. Political life was a contradictory life lived after the fact. Politics, he thought, was a futile and useless attempt to reform individual character. He believed that moral regeneration through the education of the outer man to the existence and power of the inner man was the way to achieve the goals of politics, thereby making government unnecessary. Angels, John Adams also knew, did not need government, but Adams always suspected that men were not completely angelic.

Certain qualities of Emerson's thought become highlighted in his occasional writings about politics in America. He did not usually think of himself as either politically shrewd or learned. The hard realities of politics offended both his taste and his idealism, and he regularly regretted the necessities which compelled his often grudging attention. Those necessities were always questions of morality. Loathing many of the men and issues that dominated American political life, he occasionally found his conscience forcing him to think in their terms, to come down from the secluded hilltop that he preferred. Once down on the common plain he usually grumbled about the vulgar company and unedifying problems to be found there. It took him many years to find his way, and when once found it never suited the refinement to which he had trained himself for a lifetime. He was a New Englander in the spiritual line of Edwards, not of Winthrop or Adams. Actuality was a distraction which he resented, but enough of the Puritan social conscience remained with him to force him slowly to a greater political responsibility than he cared for.

His political awareness began as opposition to Andrew Jackson and the people who made the crude Hero of New Orleans President of the United States. Early in 1828 Emerson began his political development in the privacy of his journal: "Public opinion, I am sorry to say, will bear a great deal of nonsense. There is scarce any absurdity so gross . . . which it will not bear. . . . It will bear

Andrew Jackson for President."[53]   Jackson's second presidential campaign found Emerson's position changed in no way: "we shall all feel dirty if Jackson is reelected."[54]

America's continuing and still deplorable imitation of English styles and manners extended to politics also.   Both political and cultural nationalism were desirable responses to European superiority and American servility.   The scholarly and gentlemanly Webster, an early hero for Emerson, overcame this dependence on England through the force of his native genius.   And the Jacksonians too, out of the magnitude of their ignorance, might contribute to the discovery of a more authentic American political style.   "I suppose the evil [of imitating English forms] may be cured by this rank rabble party, the Jacksonism of the country, heedless of English and of all literature . . .; they may root out the hollow dilettantism of our cultivation in the coarsest way, and the new-born may begin again to frame their own world with greater advantage."[55]   The Democrats were "demoniacal or magnetic," as "all brutes are,"[56] and their very energy might someday be turned to virtue.

The theoretical possibility that the barbarism of the Jacksonian Democrats would be a healthy purge of intellectual dependence on England was not strong enough to compensate for what Emerson saw as their immortality.   He found the unpleasantness of the Democrats unbearable, and he ran for refuge and solitude to his woods.   Should he ever become overly fond of being alive, he wrote, "I would go to a Jackson Caucus . . . and I doubt not the unmixed malignity, the withering selfishness, the impudent vulgarity, that mark those meetings would speedily cure me of my appetite for longevity.   In the hush of these woods I find no Jackson placards affixed to the trees."[57]

The Concord woods could shield him from the noise and boorishness of Jacksonian Democracy, but his mind could not ignore the problem of an ideal democracy.   Flesh and blood Democrats grated against his adopted Brahmin social code, but abstract democracy—peopled only with shadowy citizens of some City of God—had an intellectual appeal that took him some years to understand.   Why was it, for instance, that the "Whigs have the best men, Democrats the best cause"?   He was convinced that the Democrats were "destructive, not constructive.   What hope, what end have they?"[58]   The goal of the Democrats was not democracy, as

Emerson understood it. A genuine democracy required citizens more moral than any Democrat he knew. He tried to explain to his journal: "When I spoke or speak of the democratic element, I do not mean that ill thing, vain and loud, which writes lying newspapers, spouts at caucuses, and sells its lies for gold, but that spirit of love for the general good whose name this assumes. There is nothing of the true democratic element in what is called Democracy; it must fall, being wholly commercial."[59]

Emerson published his first extended essay on politics in 1844 and incorporated into it many of the random ideas he had previously been noting in his journal. As he developed his political theory he continued to rarify it, to idealize it, to make his political world unfit for any but the angels on God's right hand. Which is to say, that he began to integrate his political ideas with the rest of his Transcendental point of view.

For Emerson the individual man was all, the state was nothing. In direct opposition to the Puritans' notion of the Christian corporation, of the primacy of society over its members, Emerson argued that public morality could be achieved only one man by one man, and that the society would reflect the character of its individual constituents. John Adams had insisted that the state could force men to limit their viciousness and weakness; Emerson believed that the state could elicit only the worst in men. Thoroughly rejecting John Taylor's affirmation of the community, Emerson nevertheless agreed with Taylor that the government should recede into a dim distance, that free enterprise and individual initiative would automatically arrange both society and the state in the most natural and beneficial order.

Emerson's ecstatic Christianity led him away from the city into the woods to commune with an entire society in the abstract rather than deal with living men in the flesh. As Jonathan Edwards had found the presence of the Lord in the woods around Northampton, so Emerson fled from men to the isolation and serenity of the country around Concord. But Emerson, unlike Edwards, extracted political thought out of ecstasy. He derived a social theory out of the Protestant relationship of the isolated individual with his God. Out of his rejection of fleshly society, his preference for the calmer world of pure essence and abstraction, he developed an ethereal polis that was no polis, but one where he believed authentic individuals could live unbothered and untroubled by their neighbors. More of a Protestant than either Winthrop or Adams, more secular than Edwards, less of an agrarian than Taylor, Emerson began to fashion what was to become the standard American rhetoric about its political system, a system that existed nowhere but in the minds of those, like Emerson, who could confuse their reveries with possibilities and both with reality. His Romantic celebration of the individual, his hope that men could become heroes, led him to his antisocial society, his unpolitical polis. That he did not genuinely like his fellowmen, that he was as much of a misanthrope as John Adams, was the rock on which Emerson based his political thought.

Emerson's state rested on the shoulders of the moral heroes he imagined as its citizens. At best the state was a mere convenience invented by fallible mortals, and should always be viewed with the understanding that things should be done differently. He thought that no political institution was superior to a single true man, and no aspect of society was above reform. Every law was originally one man's idea, and the ideas of the present should always take precedence over the ideas of the past. The state was, in his view, a contrivance that should serve men; men should not serve the state.

The state existed to protect property and persons. The natural equal rights of persons demanded democracy for full protection. But persons' rights in property were not equal. Emerson, in the full flush of a primitive laissez-faire economic theory, believed that the amount of property owned by each individual was the natural and right amount for each individual. In language that the most virulent robber baron would have applauded, he explained: "One man owns his clothes, and another owns a county. This accident, depending primarily on the skill and virtue of the parties, of which there is every degree, and secondarily on patrimony, falls unequally and its rights of course are unequal."[60] The grand problem, as he saw it, was to determine the proper relationship between the equal rights of persons and the unequal rights of property.

Having articulated his crude and potentially cruel economic ideas, Emerson almost immediately made them irrelevant; "there is an instinctive sense, however obscure and yet inarticulate, that the whole constitution of property, on its present tenures, is injurious, and its influence on persons deteriorating and degrading; that truly the only interest for the consideration of the State is persons."[61] If government could contribute to the moral elevation of men, that improvement of individuals would be reflected in reformed institutions and law. He did not explain why reforms would be needed if the government were already benign enough to elevate man's moral nature.

The best that he could say of the actual function of government was that it was sometimes convenient. No actual government, he said, ever conformed either to its own claims or the legitimate demands of its citizens: "Every actual State is corrupt. Good men must not obey the laws too well. What satire on government can equal the severity of censure conveyed in the word *politic*, which now for ages has signified *cunning*, intimating that the State is a trick?"[62] This language could be fashioned into a revolutionary instrument of civil disobedience by Thoreau, but for the master, for Emerson himself, it now meant simply that government was a noisome distraction from the spiritually invigorating mysteries of Concord's woods, mysteries whose pursuit was the real business of life. Emerson's political language frequently led in one of two directions, toward revolutionary anarchism or toward apolitical withdrawal. Thoreau, as the ideal disciple, swung easily from one position to the other, while Emerson usually understood himself to mean that separation from an evil world would at least protect himself from infection.

Having basked in the divine light of the Lord that shone in his woods, having felt his spirit rise out of the flesh to meet the angels of light, Emerson was utterly convinced that the major difficulty with politics was the inability of more earthly men to cleave to eternal principle, to forget their own petty lusts and needs in the interest of the transcendent good of all. The Whigs of the 1840's had good men but bad principles. The Democrats had bad men, but democracy was a principle that even the translucent spirit of Concord could bless. The concrete result of having one party with virtue and talent and no principle, and the other party with principle but no talent or virtue, was for him the impossibility of participating in politics. Thus, again, a once revolutionary concept was now tamed to permit mere personal protection from bad manners on the one hand and bad ideas on the other.

Emerson's vision of the potential but usually unrealized divinity of men made the concept of equality difficult for him. His worship of the individual made it difficult for him to comprehend society. As he came to support a moral as well as an intellectual hierarchy of persons, the crucial doctrine of equality came to seem increasingly vague. The only equality he admitted was that rarely exercised ability of all men to live as they knew they should live. The Romantic hero was uncomfortable in a mass society, and the more equality seemed to repress the divine individuality of the moral giants, the more Emerson rejected equality. He went so far as to imply that if democracy demanded equality, and if equality demanded conformity, he would abandon democracy. But he was never thoroughly persuaded that a true democracy would destroy the fine balance between a man and his own unconscious. Though he did reject vital aspects of a mass society and the Democratic Party, he maintained a typically delicate grasp on democratic theory, after he spiritualized it to make it conform to his vision of a community of great individuals, all obedient to themselves, each man a complete moral and therefore political unit, and thus, it must be said, with no need of a community in the first place. His political ideal was a state made up of individuals who neither needed nor wanted a state.

The opportunity to judge precisely the extent of moral rot in America was given to him by the Mexican War. Many New Englanders abhorred the war as a plot on the part of Southern slave holders to extend their territories, or as an ill-concealed scheme of the Democratic Party to increase its influence. Thoreau quietly refused to pay his tax and went to jail. Emerson wrote in his journal.

Perhaps a majority of Americans, caught up in the spirit of Manifest Destiny, supported the annexation of Texas and the Mexican War. For Emerson that was a comment, not on the issue, but on the majority: "Majorities, the argument of fools, the strength of the weak."[63] The collective people was an idiot who could be led around at will; "the hordes of ignorant and deceivable natives and the armies of foreign voters who fill Pennsylvania, New York, and New Orleans" were easily manipulated "by those unscrupulous editors and orators who have assumed to lead these masses."[64] Because the idea of greatness had been debased by little men with big power, the masses could be duped into thinking that the southern expansion of the nation was a glorious adventure.

The war was a symptom, not a cause, of the meanness of American political life. "The people are no worse since they invaded Mexico than they were before, only they have given their will a deed."[65] Southerners demanded fresh lands for their slave economy, and Northerners yielded to Southern demands. To the imaginary slave owners whom Emerson maintained in the privacy of his study, he explained: "but do you know why Massachusetts and New York are so tame? —it is because we own you, and are very tender of our mortgages which cover all your property."[66] That the nation could descend to vast action on the basis of mere material considerations was all the evidence Emerson required to turn back in disgust to his woods with the firm knowledge that there he could refresh his soul and purge the vile masses from his mind.

Again, as with the Jacksonians, Emerson had a certain bitter admiration for the leaders of the war, for what he considered to be their uninhibited barbarism. After Polk's war message was accepted by the Congress, Emerson fulminated in his journal: "These—rabble—at Washington are really better than the snivelling opposition. They have a sort of genius of a bold and manly cast, though Satanic."[67] By now he had decided that the public was opposed to the war and was being manipulated by designing politicians, that the public was merely weak and perhaps stupid instead of evil. Even the once-magnificent Webster had voted for war, and Emerson began to suspect that this idol of more peaceful days had developed a low-level infection of the moral sense.

Thoreau's civil disobedience was more of a challenge to Emerson. He admired the directness of Thoreau's act and seems to have felt some discomfort at the contrast with his own passivity. He quickly found that Thoreau had erred on the side of failing to take a sufficiently large view. For the monomaniacal abolitionists going to jail was a suitable action; their single-mindedness would be served by so restricted a protest. For one who was less of a literalist than the abolitionists, for one whose view of the world was adequately encompassing and unifying, nothing short of universal moral regeneration would serve as reform. For such a political Transcendentalist, "no government short of a monarchy, consisting of one king and one subject, will appease you. Your objection [he told Thoreau in the safety of his journal], then, to the State of Massachusetts is deceptive. Your true quarrel is with the state of Man."[68] The universal reformation of man was obviously a subject worthy of attention. Much as he deplored the jingoism and aggressiveness of the Mexican War, Emerson again thought his way out of public commitment and into the accustomed serenity of his study. Thoreau became a fool in Emerson's journal: "Why should he poorly pound on some one string of discord, when all is jangle?"[69]   One must address the universe of evil or retire. Emerson seems not yet to have understood that for addressing the universe of evil retirement was essential, that the abstraction of general evil could be found not in the streets but within range of the tinkling aeolian harp.

Emerson's reflex toward synthesis and generalization now took on a political coloration that was an important move towards a more democratic position. The individual Jacksonian and expansionist deeply offended Emerson. Now he was coming to believe that the abstract body of citizens had better sense and manners than any one of its representatives or members, as Adams and Taylor had already argued. As an American Protestant and Bostonian gentlemen, it was precisely the disembodied abstraction with which he was prepared to deal. The acceptance of abstract man was his first cautious step in the direction of increased public responsibility and toward a set of mind that would not continue to frustrate action. He was finally bringing his politics into greater harmony with the boldness of his religious and literary views. Henceforth he was prepared occasionally to leave his wooded ecstasy and speak to the public good in a steadier voice than he had ever known before.

Emerson was made into a political man by the moral shock given him by the Compromise of 1850. Henry Clay had introduced the Compromise in the Senate, and almost immediately Emerson wrote that the Southerner was a more effective politician than the Northerner because the Southerner had a stronger personality than the cold and calculating Yankee. The Yankee represented only dollars and cents when a stand for absolute principle was needed. Because they represented wealth, Yankees had become smallminded and were easily manipulated. There were no great men in the political landscape, and the malignant parties thus had a free hand to perform their evil. That the North should accept the Fugitive Slave Act that became part of the final Compromise proved to Emerson that the North was as polluted as the South, that both sections were destroying their morality in favor of wealth. Fixing on this aspect of American politics for the next few years he finally concluded that

> the lesson of these days is the vulgarity of wealth. We know that wealth will vote for the same thing which the worst and meanest of the people vote for. . . . Plainly Boston does not wish liberty, and can only be pushed and tricked into a rescue of a slave. Its attitude as loving liberty is affected and theatrical.[70]

Emerson had been thinking and writing about the issue of slavery in America for quite a long time. The Fugitive Slave Act toughened his language and placed slavery in a realer political perspective; his earlier views had been vaguer and less human, as befitted a developing Transcendentalist. He had first attempted some extended analysis of slavery when he was twenty years old. He then believed that the Negro was more of a brute than a man. He argued then, as he continued to do for many years, that nature had created men unequal, and that some were natural servants of others. Thereby he approximated Aristotle's idea of the natural slave. But the young Emerson felt, though he did not know, that something was wrong with slavery as it was practiced in his own country. The best he could then do was to answer that it violated the universal and natural moral sense of men. After the natural bestiality of the Negro was appreciated, it still seemed that he was a man. As a man his enslavement was a violation of man's universal freedom of will. The argument was weak, and Emerson faced several serious refinements of his position before he was prepared to encounter the crisis of 1850.

His first step was the liberalization of his religion. By 1835, a few years after he had broken with the church, he could summon his vision of a primitive and transcendent Christianity to his aid. The earlier agonizing is completely absent as his sense of the superiority of the spirit gave some life to his new stand:

> Let Christianity speak ever for the poor and the low. Though the voice of society should demand a defence of slavery, from all its organs, that service can never be expected from me. . . . The life of this world has but a limited worth in my eyes, and really is not worth such a price as the toleration of slavery.[71]

He admitted that he was unwilling to denounce the planters because he feared the bloody consequences of such articulate dissent
in the nation, but he prayed that he might never befoul himself
by uttering a syllable of apology for slavery.

As the single-mindedness and perhaps directness of Thoreau's
protest in the Mexican War seem to have disturbed Emerson, so
the abolitionists earned many pages of similar denunciation in his
journal. His own position continued to be that slavery was a thorough evil that he should not criticize or defend in public. Slavery
was an evil, but merely one among many. The nature of significant social reform occupied an increasing amount of his attention
in the late 1830's and early 1840's, when the nation at large was
besieged by reformers of every kidney.

As one who had already enlisted in the reform of the eternal
spirit, Emerson had to make some peace with the reformers of
the here and now. He argued that any man who addressed himself to any particular evil, regardless of its malignancy, was necessarily myopic; the full range of man's essential being would open
to nothing less than Emerson's own inclusive vision of the eternal
Oversoul. Reformers, in looking too low, necessarily missed the
higher and vital nature of the transcendent human spirit. Staring
fixedly at the transcendent spirit and away from particular matter,
Emerson displayed the potential cruelty of his optimism and the
inevitable paralysis of the political reflex: "The poor . . . are only
they who *feel poor*, and poverty consists in feeling poor."[72] At this
point idealism became a solvent for ridding the world of material
misery by denying the materiality of all misery. Such idealism
constituted a change of view—from the existence of poverty to
the existence of feelings about poverty. Meaningful reform would
therefore attack not poverty, which was insignificant, but feelings
about poverty, which were of the essence. In spiritualizing the
material in this way, Emerson was still paralyzed in the face of
the misery of any single person. He believed that he understood
the agony of the race, but he was unable to encompass concrete
unhappiness in the ethereal and unkind world of spirit he was
constructing.

He was at this time unable to come to a satisfactory definition
of his own role in reform. He said that he could be wise for him-

self, but not for others. Yet he thought that his spirit was the breath needed to inspire men to lift themselves out of the swamp of matter. He could serve men in that way, but only by damaging himself: "What is good to make me happy is not however good to make me write. Life too near paralyses art."[73] Out of his desire to create beauty, to achieve the immortality of genius, he once again sundered his humanity from his mind. His definition of his role in reform was dictated, not by the problems of society, but by the needs of the self that seemed to stretch only when it was away from the limited cares of mortal men.

The experiment at Brook Farm found him consistent in his rejection of reform aimed at less than the universe and in his rejection of any organization. Still in search of the self that seemed to disintegrate in the presence of others, he found Brook Farm not responsive to the pressing problem of his life: Who was he? Would genius ever come to lift him from the slough of the ordinary? He could continue to hunt for his evasive self in the woods where he was; Brook Farm was hugely irrelevant to his problem.

Steadfast in his pursuit of the spark that would ignite his inner self and release the genius whose secret existence he felt to be real, Emerson was uncomfortable about the life of the mind. He was enough of a Yankee to honor the labor of a simple and honest farmer. He found himself in a box with no exit: he honored the spiritual life and felt guilty, by his admission, about its impracticality, its un-American quality. "I feel some shame before my woodchopper, my ploughman, and my cook, for they have some sort of self-sufficiency, they can contrive without my aid to bring the day and year round, but I depend on them, and have not earned by use a right to my arms and feet."[74] As part of himself rejected what he wanted most, he showed himself to be the ideal son of those dedicated Puritans in his own background who had perfected the knack of crying a smile. The literary class, he said to an audience of mechanics' apprentices in Boston, was "enervated and sickly" and its work was marred by "too great fineness, effeminacy, and melancholy." It was of greater moment to have better authors and worse books, if that was a necessary price. In any event an author should pay some price for excusing himself from the hard but honest Yankee ethic: "that man . . . ought to ransom himself from the duties of economy by a certain rigor and privation in his habits. . . . Let him be a caenobite, a pauper, and if need be, celibate also. Let him learn to eat his meals standing, and to relish the taste of fair water and black bread."[75] If poverty and the mortification of the flesh accompanied the monkish life of the mind he envisioned, the guilt of refusing to play the Yankee game would, hopefully, decrease.

The political meaning of his recommendation of poverty could not have been lost on the mechanics' apprentices. Perhaps he felt some bitterness in the air as he applauded a condition his audience doubtless considered in a less favorable light. He felt enough to say now that poverty was something other than the mere feeling of poverty. But he guarded against any radical political implications by surrounding himself with a vision of man that was infused with love and brotherhood:

> The State must consider the poor man, and all voices must speak for him. Every child that is born must have a just chance for his bread. Let the amelioration in our laws of property proceed from the concession of the rich, not from the grasping of the poor.[76]

As a proper Bostonian, Emerson could understand noblesse oblige while failing utterly to appreciate the demands of the American poor. If the conflict of classes could be avoided long enough, the faith he had in man's nature would be vindicated: "But one day all men will be lovers; and every calamity will be dissolved in the universal sunshine."[77] One wonders whether any of the apprentices understood that Emerson had told them of the virtues of poverty, that all must have a "just chance" to eat, that the rich should grant and the poor receive, that the poor should be patient if the rich were selfish, and that one day in the future men would truly be angels and need only the sounds of an aeolian harp for nourishment. His analysis of poverty was an ideal rationalization for maintaining things exactly as they were.

The fatal failure of reformers to see that they did not know what they were doing invalidated all effort at reform for Emerson. He suggested that all the reformers were bad Protestants who emphasized works rather than faith, and, being of little or no faith, their good works had turned rotten and collapsed. Relying on the language of his fathers Emerson tried to explain to Boston: "The young men who have been vexing society for these last years with regenerative methods seem to have made this mistake; they all exaggerated some special means, and all failed to see that the Reform of Reforms must be accomplished without means."[78] Possibly fortified by his unspoken insight into the religion of reform, Emerson could return to an extension of his earlier view that oppression consisted only of inadequate faith on the part of the oppressed; the slave was a man who felt like a slave; change his thought and you emancipate him:

> How trivial seem the contests of the abolitionist, whilst he aims merely at the circumstance of the slave. Give the slave the least elevation of religious sentiment, and he is no slave; he not only in his humility feels his superiority, feels that much deplored condition of his to be a fading trifle, but he makes you feel it too.[79]

The true scholar, Emerson admitted, must keep his mind open to every new idea, to every intellectual possibility. But faced with a concrete situation like slavery, Emerson stood solidly on a cloud and insisted that the only possibilities were intellectual ones. It was unimportant whether a man's body was enslaved as long as his mind was free. No slave owner could have desired a more satisfactory defense of slavery, a defense that insisted that the institution was too insignificant even to notice.

Never able for very long to ignore the charms and romance of knight errantry, Emerson easily saw himself flashing the Excalibur of the mind over the darkness. But his knightly vows were peculiar in that his most sacred pledge was typically to himself, a pledge perhaps to feel but not to act with others:

> If a humane measure is propounded in behalf of the slave, or of the Irishman, or the Catholic, or for the succor of the poor; that sentiment, that project, will have the homage of the hero. That is his nobility, his oath of knighthood, to succor the helpless and oppressed; always to throw himself on the side of weakness, of youth, of hope; on the liberal, on the expansive side, never on the defensive, the conserving, the timorous, the lock-and-bolt system. More than our good-will we may not be able to give. We have our own affairs, our own genius, which chains each to his proper work.[80]

Utilizing a curious amalgam of the Calvinist concept of the calling and Romantic heroism, Emerson made himself into a Quixote who, however, never needed even a physical windmill. He was prepared to tilt at the phantoms of the spirit in his own spiritual way. And that way did not yet lead away from solitude.

Merely six years before the Compromise of 1850 he was still advocating a cultivation of the self as supposedly doing more for the slave than all the combined oratory of the abolitionists. He demanded symmetry of abolition—that it should reject the products of slave labor, that it should turn toward its own moral shortcomings before pointing its finger. His notion of symmetry meant that the abolitionists "must stop all this boast and frolic and vituperation, and in lowliness free the slave by love in the heart."[81] For him there was no one worthy enough to demand the end of slavery in America. Yet when he met William Lloyd Garrison, Emerson felt respect for him as a man if not as an ideal emanation of the Holy Ghost.

Emerson put the final touches on his thought about reform as it had developed to that time in a lecture called "New England Reformers," which he delivered in the spring of 1844. Reformers had failed for two reasons: They had not understood the partial nature of their reforms, and they had relied on association to make their way. Again the test of reform was its effect not on the evil it was aimed at, but on the reformer himself. The question of association was equally clear to Emerson. His political vision of a sunlit city of lovers each of whom was complete in himself was the basis for his rejection of all cooperation until such time when cooperation would no longer be needed. The only covenant this son of Boston would countenance was one that relied on faith, was entered into by a man and himself, and had nothing to do with the creation or maintenance of society. It was the absolute Protestant covenant he dreamed of, and he would content himself with nothing less than the emergence of the sanctified and spotless Individual who could look God straight in the eye.

Brook Farm, for example, was no better than the plan of madmen who sang of heaven on their way to hell. Abolition would fail because it demanded good of evil men. All were mistaken because of the failure to see that the one was the all, that the individual was the universe. According to Emerson's vision it was possible to do genuine good for all by doing good for self, to remain in Concord with an almost clear conscience.

He defended his own passivity, in part, by insisting that not enough knowledge was available. The reasons for rejecting reform associations were not merely philosophical; they were also eminently practical. Where was the guarantee that a man's fortune would be safe in the new experimental communities? "In this new matter of association are men to blame that they will not leave their homesteads and try the hazardous experiment of a new colony in the woods of the West . . . perilling the means of living of their families? They wish well to your enterprise, but it looks to them by no means wise and secure."[82] The need for guarantees seems not quite consistent with the heroism of which he preferred to dream, but even his heroes seem to have wondered about their next meal from time to time.

When the Fugitive Slave Act became law in September 1850, as part of the Compromise, Emerson was largely unprepared for his own reaction. The first shock was that Webster had fallen and had supported the Compromise. Emerson wrote a little poem:

> Why did all manly gifts in Webster fail?
> He wrote on Nature's grandest brow, *For Sale*.[83]

Because the Fugitive Slave Act was operable in every state of the union, including Massachusetts, Emerson was forced to reconsider his own loyalty to the union. That reconsideration was not easy, but his language was sharp and his analysis had now grown less fearful: "We sneak about with the infamy of crime in the streets and cowardice in ourselves, and frankly, once for all, the Union is sunk, the flag is hateful, and will be hissed."[84] That Act and all that it meant, including the apostacy of Webster, changed Emerson's angle of vision by forcing a hateful change in the world he occupied. Now he welcomed secession as a relief from the dishonor the union had legislated. He felt that legalization of crime was demoralizing the communities of the entire nation, and now felt driven to the abolitionist platform himself.

In 1851 he delivered an abolitionist speech in Cambridge over the shouting of, perhaps, more vocal opposition than he had ever known before. His accustomed serenity of language and beatitude of vision dissolved under the fire of his rare anger: "This Slavery shall not be, it poisons and depraves everything it touches. There can never be peace whilst this devilish seed of war is in our soil.

Root it out, burn it up, pay for the damage, and let us have done with it."[85]

Back in Concord in the same year, he spoke again on "The Fugitive Slave Law," and announced that the Compromise had made him into a political creature:

> The last year has forced us all into politics, and made it a para-
> mount duty to seek what it is often a duty to shun. We do not
> breathe well. There is infamy in the air. I have a new experience.
> I wake in the morning with a painful sensation, which I carry about
> all day, and which, when traced home, is the odious remembrance
> of that ignominy which has fallen on Massachusetts, which robs the
> landscape of beauty, and takes the sunshine out of every hour. I
> have lived all my life in this state, and never had any experience of
> personal inconvenience from the laws, until now. They never came
> near me to any discomfort before.[86]

He told his neighbors that an attempt to abrogate the Act must be their first step, to be followed by some policy that would confine slavery to the states where it then existed, and where it should be encouraged to die. In some way the Fugitive Slave Act had to be made inoperative. Should attempts at abrogation fail, and while abrogation was being sought, Emerson told his audience to disobey the Act. The version of abolition he now supported was compensatory. It would reimburse the owner for his lost property. "I say buy, —never conceding the right of the planter to own, but that we may acknowledge the calamity of his position, and bear a countryman's share in relieving him; and because it is the only practicable course, and is innocent."[87]

On the fourth anniversary of Webster's speech in favor of the Slave Act, Emerson spoke in New York City, and some of the earlier intellectual palsy began to assert itself again. The inward quest for self and genius would not absolutely retire. "I do not often speak to public questions; —they are odious and hurtful, and it seems like meddling or leaving your own work. I have my own spirits in prison; —spirits in deeper prisons, whom no man visits if I do not."[88] He confessed that slavery had been unreal to him until the Slave Act because he had never suffered any inconvenience from it until then. But by now his abolitionist zeal had cooled. No longer demanding the immediate end of slavery, he also now began once more to rely on his faith in the compensations of an eventually benign natural order.

A few years earlier he had confided to the privacy of his journal that his participation in the slavery issue was madness at best and sinfulness at worst. By the summer of 1852 he was no longer certain that the role he had played was consistent with what he most wanted:

> I waked at night, and bemoaned myself, because I had not thrown myself into this deplorable question of slavery, which seems to want nothing so much as a few assured voices. But then, in hours of sanity, I recover myself, and say, "God must govern his own world, and knows his way out of this pit, without my desertion of my post, which has none to guard it but me. I have quite other slaves to free than those negroes, to wit, inprisoned spirits, imprisoned thoughts, far back in the brain of man, —far retired in the heaven of invention, and which, important to the republic of Man, have no watchman, or lover, or defender, but I."[89]

His tentative New York City speech was therefore the partial publicizing of a position he held more enthusiastically in private. For a moment his disgust at Webster and outrage over the issue seemed likely to bring him out of himself. He did emerge, and with honor, for that moment, but almost at once went back to the earlier occupation of musing and rhapsodizing in the woods. Coming events also would leave him no peace. Kansas, John Brown, and Civil War forced him to return to the life of mortal flesh, to speak his words about the City of Man.

As the war came closer and as he thought about man in society, an earlier idea began to assume new significance. Government was the source of all, or most, social evil. What men would never dream of doing singly, they seemed glad to do in Congress. Political association, as reform association, somehow seemed to drain the morality out of the members. Free and private enterprise was the only mechanism suited to a society of potentially great individuals. Laissez-faire was designed as a reflection of growing individualism, and as Emerson made a religion out of the latter he was glad to oversubscribe to the former. "In a free and just commonwealth, property rushes from the idle and imbecile to the industrious, brave and persevering."[90] The hierarchy of wealth thus became identical with the hierarchy of virtue, all of which conformed to the natural order, and any attempt to rearrange the balance could only result in social chaos.

Looking for so long at the individual, Emerson had grown blind to society. He later concluded that the distinction of his milieu had been the discovery of the individual. The corporatism of earlier American society had dissolved and man had been freed from his fellows; the Christian corporation of the Puritans and the republics of virtue of Adams and Taylor had supposedly prepared authentic men to stand alone and be all: "The former generations acted under the belief that a shining social prosperity was the beatitude of man, and sacrificed uniformly the citizen to the State. The modern mind believed that the nation existed for the individual."[91] Romanticism, in his mind, demanded the atomization of society, the freedom of each individual in order that he achieve heroism. Idealism, in his mind, demanded the absolute unity of mankind. The rapidly developing individualism of liberal capitalism reinforced his Romanticism, and the rhetoric of liberal Christianity supported his idealism. The two convictions could easily have paralyzed a more orderly mind, but he continued to assert that unity could be achieved only through atomization.

The individual, not the community, was the source of power and wisdom. The mass of people, as he had earlier half-suggested, was a mere obstacle to the flight of genius; the people had associated and had gone mad:

Leave this hypocritical prating about the masses. Masses are rude, lame, unmade, pernicious in their demands and influence, and need not to be flattered but to be schooled. I wish not to concede anything to them, but to tame, drill, divide and break them up, and draw individuals out of them. The worst of charity is that the lives you are asked to preserve are not worth preserving. Masses! the calamity is the masses. I do not wish any mass at all, but honest men only, lovely, sweet, accomplished women only, and no shovel-handed, narrow-brained, gin-drinking million stockingers or lazzaroni at all.[92]

Starting with an idea of a sacrosanct individual, Emerson continued to search for a formula that would protect his self-sufficient demigod from the incursions of community. Laissez-faire economics, the rejection of social in favor of personal reform, and physical isolation or perhaps elevation were the steps on his path to his ideal of an antisocial society. America, on the verge of war, offended his mind and taste. But he continued to have his mind changed by changing national affairs.

Emerson experienced the initial years of Civil War with no clear picture of the aims either of the North or of Lincoln's administration. He hoped that moral rectitude was on the side of the North, but he feared its "timorous literalism" as a dangerous weakness. The resources of the South were completely occupied in the war, but Northern materialism and sensualism would not be thoroughly diverted even by such a contest. Abolition of slavery as a distinct goal of Northern policy was the missing ingredient that kept Emerson, and others of his persuasion, in a moral limbo during the early years of Civil War.

Eight months before the Emancipation Proclamation, Emerson appealed for official abolition in an address at Washington. He contrasted the ideal with the experienced America, and the ideal for him was as lofty as it had been for the participants of the great migration to the west: "Our whole history appears like a last effort of the Divine Providence in behalf of the human race."[93] America had been intended to offer opportunity to men, but a sniveling Congress, ineffectual President, and corrupt populace seemed perilously close to destroying God's country. In failing to proclaim emancipation as the keystone of Northern policy, the Congress was making a sham of a war that might otherwise have been a glory. Lincoln seemed to have no practical goal and no ideal. The President's humanitarianism was no substitute for a morally grand vision: "President Lincoln should remember," Emerson wrote in his journal, "that humanity in a ruler does not consist in running hither and thither in a cab to stop the execution of a deserter."[94] Still convinced of the validity of the national mythology, but adapting it to his idealism, he viewed the potential role of America as the example of moral superiority to all nations, and the history of America as a descent into common evil. Emerson found himself in his accustomed position of having to choose between a lovely ideal and a base actuality.

The President's Emancipation Proclamation changed everything for Emerson. Now the North was clean, the war heroic, and the outcome predestined. With his refreshed view of the War and of the North he discovered that the intellectual had a positive obligation to relate to politics in a specific manner. "A scholar defending the cause of slavery, or arbitrary government, of monopoly, of the oppressor, is a traitor to his profession. He has ceased to be a scholar. He is not company for clean people."[95] The war could shake men from their comfort and selfishness and make them stretch farther than their reach. Emerson's romance of the war was made possible and probably inevitable by Lincoln's decision to support emancipation.

Lincoln himself was never quite Emerson's idea of a heroic leader of a moral crusade. His crudeness and boorishness recalled the hated Jackson. But Lincoln, as a consequence of Emancipation, came finally to rest in Emerson's mind as the perfect example of the American primitive, a type that suited his philosophy but not his taste. As a primitive, Lincoln had the animal force of a Jackson, which, however, he, unlike Jackson, had turned to high purpose. If the choice were between morality and manners, Emerson was compelled to applaud Lincoln:

> You cannot refine Mr. Lincoln's taste, extend his horizon, or clear his judgment; he will not walk dignifiedly through the traditional part of the President of America, but will . . . cheapen himself. But this we must be ready for, and let the clown appear, and hug ourselves that we are well off, if we have got good nature, honest meaning, and fidelity to public interest, with bad manners, —instead of an elegant *roué* and malignant self-seeker.[96]

In the memorial service Emerson read at Concord four days after Lincoln's death, the theme of the American moral savage was quietly present again. Lincoln "was thoroughly American, had never crossed the sea, had never been spoiled by English insularity or French dissipation; a quite native, aboriginal man, as an acorn from the oak; no aping of foreigners, no frivolous accomplishments."[97] That simmering spiritual power which Emerson had always believed to be an American characteristic, even though it had usually been diverted to petty materialism, found its outlet in Lincoln who was "the true history of the American people in his time . . ., the true representative of this continent."[98]

The transcending unity Emerson had never before found in politics was completed. America became heroic in Lincoln, who was the voice and body of the people. As the one and all merged into an almost ineffable vision, Emerson finally came close to the attitude of Whitman. Equality oppressed the individual hero unless that hero was the people and the self simultaneously. More repressed than Whitman, Emerson could not find the people in himself, but he did find America in the heroic and barbaric Lincoln. The circle was thus completed. Equality submerged greatness in a deadening level of sameness; the people as a political body was infected with partiality and meanness; purified in the holy fires of affliction, and given the appropriate voice and form, the people could rouse itself to deeds no single hero would dare. The people, therefore, was worthy of celebration because it could throw up out of itself an authentic man when needed. So Emerson ended almost where he began: The abstract people could be made heroic and therefore poetic, even though no part or member of that society was worthy of the proper society of gentlemen.

Emerson's idea of the nation, his several moods of nationalism, both reflected and contributed to the national mythos. His political development was his response to the actual America, while the growth of his version of nationalism was a consequence of the changing vision of his inner eye, his response to an ideal America. The necessary tension between the actual and the ideal resulted in tension between politics and nationalism. The nature of his ideal nation was the standard by which he could judge its actual political life. Regardless therefore of his dismay at political events, he kept a cleaner and more noble America always ready at hand for his steady admiration.

Emerson's specific contribution to American nationalism was his affirmation of the abstract people, not a specific group or class, but the totality of the disembodied corpus. Moving beyond the relative exclusiveness of Winthrop's chosen people, Edwards' elect, Adams' republic of virtue, and Taylor's community of pure farmers, Emerson discovered the heroism and poetry in the complete whole which was bigger than the sum of its parts. The idealistic need to unify and the Romantic urge to separate and differentiate came together in his sense of the nation: Unification of the ideal people constituted the real, that is, the spiritual homeland whose nobility and morality differentiated it from the other nations of the earth. His political difficulties with the concept of equality disappeared in his ideal nationalism; if equality meant that men would fail as heroes, at least the nation was heroic, and as such alone among the nations. Equality therefore served his intellectual though not his political reflexes. Equality was acceptable only as idea. He served democracy intellectually, if not politically. The intellectual and fleshless democracy to which he was loyal satisfied both idealism and Romanticism, as well as the popular national spirit. The widespread expansiveness and optimism of the era of Manifest Destiny found Emerson most congenial when he sketched the America that might yet be, when he assured the nation that beyond the muck of daily experience the Oversoul sweetly smiled.

Emerson knew the mythology of the west that had been central to the nationalism of an earlier America. As a young man his use of the idea of the west was conventional: "There is everything in America's favour, to one who puts faith in those proverbial prophecies of the Westward progress of the Car of Empire."[99] Turning to verse he showed that he had such faith himself:

> Far in the East when Time was young
> The Spirit of Empire loved to dwell
> In Egypt Arts and Learning sprung
> And Music woke her choral shell.
>
> There in the palace of the Sun
> The gorgeous Day, to earth, is born
> And o'er the world, its chariot rolls
> Towards the rich West in triumph drawn
>
> And to the West shall Empire come
> Amid our mountains, stall his steeds.
> Here Glory finds his final home
> And Grandeur write immortal deeds.[100]

He seems to have found the imperial west of glory and grandeur more attractive than the west of happiness and virtue. Yet two years later he went further, with the ancient Puritans, and found his land to be the hope of the world, a city on a hill:

> Heave gently, dark Ocean! thou bear'st on thy breast
> The hope of mankind to its home in the West
> If the tempest should bury that ship in the deep
> The fortunes of nations beside it should sleep
> For she brings thro' the vast solitudes of the sea
> The pride of old England, the [sic]
> The pilgrims of England[101]

Emerson early felt the presumed validity of the old idea that God had hidden the New World until men were equal to its promise. America was thus an essential step on the path of human progress, and as such it commanded world attention. Its greatness was the discovery of ways to achieve peace without coercion. England had known, but had lost through age, the blessing of fearless serenity. America had inherited the once free step of her now decrepit parent.

Before he was ready to float into idealism, the young Emerson shared in the popular national pride in actuality: "the Utopian dreams which visionaries have pursued and sages exploded, will find their beautiful theories rivalled & outdone by the reality, which it has pleased God to bestow upon United America."[102] So far he was limited to the usual notions of a superior people living in a land specially favored by isolation from the past and the sins of age: "Separated from the contamination which infects all other civilized lands this country has always boasted a great comparative purity."[103]

The actuality of frontier lawlessness was a disturbing note. Pioneers who had been driven out of settled society by bankruptcy, debasement, or licentiousness, might retard and perhaps frustrate the Americanization of the world. The actual westward movement *in* America, as opposed to the ideal westering *to* America, gave him pause. He hoped that government could encourage morality and intelligence in the American west, and knew that "if the senates that shall meet hereafter in those wilds shall be made to speak a voice of wisdom & virtue, the reformation of the world would be to be expected from America."[104] He hoped that the magnitude and significance of the task would be a sufficient motivation to greatness. To make the world free by perfecting the American example was an American idea whose lineage traced back through Taylor and Jefferson, Adams, Edwards in his unique way, to Winthrop and the city on a hill. Emerson was merely playing minor variations on an antique theme, but a theme that was growing increasingly popular during the era of Manifest Destiny. He had not yet found his own voice of nationalism.

He shared too in the popular American defensiveness and nervousness about obvious and actual national shortcomings. American history was dull? Yes, but only because misery and interesting history went together. The American Revolution, as he understood it, had resulted in more political freedom, economic abundance, and moral and religious improvements than any other nation had. America's dramatic deficiency was merely proof of her actual adequacy. But actual adequacy was not ideal adequacy.

Throughout the first of Jackson's administrations, Emerson continued to worry about American braggadocio and lack of fixed national principles. Was not the President himself proof that the wild men of the American west, so far from being tamed by civilization, were on the verge of capturing the entire nation? He did not know it at the time but his developing Transcendentalism was nearly ready to rescue him from the Jacksonian barbarism, to take him from malodorous matter to the sweet scent of spirit. The whisper of the Oversoul was preparing to drown out the mad roaring of the Democratic Party.

As an ideal world grew increasingly real to Emerson, the material or political America grew increasingly dim, except for those moments in the 1850's when he was moved to outrage. With idealism, Emerson began to find his own resonance. The genuine America was one of intellect and spirit. Political independence had been won more easily than intellectual independence could be. America had been unable to free itself from the dominion of the English and European mind. And Europe had produced intellectual and spiritual masters who could only be served in the unheroic posture of a disciple.

The authentic American scholar, according to Emerson, must search the unexplored extent of human power. But the scholar would fail unless he were also and primarily an authentic man, true to his own unconscious, and with the moral courage of radical individualism. The Romantic ego demanded satisfaction even as it was drifting in the land of transcendent essence. As the separate selves of American scholars all asserted their own integrity, there would arise a new community of heroes united in the source of their inspiration and the consequences of self-reliance. A serene and Christian idealism was thus made to live with the demonism of the Romantic demand for glory, for stature, and for the worship of the heroic self.

A broken and servile spirit did not seem to characterize the western pioneers whose very energy and independence worried Emerson in other ways. The romance of man against nature in the American west was not lost on him, and he wondered whether those American primitives might hold the key to the whole. His grudging admiration of the sheer force of Jackson and the early Lincoln was a consequence of his view of the authenticity of western man. When that genuine force of ego would find its proper expression, the hope of mankind would be vindicated and the mission of America realized:

> This country has not fulfilled what seemed the reasonable expecta-
> tion of mankind. Men looked, when all feudal straps and bandages
> were snapped asunder, that nature, too long the mother of dwarfs,
> should reimburse itself by a brood of Titans, who should laugh
> and leap in the continent, and run up the mountains of the West
> with the errand of genius and love.[105]

That potential titans should willingly consent to dwarf themselves through a failure of mind did not detract from the idealization of the nation. The finite details of material America were the stuff of poetry, as later Whitman agreed and Henry James did not. But the ostensibly common and sometimes base nature of the details of America required a spirit already uplifted for proper appreciation, as Whitman and James both knew. Emerson grieved that America had yet not had its genius "with tyrannous eye" who could see "in the barbarism and materialism of the times, another carnival of the same gods whose picture he so much admires in Homer." Despite the absence of poetry, "America is a poem in our eyes . . . and it will not long wait for metres."[106]

During the Mexican War Emerson first experienced his periodic confusion of his politics and his nationalism, when the latter always suffered. On the few occasions when indignation compelled him to attend to the finite details of political matter, his ideal nation contracted under the press of hard facts. A trip to England reinforced his momentary politicization of nationalism; he admired the gentility and stability of the English and felt that America "is the Paradise of the third class; here everything is cheap; here everything is for the poor. England is the Paradise of the first class; it is essentially aristocratic, and the humbler classes have made up their minds to this, and do contentedly enter into the system."[107] America as poem receded as she was led, according to his view, to expansiveness and aggression in the interest of satisfying the insatiable planters of the South.

England and Europe should be and usually were as foul as America was at war with Mexico. But America had fewer excuses. Her people had been Europe's most desirable inhabitants. In a not untypical burst of chauvinism and racism, Emerson congratulated America on her fair-haired people:

In the distinctions of the genius of the American race it is to be considered that it is not indiscriminate masses of Europe that are shipped hitherward, but the Atlantic is a sieve through which only or chiefly the liberal, adventurous, sensitive, *America-loving* part of each city, clan, family are brought. It is the light complexion, the blue eyes of Europe that come: the black eyes, the black drop, the Europe of Europe, is left.[108]

The Emancipation Proclamation made it possible for Emerson to retire politically and thus released his nationalism from its intermittent confusion with politics over the last thirteen years. In and after 1863 he was free to return to the ideal America he had occupied before the Compromise of 1850. In 1863 America suddenly became the poem again: "At every moment some one country more than any other represents the sentiment and the future of mankind. None will doubt that America occupies this place in the opinion of nations,"[109] as was proved to him by mounting numbers of blue-eyed immigrants. With the end of legal slavery the poem without poets asserted itself again. There were those who found America insipid, flat, with neither illusions nor romance. Such had been spoiled by London and Paris, and were not really Americans. Any true lover of the ideal America could see both the problem and its solution:

> Let the passion for America cast out the passion for Europe. Here let there be what the earth waits for, —exalted manhood. What this country longs for is personalities, grand persons, to counteract its materialities.[110]

Two years later he confessed to an admiration of the phrase "Manifest Destiny," which earlier had summarized for him the ultimate evil of the nation. Now the phrase signified "the sense all men have of the prodigious energy and opportunity lying idle here. The poor Prussian or Austrian or Italian, escaping hereto, discovers that he has been handcuffed and fettered and fast-tied all his lifetime."[111]

The war finally taught Americans to rely on themselves, to abandon European and especially English criteria of excellence. As this new self-reliance began to express itself in the postwar commercial and industrial expansion, Emerson, perhaps despite himself, was impressed. And he began happily to applaud the work of the masters of matter. "Here is man in the Garden of Eden; here the Genesis and Exodus." The language has the old ring, but the meaning was new. Eden now meant the cornucopia to which the world's hungry—in their flesh, not their spirit—came to feed. "All is ductile and plastic," he enthused, in the Whitmanesque mood that had seized him:

> America is such a garden of plenty, such a magazine of power, that at her shores all the common rules of political economy utterly fail. Here is bread, and wealth, and power, and education for every man who has the heart to use his opportunity. The creation of power had never any parallel.[112]

As the Oversoul had faded under pressure from politics, so it could not withstand the brute fact of industrial expansion. America as poem now sang of material power and material plenty. The spirit, evidently, could wait while the blond immigrants were fed, housed, and schooled. The whirring of American industry became the poem's refrain, as even the mythology of the west was put to the new work: "That cosmical west wind . . . is alone broad enough to carry to every city and suburb, to the farmer's house, the miner's shanty and the fisher's boat, the inspiration of this new hope of mankind."[113]

So Emerson's notion of America's mission ended on the note that had been characteristic of John Adams. The conversion of good ideas to practice was to be America's contribution to mankind. In his journal Emerson quietly noted what was a dramatic reversal in his thought. "I have the belief that of all things the work of America is to make the advanced intelligence of mankind in the sufficiency of morals practical."[114] The nation was still to be "the leading Guide and Lawgiver of the world"[115] because of its hard political insights. America was to ease the actual pain of the world.

To be sure, the old American poem of spirit sounded behind the excitement of industrialization and increasing immigration. But Emerson, in his middle sixties, had lost his youthful certainty about the sufficiency of the spirit. He had turned to an actual America and left it to others to criticize its worst excesses of materialism. Throughout his political and nationalistic thinking Emerson himself had been, as he said of Lincoln, "the true history of the American people in his time." That the rhapsodic worshipper at the shrine of the aeolian harp ended his prayer in a boiler factory is proof of how completely he had marched in time with his nation.

The conclusion to which one must come is that for Emerson only a total truth could be true. Bits and pieces of truth could amuse, enlighten, perhaps even uplift, but the piece was necessarily false. The precise meaning of Emerson's wholeness can never be extracted from his work because of his rejection of precision in favor of rapture. There is that in Emerson which validates John Dewey's estimate: "Emerson is not only a philosopher, . . . he is the Philosopher of Democracy."[116] There is that in Emerson which validates the exact opposite. He will not sit still for one substantive portrait, though the direction of major drift in his thought is apparent.

Emerson began his intellectual quest as a search for a cure for Unitarian sterility. The problem was intellectual and so was the answer. Rejecting mind at almost every turn, his preoccupation with the answer to Unitarianism unfitted him to write the language of Hawthorne, Poe, or Melville. He was, as he said, a spectator, not, one supposes, the most advantageous role for a poet, as Emerson's poetry may prove. Approaching poetry as an aspect of his intellectual quest, he had feelings about poetry rather than poetic feelings. He was afflicted, in short, with the worry of his entire career: The spirit did not come, and one could do nothing to get a response to an earnestly issued invitation. Celebrating sparks and flashes, Emerson seems never to have caught the fire he knew necessary to his art, and his poems were therefore essays. Nonetheless, one scholar has shown that "Emerson's theory of expression was that on which Thoreau built, to which Whitman gave extension, and to which Hawthorne and Melville were indebted by being forced to react against its philosophical assumptions."[117] From his own prison, Emerson could help to liberate others. Hawthorne could be devastating about "Mr. Emerson—the mystic, stretching his hand out of cloudland, in vain search for something real,"[118] but Mr. Hawthorne grew artistically richer because of his need to devastate Mr. Emerson. Emerson was, in short, the intellectual catalyst of his time.

His power came from the common enemy against which most intellectual and artistic Americans at the time had to struggle, from the continuity and divergencies of the New England tradition in his work. With the collapse of old dogma, New England mystics were now "free to carry on the ancient New England propensity for reeling and staggering with new opinions. They could give themselves over, unrestrainedly, to becoming transparent eyeballs and debauchees of dew."[119]   Emerson was at the very heart of that movement to release the human spirit from its old New England determinism into the light of day. And though Emerson's way into light was slightly ridiculous according to Hawthorne and Melville, both agreed that there was darkness where Emerson had pointed. They had to find their own light, such as it was, elsewhere.

He was even more than an inspiration or a productive irritant to his fellows. Emerson was the American spirit, as many of the tensions and contradictions of the nation found embodiment in him. He could sustain an optimism that hid a demon, could speak of the good of the universe in a nation of slavery, could justify actual evil in the name of a higher good, could defend spiritual equality but long for heroes, could speak for abstract democracy and find most actual men offensive. Most important, Emerson's voice was that of individualism at a time of developing individualism in both political and economic life. The political economy of laissez-faire capitalism found philosophical and spiritual sustenance in Emerson's essays, lectures, and poetry. The new idea in the American intellectual tradition—that society was smaller and more evil than one man—was soon to become orthodoxy for the successful entrepreneurs of the industrial revolution.

That Emerson's idealism was prepared to find the real and enduring symbol in the commonplace, including the smoke and steam of an expanding economy, allowed him to sing the American hymn to power. His mind was the single most useful mind ever offered to a nation trying to explain the gulf between its ideal and actual self, between its theory and practice, between its history and mission: The ideal was real and the actual false. America was therefore not its past, but its future. The darkness was gone, and man was free to follow his instinct even into the marketplace, where he would be a god. Whatever was, might or might not be right, but the eternal future was holy. Despite the record made by American men, the American man could stand erect with pride in the life he would live tomorrow.

SELECT BIBLIOGRAPHY

Kenneth W. Cameron. *Emerson the Essayist.* 2 vols. Raleigh, N. C., 1945.

Arthur E. Christy. *The Orient in American Transcendentalism.* New York, 1932.

Merle Curti. *American Paradox.* New Brunswick, N. J., 1956.

R. W. B. Lewis. *The American Adam.* Chicago, 1955.

F. O. Matthiessen. *American Renaissance.* New York, 1941.

Sherman Paul. *Emerson's Angle of Vision.* Cambridge, 1952.

Mario Praz. *The Romantic Agony.* London, 1933.

Ralph L. Rusk. *The Life of Ralph Waldo Emerson.* New York, 1949.

Alexis de Tocqueville. *Democracy in America.* 2 vols. New York, 1954.

Albert K. Weinberg. *Manifest Destiny.* Baltimore, 1935.

Stephen E. Whicher. *Freedom and Fate.* Philadelphia, 1953.

Conrad Wright. *The Beginnings of Unitarianism in America.* Boston, 1955.

VI

THE DEMONIC ❃ *Herman Melville*

> With the soul of an Atheist, he wrote down
> the godliest things; with the feeling of death
> and misery in him, he created forms of gladness
> and life. For the pangs in his heart, he put
> down hoots on the paper. And everything else
> he disguised under the so conveniently adjust-
> able drapery of all-stretchable Philosophy.
>
> *Pierre*

Rage was perhaps one inevitable reaction to the pietistic optimism of nineteenth-century America. With the continuing definition of the nation, and the continuing achievement of attainable goals along the way, America had seemed actually to become the nation of the future, the natural asylum for the party of hope. As the solemn rhetoric of the founding fathers gave way to tub-thumping political revivalism from Jackson on, an increasingly democratic people came, and saw, and conquered. Dreary old phrases about the limitation of human power or, even worse, about original sin were evidently shown to be both false and pernicious by the unprecedented march of the American people. When political leaders actually talked about and perhaps even believed in popular sovereignty, and when national policies presumably based on the collective people's power and wisdom resulted in one apparent success after another, it was undoubtedly tempting for the nation to sit back on occasion and complacently view the monuments it had thrown up in its own honor.

271

Emerson seemed less a prophet of hope than a chronicler of hope's actual achievement. His instinctive recoil from ugliness or pain was shared by many. Evil had become un-American. The borders were stretched, railroads built, and peace won on American terms. The new American man with his musket over his shoulder was, in his collective mass, invincible. The even newer American man, designing, building, and sailing the proud clipper ships, made profits today by building for tomorrow. The universe seemed especially kind to the western heroes who were still at that old American task of refashioning the earth for the betterment of humanity. The task was as old as Winthrop, but the tools of the nineteenth century were new. The railroad spike had replaced the Bible as the (hopefully) irresistable American talisman.

The secret of the laws of nature and of nature's God seemed to be revealed, and apparently limitless power was entrusted to the nation. The power to be and to do, the power to make and to stand erect, the power to be free in a world enslaved by its own history—Americans commanded the powers of the earth for the benefit of those who were strong enough and wise enough to come and share in the work and the profit of building a different and more humane earth.

The idea of human perfectibility could presumably be finally validated merely by looking around. Looking away from the less sanguine view of man that had been held by Winthrop, Edwards, Adams, and Taylor, Americans applauded themselves by applauding Emerson. The conviction of man's depravity or weakness or stupidity, which had been basic to the richest strain of the American intellectual tradition before Emerson, had presumably been superannuated by actual physical and ideological achievement. Or had it?

In one transcendent swoop, Emerson could deny the reality of poverty and slavery, could ignore institutional weaknesses and politics altogether. Steadfastly glued to the ideal, Emerson could intellectualize the actual to conform to his gentle self. But there were also less gentle selves who lived a subterranean life in God's country, men who saw pain when they looked at it. There were some few artists like Poe, Hawthorne, and Melville who were driven underground by a society that would not or could not tolerate a serious threat to complacency. As rightful descendants of a once dominant mood, the nay-sayers of nineteenth-century America were enraged at the dilution of what they too took to be America's ideal; but that ideal was being destroyed, as they saw it, by the blindness of idealism. They could rail at the easy acquiescence of their time and place, they could drink themselves to death or lash themselves into demonic aggression in their art, but they could not acquiesce. Forced into a hated alienation, their art was nourished by their rage. They dipped their pens in venom and produced America's best literature.

To read Melville's work from start to finish is to see him climb to a high plateau of art and excellence; it is to watch him take an emotional and intellectual journey that began in the buoyant temper of young America and ended in a private world of unmitigated and unmediated torment. He completed that journey in a few short but inhumanly intense years. Melville's growth as an artist was a development from the writer as American to the writer as Melville. His greatness was achieved by finding his own voice in the American chorus, by isolating himself from the rhythm and tempo of his time and place. But his spiritual isolation occured in a specific American context which at least contributed to the timbre of his deepening voice. Fighting to free himself from his nation, he had to keep his nation in his art. As he found his solo voice, an American harmonic or contrapuntal note was still always audible. His work became finally so purely American because of the depth of his rejection of America.

Melville's first work, of course, was not entirely premonitory. *Typee*, published in 1846 when he was twenty-seven years old, was a book of both exuberant and shocked discovery. As the first literary white man to explore parts of the South Seas, Melville himself actually entered into a warm and soft and green world of innocence and joy. He discovered genuine primitivism and was thoroughly charmed by it. But he also saw the work of the Christian missionaries, who, in bringing civilization to the islanders, also brought, perhaps without intention, the end of charm and the beginning of misery. *Typee* is a narrative of Melville's own and imagined experiences as a captive in the valley of the innocent and lovely Typee cannibals of the Marquesas. It is also a description of the ugly consequences of evangelical Christianity in an authentic earthly paradise.

Typee was an integral part of the romantic passion for the exotic, but its mood was not quite of a piece with the widespread celebration of strangeness, of the picturesque and the remote in time. In what had become a characteristic American reflex, Melville could not look backward to find the exotic. In *Typee* he reached out in space in order to avoid affirming time; to Polynesia, not to the middle ages. Yet he could lapse into quite conventional romantic excess: "The Marquesas! What strange visions of outlandish things does the very name spirit up! Lovely houris—cannibal banquets—groves of cocoa-nuts—coral reefs—tattooed chiefs—and bamboo temples . . . *heathenish rites and human sacrifices.*"[1] Merely chanting the strange names and sounds was enough to satisfy the most superficial requirement of the romantic sensibility.

The American firm of Harper and Brothers rejected the manuscript because "it was impossible that it could be true and therefore was without real value."[2] Melville's brother, who had been rewarded for political services with an appointment as Secretary of the Legation in England, sold the book to John Murray and showed it to Washington Irving, who thought it exquisite and who predicted its success. After the English sale, Wiley and Putnam contracted to publish *Typee* in America.

Because it did speak to a popular desire to be titillated by the exotic, *Typee* became a commercially successful book and made Melville famous. Even in this first work, however, Melville worried many critics in both England and America. He was on relatively safe territory in the simple narrative portions of the book, but when he turned to genuine praise of actual primitivism, when he lashed out at the Christian missions, his critics had fair warning that Melville was not altogether a mere spokesman of an innocuous and false commitment to romantic ghosts who could be relied on to mind their own business. *Typee* was real, and so was Melville, though many, especially in England, doubted both.

The primitive life Melville discovered in the Typee valley was voluptuous, simple, carefree, and energetically happy. The natives seemed to think and act spontaneously together. He presumed them to be governed by a firm moral sense; and therefore he assumed that sense to be an innate human attribute, the Puritans notwithstanding: "It is to this indwelling, this universally diffused perception of what is *just* and *noble,* that the integrity of the Marquesans in their intercourse with each other is to be attributed."[3] The natives taught Melville that men were better than he had supposed them to be from his knowledge of civilization.

The sensuous and sensual aspects of primitivism gave the somewhat prim and proper American some trouble, but he guiltily had a roaring good time. He found the dances of the Marquesan girls "beautiful in the extreme, but there is an abandoned voluptuousness in their character which I dare not attempt to describe."[4] He could bring himself to describe the experience he and Toby, his companion in Eden, endured on their first morning in the valley:

> As these unsophisticated young creatures were attended by no jealous duennas, their proceedings were altogether informal, and void of artificial restraint. Long and minute was the investigation with which they honoured us, and so uproarious their mirth, that I felt infinitely sheepish; and Toby was immeasurably outraged at their familiarity.... My feelings of propriety were exceedingly shocked, for I could not but consider them as having overstepped the due limits of female decorum.[5]

He did not say so, of course, but he fell in love in his happy valley. Strolling, canoeing, bathing with and being attended by lovely Fayaway, Melville was probably happier than at any time during his life. The image of the almost nude girl standing in the bow of their canoe, holding her robe in her outstretched arms for a sail, is drawn with such tender passion that the reader is lulled into Melville's incredulous but yielding mood. How to describe a golden and innocent lover like Fayaway? "The easy unstudied graces of a child of nature like this, breathing from infancy an atmosphere of perpetual summer, and nurtured by the simple fruits of the earth; enjoying a perfect freedom from care and anxiety, and removed effectually from all injurious tendencies, strike the eye in a manner which cannot be portrayed."[6] More than his eye was struck. No wonder that the reviewer of the book in the London *Times* exclaimed: "Enviable Herman! A happier dog it is impossible to imagine than Herman in the Typee Valley."[7]

Witnessing some of the earliest incursions of civilization and Christianity into the dream-like emerald islands, Melville was indignant at what he took to be a deliberate war against happiness in the name of morality. White men had first goaded the simple natives into savagery and then set out to destroy the savages in the name of civilization, as heathenism in North America had been destroyed by destroying the heathens. Opposing natural freedom, the missionaries stood for repression. The primitive whose physical wants were unsatisfied by nature could profit from civilization if at least his hunger would be alleviated. But the well-fed islander had nothing to gain from civilization except a cultivation of his mind, nothing to gain except repression resulting in sublimation: ". . . despite the disadvantages of his condition, the Polynesian savage, surrounded by all the luxurious provisions of nature, enjoyed an infinitely happier, though certainly a less intellectual existence, than the self-complacent European."[8]

As Melville's understanding deepened, his attack swelled to a general though only partially articulated criticism of civilization and its discontents: "In a primitive state of society, the enjoyments of life, though few and simple, are spread over a great extent, and are unalloyed; but the heart-burnings, the jealousies, the social rivalries, the family dissensions, and the thousand self-inflicted discomforts of refined life, which make up in units the swelling aggregate of human misery, are unknown among these unsophisticated people."[9] The islanders had no money and therefore knew none of its attendant miseries, no contention, and but little illness.

The twin forces of civilization and Christianity had nothing to offer except the total destruction of an unrepressed Eden, nothing except turning utterly free and childlike men into corpses or slaves. Sexual freedom, in its widest sense, evidently constituted a sufficiently radical rebuke to civilization to force white men to war against the innocent savage mind with Christianity and against the innocent savage body with civilization:

> Among the islands of Polynesia, no sooner are the images overturned, the temples demolished, and the idolaters converted into *nominal* Christians, than disease, vice, and premature death make their appearance. The depopulated land is then recruited from the rapacious hordes of enlightened individuals who settle themselves within its borders, and clamorously announce the progress of the Truth. . . . The spontaneous fruits of the earth, which God in His wisdom had ordained for the support of the indolent natives, remorselessly seized upon and appropriated by the stranger, are devoured before the eyes of the starving inhabitants, or sent on board the numerous vessels which now touch on their shores. When

the famished wretches are cut off in this manner from their natural supplies, they are told by their benefactors to work and earn their support by the sweat of their brows![10]

The sad process was already well advanced in Honolulu, where "the small remnant of the natives had been civilized into draught horses, and evangelised into beasts of burden."[11]   He concluded that all of the islanders would have been infinitely better off if they had never seen the face of the white man.

Typee obviously would worry some of its readers. America was certainly not the nation to approve apostrophes to savagery or probings beneath the white skin of Christian civilization. An expurgated American edition was prepared; it omitted Melville's more luscious passages as well as his attacks on the missionaries. But even though the original *Typee* went against the grain, its gaiety was infectious and Melville was almost applauded. Mixed with that applause there was, however, a steady American carping that something, something was wrong with the book and its author. Horace Greeley perfectly expressed this sense of slightly bewildered sanctimoniousness; in a New York newspaper Greeley said that *Typee* was "unmistakably defective, if not positively diseased in moral tone, and will very fairly be condemned as dangerous reading for those of immature intellects and unsettled principles. Not that you can put your finger on a passage positively offensive; but the *tone* is bad."[12]

Melville spent his happiest days in the Typee valley; and he desperately wanted to get away while he was there. First of all a leg infection would not heal. Second, he was held a captive by the natives, a fact that encouraged a desire to escape even into a meaner world. And most important, he was a civilized white man who could not endure pure pleasure, who could not de-sublimate. Constantly distracted by his mind, Melville knew that a reversion back into prehistory, back into timelessness, was impossible for him despite his wide-eyed appreciation of naked happiness.   Being white and refined he was unable to become brown and simple; living in a veritable Golden Age he became monomaniacal in his passion to escape to a world he already hated.

He did escape, and his first reaction was nostalgic. *Omoo* (1847) begins with his regrets over leaving the happy valley he could not endure while he was there:

> Safe aboard of a ship—so long my earnest prayer—with home and
> friends once more in prospect, I nevertheless felt weighed down
> by a melancholy that could not be shaken off. It was the thought
> of never more seeing those who, notwithstanding their desire to
> retain me a captive, had, upon the whole, treated me so kindly. I
> was leaving them forever.[13]

But the romantic rover could not long resist the lure of a sea breeze
or of other islands. As the winds freshened, his spirits rose; and he
was on his way from Nukuheva to Tahiti, from untouched nature
to semicivilization. That is the story of *Omoo.*

Melville's second book was his most light-hearted. For once, in
Omoo, he was a simple and guiltless bum in company with the
amoral and reckless Dr. Long Ghost. Their aimless and happy
wanderings make up Melville's only picaresque tale in which he
seems to have been convinced that there was something essentially
absurd and amusing about both himself and the situations in which
he found himself. To be sure, he continued his attack on civilization
and the Christian missionaries, and found the semicivilized Tahitians
less to his liking than the purer savages of Typee, but in *Omoo* it
was the adventure that mattered and he threw himself into it with
gusto.

It was merely a matter of time before the urge to move again
would assert itself. He and Dr. Long Ghost decided to quit the
islands by shipping in an American whaler then in Tahiti's harbor.
The doctor was forced to remain because the captain refused to
sign him, so Melville was off and on his own once more. He had
heard that the ship was unlucky in her hunt for whales, but the
lure of new sights and sounds was irresistible. Romance was the
thing. Unlucky? Unprofitable? "But what of that? We would
have all the sport of chasing the monsters, with none of the detestable work which follows their capture. So, hurrah for the coast of
Japan! Thither the ship was bound."[14]

Melville was annoyed when *Typee* and *Omoo* were often dismissed as fancies of his imagination, when his English publisher
asked for some proof that he actually existed and had really traveled in the South Seas. He decided to write a thoroughgoing
romance of Polynesian adventure partly in order to see whether
his earlier critics would be able to tell the difference between fact

and fancy. "This thought," he said, "was the germ of others, which have resulted in *Mardi*,"[15] published in 1849.

Mardi is an allegorical tale of a canoe trip to the many islands composing the great archipelago of the world. It is the tale of a quest, or rather several simultaneous quests: a search for love, for truth, and for community. The structure of the story allowed Melville to make a start towards a kind of expression not to be found in *Typee* or *Omoo*. He wrote *Mardi* in a spirit of an intellectual adventure whose terminus he did not know; he evidently had decided to try his philosophical wings despite the clear fact that he did not know where to fly. The result, as one critic expressed it, "is the drifting and eddying fog of intellectual worry, vacillation, and indecision."[16]

The philosophical categories that were relevant to Melville were those that had been long debated by Americans, as well as by many others. He was concerned with theology, nature, and idealism, as Emerson and Edwards had been. By the middle of the nineteenth century that triple concern was peculiarly American, less in the fact of the concern than in the substance of the argument itself. Emerson had set the tone, and yet he had merely followed the lead of the Puritans. Melville understood his own intellectual milieu, and though he rejected the accepted views he continued to think along those well-worn lines.

Perhaps it was the physical pleasures of the Typee valley that convinced him that any form of idealism was essentially wrong, that undiluted intellection, if carried far enough, must result in a form of madness. The Typee natives experienced ecstasy instead of thought, physical instead of intellectual life. Freed instincts apparently meant laughter and health, while the hegemony of mind meant gloom and sickness. Mind and health were becoming polarized for Melville. In Typee life was a long, occasionally interrupted nap. He seems to have feared that idealism, as a logical consequence of repressive civilization, was some kind of disguise of the fact that men of the city had forgotten how to live, and had invented a new dream world of the mind to take the place of the real world of pleasure out of which they had chased themselves. Whatever the source, Melville was already convinced that reality consisted in something more than idea, even if he could not make that something precise. "Sublimate, as you will," he explained, "the idea of our ethereality as intellectual beings; no sensible man can harbour a doubt, but that there is a vast deal of satisfaction in dining."[17] Pleasure and idealism were mutually exclusive, and idealism, on that account, was opposed to something valuable in human life.

As the transcendentalists, and especially Emerson, had used idealism as their mode of analysis, they applied that mode to nature as their major source of truth. Nature, for them, had been a metaphor of the human mind, filled therefore with human significance and relevance. Again it is probable that Melville learned to reject the American idealization of nature in the cannibalistic Typee valley or on the ships that carried him to and from that idyllic prison. He had weathered the natural fury of Cape Horn, had come close to starvation in nature, and yet was keenly alive to the beauty and majesty of the natural world. Babbalanja, the philosopher in *Mardi*, expressed an idea that was to grow increasingly important to Melville: "All vanity, vanity . . . to seek in nature for positive warranty to these aspirations of ours. Through all her provinces, nature seems to promise immortality to life, but destruction to beings. Or . . . if not against us, nature is not for us."[18]

In rejecting idealism, Melville found himself without what had become the usual American understanding of God's created universe. Nature seemed to him a gigantic fact whose existence and content might signify nothing about man's fate. Without idealism he was coming to what was for him a vital idea: Nature was neutral. Men were compelled to make their way as best they could through the natural world, but the ease or difficulty of their progress did not mean that that world had man's pain, comfort, or even edification in view. Nature was real, not metaphoric, and men who assigned some motive to nature created a world in their own image and thus blinded themselves to reality. Idealism was necessarily anthropomorphic and thus necessarily unable to comprehend the nonhuman universe in its own terms. To describe the facts of nature with the language of morality or emotion was to miss the essential neutrality of the whole: "As well hate a seraph as a shark. Both were made by the same hand."[19]

The total universe really existed, was all created by God, and men could dream about creating the world through idea only at their own peril, at the price of losing a genuine relationship with a genuine but morally neutral universe. That universe of course offered men both comfort and pain, life and death, but without intention. Melville, unlike Emerson, could not view a storm at sea as big with cosmic and human meaning, and unlike Winthrop and Edwards could not think of it as a consequence of human thought and conduct. Both malignity and benignity had disappeared for Melville, and he was left with the perhaps awesome fact of a storm or a shark that men must learn to endure.

Nature was created by the Lord God of the universe, and in *Mardi* Melville publicly began his life-long and futile search for an acceptable theological position. His overpowering need to come to some understanding with earlier, especially American, theology began now to lend a certain national color to his best books. Calvinism, in which he had been raised, and idealism were his central enemies in his quest for religious peace; Edwards and Emerson explicitly personified the convictions with which he was virtually obsessed and from which he spent a life trying to escape. In *Mardi* he made only a hesitant start, asserting that predestination and free will were irreconcilable, and that free will was necessary in order for men to be held morally accountable for what they did or failed to do, Jonathan Edwards evidently notwithstanding. Babbalanja found peace on an island called Serenia by giving himself over to love in Christ; he counseled the questing sailor to do the same, to stop roving and searching for what was finally to be found in his own heart, to become resigned to mystery. The young sailor sailed away, and with hindsight we know that the theological voyage was to last as long as Melville lived. In *Mardi* some of the problems were suggested; none of the solutions were.

Fighting to free himself from America's intellectual tradition, Melville was still deeply involved in the national mythology that had been elaborated earlier. He knew every ingredient in that mythology, and was troubled by each. For every illusion he felt disillusion, but he could not yet shake free from the idea that his land might yet live up to its promise. Knowing the national sense involved in Winthrop's city on a hill, Adams' republic of virtue, Taylor's garden of America, and Emerson's hymn to the collective people, Melville was worried about slavery, imperialism, democracy, hypocrisy, and pride.

Melville still continued to accept the notion of the uniqueness of America, the fact that in some sense the land was promised, that the idea of the west presaged what might still be America's destiny if her people would but honor the national pledge. The idea of the west was as alive to him as it had been for any other American:

> West, West! West, West! Whitherward point Hope and prophet-fingers; whitherward, at sunset, kneel all worshippers of fire; whitherward in mid-ocean, the great whales turn to die; whitherward face all the Moslem dead in Persia; whitherward lie Heaven and Hell! —West, West! Whitherward mankind and empires—flocks, caravans, armies, navies; worlds, suns, and stars all wend!   —West, West! —Oh boundless boundary!   Eternal goal!   Whitherward rush, in thousand worlds, ten thousand keels! Beacon, by which the universe is steered! —Like the north star, attracting all needles! Unattainable forever; but forever leading to great things this side of thyself! —Hive of all sunsets! —Gabriel's pinions may not overtake thee![20]

Even the idea of the west that had sustained much of America's mythos was grown ambiguous in Melville's complex sense of the nation. It was possible, he thought, that the course of empire and happiness could reverse itself, as Babbalanja said: "'Tis the old law: —the East peoples the West, the West the East; flux and reflux. And time may come, after the rise and fall of nations yet unborn, that, risen from its future ashes, Popheero [Europe] shall be the promised land, and from her surplus hordes Kolumbo [America] people it."[21]

Written during the Mexican War, *Mardi* warned America that lusting for empire, striking bargains at the point of a spear, was a violation of national mission. It lectured Americans that "yours is the best and happiest land under the sun,"[22] not wholly because they had willed it to be so, but because the history and geography of their land required them to be free. The nation had been independent before independence was declared: "Your ancient pilgrims fathered your liberty; and your wild woods harboured the nursling."[23] The nation's past tended towards freedom, but the present did not.

Socially, and thus more important than politically, Americans were becoming unfree. They were cringing. They cheered on their own number to national folly because they could not wait for time to bring them the secrets it contained:

> Expand not your area too widely, now. Seek you proselytes? Neighbouring nations may be free, without coming under your banner. And if you cannot lay your ambition, know this: that it is best served by waiting events. Time, but Time only, may enable you to cross the equator; and give you the Arctic Circles for your boundaries.[24]

Slavery, like imperialism, ran counter to what Melville believed to be the right national purpose. And he knew no immediate solution to slavery, arguing that, again, time was the answer, that time must bring abolition. He knew that "these South savannahs may yet prove battlefields,"[25] but he also feared that war might produce unintended, unpredictable, and unbearable consequences. Though he was unequivocal in his condemnation of the central fact of southern history, he was in *Mardi* unable to speak for immediate abolition in a clear voice.

Though the sins against the national Holy Ghost loomed large and black to Melville, the national promise was still meaningful to him. The idea of America could be and was subverted by experience in America, subverted but not destroyed:

> Vivenza [United States] was a noble land. Like a young tropic tree she stood, laden down with greenness, myriad blossoms, and the ripened fruit thick-hanging from one bough. She was promising as the morning. Or Vivenza might be likened to St. John, feeding on locusts and wild honey, and with prophetic voice crying to the nations in the wilderness. Or, child-like, standing among the old robed kings and emperors of the Archipelago [of the world], Vivenza seemed a young Messiah, to whose discourse the bearded Rabbis bowed.[26]

America was young, and though she suffered from the impetuosity and recklessness of youth, yet she promised saner and wiser things to come. She offered strength in an enfeebled world, potential innocence amid urbane decay. It was the newness of the new world that caught his imagination. His nation, though corrupted in the present, might yet function as the republic of virtue, as the city on a hill, as the asylum for the poor and brave of all the earth, as the sanctuary for all those who were too good for life in hoary Europe:

> Here [in the United States] lie plantations, held in fee by stout hearts and arms; and boundless fields, that may be had for seeing. Here, your foes are forests, struck down with bloodless maces. —Ho! Mardi's [world's] Poor, and Mardi's Strong! ye, who starve or beg; seventh sons who slave for earth's firstborn—here is your home; pre-destinated yours; Come over, Empire-founders! fathers of the wedded tribes to come! —abject now, illustrious evermore: —Ho: Sinew, Brawn, and Thigh![27]

In *Mardi,* Melville, like Emerson, judged the actual America by an ideal America, and found the actual severely wanting. Still nourished by hope, he was not yet what he was to become.

Mardi was a disappointment to Melville's public. His readers had identified him with apparently light and entertaining though somewhat wicked tales of exotic adventure. What could that public make of the awkward and aimless physical and metaphysical wanderings in Melville's sprawling allegory? The London *Athenaeum* described the book for its readers: "Matters become crazier and crazier—more and more foggy—page by page—until the end is felt to be a happy release." *The Literary Gazette* was perhaps more candid: "As for giving any idea of it, we have none ourselves."[28] Melville himself had recourse to what was then his typical response to a problem: "Time, which is the solver of all riddles, will solve 'Mardi.'"[29]

Melville did not have time to wait; *Mardi* failed to bring him the money he needed, and that need drove him to write books hopefully designed to realize a profit though perhaps to fail as art. He also published *Redburn* in 1849, and *White Jacket,* which seems to have been written in less than three months, in 1850. In a private letter he came close to disowning both books:

> no reputation that is gratifying to me, can possibly be achieved by either of these books. They are two *jobs,* which I have done for money—being forced to it, as other men are to sawing wood. And while I have felt obliged to refrain from writing the kind of book I would wish to; yet, in writing these two books, I have not repressed myself much—so far as *they* are concerned; but have spoken pretty much as I feel. —Being books, then, written in this way, my only desire for their 'success' (as it is called) springs from my pocket, & not from my heart. So far as I am individually concerned, & independent of my pocket, it is my earnest desire to write those sort of books which are said to 'fail.'[30]

Redburn is a simple story of the initiation of a young and innocent American sailor into the darker ways of the world than those he had known at home. He disembarked at Liverpool and discovered misery, evil, and vice, and learned something about his homeland in contrast. The virtual ubiquity of poverty struck him as a dominant feature of life in Liverpool, and the paupers and beggars were mostly native Englishmen. In America, he remembered, a native beggar was almost never to be seen: "to be a born American citizen seems a guarantee against pauperism; and this, perhaps, springs from the virtue of a vote."[31] The old world was more sordid and less romantic than the young sailor had imagined, and he suffered from self-pity as he tried to make his way around the city with a superannuated guide book. He was alone, impoverished himself, and repeatedly shocked by the depth and breadth of human suffering.

The callousness and enmity the young sailor thought to be characteristic of life in the old world emphasized strands of the mythology of America which he recalled with pride. The new world was new and was mankind's fairest hope; it was the proper locale for the reestablishment of a lost community and of paradise lost:

> We [Americans] are the heirs of all time, and with all nations we divide our inheritance. On this Western Hemisphere all tribes and people are forming into one federated whole; and there is a future which shall see the estranged children of Adam restored as to the old hearthstone in Eden. The other world beyond this, which was longed for by the devout before Columbus' time, was found in the New; and the deep-sea lead, that first struck these soundings, brought up the soil of Earth's Paradise. Not a Paradise then, or now; but to be made so at God's good pleasure, and in the fulness and mellowness of time.[32]

The sailor had not moved beyond Melville's cautious yet positive national hope as expressed in *Mardi*. America was not but could become God's country if her people would cleanse the land of evil, which, in the context of Melville's nationalism, was both sinful and treasonous.

One manifestation of that evil was the occasion for writing *White Jacket*. Melville had returned from his South Sea travels in a man-of-war of the United States navy and had been horrified by the floggings he had witnessed. *White Jacket* dramatized that horror and Melville hoped that actual reform would result when his story was told. He admitted that English captains had even greater legal authority to inflict more lashes than an American captain, but he said that the English were more restrained. He remembered that a prominent Virginian once declared in Congress that he had seen more flogging on a single cruise of an American man-of-war than had occurred on his own plantation of five hundred slaves in a decade. The trouble with American captains was that they had not been bred for authority, and that was truer of northeners than southerners. The very political democracy of the United States made the necessary autocracy of a ship at sea even more onerous than it was on the ships and navies of less democratic nations. That no sailor before the mast could hope to rise to the rank of a commissioned officer seemed to Melville to contradict the national spirit. And flogging, sometimes arbitrary and often severe, was, to his mind, absolutely irreconcilable with his own nationalism.

The national mythology articulated in *White Jacket* was still part of a long tradition, one for which Emerson had done so much. America must free herself from time, from the past, in order to be what she must be. Flogging, for instance, was sustained by precedent, but what had a unique land and a special people to do with precedent?

> The world has arrived at a period which renders it the part of Wisdom to pay homage to the prospective precedents of the Future in preference to those of the Past. The Past is dead, and has no resurrection; but the Future is endowed with such a life, that it lives to us even in anticipation. The Past is, in many things, the foe of mankind; the Future is, in all things, our friend. In the Past is no hope; the Future is both hope and fruition. The Past is the text-book of tyrants; the Future the Bible of the Free.[33]

The past had been rejected by most of America's most serious architects of the national mythos. America was new, and that fact could mean either unprecedented virtue or intelligence or power, or all three at once. The sense of the irrelevance of time led Melville, as it had led Winthrop, Adams, and Emerson, for instance, to an analogy with Israel, to a sense that America was the promised land occupied by the chosen people. Perhaps never in our literature has the theme of God's country been sung with a fervor to match Melville's:

Escaped from the house of bondage, Israel of old did not follow
after the ways of the Egyptians. To her was given an express dispen-
sation; to her were given new things under the sun. And we Americans are the peculiar, chosen people—the Israel of our time; we bear
the ark of the liberties of the world. Seventy years ago we escaped
from thrall; and, besides our first birthright—embracing one continent
of earth—God has given to us, for a future inheritance, the broad
domains of the political pagans, that shall yet come and lie down
under the shade of our ark, without bloody hands being lifted. God
has predestinated, mankind expects, great things from our race; and
great things we feel in our souls. The rest of the nations must soon
be in our rear. We are the pioneers of the world; the advance-
guard, sent on through the wilderness of untried things, to break a
new path in the New World that is ours. In our youth is our strength;
in our inexperience, our wisdom. At a period when other nations
have but lisped, our deep voice is heard afar. Long enough have
we been skeptics with regard to ourselves, and doubted whether,
indeed, the political Messiah had come. But he has come in *us,* if
we would but give utterance to his promptings. And let us always
remember that with ourselves, almost for the first time in the history
of earth, national selfishness is unbounded philanthropy; for we cannot do a good to America, but we give alms to the world.[34]

The United States was now the *nation* on a hill, the hope of
the world, the scene of peace and glory and wisdom. But as Melville's language took flight, as his hymn to the nation was sung with
increasing passion, he merely felt the actual abuses of Americans
more deeply. As he raised America's promises, he was crushed by
her performances. May flogging be practiced in God's country?

The hero of *White Jacket* was himself lashed to the rigging on
one occasion in order to be scourged. He was saved at the last
minute, but as he waited to feel the whip his reflections led to
thoughts of murdering the captain and then killing himself in order
to avoid the humiliation of the whip. He was driven to the extrem-
ity of including murder and suicide among man's natural rights:
"The privilege, inborn and inalienable, that every man has, of dying
himself, and inflicting death upon another, was not given to us without a purpose. These are the last resources of an insulted and
unendurable existence."[35] His flogging was narrowly averted, and
so his privileges of death were not exercised, but that central event
of the story radiated throughout the book as Melville once more
decided to try to face the metaphysics of Calvinism in order better

to understand man's fate in the man-of-war world he occupied.

In *White Jacket,* Melville was more sure of his theology than he was ever to be again. He extended his earlier conception of nature to include fate; both were now thought to be neutral. Fate was both "heartless and impartial; not a fiend to kindle bigot flames, nor a philanthropist to espouse the cause of Greece. We may fret, fume, and fight; but the thing called Fate everlastingly sustains an armed neutrality."[36] No man, certainly not a philosopher nor a theologian, could know the destiny of men, all of whom sail under sealed orders and head for unknown ports, but even so the end of each man's voyage "was predestinated ere we slipped from the stocks at Creation."[37] He was certain, he said, that there was some destination, and that those who thought that there would only be an eternal drifting were mad. He was equally certain that ideas of free will were all delusions.

Melville was not making full obeisance to the God of Edwards. Life was mysterious and determined, but the mystery, for Melville, was not in God's secret ways but in man himself; "in our own hearts we fashion our own gods. . . . Ourselves are Fate."[38] Again: "There are no mysteries out of ourselves."[39] Men were not free because they were slaves to themselves, were both governor and governed, agent and principal, perhaps jailer and prisoner. It was no new idea that a man's character is his destiny, and no new idea that the enigma of life on earth is contained in the darker recesses of the human psyche. Melville had so far accepted, perhaps unknowingly, Edwards' analysis of man while rejecting Edwards' theology. Now God was not in His heaven, and man was as unfree as he had ever been in the colder and earlier New England climate. The Typee valley had lost its echo and its outline. Melville was prepared to write his masterpiece.

Moby-Dick (1851) is neither a novel nor a philosophical treatise. It is not a novel in the sense that a novel is a reconstruction in dramatic form of the author's vision, that its story is told by its characters in situation or action. It is Melville, not his characters, who tells us about *Moby-Dick.* In large measure, the book is precisely a telling *about,* rather than a creation of dramatic imagination which confronts us with action as acted. Melville makes assertions about his characters and their activity, rather than showing them in motion. There is furthermore no narrative center in *Moby-Dick*, though Ishmael is the organizing consciousness of the first fifteen chapters; but Ishmael is abandoned as narrator for a time with neither explanation nor justification, only to be used again, and dropped again. Sometimes technical dramatic organization elimi-nates a single narration altogether, and sometimes an omniscient observer addresses the reader. Melville's seeming formal care-lessness was a result of his unwillingness or inability to adopt a single form, and that was a result of the essential inappropriateness of the novel as form for what he wanted to say. But he had, of course, to contend with his sensibilities and imagination as well as with his mind. He was not a philosopher because he was a novelist, and not a novelist because he was a philosopher. That he has had no direct influence on the course of subsequent literature may be explained by the confusions in the center of his craft.[40]

Melville could have had his say, as Emerson did, in essays, or perhaps more comfortably in sermons, than in the novel formally defined. Given, however, the substance of what he had to say, the intellectual clarity possible in an essay or a sermon would have encouraged his age to damn him not merely with the neglect he actually suffered, but with something presumably more frightening to him. It seems at least plausible to assume that Melville had a point he wanted to make to his world but was unwilling to make in the light of day; he chose to hide in the novel, and yet must have hoped that his disguise would be penetrable.

To strike through the masks of *Moby-Dick* in order to discover Melville as philosopher seems like a perfect technique for destroying the art of the book. The book is simply there and is accessible to experience. The intention here is not to assume that the arguments of the book are the whole or even its most important part. That Melville was an artist no longer needs to be said. But he was an American artist, and he can be approached through his most Ameri-can aspect, his mind. It is assumed that an understanding of his mind will contribute to an understanding of his art and hoped that intellectual analysis will not destroy magic. It is an impertinent hope because he was a master magician, a virtuoso at juggling the pasteboard masks he hid behind, and his art is his own security that critics will never reduce him to a pedant himself. There are corners that will not be lighted and edges that cannot be sharpened. Uncontrolled reverberations are not controllable, and Melville's sometimes blinding protective coloration will always produce academic quibbles about what he really meant. Some of his masks were designed to be pierced, others were not; and most were fashioned with other ends in view, and thus occupy some middle and maddening ground.

Ishmael is Melville's first mask in *Moby-Dick*. Sensitive Ishmael, with neither money nor interest in life on shore, naturally turns seaward in order to be free of the land's dust on his body and land's weight on his spirit:

> Whenever I find myself growing grim about the mouth; whenever it is a damp, drizzly November in my soul; whenever I find myself involuntarily pausing before coffin warehouses, and bringing up the rear of every funeral I meet; and especially whenever my hypos get such an upper hand of me, that it requires a strong moral principle to prevent me from deliberately stepping into the street, and methodically knocking people's hats off—then, I account it high time to get to sea as soon as I can.[41]

Somehow the land meant melancholy and could lead to suicide. The sea was Ishmael's alternative, and Melville's second mask.

The sea dialectically explains the land. As everyone knows, Ishmael says, "meditation and water are wedded forever."[42] To lose sight of land was to gain sight of, if not into, mystery. Somewhere deep in the pool into which Narcissus looked, and into which we may look, "is the image of the ungraspable phantom of life; and this is the key to it all."[43] As the phantom slipped through his fingers on land, Ishmael sought to grasp the ungraspable at sea, where it could be most readily found. To search for relief from cosmic depression at sea made sense to Ishmael because his earlier experience as a merchant seaman had taught him at least that much. But why ship in a whaler?

Evidently Ishmael had been raised as a proper Calvinist, as had Melville, for, he explains, he turned to whaling as a simple manifestation of the divine economy that had been perfected before time itself began. Though Melville later tried to qualify his rigid determinism by saying that free will did operate within the limits established by necessity, and that chance, though limited by freedom and fate, "has the last featuring blow at events,"[44] he continued rather consistently to think of volition as being utterly determined by the demons hiding in each man's own psyche. Ishmael danced to a tune he neither played nor was certain he could hear. But he was certain of his own dancing and could deduce the tune from that fact. Since he decided to go whaling, it must have been that it had been decided that he should so decide: "I think I can see a little into the springs and motives which, being cunningly presented to me under various disguises, induced me to set about performing the part I did, besides cajoling me into the delusion that it was a choice resulting from my own unbiased freewill and discriminating judgment."[45] The theology of *White Jacket* was still intact.

Ishmael went to sea as a whaling man because of who he was, as Jonathan Edwards would have understood. He was lured by exotic prospects and tantalized by the tumbling mysterious images whaling brought to mind. Hopelessly romantic, Ishmael's decision was compelled by Ishmael's intellectual and psychological organization. Unable, of course, to escape his own perception of the greatest apparent good, he freely acted as he willed, but was not free to will otherwise. "I am tormented with an everlasting itch for things remote,"[46] he said, and the escape to the sea in search of the overwhelming whale was demanded because Ishmael was Ishmael. Having made his decision he was freed from the mean drabness of land life that stultified his spirit and produced the tormenting itch. When he decided, "the great flood-gates of the wonder-world swung open, and in the wild conceits that swayed me to my purpose, two and two there floated into my inmost soul, endless processions of the whale, and, midmost of them all," he explained portentously, "one grand hooded phantom, like a snow hill in the air."[47]

Ishmael does what he is. Though his freedom of action is radical, he perceives as he is, and can do no other. He is driven by the fact of his existence. In Jonathan Edwards' sense, which has other than Christian application, to exist is to perceive is to choose is to will is to act. Ishmael's necessitated whale hunt is thus not, as seems apparent at first blush, a vindication of Puritan orthodoxy, but a repudiation of it. The irony of using an apparent piety against itself is one of Melville's basic strategies. In explaining Ishmael's seaward move in terms of predestination, Melville gives his first clue to Ishmael's goal: Necessitated by existence, Ishmael sails to find the answers to the absurdity of existence. Both life and death can be found at sea, and as Ishmael mockingly said, only his mere body could be killed at sea. Since existence is delimited by death, it is death that must be probed. Cato took his sword, and Ishmael took the sea.

Behind his first two masks, Melville began to say what he could not help saying. Speaking through Ishmael and about the sea, he began to explain where *Moby-Dick* was finally to go. On board the little boat carrying him from New Bedford to Nantucket, where he hoped to find a whaling ship on which to sign, Ishmael felt a surging release. The safe but ugly land slipped away as Ishmael was carried from a faceless and enervating struggle for animal existence toward manhood and significance. Little men had scratched in the earth and scarred its surface with enduring marks of their own squalor; the sea marked men, not men the sea: "how I spurned that turnpike earth! —that common highway all over dented with the marks of slavish heels and hoofs; and turned me to admire the magnanimity of the sea which will permit no records."[48]

Man lives fleshily of the flesh on land where both his comforts and fears may be attended to. It is a pitiful life that is dedicated to "safety, comfort, hearthstone, supper, warm blankets, friends, all that's kind to our mortalities."[49]   But survival in a storm at sea depends on avoiding the emasculated land that cushions and soothes and induces narcosis in its supine inhabitants. To be safe at sea in a storm, the ship must fly from the land which constitutes the direst menace.

So it is with the mind at sea, for which the sea is a limpid mask. To think is to sail. To think hazardously is to face the sea as a man. To think deeply is to sail far. "All deep, earnest thinking is but the intrepid effort of the soul to keep the open independence of her sea."[50]   To let the mind loose on the deep is to run the risk of destruction. But to court destruction in the search for the secret meanings which taunt a mind strong enough to be taunted is also to court manly independence from the God who sneers at man's fragility. If such freedom meant death, the slavery of land meant the same. The alternative was standing upright on a rolling ship or groveling in a steady earth: "But as in landlessness alone resides the highest truth, shoreless, indefinite as God—so, better is it to perish in that howling infinite, than be ingloriously dashed upon the lee, even if that were safety! For worm-like, then, oh! who would craven crawl to land!"[51]

Melville was singing of course of no soft summer cruise. To hazard the recesses of the mind, to call up the deep swimming monsters of the psyche, was absolutely to risk being devoured by them, perhaps in a ghastly cycle of autocannibalism ingesting its own guts like wounded sharks, which "viciously snapped, not only at each other's disembowelments, but like flexible bows, bent round, and bit their own; till those entrails seemed swallowed over and over again by the same mouth, to be oppositely voided by the gaping wound."[52] The chartless sea voyage into the self was therefore as frightening as God, and had to be made for that very reason. The horror of discovering the new world of the ego was countered with the horror of enduring a life not truly lived, of enduring an idiot existence of acquiescence. To begin the voyage was to end it; no man could turn his back to safety once and ever embrace it again, even though his own audacity might occasionally batter his resolution into regret:

> . . . turn to this green, gentle, and most docile earth; consider them both, the sea and the land; and do you not find a strange analogy to something in yourself? For as this appalling ocean surrounds the verdant land, so in the soul of man there lies one insular Tahiti, full of peace and joy, but encompassed by all the horrors of the half known life. God keep thee! Push not off from that isle, thou canst never return![53]

It was human to tire, and the voyage was exhausting, but one point of the voyage was to endure the unendurable in order to be free of man's dependence on a cozy mother who would dry both his tears and his spirit. One price of independence was the torture of peering deep into the unmarked waves, and seeing there some vague moving shapes that proved that man was afraid.

The face of the primitive was Melville's third mask. The dialectic between the sea and the land was extended to one between savagery and civilization. In New Bedford, Ishmael found himself in bed with Queequeg, a prince and a cannibal from some true and therefore uncharted island in the South Seas. Hideously tattooed, Queequeg first repelled but then pleased Ishmael when they found themselves entwined in love in their great bed. Ishmael saw quiet and instinctive qualities in the savage which civilization of the land had quashed in its white man. Ishmael saw that Queequeg was simple, direct, and free:

> You cannot hide the soul. Through all his unearthly tattooings, I thought I saw the traces of a simple honest heart; and in his large, deep eyes, fiery black and bold, there seemed tokens of a spirit that would dare a thousand devils. And besides all this, there was a certain lofty bearing about the Pagan, which even his uncouthness could not altogether maim. He looked like a man who had never cringed and never had had a creditor.[54]

Primitivism meant the presocial condition of an innocence lost to the dusty white inhabitants of a falsely secure and numbing earth. The outlandish outlander was peaceful where a landsman was inwardly churning, self-contained where a white stupidly chattered, unconscious of his genuine wisdom where the socialized man mistakenly took his conventions for knowledge. Unconscious and instinctive as the sea, the savage would not deceive. He was guilty of "no civilized hypocricies and bland deceits."[55] For the reasons that Queequeg repelled others, he appealed to Ishmael, who was already preparing to hazard the sea in rejection of the land. Not all sailors were true sailors, and some were too blind to see a man behind the pagan skin. "I'll try a pagan friend," Ishmael thought, "since Christian kindness has proved but a hollow courtesy."[56] With deepening spiritual involvement, the pagan in search of a true Christianity, and the Christian in search of the pagan unconscious, tried to lead each other to the desired vision. Queequeg loved and made love to Ishmael easily and simply; Ishmael clumsily and haltingly reached for Queequeg with the guilt of his whiteness. The pagan taught him how to love as a primitive, though the Christian had been trained away from love as a member of a progressive social order. A white man, Melville knew, could not endure the direct pleasures of the Typee valley. Ishmael offered his body (all that a Christian had), and Queequeg offered his pure spirit (all that a pagan had).

Two other savages completed Melville's third mask. Tashtego, a full-blooded Indian from Martha's Vineyard, and Daggoo, a gigantic African Negro, became, with Queequeg, the three harpooners on the voyage to which Ishmael was destined. The nobility of these particular savages was heightened by the American lesson about the meaning of civilization in its dealing with the two races represented. The Indian and the Negro, along with the cannibal, felt no guilt because they had none. But the repressed and depraved white man cringed in the noble presence of the savages. Of Daggoo it was said that "there was a corporeal humility in looking up at him; and a white man standing before him seemed a white flag come to beg truce of a fortress."[57] When a white man climbed on Daggoo's back the bearer looked nobler than the rider. The pallor of civilization stood out in more sickly relief when those three savages placed their warm flesh in its presence.

With the directness of the unconscious, these three became the harpooners whose function was to hurl the iron that fastened the whaleboats to their quarry. With the manliness of unconscious strength, they could perch in the prows of the tossing small boats and dare to strike man's first blow. Pitting their own unconscious strength against the unconscious strength in and of the sea, the savages were distillations of the sea with whose creatures they formed a fraternity of unencumbered power. Because he was less of a true sailor, Ishmael needed to lose his whiteness in seas Queequeg carried within himself.

The savage was a distillation of the sea, as was also the whale, Melville's fourth mask. Ishmael was not only sailing, but hunting. Signing on a whaler, he had consigned himself to keep company and to do business with a society of heroes who sought to find, kill, and butcher the world's most prodigious creature, who sought to reduce its magnificence to oil and fragrance for the pleasures of shore people and the profit in cash for themselves. For Melville, unlike most of his characters, the whale was a whale, not a symbol; the whale was neither God nor nature nor the forces of evil, but was a neutral fact of a nature whose total neutrality he had earlier defined. As he later said in *Benito Cereno*, ". . . skulk as he might, and go mad with it, nature cared not a jot; since, whose fault was it, pray?"[58]

His lavish attempts to portray the actuality of the whale in his long chapters on cetology are not mere digressions from the main story line, but his way of rendering the reality of the whale. Obviously his characters attached symbolic significance to the whale, especially to the hoary white one called Moby-Dick, but to identify Melville with his masks is to miss the power and relevance of his cetology and to miss the direction of the book's intelligence. His best explanation was characteristically devious: "So ignorant are most landsmen of some of the plainest and most palpable wonders of the world, that without some hints touching the plain facts, historical and otherwise, of the fishery, they might scout at Moby-Dick as a monstrous fable, or still worse and more detestable, a hideous and intolerable allegory."[59]

One of Melville's techniques for disguising himself was simply to deny what he believed in one place and not in another. It proves nothing that he explicitly denied that Moby-Dick was fabulous or allegorical. The proof must reside in the execution of the book, rather than in his description of that execution; must reside in what he did, not in what he said about what he was doing. To read him otherwise is to deny him the penetrability of those masks which he must have designed to be penetrated. His statement about the actuality of Moby-Dick is borne out by the book, by the cetology, and by significant responses of significant characters, as we will see. Obviously, however, that the whale Moby-Dick was actual does not in itself mean that the book *Moby-Dick* is not an allegory.

One question that informs vital aspects of the whole work refers to the nature of whales in general and Moby-Dick in particular, or, to put it differently, refers to the meaning of symbols or the meaning of nature. The answers to such questions define the fact or allegory of the whale for the speaker; they define the point of view, not the point viewed. But, again, the whale can be, and was, discussed with reference to no particular point of view in the cetological excursions, where the crucial questions had to do with anatomy and classification. Either ignorant of or forgetting about the objective whale, various characters deal with Moby-Dick as a vast white ink-blot into which they project themselves. In *Pierre*, Melville's next book, the discovery that the universe did not care about men was put with the full shock of a fresh death: ". . . Nature is not so much her own ever-sweet interpreter, as the mere supplier of that cunning alphabet, whereby selecting and combining as he pleases, each man reads his own peculiar lesson according to his own peculiar mind and mood."[60]

There can be but little doubt that Melville intended to divest symbols of any intrinsic meaning. Different men saw different worlds, and the objective world was unaffected. The elaborate treatment of the color white, which Melville explained was the absence of color, is a clue to his meaning; men responded to whiteness because nothing was the very thing men could invest with everything they either feared or loved. The ambiguity of whiteness, not its transcendent meaning, was what charged it with meaning for the generations of men.

So with the crude symbolism of the doubloon which Ahab nailed to a mast as a reward for the man who would first sight Moby-Dick. The various interpretations of that coin demonstrate that the coin, of itself, was merely a coin, but that men saw themselves in its moulded face. Ahab saw his own strength, pride, courage, stormy life, and stormy death; Starbuck saw the three mountain peaks as the Trinity as well as seeing the sun of righteousness, but first he saw the valley of death; Stubb got an almanac to interpret the zodiac, and made a game of it; Flask saw a gold coin worth sixteen dollars that could buy 960 cigars; Queequeg compared his tattooing with the design of the coin; Fedallah made a mystical sign to the mysterious symbols; crazy Pip saw it as the ship's navel, and chattered that all saw, all saw. The coin was no symbol until men made it so, and men made it into themselves.

The certainty with which Edwards and Emerson saw God in nature was gone. Now the world was not made for men but was simply an existential fact with neither essence nor transcendence. The meaninglessness of nature now began to horrify: Without meaning there was no purpose, and puny man was merely adrift in a violent sea with no reason to stay afloat and no assistance more useful than the realization of his total isolation from men and God and nature. Looking behind the symbolism that had sustained Edwards and Emerson, Melville found simply a frigid void that could not support human life, a void that made man's predicament absurd.

Melville steadily kept the objectivity of the whale in view. He rejected the aspect of Emersonian transcendentalism that vaporized hard reality into a dream world which was more acceptable to fearful men who had willed themselves into blindness; his opposition to transcendentalism was partially expressed in the cetology. The whale's material existence was presented to the limit of Melville's scientific knowledge. It was left to others in the book to perform the mental operation on the whale's flesh so that the whale could

become a god or a fiend, but no longer a whale. Bringing idealism
to bear on the whale made the whale more obviously relevant to
men and less a gigantic fact of a morally neutral and ghastly natural
world.

In a chapter called "The Affidavit," Melville had Ishmael testify
to the literal truthfulness of the whale's power. But Ishmael is
not Melville, and he is unable to dissociate the whale completely
from ideas about its presumed intelligence, malice, or vengeance.
In trying to present evidence about the ability of a whale to destroy
a whale ship, Ishmael also presents evidence about his own inability
to avoid ascribing motives and qualities to the whale which conform
to his own distracting itch to confront the mysterious depths of
the natural world: "The sperm whale is in some cases sufficiently
powerful, knowing, and judiciously malicious, as with direct afore-
thought to stave in, utterly destroy, and sink a large ship; and what
is more, the sperm whale *has* done it."[61] Melville described the
unconscious strength of the whale, which Ishmael acknowledged,
of course; but in the very moment of his acknowledgement Ishamel
was carried further by his adjectives: "That Himalayan, salt-sea
mastodon, clothed with such portentousness of unconscious power,
that his very panics are more to be dreaded than his most fearless
and malicious assaults!"[62] Though the strength of the whale was
brutal, an objective fact of whalehood, yet Ishmael assumed that
the whale was capable of intrepidity and malice. Any such anthropomorphic attribution discloses much about the speaker and nothing
about the whale.

The whale was part of God's created universe; properly understood, then, the whale could teach men about the Lord. Nature,
as Edwards had said, was an image of divine things, and Emerson
had reported that the created world was the material sediment of
the divine mind. According to Ishmael, the business of whaling
was more frightening than the business of human warfare because
the whale could display more than human ferocity and terror,
could show the wonderful terror of God. But Ishmael was repeatedly
restrained by Melville's vision that to peer behind a symbol may be
to discover precisely nothing. Thus even Ishmael suggested that
the whale was incomprehensible as a symbol:

But if I know not even the tail of this whale, how understand his head? much more, how comprehend his face, when face he has none? Thou shalt see my back parts, my tail, he seems to say, but my face shall not be seen. But I cannot completely make out his back parts; and hint what he will about his face, I say again he has no face.[63]

Though Ishmael was restrained by Melville's intensifying despair of discovering any transcendent meaning or human relevance in the universe, he sometimes attempted to get the whale more firmly fixed in his own mind. Phrenology was based on the assumption that there was human significance in facts of nature; the bumps and lumps of a human skull could tell of human destiny. Ishmael decided that whalish bumps were as eloquent as human ones. The whale, thus interpreted, was a genius, even though it never wrote a book. "No, his great genius is declared in his doing nothing particular to prove it."[64] Carrying his anthropomorphism to its absurd limit, Ishmael described the personality of his lumpy man-whale: "This man had no self-esteem and no veneration. And by these negations, considered along with the affirmative fact of his prodigious bulk and power, you can best form to yourself the truest, though not the most exhilarating conception of what the most exalted potency is."[65] Potency meant a lack of consciousness of self, a radical freedom in the universe, and physical force. The whale's bumps proved that the whale was a thoroughgoing actual whale; Ishmael's anthropomorphism finally turned the whale back into a whale whose profoundest meaning was that it, the whale, existed. Ishmael came finally to learn from Melville that existence is the fundamental fact and that transcendence is a fraud.

But Ishmael was not steady in his hold on radical existence; that is why he went to sea. Going aloft could jeopardize his vision of reality. As Father Mapple signified his "spiritual withdrawal for the time, from all outward worldly ties and connections"[66] by climbing into his high pulpit, so Ishmael was sometimes lulled into a dreamy and luxurious immersion in transcendence when he had separated his physical self from the reality of the deck when keeping his watch high in the masts. There he became a perfect Emersonian rhapsodist of the Oversoul:

Lulled into such an opium-like listlessness of vacant, unconscious revery is this absent-minded youth by the blending cadence of waves with thoughts, that at last he loses his identity; takes the mystic ocean at his feet for the visible image of that deep, blue, bottomless soul, pervading mankind and nature. . . . In this enchanted mood, thy spirit ebbs away to whence it came; becomes diffused through time and space. . . .[67]

Precisely the same drifting into Emersonian transcendence was experienced by the heroes of *Mardi* and *White Jacket* when they were sent aloft.[68]

There were two essential consequences of this fading reality. When Ishmael was so afflicted, he would sight no actual whales; he was also very likely to lose his grip on the ropes along with his grip on reality, and fall to actual death on the actual deck or in the actual sea. Shipowners, he counseled, should beware of enlisting as hands young men with "Phaedon instead of Bowditch in his head. Beware of such an one, I say: your whales must be seen before they can be killed; and this sunken-eyed young Platonist will tow you ten wakes round the world, and never make you one pint of sperm the richer."[69] It was at least partly amusing to lose the hunted whale in the fog of a transcendent mood. There was nothing amusing about the concrete threat transcendence was to existence:

But while this sleep, this dream is on ye, move your foot or hand an inch; slip your hold at all; and your identity comes back in horror. Over Descartian vortices you hover. And perhaps, at mid-day, in the fairest weather, with one half-throttled shriek you drop through that transparent air into the summer sea, no more to rise for ever. Heed it well, ye Pantheists.[70]

Tashtego once fell into the sweet-smelling head of a sperm whale and Melville improved the event with another warning about the dangers of transcendentalism; he wondered how many men had "likewise fallen into Plato's honey head, and sweetly perished there?"[71] It was necessary for men to free themselves from slavery to transcendence, from Kant, as well as from John Locke's empiricism, who Melville took to be the opposite of Plato, Kant, and Emerson. Intellectual independence was necessary in order to see in what ways men were not independent.

The existence of material reality did not depend on perception.

The depth of the sea and the hardness of the deck were objective. That objectivity could awaken the sweetly smiling dreamer to perceive the pain of his own self-induced destruction.   Perched one hundred feet in the air on a careening mast required a sense of the real, put an intolerable price on fusing with the universal spirit, and demanded comprehension of existence, not seduction by symbols. Melville used the ascended sailor as an anti-symbolic symbol when he implied that all the world was perched on that crazy mast, whether the world knew it or not. Survival depended on each man's ability to see the deck and sea and his own precariousness as actual, and his knowledge that no one and nothing could help him cling to the yard except his own fundamentally isolated self and his own accuracy of perception.   To reach out for a savior when high in the rigging would result only in another morsel for the sharks, or another shattered skull to be swept off the deck.

Set against young Ishmael was old Ahab. Ahab was the namesake of the wickedest king of Israel, who worshipped Baal, the false god, and provoked God more severely than all the line of kings before him. Ahab, Melville's fifth and densest mask, walks gloomily and tragically through the book in search of something. He was a hunter too. His prey was Moby-Dick, not the whales of the sea. What Ahab meant to Ahab in hunting and hating the great white whale is the crux. Melville shrouded Ahab in the form of madness, but a madness of some lucidity. Ishmael knows more than he says, and he knows how to hide his meaning. Ahab struggles to explain himself as no other character does, and Melville both assists and deliberately hinders his dark captain: ". . . as touching all Ahab's deeper part, every revelation partook more of significant darkness than of explanatory light."[72]   Ahab is the path to Melville, the reason for Melville's fear, the fact requiring disguise.

Melville sets the transcendentalism of old Ahab against the existentialism of young Ishmael. Ahab, unlike Ishmael, is a devout believer in an inverted but still Christian sense; he worships Idea and Essence, and thinks he knows how to read the meaning of the symbolic cosmos. But he worships some Baal, not God; his profound religiosity is based on faith in the existence of God who is, however, malignant and foul.   Only the death of God will herald Ahab's release from the agony of his own mortality. Ahab's humanity was a lifelong torment and taunt. He hates the God whose existence he accepts; he will thrust his barbed iron into God's heart, and revel in the blood streaming from what he will acknowledge to be the one true God. Old Ahab forces transcendence to its final verge, and discovers madness there. But his motives are complex and ambiguous, and one must allow Ahab to assist at his own autopsy.

It is strange to find Ahab's demonism as a legitimate offspring of sweet Emerson's affirmative transcendentalism or of Edwards' profoundly pious idealism. Ahab's idealism is explicit, as from his own mouth he confesses: "Oh! how immaterial are all materials! What things real are there, but imponderable thoughts?"[73] As both Edwards and Emerson had said, nature was simply an analogy of divine idea, and the key to the human soul was an accurate interpretation of nature. Precisely so for Ahab: "O Nature, and O soul of man! how far beyond all utterance are your linked analogies! not the smallest atom stirs or lives on matter, but has its cunning duplicate in mind."[74] Old orthodoxy was now to fester into madness, but never to grow so misshapen as to obscure its ostensibly pious origins.

Ishmael goes whaling in order to confront himself in the actual sea-world whose very dangers would emphasize being. Ahab goes whaling in order to confront idea and essence. He will pit himself not against a whale, not even against one particular whale, but against the flesh which was made from the Word. In his monomaniacal hunt for Moby-Dick, Ahab hunts not the particular white flesh of that particular whale; he hunts the Word in the flesh. He does not intend to silence the Word, but to replace it with another. He is obsessive, obviously, but the target of his obsession is Ahab, or rather Ahab's own teeming brain, or rather his own elevation of Moby-Dick to that transcendental realm where nature signifies God, where reality is idea. Seeing the white whale, but hearing the Word in the Puritan and Emersonian traditions, Ahab was tortured by the Word he first conceived himself, then heard, then loathed. Moby-Dick was an essence to Ahab, not a whale. That essence patricidally killed him.

Ahab is a madman. His world was encased in his own skull, and his soul "shut up in the caved trunk of his body, there fed upon the sullen paws of its gloom."[75] Sometimes he would fly with a scream from his hammock, trying to elude himself:

. . . in Ahab's case, yielding up all his thoughts and fancies to his one supreme purpose; that purpose, by its own sheer inveteracy of will, forced itself against gods and devils into a kind of self-assumed, independent being of its own. . . . God help thee, old man, thy thoughts have created a creature in thee; and he whose intense thinking thus makes him a Prometheus; a vulture feeds upon that heart forever; that vulture the very creature he creates.[76]

The nature of Ahab's reality was personal and private, a definition of both transcendentalism and insanity. The meaning he gave to symbols, the essence he saw in matter, was his own meaning and his own essence. As his mind had transformed Moby-Dick from a whale into an idea, so he had similarly transformed himself. Ahab was an essence, not a man, even though he had once had "his humanities" and still could drop a single tear into the sea. His stature was nourished by immateriality: "Oh, Ahab! what shall be grand in thee, it must needs be plucked at from the skies, and dived for in the deep, and featured in the unbodied air!"[77] He lived *in* but not *of* the world, as he sadly saw himself: "Ahab stands alone among the millions of the peopled earth, nor gods nor men his neighbours."[78]

Alone in his hate, but in need of others for their strength, private Ahab had to inspire if not to convince the crew to hunt with him for his creature, Moby-Dick. He was compelled to expose his madness. Starbuck, the piously Christian first mate, was horrified because he understood part of the nature of Ahab's quest: "'Vengeance on a dumb brute!' cried Starbuck, 'that simply smote thee from blindest instinct! Madness! To be enraged with a dumb thing, Captain Ahab, seems blasphemous!'"[79] At the moment Starbuck saw the whale as a whale, as one of God's stupid creatures, and in the simplicity of his traditional faith he raised the crucial issue, a definition of reality. But because Starbuck's challenge to Ahab was a reflex and could not come with a passion to match Ahab's, the mate was unprepared for Ahab's answer, and unable to oppose his own half-formed will to the rigidity of Ahab's own. Starbuck was struck dumb by the flashing words Ahab hurled at him, words which convict Ahab of his madness and which infected the crew with a glimpse into the old man's inner and total world:

All visible objects, man, are but as pasteboard masks. But in each event—in the living act, the undoubted deed—there, some unknown but still reasoning thing puts forth the mouldings of its features from behind the unreasoning mask. If man will strike, strike through the mask! How can the prisoner reach outside except by thrusting through the wall? To me, the white whale is that wall, shoved near to me. Sometimes I think there's naught beyond. But 'tis enough. He tasks me; he heaps me; I see in him outrageous strength, with an inscrutable malice sinewing it. That inscrutable thing is chiefly what I hate; and be the white whale agent, or be the white whale principal, I will wreak that hate upon him. Talk not to me of blasphemy, man; I'd strike the sun if it insulted me. For could the sun do that, then I could do the other; since there is ever a sort of fair play herein, jealousy presiding over all creations. But not my master, man, is even that fair play. Who's over me? Truth hath no confines.[80]

That is the old man's confession. The sensible world is a trick consciously and evilly designed to force him to see that he cannot truly see. Because the living essences of things are hidden, Ahab is a prisoner of sense. Demanding freedom, he is duped by appearances. Refusing to acquiesce in the role of a victim, he wills to discover God's malicious trick. Occasionally, he glimpses what Ishmael knows, and says that behind the mask may be nothing, that the alternatives are being and nothingness, not one idea or another. But his outrage at being made to play the fool for God's entertainment is irrepressible, and he will strike at essence with essence, will take vengeance on his whale because it is not a whale, but a hidden truth. How may truth dare to hide from Ahab? How may Moby-Dick, the embodiment of the disguise worn by the insulting deception, continue to swim into Ahab's inner vision as a living taunt that God continues to play His ugly game with impunity?

Others, as well as Starbuck, tried to persuade Ahab that the whale Moby-Dick was not what Ahab hated. Repeatedly he was told that the white whale was a monstrous but not a marvelous fish that could not be guilty in any human sense. A surgeon aboard an English whaler tried to explain to Ahab: "what you take for the White Whale's malice is only his awkwardness."[81] And Starbuck would not desist: "Moby-Dick seeks thee not. It is thou, thou, that madly seekest him!"[82] All to no avail, because the old man had learned to trust his inner vision rather than continue to rely on his mortal eyes to see through the tricks and cheats God had designed in order to keep men stumbling through their lives until each would finally trip for the last time.

The whale, above all, was convenient. Ahab could protest his blindness by destroying that white mask which had crippled him, had grimly "reaped" off his leg as the Grim Reaper. But Ahab's life did not drain out of his torn flesh, and his will was born in the pain: "He piled upon the whale's white hump the sum of all the general rage and hate felt by his whole race from Adam down; and then, as if his chest had been a mortar, he burst his hot heart's shell upon it."[83] Man's rage at his own destiny became, in Ahab's monomania, his weapon. Flinging his hate along with his harpoon, he would destroy the whale whose essence was hidden deep within the gigantic flesh. That his harpoon should carry his message of raging hate Ahab baptized it in the blood of his three pagan harpooners, and he cried the defiance of the Black Mass which was also the secret motto of the book: "Ego non baptizo te in nomine patris, sed in nomine diaboli!"[84] Such a harpoon, now also raised to transcendence, would speak clearly to the deceitful whale, and if Ahab could kill the deceit he would demonstrate man's ability to protest against God's cruelty in creating a world all hidden and secret so that men could but limp and stumble through their short and tormented lives.

Defiantly seizing a lightning rod during a lightning storm, Ahab explained himself to the taunting disembodied essence of the cosmos, to the "clear spirit" of fire:

I now know thee, thou clear spirit, and I now know that thy right worship is defiance. To neither love nor reverence wilt thou be kind; and e'en for hate thou canst but kill; and all are killed. No fearless fool now fronts thee. I own thy speechless, placeless power; but to the last grasp of my earthquake life will dispute its unconditional, unintegral mastery in me. In the midst of the personified impersonal, a personality stands here. Though but a point at best; whencesoe'er I came; wheresoe'er I go; yet while I earthly live, the queenly personality lives in me, and feels her royal rights. But war is pain, and hate is woe. Come in thy lowest form of love, and I will kneel and kiss thee; but at thy highest, come as mere supernal power; and though thou launchest navies of full-freighted worlds, there's that in here that still remains indifferent. Oh, thou clear spirit, of thy fire thou madest me, and like a true child of fire, I breathe it back to thee.[85]

Ahab could worship the basest form of that spirit—Christ Himself, love. But the pure essence, without personification or personality, that was the maddening trickster. If it were not for God, Ahab could worship Christ, and might, perhaps, when God was dead. And Ahab's iron will had already shaken God loose from His accustomed throne. Ahab, through his sheer daring to be, had as he thought, started the grim execution of the Divine:

> The prophecy was that I should be dismembered; and—Aye! I lost this leg. I now prophecy that I will dismember my dismemberer. Now, then, be the prophet and the fulfiller one. That's more than ye, ye great gods, ever were. . . . I will not say as schoolboys do to bullies, —Take some one of your own size; don't pommel *me!* No, ye've knocked me down, and I am up again; but *ye* have run and hidden. Come forth from behind your cotton bags! I have no long gun to reach ye. Come, Ahab's compliments to ye; come and see if ye can swerve me. Swerve me? ye cannot swerve me, else ye swerve yourselves! man has ye there.[86]

Ahab's resolution could falter, his obsession could grow momentarily weak, and he could protest that he was innocent, that even in his search to end his victimization he was a victim. He said to Starbuck:

> Is Ahab, Ahab? Is it I, God, or who, that lifts this arm? But if the great sun move not of himself; but is an errand-boy in heaven; nor one single star can revolve, but by some invisible power; how then can this one small heart beat; this one small brain think thoughts; unless God does that beating, does that thinking, does that living, and not I. By heaven, man, we are turned round and round in this world, like yonder windlass, and Fate is the handspike.[87]

But protest as Ahab would, Melville protested about Ahab. To speak of fate and escape accountability had been denied to Ishamel and was now denied to Ahab, as Melville explained once more, as he had in *White Jacket:* "For with little external to constrain us, the innermost necessities in our being, these still drive us on."[88] Melville made both characters play by the same rules; necessity is the key, but a necessity of being. Ahab saw and thought and willed and therefore acted as Ahab, and could do no other. "What I've dared, I've willed; and what I've willed, I'll do!"[89] He necessarily acted out his inner drama; he was not free to change the play, the idea, or the man. Given who Ahab was, we are therefore also given what he was. It was the Edwardsean formula again. But old Ahab saw only dimly: "Ahab is for ever Ahab, man. This whole act's immutably decreed. 'Twas rehearsed by thee and me a billion years before this ocean rolled. Fool! I am the Fates' lieutenant; I act under orders."[90] He was always exactly Ahab, and he did act under orders. But the fates who issued the orders lived in his own tormented mind. He was his own creature, and could not disobey.

Recognizing that he was fighting a personal war, Ahab resented the human weakness that forced him to enlist the aid of others. He needed the muscle and skill of his crew, and hated the fact of his need. He required a carpenter to make him a new leg and saw that the carpenter reduced his own stature:

> Oh, Life! Here I am, proud as a Greek god, and yet standing debtor to this blockhead for a bone to stand on! Cursed be that mortal inter-indebtedness which will not do away with ledgers. I would be free as air; and I'm down in the whole world's books.[91]

Most of all Ahab needed his crew. But he needed his men not as mere hands on a whaler, but as agents of his madness. He had to charge them with his own energy, fill them with his own purpose, ignite them with a spark from his own flame, teach them to see with his own internal and infernal eye. He needed them to be the muscle to bring his lance to the white fish's life. How it was that he succeeded was more than Ishmael knew:

> Such a crew, so officered, seemed specially picked and packed by some infernal fatality to help him to his monomaniac revenge. How it was that they so aboundingly responded to the old man's ire—by what evil magic their souls were possessed, that at times his hate seemed almost theirs; the White Whale as much their insufferable foe as his; how all this came to be—what the White Whale was to them, or how to their unconscious understandings, also, in some dim, unsuspected way, he might have seemed the gliding great demon of the seas of life, —all this to explain, would be to dive deeper than Ishmael can go.[92]

But the old man did succeed, and easily too, in welding his men into his most carefully prepared instrument of hate.

Since the source of inspiration for the men would be his own fury, Ahab worried that their committment would diminish his own. He was afraid that his demons would desert him if the crew required too much of him. When the mates could not look him in the eye Ahab feared that they had not caught his vibration; but quickly he changed his mind: ". . . did ye three but once take the full-forced shock, then mine own electric thing, *that* had perhaps expired from out me. Perchance, too, it would have dropped ye dead. Perchance ye need it not."[93] He learned that the crew did not need to match the temperature of his will degree for degree; he discovered that he did not need to exert his personal force to the point of its own exhaustion in order to take command of the crew's collective will. Not one man among them could resist the old captain's power, and he exulted: "'Twas not so hard a task. I thought to find one stubborn, at the least; but my one cogged circle fits into all their various wheels, and they revolve."[94]

Each man on board found himself snared as Ahab sprung his mysterious trap. They did not know why his charisma charmed or forced them to act, perhaps against their wills. Some complained in private, but none could face the captain with resolution. Ishmael, too, along with the rest, was swept into the old man's orbit: "I, Ishmael, was one of that crew; my shouts had gone up with the rest; my oath had been welded with theirs; and stronger I shouted . . . because of the dread in my soul."[95] Why? Why did the young sailor whose not yet completed but still certain approach to meaning, an approach which should have been an impregnable defense, why did he succumb? "A wild, mystical, sympathetical feeling was in me; Ahab's quenchless feud seemed mine."[96]

Ahab was the quintessential totalitarian. Combining the objective power of his office as absolute master of his ship with the subjective power of his monomania, and both with the dedication to and rhetoric of an inspirational transcendence, he was irresistible. When he concentrated his special and directed obsession at the weaker because more diffuse wills of his actual subordinates, the result was inevitable. The shouts of the crew were raised in affirmation of the leader's command of material force as a captain, his magnetism as a madman, and his eloquence as a transcendentalist. Melville wants us to understand that Ishmael shouted his *Sieg Heil* along with the rest not because his intellectual position was fundamentally weak but because Ahab could force a suspension of will and judgment.

Because Ishmael was strong, in one sense stronger than Ahab, that suspension of Ishmael's will was temporary. There came a time when the young sailor could take a second breath and recover. But Ahab remained the master of the ship regardless of the state of

Ishmael's ego, and the hunt had to continue. The scar left on Ishmael's authenticity by Ahab's burning power was indelible. And Melville made Ishmael know it in the dark of one dangerous and critical night.

So far Ishmael had lost himself twice: when he was aloft and when he faced Ahab's fire. His understanding was shattered yet a third time because of a blinding fire in the night. While he was at the helm one midnight the flames from the tryworks threw a red glare over the scene he surveyed from the quarterdeck. He dreamed Ahab's kind of dream and saw the fire-carrying ship as a portentous symbol: ". . . as the wind howled on, and the sea leaped, and the ship groaned and dived, and yet steadfastly shot her red hell further and further into the blackness of the sea and the night, and scornfully champed the white bone in her mouth, and viciously spat round her on all sides; then the rushing *Pequod*, freighted with savages, and laden with fire, and burning a corpse, and plunging into that blackness of darkness, seemed the material counterpart of her monomaniac commander's soul"[97]

When earlier Ishmael had lost his hold on meaning disaster had come close, and so again. As he watched the fire cast eerie light into the night he fell asleep, awoke, and found himself facing backwards, an enchanted and hallucinating helmsman guiding the ship by peering into the black night over the stern: "Lo! in my brief sleep I had turned myself about, and was fronting the ship's stern, with my back to her prow and the compass. In an instant I faced back, just in time to prevent the vessel from flying up into the wind, and very probably capsizing her."[98] Drifting into transcendence when aloft had endangered his life, when succumbing to Ahab had endangered his self, and when at the helm had endangered the entire ship. Each time he learned anew that the consequences of wafting into the universal spirit could be fatal. This time Ishmael preached: "Look not too long in the face of the fire, O man!" As Ahab was by his own description "a true child of fire,"[99] Ishmael, when he shook free from his hallucination, knew what face it was he had to avoid. The physical separation from reality of height or night, and the psychological separation that Ahab compelled, all threatened the young sailor. As he survived each shock, he became increasingly and radically free, even though he necessarily remained a hand under Ahab's mad captaincy.

As Ishmael endured he learned to see something in Ahab that helped to explain the old man's tragic greatness. Ahab lived with woe and sought for release through the execution of his own will. Not even the natural sunlight, according to Ishmael, could gaily light the actual grief of this world. To acknowledge pain and not hide from it was a natural attitude of one trying to reel away from Emersonian callousness. There was wisdom in the acknowledgement of existential pain. To see woe truly as woe required the manly courage to face a reality too grim for weaker men. Ishmael explains:

> . . . that mortal man who hath more of joy than sorrow in him, that mortal man cannot be true—not true, or undeveloped. . . . The truest of all men was the Man of Sorrows, and the truest of all books is Solomon's, and Ecclesiastes is the fine hammered steel of woe. 'All is vanity.' ALL. This wilful world hath not got hold of unchristian Solomon's wisdom yet. But he who dodges hospitals and jails, and walks fast crossing graveyards, and would rather talk of operas than hell . . . not that man is fitted to sit down on tombstones, and break the green damp mould with unfathomably wondrous Solomon.[100]

The individual who has not and does not seek understanding is truly dead. There was the greatness of the proper search in Ahab's lunatic hunt. But though Ahab had the strength to acknowledge pain, he had also the madness to call pain wisdom. Yet Ahab flew to heights few men could reach:

> Give not thyself up, then, to fire, lest it invert thee, deaden thee; as for the time it did me. There is a wisdom that is woe; but there is a woe that is madness. And there is a Catskill eagle in some souls that can alike dive down into the blackest gorges, and soar out of them again and become invisible in the sunny spaces. And even if he forever flies within the gorge, that gorge is in the mountains; so that even in his lowest swoop the mountain eagle is still higher than other birds upon the plain, even though they soar.[101]

Ishmael regained his balance in time to see the heroic stature of Ahab's own inversion, and in time to admire the probable agent of his own destruction. Ishmael had learned what Ahab could never know: Wisdom is pain, but pain is not wisdom. Ishmael could become physically and momentarily reversed, but Ahab's reversal was permanent and pervasive. In deriving his vision from the aching stump of his torn leg, Ahab had consigned himself to the world of the heroically dead.

The middle term between Ishmael and Ahab was the savage heart. The harpooneers did as they were told, to be sure, but they were never completely Ahab's victims. They followed orders as they were paid to do, and though Ahab could occasionally cause them to respond partially to his charisma, their wills were not broken by him. Neither resisting nor accepting transcendence, the savages would not shudder at the dark omens that frightened the more enlightened Christian sailors, and were not amazed at Ahab's command of the power of blackness. For example, an electric storm reversed the ship's compass and Ahab mysteriously made a new one:

> As for the men, though some of them lowly rumbled, their fear of Ahab was greater than their fear of Fate. *But as ever before,* the pagan harpooneers remained almost wholly unimpressed; or if impressed, it was only with a certain magnetism shot into their congenial hearts from inflexible Ahab's.[102]

The simple humanity of the pagans made them respond to Ahab, but their response was less than the others. Like Ishmael, they had a different vocabulary and a different vision from the captain and his crew. The pagans were protected, however, by primitive simplicity, while Ishmael was saved by knowledge. There is a difference between protection and salvation. It was eminently fitting that Ishmael's life should be saved by the floating coffin of the pagan Queequeg. The bond between Ishmael and the savage began in the marriage bed in Peter Coffin's inn, and continued to the ultimate scene with Ishmael clinging to the savage's coffin.

For Ahab the world, as has been said, was a malicious trick played by God in order to torment and frustrate men. Ishmael learned to see in a related way. Out of his knowledge that there was nothing behind sheer existence, Ishmael developed a reflex of the absurd, learned to act with the tragicomic posture of an actor in some theater of the absurd: "There are certain queer times and occasions in this strange mixed affair we call life when a man takes this whole universe for a vast practical joke, though the wit thereof he but dimly discerns, and more than suspects that the joke is at nobody's expense but his own."[103] Ahab agonized at the trick played on him by his tormenting God; Ishmael was sustained by the absurdity of his relation to a life whose gravest moments were also the most ridiculous. It was, after all, absurd that his existence should be imperiled by some other who was a lunatic; it was ridiculous that his freedom of choice should be nullified by Ahab, who acted from compulsion, not freedom. Ishmael's earlier knowledge that freedom was illusory was now reinforced. He explained as best he could:

> And as for small difficulties and worryings, prospects of sudden dis-aster, peril of life and limb; all these, and death itself, seem . . . only sly, good-natured hits, and jolly punches in the side bestowed by the unseen and unaccountable old joker. That odd sort of wayward mood I am speaking of, comes over a man only in some time of extreme tribulation; it comes in the very midst of his earnestness, so that what just before might have seemed to him a thing most momen-tous, now seems but a part of the general joke. There is nothing like the perils of whaling to breed this free-and-easy sort of genial, des-perado philosophy; and with it I now regarded this whole voyage of the Pequod, and the great White Whale its object.[104]

Having *Angst* break into absurdity, Ishmael made a leap into the ridiculous in order to insulate himself from further contagion from Ahab, knowing all the while that he must continue to sail with his captain on the insanely compulsive voyage. That knowledge rein-forced his sense of absurdity rather than added to his store of despair.

That Ishmael's existence should depend upon Ahab's will was ridiculous. But no more so than the peril every man endured at the hands of others. Once, when Queequeg was standing on a whale tied alongside the ship, Ishmael was tied to the savage in order to fish him out of the shark-infested waters should he lose his footing on the slippery carcass. Should Queequeg slip, Ishmael, so far from saving him, would be likely to be pulled into the water too. He said that his free will "had received a mortal wound; and that another's mistake or misfortune might plunge innocent me into unmerited disaster and death."[105] He thought that such a situation must be an interregnum in Providence, which Ishmael, as he pon-dered his precarious relationship, came to see as the normal human condition. Every mortal was tied to many others, and every mortal controlled only one end of the relationship. A banker's folly could throw a man into bankruptcy; a druggist's carelessness could send a man to his death. There was no greater danger at sea than on land; death was everywhere, and men were compelled to depend on others who were not dependable for security: "And if you be a philosopher, though seated in the whale-boat, you would not at heart feel one whit more of terror, than though seated before your evening fire with a poker, and not a harpoon, by your side."[106] Precisely because of its omnipresence, terror was absurd.

Because Starbuck was a traditional Christian he spoke Ahab's language and was therefore an easy mark for the captain. Already committed to transcendence, the first mate was courageous enough in the face of merely ordinary horror, but was unable to withstand the spiritual terror which menaced him from Ahab's glaring eye. When once Ahab captured Starbuck, the mate was forever a slave to madness, as he confessed himself: "My soul is more than matched; she's overmanned; and by a madman! Insufferable sting, that sanity should ground arms on such a field! But he drilled deep down, and blasted all my reason out of me!"[107] He was an easy victim because he thought and lived with Ahab's own categories; Christianity could not withstand antichristianity. Stubb, and the others, broke under Ahab's thunder because they were lesser men than the captain, because they were stupid and blind. Starbuck was the crucial test to Ahab—not Ishmael, who was unknown to Ahab—because of Starbuck's avowed piety. Ahab did not realize until it was all over with the crew how easy it would be for him to stand that piety on its head. Though the mate would protest the whole voyage through, though he would skulk in corridors trying to work up the courage to kill the old devil, he was forever lost when he was first lost.

Christianity was no help to Starbuck because he did not understand it, and if he had he would have seen its uselessness. Ahab had already intimated that he could worship love but not power, the feminine but not the masculine, personification not abstraction, Christ not God. In one resounding sentence, the narrator came as close as he dared to asserting that Christ was a woman: "And whatever they may reveal of the divine love in the Son, the soft, curled, hermaphroditical Italian pictures, in which his idea has been most successfully embodied; these pictures, so destitute as they are of all brawniness, hint nothing of any power, but the mere negative, feminine one of submission and endurance, which on all hands it is conceded, form the peculiar practical virtues of his teachings."[108] How could Starbuck, or any man, who became soft and yielding and resigned through Christianity hope to resist Ahab's concentrated power? As the word became flesh in Christ it became radically altered; with embodiment it became merciful and tender instead of wrathful and vengeful as in Israel. As the abstract took form it became, for Ahab, baser because more human. He could worship queenly personality if impersonal thought did not rage behind her. Blindly worshipping the feminine Christ with no care for the anterior force, poor Starbuck yielded because, not in spite, of his belief, even if he did not know what it was that he did believe.

Starbuck was not alone. Wherever formal and orthodox Christianity flourished, men were literally forced to become effeminate or hypocritical. Ishmael and Ahab actually agreed. Let a ship once sight and report an ostensible obstacle and ships would for long avoid the place: "There's your law of precedents; there's your utility of traditions; there's the story of your obstinate survival of old beliefs never bottomed on the earth, and now not even hovering in the air! There's orthodoxy!"[109] Rejecting the past, transcendence, formalism, and the tenderness of Christ in a clawing world, Melville, through his characters, rejected the whole of religion. In so doing, Melville and Ishmael were drawing closer together.

The savages on board the *Pequod* presented both a foil and an alternative to Christianity. In *Mardi* Melville had argued that it was senseless actually to hate a shark, as much a creature of God as an angel; now Queequeg, in his primitive simplicity, said: "Queequeg no care what god made him shark . . . wedder Feegee god or Nantucket god; but de god wat made shark must be one dam Ingin."[110] Queequeg realized that Christianity was not the answer he had hoped it would be and decided that "it's a wicked world in all meridians; I'll die a pagan."[111] He recognized the interdependence of all men and resolved simply to do good when he could; he seemed to say that "It's a mutual, joint-stock world in all meridians. We cannibals must help these Christians."[112]

Ishmael gaily decided to leave Queequeg and his funny black idol-god alone, at least until the savage began to fast. Ishmael required nothing of any man's religion except that it do no harm to himself or others. He thought that the idea of going hungry to please a god was excessive: "But when a man's religion becomes really fanatic; when it is a positive torment to him; and, in fine, makes this earth of ours an uncomfortable inn to lodge in; then I think it high time to take that individual aside and argue the point with him."[113] There is no doubt that Melville was thinking of the God of Edwards, described in Father Mapple's sermon, when he had Ishmael debate theology with the cannibal.

That Christianity demanded hypocrisy as well as effeminacy was left to the illiterate Negro cook finally to demonstrate. Stubb ordered the cook to deliver a sermon to a writhing mass of sharks who were gorging on the carcass of a whale tied alongside of the *Pequod*. The old cook leaned over the bloody and boiling sea, and sermonized the feeding sharks: "Your woraciousness, fellow-critters, I don't blame ye so much for; dat is natur, and can't be helped; but to gobern dat wicked natur, dat is de pint." He conceded that sharks were sharks, but if they would govern their more sharkish urges, they would become angels. Stubb was delighted and announced that that was true Christianity, and ordered the cook to continue. The Negro protested: "No use goin' on; de dam willains will keep a-scrougin' and slappin' each oder, Massa Stubb; dey don't hear one word; no use a preachin' to such dam g'uttons as you call 'em, till dare bellies is full, and dare bellies is bottomless; and when dey do get 'em full, dey won't hear you den; for den dey sink in de sea, go fast to sleep on de coral, and can't hear not'ing at all, no more, for eber and eber." The utter pointlessness of urging sharks to repress their sharkishness, and of trying to inculcate moderation in gluttons, drove the frantic cook to his final benediction: "Cussed fellow-critters! Kick up de damndest row as ever you can; fill up your dam' bellies till dey bust—and den die."[114]

With Melville's deepening bitterness, with his developing hatred of Christianity, his view of America began also to change. While he was voiding symbols of intrinsic meaning, and continuing to free himself from attachment to supposedly eternal and immutable truths, he was preparing himself to question his earlier participation in the then conventional national mythology. America was to become neither a symbol nor a promise, but a mere nation where men raved as men always and everywhere raved. He was coming to see that America was an integral part of the civilization he had rejected in *Typee*. Brother Jonathan had proved that he was an "apostolic lancer"[115] in the Mexican War. The hypocrisy of clothing avarice and ambition in the rhetoric of piety was a long human and national tradition. The Quaker owners of the *Pequod*, exemplifying the Protestant ethic of profit in the name of piety, seemed to conclude "that a man's religion is one thing, and this practical world quite another. This world pays dividends."[116] Bildad, one of the owners, epitomized the Puritan formula that it was necessary to love the world with weaned affections, as well as the deceit built into that formula; he advised his men to keep the Sabbath at sea but not if it proved expensive: "Don't whale it too much a' Lord's days men; but don't miss a fair chance either, that's rejecting Heaven's good gifts."[117]

Melville's disgust was elicited by the facts of civilization rather than by any particular fact of America, except that he now saw America as civilized rather than as the relatively primitive hope of the world he had earlier envisaged. He had learned on Typee that civilization was repression, that history was made by men who were driven by themselves to leave the shade of a palm tree and the hand of a lover. Happy men did not do, they simply were. Ambition and success thus began time and history and something called progress. History was the story of the doings of demonic men who might lament their expulsion from the Garden but who were driven by their own imprisoned energy to be great: "For all men tragically great are made so through a certain morbidness. Be sure of this, O young ambition, all mortal greatness is but disease."[118] Ahab was civilized to an ultimate degree; he was almost pure mind. Even though he had once had "his humanities" he recognized that humanity was as much his enemy as he was himself. Ahab felt some human sympathy for the mad little Negro, Pip, and Ahab had to avoid every emotion in order to remain the concentrated intelligence he was. He explained to Pip that "there is that in thee, poor lad, which I feel too curing to my malady. Like cures like; and for this hunt, my malady becomes my most desired health."[119]

Ahab, as civilization, as America, had to cultivate his madness in order to achieve the mad goals he had set himself. But Ahab, unlike civilization or America, had enough self-consciousness to know what he was doing. His memory of his own warmer past could bring a solitary tear to his eye. Instead of even a single tear, lesser men of civilization applauded themselves, and prated of amelioration and progress, while hypocritically condemning those who knew better:

Go to the meat-market of a Saturday night and see the crowds of live bipeds staring up at the long rows of dead quadrupeds. Does not that sight take a tooth out of the cannibal's jaw? Cannibals? who is not a cannibal? I tell you it will be more tolerable for the Feegee that salted down a lean missionary in his cellar against a coming famine . . . in the day of judgment, than for thee, civilized and enlightened gourmand, who nailest geese to the ground and feastest on their bloated livers in thy paté-de-foie-gras.[120]

Melville's milieu with its mid-Victorian proprieties had not been structured for either his physical or his intellectual comfort. He already knew that he must live in but not of the world, and, like the whale, "remain warm among ice."[121] Of course *Moby-Dick* failed to bring him either appreciation or cash, and he needed both. "Dollars damn me," he wrote to Nathaniel Hawthorne, "what I feel most moved to write, that is banned, —it will not pay. Yet, altogether, write the *other* way I cannot. So the product is a final hash, and all my books are botches."[122] Hawthorne understood and praised *Moby-Dick,* and constituted for Melville at least an audience of one. Because Hawthorne understood, Melville enjoyed "a sense of unspeakable security," and was prompted to write his now famous sentence: "I have written a wicked book, and feel spotless as the lamb."[123] He was grateful to Hawthorne, he said, for explaining that *Moby-Dick* was one vast and integrated allegory which Melville said he had vaguely felt but had not really known.

Melville had found a sympathetic and sensitive intelligence in Hawthorne. Hawthorne understood because he too "says no! in thunder,"[124] while those who affirm necessarily lie. Hawthorne understood because, as Melville had earlier said in print, there was "a touch of Puritanic gloom" about him, a "great power of blackness in him [which] derives its force from its appeals to that Calvinistic sense of Innate Depravity and Original Sin, from whose visitations, in some shape or other, no deeply thinking mind is always and wholly free." Hawthorne understood because he, too, had disguised himself in his work, had made himself appear harmless, and the world had been wrong in its assessment of him. "This Man of Mosses," Melville said about Hawthorne and could have equally well said about himself, "takes great delight in hoodwinking the world, —at least, with respect to himself."[125] Given his view of Hawthorne's art, it was fitting that Melville should have warmed to Hawthorne's friendship, and not surprising that Hawthorne evidently could not quite understand Melville.

Perhaps sensing Hawthorne's bewilderment, Melville tried to explain himself to his friend. He wrote in a letter that the world found truth ridiculous and clung to its soothing lies. It was therefore necessary to resist the world even though that would mean poverty. Among those frightful lies was the notion that the brain could be developed only at the expense of the heart. It was not so, Melville said, and he stood for the heart. "To the dogs with the head!"[126] Ahab was pure head, and Melville was not. Men feared and disliked God because they did not trust His heart, thinking Him unmixed brain. He concluded his explanations to Hawthorne by apologizing for capitalizing the pronouns for God, saying that it was the usage of a flunky.

Melville had found what he thought was a soulmate, but that did not lessen his need for money or his deepening isolation and alienation. In *Pierre,* published the year after *Moby-Dick,* he now expressed himself more explicitly than had been his custom; for once, the critics understood and hissed in chorus. An American review of Pierre said "that Mr. Melville is a man wholly unfitted for the task of writing wholesome fictions; that he possesses none of the faculties necessary for such work; that his fancy is diseased, his morality vitiated, his style nonsensical and ungrammatical, and his characters as far removed from our sympathies as they are from nature."[127] *Pierre* is the story of how the evil of the world can force innocence into incest, murder, and suicide. The power of blackness was continuing to charge Melville's internal world.

The hero, Pierre, begins as a thorough innocent who learns that his father had had a daughter whose birth was hidden from the world. That daughter, Isabel, appears and Pierre vows to care for her though he has to reject his inheritance, his mother, and his lover. Isabel and Pierre, pretending they are married, go to New York City where Pierre hopes to make a living by writing. In time Lucy, Pierre's former fiancée, comes to live with them. In a street brawl Pierre commits a crime, is jailed, and kills himself. He had directly or indirectly been responsible for the deaths of his mother, Lucy, and Isabel, all as a result of his vow to do the Christian

thing by his poor sister Isabel. At his death Pierre had been transformed from an engaging naïf into a raging cynic.

By making his hero a writer, Melville gave himself the opportunity to write about a writer in mid-nineteenth-century America.
Though the precise identification of Melville with Pierre must remain
moot, it is undeniable that at least part of *Pierre* was Melville's
own spiritual autobiography. Pierre was young, fresh, and effer-
vescent with life and health. He started the novel as a youth who
could have appreciated the valley of the Typees and had, through
his vow to remain true to the dark Isabel, turned to writing, "the
most miserable of all the pursuits of a man."[128] The radiant health
of the vital youth had been squelched in order for him to find truth,
to pour his soul onto paper; the earlier *joie de vivre* had been tamed,
civilized, and Melville was once again reminded of the sickening
contrast between happiness and society:

> Oh, I hear the leap of the Texan Camanche, as at this moment he
> goes crashing like a wild deer through the green underbrush; I hear
> his glorious whoop of savage and untamable health; and then I look
> in at Pierre. If physical, practical unreason make the savage, which
> is he? Civilization, Philosophy, Ideal Virtue! behold your victim![129]

The security of Pierre's early life had been utterly shattered as a
result of learning about Isabel's existence. He resolved never again
to succumb to illusion: "Henceforth I will know nothing but Truth;
glad Truth, or sad Truth; I will know what *is*, and do what my deepest angel dictates."[130] With Ahab and in a sense with Ishmael,
Pierre now, in order to avoid a continued life of comfortable deceit,
was committed to breaking through the pasteboard masks that
disguised all reality: "Let me go, ye fond affections; all piety leave
me; —I will be impious, for piety hath juggled me, and taught me
to revere, where I should spurn. From all idols, I tear all veils;
henceforth I will see the hidden things. . . ."[131]

It was natural that Pierre should occasionally regret his decision
to repudiate the sweet illusions of his past so that "he might not
feel himself driven out an infant Ishmael into the desert, with no
maternal Hagar to accompany and comfort him."[132] The seeker
after life's hidden truths was precisely such a rootless and friendless
wanderer for Melville, as every one of his earlier books had shown.
Pierre was destined to repeat the quests of Melville's earlier rovers,

except that his journey was to occur in a dingy study, was not to be a physical journey, and was not, therefore, to be mitigated by any romance or adventure. Pierre, like Melville at that stage, was to travel by sitting still, and was to suffer only more intensely as a result.

Melville's earlier attitude about the concept of fate was still unchanged. Pierre was caught by his ideas, attitudes, and beliefs, and could not escape. He had brought his entire self to the problem of Isabel, and that self demanded that he act in one way rather than another: "But Pierre was not arguing Fixed Fate and Free Will now; Fixed Fate and Free Will were arguing him, and Fixed Fate got the better in the debate."[133] He was fated by his own psychological organization to pursue a reality that could only be illuminated by the "flashing revelations of grief's wonderful fire. . . ."[134] Moved by a compassion he would not and could not stifle, Pierre was led by his heart to embark on a journey of the head. The inevitable woe of exploring the darker recesses of reality was the necessary price of truth.

It should now come as no surprise that Pierre learned that the kind of hopeful transcendentalism best represented by Emerson was his greatest obstacle to reality. Analogies were essential to Emerson's world view, and Pierre exploded: "Quit thy analogies; sweet in the orator's mouth, bitter in the thinker's belly." Emersonian theories of optimism and compensation were especially blinding. The compensations of evil, Emerson believed, would teach that evil was merely negative and partial while good was positive and universal. Emerson had argued that evil and pain, properly understood, would be seen as a stage of good unfolding. Emerson had written that the poet "disposes very easily of the most disagreeable facts," and Melville wrote in the margin of Emerson's book: "So it would seem. In this sense Mr. E. is a great poet."[135] In the manuscript he was writing, Pierre exploded again: "Away, ye chattering apes of a sophomorean Spinoza and Plato, who once didst all but delude me that the night was day, and pain only a tickle."[136] Emerson had said that poverty consisted in feeling poor, that the poor lent shadow to a sunny landscape that would have been less beautiful in only bright colors. There were those, Pierre said, who required a "povertiresque" ingredient in the social landscape as they needed a picturesque one in the natural:

> To such an one, not more picturesquely conspicuous is the dismantled thatch hut in a painted cottage of Gainsborough, than the time-tangled and want-thinned locks of a beggar, *povertiresquely* diversifying those snug little cabinet-pictures of the world, which, exquisitely varnished and framed, are hung up in the drawing-room minds of humane men of taste, and amiable philosophers of either the 'Compensation,' or 'Optimist' school. They deny that any misery is in the world, except for the purpose of throwing the fine *povertiresque* element into its general picture.[137]

The philosophers of optimism had never experienced poverty, and their theories rendering poverty acceptable were mere parlor games that could, however, become dangerous if taken for the real thing. In a private letter, Melville had earlier said that he had been "very agreeably disappointed in Mr. Emerson" because the Concord sage had been comprehensible. The trouble with Emerson was that "his belly . . . is in his chest, and his brains descend down into his neck." Melville could tolerate only a limited quantity of Emerson: "But enough of this Plato who talks thro' his nose."[138]

The profoundest error of the transcendentalists was their inability to see that men were human, not divine, and that absolute and universal ideas and codes of conduct were inapplicable to them. In *Pierre*, Melville called absolute standards "chronometrical," and relative ones "horological." The earth was not heaven, "and thus, though the earthly wisdom of man be heavenly folly to God; so also, conversely, is the heavenly wisdom of God an earthly folly to man."[139] The reason Christ suffered on earth was that He was unfit for the earth. "With inferior beings, the absolute effort to live in this world according to the strict letter of the chronometricals is, somehow, apt to involve those inferior beings eventually in strange, *unique* follies and sins, unimagined before."[140] An attempt to live a truly Christian life might end in the individual's own crucifixion, but would more likely result in that individual crucifying others, or perhaps both, as in the examples of Pierre and Billy Budd. Pierre had vowed to be a better man than society could understand or tolerate, and through its reaction to him he was led to black crime by both his own and society's standards. The consequences of genuine virtue in American civilization could only be incestuous lust, murder, and suicide.

Pierre was the end of Melville's intense and even frantic period of writing. In six years he had published seven novels. He had written and thought himself into exhaustion which his own family suspected to be insanity, though the physicians who examined him did not. He was now at his most dangerous crisis, and it seems a prudent guess to say that if he had continued to write in the vein of *Moby-Dick* and *Pierre* he would have destroyed himself. He did continue to write, but more leisurely, more carefully, with greater attention to his own mental health. America contributed to his decision to slacken his pace; all of his books together were not producing sufficient income for him to continue writing.

His sense of poverty now became nearly obsessive, as "Poor Man's Pudding and Rich Man's Crumbs," a story he published in 1854, will show. He tried to obtain a position in American consulates in Honolulu, Florence, and other places, but although Hawthorne tried to help him, he failed. Literally driven to his desk, Melville published *Israel Potter* in 1855, and collected a series of his short stories in *The Piazza Tales* in 1856. In *Israel Potter* he tried to write a simple adventure story of the American Revolution, a story that apparently would not put too heavy a burden on his energies; he tried to recapture his now lost nationalism, saying that "America is, or may yet be, the Paul Jones of nations . . . civilized in externals but a savage at heart. . . ."[141] The attempt to reach back, to recapture the excitement of his youth, to search for the language of gayety, is pathetic. He had climbed to where he was and he could not find his way back into the more comfortable valley he had once known. The novel was another commercial failure, as were *The Piazza Tales*. He managed to survive on the income he received for writing for magazines. Melville's now chronic melancholia seemed bottomless.

In order to find cheer or, at least, a change of scene that hopefully would do him some good, he set out with borrowed money to tour the Holy Land in 1856. On the way he stopped to see Hawthorne at Hawthorne's consulate in England. They took a walk and Hawthorne recorded his impressions and their talk in his private notebook:

Melville as he always does, began to reason of Providence and futurity, and of everything that lies beyond human ken, and informed me that he had "pretty much made up his mind to be annihilated"; but still he does not seem to rest in that anticipation; and, I think, will never rest until he gets hold of a definite belief. It is strange how he persists—and has persisted ever since I knew him, and probably long before—in wandering to-and-fro over these deserts. . . . He can neither believe, nor be comfortable in his unbelief; and he is too honest and courageous not to try to do one or the other. If he were a religious man, he would be one of the most truly religious and reverential; he has a very high and noble nature, and better worth immortality than most of us.[142]

The subsequent trip did Melville little genuine good. He found Jerusalem barren and oppressive; Pompeii seemed "like any other town. Same old humanity. All the same whether one be dead or alive." Rome was no exception: "Rome fell flat on me. Oppressively flat."[143] But from his gloomy travels he found material to work into a lecture on ancient statuary that he gave, and got paid for, when he returned to America, and inspiration for a long narrative and metaphysical poem he was to call "Clarel."

When he returned, little better for his moment of hollow recreation, and still desperate for funds, he published *The Confidence Man* (1857). An obscure work, *The Confidence Man* was, among other things, Melville's spit of hate against America and what it stood for. It was his most venomous attack on both Emerson and Thoreau. It was the limit of his misanthropy.

The story takes place on a Mississippi steamer called the *Fidèle*, and begins with the appearance of a dreamy, innocent, deaf and dumb stranger dressed in white who writes Christian phrases on a slate: "Charity thinketh no evil." The crowd of passengers jeers and attacks him, and accepts the sign hung up by a barber: "No Trust." In a rapid series of scenes, a succession of confidence men appear on the boat, each exploiting the stupidity, credulity, or avarice of the passengers. Money is collected by the confidence men for a number of fake organizations and purposes, including the Black Rapids Coal Company, the Seminole Widow and Orphan Asylum, the New Jerusalem reform colony, the Omni-Balsamic Reinvigorator, and the Philosophic Intelligence Office. Fraud is perpetrated for its own sake as well as for profit: "How much money did the devil make in gulling Eve?"[144] In brief compass, Melville ran up his list of sharp business practices in America, gullibility, and hypocrisy.

He could not avoid the subject of slavery in 1857. One of the confidence men was asked if he was an abolitionist; in his answer, Melville indicted that vital aspect of his time and place for its trimming, insincerity, callousness, and folly:

> As to that, I cannot so readily answer. If by abolitionist you mean a zealot, I am none; but if you mean a man, who, being a man, feels for all men, slaves included, and by any lawful act, opposed to nobody's interest, and therefore rousing nobody's enmity, would willingly abolish suffering (supposing it, in its degree, to exist) from among mankind, irrespective of colour, then I am what you say.[145]

Two of the passengers on the *Fidèle* were Mark Winsome and his disciple, Egbert. There is no doubt that Melville intended these two to represent Emerson and Thoreau. Winsome was first known as "the mystic," and was described this way: "Toning the whole man, was one-knows-not-what of shrewdness and mythiness, strangely jumbled; in that way, he seemed a kind of cross between a Yankee peddler and a Tartar priest, though it seemed as if, at a pinch, the first would not in all probability play second fiddle to the last."[146] The glance of his pale blue eye seemed as if it could come from no feeling, living man. Invited to sit down to a glass of wine, Winsome replied: "But, as for the wine, my regard for that beverage is so extreme . . . that I keep my love for it in the lasting condition of an untried abstraction."[147] He drank ice-water instead. When pressed on a point, the mystic solemnly announced: "I seldom care to be consistent."[148]

Melville's fullest measure of scorn for virtually everything Emerson stood for was concentrated in Winsome's answer to the question of whether his philosophy conformed to the world: "It does; and that is the test of its truth; for any philosophy that, being in operation contradictory to the ways of the world, tends to produce a character at odds with it, such a philosophy must necessarily be but a cheat and a dream."[149] Melville's disgust can be measured by his praise of Hawthorne for saying "No! in thunder." Affirmation and acquiescence were always and everywhere fraudulent for Melville, and Emerson's merging with the mainstream of American life was therefore not merely wrong but also vicious.

Egbert, Winsome's disciple, appears, and a confidence man tries to borrow money from him by making an appeal to friendship. The philosophy of Winsome allows Egbert to resist all appeals because, he says, real friendship exists only in celestial realms and has contempt for eathly pain and need. The confidence man has finally met his match, and he bursts out at Egbert:

> Why wrinkle the brow, and waste the oil both of life and the lamp, only to turn out a head kept cool by the under ice of the heart? What your illustrious magian [Winsome-Emerson] has taught you, any poor, old, broken-down, heart-shrunken dandy might have lisped. Pray, leave me, and with you take the last dregs of your inhuman philosophy. And here, take this shilling, and at the first wood-landing buy yourself a few chips to warm the frozen natures of you and your philosopher by.[150]

In the final scene an old man asks one of the confidence men for a life preserver. The confidence man gives him "a brown stool with a curved tin compartment underneath."[151] The distance between Melville's two life preservers, from Queequeg's coffin to a portable toilet, is the distance he had traveled from tragedy to hate. To a frightened and gullible old man, the American operator had nothing to give but false hope and a stinking toilet. "Pah! what a smell," the confidence man complained as the *Fidèle* continued to steam down the great American river with her assortment of great American types. But Melville had not yet completed expressing his disenchantment with the nation that had turned him into a stranger.

His personal plight was worsened by the Civil War. Again he tried to obtain a consulship, and again he failed. In 1863 he moved his family from Massachusetts to New York City, where he scratched out a living. He wrote poetry about the war, collected in *Battle Pieces*. It referred mostly to the agony and tragedy of individual battles and scenes of the war. In a supplement to his war poetry, written more than a year after Lee's surrender, he pleaded with northerners to exercise common sense and charity, though he had no hope that his compatriots were capable of either. Finally, in December, 1866, he found a job after looking for a decade. He was appointed out-door customs inspector at the Port of New York for four dollars a day. He held that post for nineteen almost silent years.

He seems willingly to have accepted the obscurity as, perhaps, a necessary price of sanity and survival. Readers who tried could not locate him. Abandoning himself to inspecting the luggage of those wealthy enough to travel, he almost stopped inspecting the spiritual baggage of his time and place. Almost, but not quite. In a private letter of 1877 he tried to explain himself:

> ... at my years, and with my disposition, or rather, constitution, one gets to care less and less for everything except downright good feeling. Life is so short, and so ridiculous and irrational (from a certain point of view) that one knows not what to make of it, unless—well, finish the sentence for yourself.[152]

Melville did continue to write in his spare time, mostly poetry now. *Clarel* was published in 1876, and two volumes were privately printed: *John Marr and Other Sailors* in 1888, and *Timoleon* in 1891. The manuscript of *Billy Budd* was completed three months before his death, but was not published until 1924. Melville's final intellectual development can be seen in *Clarel* and *Billy Budd,* two works which should dispel the older idea that Melville, at this stage of his life, had nothing left to say.

In the Standard Edition of Melville's *Works, Clarel* is a poem of 630 pages. It is the narrative of a young student's quest for truth in the Holy Land, his discovery of others similarly anguished, and his ultimate recognition that there may be nothing to replace the lost, remembered peace. One critic has well said that "the loss of faith is the basic assumed fact of the poem, and its larger problem is how to endure the overwhelming sense of a shattered vision."[153] Among the visions shattered in *Clarel* were the many ingredients that had made up the mythology of America. What made an American leave home?

> Is't misrule after strife? and dust
> From victor heels? Is it disgust
> For times when honour's out of date
> And serveth but to alienate?[154]

It was not only the concrete practices of post-war America that Melville repudiated, not merely experience, but the full set of illusions and promises that had constituted the national myth. Step by step, Melville now also cries "No! in thunder" to the complex of ideas and attitudes that he had earlier accepted and had been nourished by, had come to suspect, and now vehemently rejected. Seizing the ideas that had been slowly developed in the stretch of time from Winthrop to Edwards, Adams, Taylor, Emerson, and his own earlier life, Melville now forced American myth to come through the filter of his own experience, to stand the test of his own life and his own knowledge. He closed the circle in *Clarel,* and a vital development of American thought ended. God's country could not survive in his jaundiced but acute eye, and though others were to continue the hymn to the city on a hill, they could do so only out of ignorance of Melville and *Clarel;* they could continue to celebrate the development of the national mind only by turning their backs on a central aspect of that development.

The idea that America had abolished time had been crucial to the earlier myth, that the old world was the past and therefore evil, and, as the past, irrelevant to the land of the future. Melville now answered:

> Our New World bold
> Had fain improved upon the Old;
> But the hemispheres are counterparts.[155]

He accused the age of superficiality, opportunism, and arrogance. The world had failed the searching youth in *Clarel* who wondered whether there might not be some other world:

> well, there's the *New*—
> Ah, joyless and ironic too![156]

Men had thought that the new world was a special place unrelated to time, had believed that the innocent virginity and power of the new had been guaranteed by the immemorial idea of the west:

> They vouch that virgin sphere's assigned
> Seat for man's re-created kind:
> Last hope and proffer, they protest.
> Brave things! sun rising in the west;
> And bearded centuries but gone
> For ushers to the beardless one.
> Nay, nay; your future's too sublime:
> The Past, the Past is half of time,
> The proven half.[157]

Winthrop had sermonized about the assignment of the new world as the home of the saints, recreated men; Edwards had taught of the sunrise in the west, with all that implied; Adams had written of the wisdom of the past as merely preparatory for the grand climax of America; Taylor had argued that his land could recapture Eden; and Emerson had sung and sung his hymns to the present.

The idea of America as a city on a hill, as God's country, now emerged as a "satire of the heaven."[158] A character in *Clarel* protested that America did have at least a political secret based on her natural abundance:

> The vast reserves—the untried fields;
> These long shall keep off and delay
> The class-war, rich-and-poor-man fray
> Of history. From that alone
> Can serious trouble spring.[159]

The ancient idea that the relatively wide distribution of property in America would protect the people from the most violent excesses of the Old World was there unearthed as new ammunition in defense of the nation. The idea was that the founding fathers had built well, and that the plenty of the place would sustain their work. The answer came in solemn cadence. America lived fast, and would die quickly:

> 'Twill come, 'twill come!
> One demagogue can trouble much:
> How of a hundred thousand such?
> And universal suffrage lent
> To back them with brute element
> Overwhelming?[160]

America's destiny was but the destiny of the past, and "Your Thirty Years (of) War" would surely come; there would be "New confirmation of the fall/Of Adam." Democracy and equality were but new engines to generate ancient crime:

> Myriads playing pygmy parts—
> Debased into equality:
> In glut of all material arts
> A civic barbarism may be:
> Man disennobled—brutalised
> By popular science—atheised
> Into a smatterer—[161]

There was no possible answer to this utter rending of the national myth, as the listeners themselves concluded:

Columbus ended earth's romance:
No New World to mankind remains![162]

With the end of the new came the end of hope. America thus, so far from signifying mankind's fairest hope, represented the end of all hope that had been based on a faith that something new could yet be found.

Melville's last word has been often read as his final act of acceptance and resignation. *Billy Budd* has been understood to be his discovery that some kind of Christian submission was finally the answer to his life's quest. It is, perhaps unfortunately, not possible to see *Billy Budd* in that way. The tale is an integral part of Melville's total work, it but continues the great themes that had occupied him from the first.

Billy himself must be seen as a Melvillean savage, not as Christ. He had no memory of his own past; he was a foundling, illiterate, unselfconscious, naïve, and beautiful. He was, as Melville wrote, "little more than a sort of upright barbarian."[163] Perhaps to underscore his point, which has so often been missed, Melville tried again: "a barbarian Billy radically was."[164] Billy's profound innocence was recognized by the crew who called him "Baby," and who, almost to a man, loved him. As an innocent barbarian, Billy was simply incapable of living by civilized rules. He was beyond good and evil in any social sense.

Claggart, the master-at-arms, was first offended by Billy's beauty, and finally roused to hatred by his insight that Billy had never willed malice. Claggart was innately evil, Melville said, and in his mysterious way seemed to sense in primitive Billy some kind of personal rebuke. Claggart lied to the captain about Billy, and Billy, falling victim to the savage's inarticulateness, to his stammer, struck Claggart a single but fatal blow.

Captain Vere was the best that civilization could produce. A thoroughly sublimated man, he "had a marked leaning toward everything intellectual."[165] He read a great deal, but avoided romance and fantasy in favor of hard fact. He was somewhat pedantic, honest, and even compassionate. But he was civilized and, being such, was fated to destroy the radical innocence of the barbarian. When Claggart's death was verified, Vere exclaimed: "Struck dead by an angel of God. Yet the angel must hang!"[166]

That Vere confused divine with human goodness did not alter his own plight. He was a sensitive man of the city and was compelled by the rules he lived by to acknowledge that "innocence and guilt, personified in Claggart and Budd, in effect changed places."[167]

The very civilization of the captain forced him to reverse his own deepest sense of justice. He knew that he was violating nature, but what of that? "Do these buttons that we wear attest that our allegiance is to Nature? No, to the King."[168] As a civilized man, Vere, like Ahab in this one sense, saw that he must hold to intellect and fear femininity, to maintain abstraction and reject the common though usually distorted feelings of humanity: "The heart is the feminine in man, and hard though it be, she must here be ruled out."[169] He knew that "with mankind . . . forms, measured forms, are everything,"[170] but he confused, as he had to, mankind with civilization. He represented Winthrop's sense of the Christian corporation, Adams' sense of the republic of virtue, and Taylor's sense of the Garden of the South. As a good civilized man Vere, was, however, unable to avoid profound crime in the name of justice.

And so Billy was sentenced to a death which he, as a savage, did not fear, but which the crew did. Melville hinted at the reason why the crew dreaded death when he wrote the name of Jonathan Edwards in the margin of the manuscript. The chaplain failed to bring Billy to a Christian understanding and fear of death, or to any thoughts of salvation or of a savior. Billy seemed content to die, and even the chaplain was forced to conclude that pagan Billy was angelic, "that innocence was even a better thing than religion wherewith to go to judgment."[171] All of the crew heard Billy bless the captain with his final breath, and the crew involuntarily repeated the blessing. All, that is, blessed the honorable hangman of innocence for doing his civilized duty. So far from being Melville's final word of submission and peace, *Billy Budd* may stand with *Pierre* and *The Confidence Man* as his still unabated condemnation of a life that must make war on the memoryless, innocent, and happy, make war on the Baby Budds who were eternally new.

Melville understood the idea of the new; he understood that the discovery of the final New World ended, rather than began, man's eternal dream of a happy land where sorrow and pain would be no more. He knew that the New World, because it was the last, would necessarily be the place where men would have to face themselves without the comfort of that ancient faith that elsewhere life could be better. America meant that there was no place left to go, no more escapes, no more freedom growing in virgin lands. The gift of new space was finished, and henceforth men would have to make instead of receive their felicity. Melville knew that they would fail. American comfort had been genuine so long as Americans received it, so long as the land had been fertile and unoccupied. With the end of land came the beginning of true civilization, came men's need to fashion ways to live together. Melville's own life overlapped the lives of both John Adams and Franklin Roosevelt. He had witnessed the growth of America from a primitive to an industrial order. He had seen the passing of the land and the development of civilization. With civilization in America came the ultimate tragedy: the eternal passing of the Typee valley from mankind's sober hope. America now took her place among the nations as a land like any other. Americans now were merely men. The land had come of age, and age was time and tragedy and the end.

SELECT BIBLIOGRAPHY

Charles R. Anderson. *Melville in the South Seas*. New York, 1939.
Newton Arvin. *Herman Melville*. New York, 1950.
W. H. Auden. *The Enchaféd Flood*. New York, 1950.
Warner Berthoff. *The Example of Melville*. Princeton, 1962.
Merlin Bowen. *The Long Encounter*. Chicago, 1960.
William Braswell. *Melville's Religious Thought*. Durham, 1943.
Richard Chase. *Herman Melville*. New York, 1949.
Merrell R. Davis. *Melville's Mardi*. New Haven, 1952.
Charles Feidelson. *Symbolism and American Literature*. Chicago, 1953.
H. Bruce Franklin. *The Wake of the Gods*. Stanford, 1963.
William H. Gilman. *Melville's Early Life and Redburn*. New York, 1951.
A. N. Kaul. *The American Vision*. New Haven, 1963.
D. H. Lawrence. *Studies in Classic American Literature*. New York, 1923.
Harry Levin. *The Power of Blackness*. New York, 1958.
R. W. B. Lewis. *The American Adam*. Chicago, 1955.
F. O. Matthiessen. *American Renaissance*. New York, 1941.

Perry Miller. *The Raven and the Whale.* New York, 1956.
Charles Olson. *Call Me Ishmael.* New York, 1947.
Ellery Sedgwick. *Herman Melville.* Cambridge, 1944.
Milton R. Stern. *The Fine Hammered Steel of Herman Melville.* Urbana, 1957.
Lawrance Thompson. *Melville's Quarrel with God.* Princeton, 1952.
Nathalia Wright. *Melville's Use of the Bible.* Durham, 1949.

GENERAL BIBLIOGRAPHY

D. W. Brogan. *The American Character*. New York, 1944.

Oscar Cargill. *Intellectual America*. New York, 1948.

Morris R. Cohen. *American Thought*. Glencoe, Ill., 1954.

Merle Curti. *The Growth of American Thought*. New York, 1943.

Joseph Dorfman. *The Economic Mind in American Civilization*. 5 vols. New York, 1946–1959.

Leslie A. Fiedler. *Love and Death in the American Novel*. New York, 1960.

Ralph Henry Gabriel. *The Course of American Democratic Thought*. New York, 1940.

Louis Hartz. *The Liberal Tradition in America*. New York, 1955.

Richard Hofstadter. *Anti-intellectualism in American Life*. New York, 1963.

———— *The American Political Tradition*. New York, 1948.

Reinhold Niebuhr. *The Irony of American History*. New York, 1952.

H. Richard Niebuhr. *The Kingdom of God in America*. Chicago, 1937.

Saul K. Padover. *The Genius of America*. New York, 1960.

Henry Bamford Parkes. *The American Experience*. New York, 1955.

Vernon L. Parrington. *Main Currents in American Thought*. New York, 1927, 1930.

Stow Persons. *American Minds*. New York, 1958.

Charles L. Sanford. *The Quest for Paradise*. Urbana, 1961.

A. M. Schlesinger, Jr., and Morton White, eds., *Paths of American Thought*. Boston, 1963.

Herbert W. Schneider. *A History of American Philosophy*. New York, 1946.

Harvey Wish. *Society and Thought in Early America*. New York, 1950.

REFERENCES

CHAPTER I

POLITICAL THEOLOGY ❋ *John Winthrop*

1. Robert C. Winthrop, *Life and Letters of John Winthrop* (Boston, 1864–1867), I, 57.
2. John Winthrop, *Papers*, A. B. Forbes, ed. (Boston, 1929–1947), I, 159.
3. *Ibid.*, I, 209.
4. Jan. 14, 1626, *Life and Letters*, I, 214.
5. May 15, 1629, *ibid.*, I, 295–296.
6. *Ibid.*, I, 298.
7. *Ibid.*, I, 301.
8. *Papers*, II, 114–115.
9. *Ibid.*, II, 116.
10. *Ibid.*
11. *Ibid.*, II, 117.
12. *Ibid.*
13. *Ibid.*, II, 137.
14. *Ibid.*, II, 136.
15. *Ibid.*, II, 137.
16. *Ibid.*, II, 152.
17. Oct. 15, 1629, *Life and Letters*, I, 338.
18. *Papers*, II, 152.
19. *Ibid.*, II, 161.
20. *Ibid.*, II, 232.
21. *Ibid.*, IV, 170.
22. *Ibid.*, II, 282.
23. *Ibid.*, II, 282–283.
24. *Ibid.*, II, 287.
25. *Ibid.*, II, 288.
26. *Ibid.*, II, 290.
27. *Ibid.*, II, 292.

28. *Ibid.*, II, 293.
29. *Ibid.*, II, 295.
30. John Winthrop, *Journal, 1630–1649*, James K. Hosmer, ed. (New York, 1908), II, 83.
31. *Papers*, II, 152.
32. *Journal*, II, 83–84.
33. *Ibid.*, II, 238.
34. *Ibid.*, II, 239.
35. *Ibid.*
36. *Ibid.*
37. *Papers*, III, 422 n.
38. *Ibid.*, III, 423.
39. *Ibid.*, III, 423, 424.
40. *Ibid.*, III, 465.
41. *Ibid.*, III, 475.
42. *Ibid.*, III, 467.
43. *Ibid.*, IV, 385.
44. *Ibid.*, IV, 382.
45. *Ibid.*, IV, 383.
46. *Ibid.*, IV, 386.
47. *Ibid.*, IV, 383.
48. *Ibid.*, IV, 385.
49. *Ibid.*, IV, 390, 391.
50. *Journal*, II, 238.
51. *Ibid.*
52. *Papers*, IV, 476.
53. *Ibid.*, IV, 468.
54. *Ibid.*, IV, 468–469.
55. *Ibid.*, IV, 471.
56. *Ibid.*, IV, 482.
57. *Ibid.*, IV, 471.
58. *Ibid.*, IV, 472.
59. *Ibid.*, IV, 472 n.
60. *Ibid.*, IV, 473.
61. *Ibid.*, IV, 476.
62. *Ibid.*, IV, 473.
63. *Ibid.*, IV, 54.
64. "Libertye," Thomas Hutchinson (ed.), *Collection of Original Papers Relative to the History of the Colony of Massachusetts-Bay* (Albany, 1865), I, 78.
65. *Journal*, II, 36–37.
66. Edmund S. Morgan, *The Puritan Dilemma* (Boston, 1958), 96.
67. *Papers*, III, 505–507.
68. *Ibid.*, II, 267.
69. *Ibid.*, III, 13.
70. J W to Sir Simonds D'Ewes, July 21, 1634, *ibid.*, III, 171.
71. *Ibid.*, IV, 169–171.

72. *Ibid.*, IV, 171.
73. *Ibid.*, II, 274.
74. Frederic W. Maitland, "Introduction," in Otto Gierke, *Political Theories of the Middle Ages*, tr. F. W. Maitland (Cambridge, Eng., 1900), xxx, xxi.
75. *Records of the Governor and Company of the Massachusetts Bay in New England*, N. B. Shurtleff, ed. (Boston, 1853–1854), I, 10.
76. Maitland, *op. cit.*, xxxi.
77. *Journal*, II, 99.
78. C. M. Andrews, *The Colonial Period of American History* (New Haven, 1934–1938), I, 435 n.
79. *Journal*, II, 24.
80. Hutchinson, *Papers*, I, 216–219.
81. *Journal*, II, 290, 291, 294.
82. *Ibid.*, II, 300, 304.
83. *Ibid.*, II, 301.

CHAPTER II

THEOLOGY ✻ *Jonathan Edwards*

1. *The Lesson of the Covenant*, in Perry Miller (ed.), *The American Puritans* (Garden City, N.Y., 1956), 152.
2. *Ibid.*, 148.
3. Perry Miller, *Jonathan Edwards* (N.P., 1949), 39–40.
4. *A Faithful Narrative of the Surprising Work of God, in the Conversion of Many Hundred Souls, in Northampton*, in *The Works of President Edwards* (New York, 1830), IV, 17. Hereafter this collection will be cited as *Works*.
5. *Ibid.*, 39.
6. *Ibid.*, 62.
7. *Ibid.*, 31–32.
8. *Ibid.*, 70–71.
9. *Ibid.*, VII, 166.
10. *Ibid.*, 170.
11. *Ibid.*, 170, 171, 173.
12. *Ibid.*, IV, 128.
13. *Ibid.*, 129.
14. *Ibid.*, 130.
15. *Ibid.*, 131.
16. *Ibid.*, 132.
17. *Ibid.*, 132–133.
18. Miller, *Jonathan Edwards*, 177.
19. *A Treatise Concerning Religious Affections*, John E. Smith, ed. (New Haven, 1959), 84.
20. "Miscellanies," in Harvey G. Townsend (ed.) *The Philosophy of Jonathan Edwards from His Private Notebooks* (Eugene, Ore., 1955), 209.
21. *Affections*, 96.

22. *Ibid.*, 108.
23. *Ibid.*, 142.
24. *Ibid.*, 151.
25. *Ibid.*, 165.
26. *Ibid.*, 197.
27. *Ibid.*, 240.
28. *Ibid.*, 253.
29. *Ibid.*, 266.
30. Miller, *Jonathan Edwards,* 188–189.
31. *Affections,* 365.
32. *Ibid.*, 420.
33. J E to Rev. Peter Clark, May 7, 1750, *New England Quarterly,* XXIX, 2 (June, 1956), 229–230.
34. *Ibid.*, 229.
35. *Freedom of the Will,* Paul Ramsey, ed. (New Haven, 1957), 131.
36. *Ibid.*, 137.
37. *Ibid.*
38. *Ibid.*, 139.
39. *Ibid.*, 140.
40. *Ibid.*, 141.
41. *Ibid.*
42. *Ibid.*, 142.
43. *Ibid.*, 147.
44. *Ibid.*, 145.
45. *Ibid.*, 144.
46. *Ibid.*, 152.
47. *Ibid.*
48. *Ibid.*
49. *Ibid.*, 153.
50. *Ibid.*
51. *Ibid.*, 153.
52. *Ibid.*, 158–159.
53. *Ibid.*, 159.
54. *Ibid.*, 160.
55. *Ibid.*, 163.
56. *Ibid.*, 304.
57. *Ibid.*, 225.
58. *Ibid.*, 301.
59. *Ibid.*, 309.
60. *Ibid.*, 367.
61. *Ibid.*, 370.
62. *Ibid.*, 399.
63. *Ibid.*, 402.
64. "Miscellanies," in Townsend (ed.), *op. cit.,* 157n.
65. *The Great Christian Doctrine of Original Sin Defended,* in *Works,* II, 546.

66. "Miscellanies," in Townsend (ed.), *op. cit.*, 257.
67. *Ibid.*
68. Quoted in Miller, *Jonathan Edwards*, 328.

CHAPTER III

POLITICAL THEORY ❖ *John Adams*

1. George Berkeley, *Works*, A. C. Fraser, ed. (Oxford, 1871), III, 232.
2. Leon Howard, *The Connecticut Wits* (Chicago, 1942), 136.
3. Rutherford E. Delmage, "The American Idea of Progress," *Proceedings* of the American Philosophical Society, XCI (Oct., 1947), 310.
4. Andrew Burnaby, *Travels through the Middle Settlements in North America*, in John Pinkerton, *Voyages and Travels in All Parts of the World* (London, 1812), XIII, 750.
5. John Galt, *The Life, Studies, and Works of Benjamin West* (London, 1820), 114–117.
6. *Boston Gazette* (May 6, 1782), quoted in Perry Miller, "The Garden of Eden," *American Heritage*, VII, 1 (Dec., 1955), 58.
7. Ezra Stiles, *The United States Elevated to Glory and Honour* (2d ed.; Worchester, 1785), 9, 60, 63, 75.
8. Richard Price, *Observations on the Importance of the American Revolution* (London, 1784), 7.
9. Quoted in Merrill Jensen, *The New Nation* (New York, 1950), 90.
10. David Tappan, *A Discourse Delivered at the Third Parish in Newbury* (Salem, 1783), 12.
11. John Rodgers, *The Divine Goodness Displayed in the American Revolution* (New York, 1784), 30.
12. Price, *Observations*, 5–6.
13. T P to B F, Feb. 28, 1783, in B F, *Works*, J. Sparks, ed. (Boston, 1840), IX, 491.
14. Thomas Paine, *Life and Works*, W. M. Van Der Weyde, ed. (New Rochelle, 1925), II, 179.
15. T J to Edward Livingston, April 4, 1824, T J, *Writings*, P. L. Ford, ed. (New York, 1899), X, 301.
16. Joel Barlow, July 4, 1787, quoted in Howard, *op. cit.*, 200.
17. T J to William Ludlow, Sept. 6, 1824, in T J, *Writings*, H. A. Washington, ed. (New York, 1857), VII, 377–378.
18. J. H. St. John de Crèvecoeur, *Letters from an American Farmer* (London, 1912), 47.
19. *Ibid.*, 43, 45.
20. Quoted in Merrill Jensen, *The Articles of Confederation* (Madison, 1940), 34–35.
21. H. D. Foster, "International Calvinism through Locke and the Revolution of 1688," *American Historical Review*, XXXII, 3 (April, 1927), 492.

22. April 24, 1756, *Diary and Autobiography*, L. H. Butterfield *et al.*, eds. (Cambridge, 1961), I, 22.
23. Spring, 1759, *ibid.*, 95.
24. *Ibid.*, III, 272–273.
25. "On Private Revenge," *Boston Gazette*, Aug. 1, 1763, *Works*, C. F. Adams, ed. (Boston, 1850–1856), III, 427.
26. Sept. 5, 1763, *ibid.*, 443.
27. Aug. 29, 1763, *ibid.*, 432.
28. *Ibid.*, 449.
29. *Ibid.*, 450.
30. *Ibid.*, 452 n.
31. J A to Benjamin Rush, May 23, 1807, *ibid.*, IX, 600.
32. *Ibid.*, III, 453.
33. *Ibid.*, 454.
34. *Ibid.*, 463.
35. *Diary and Autobiography*, I, 264–265.
36. Jan. 1, 1766, *ibid.*, 283.
37. Dec. 1765, *ibid.*, 282.
38. *Boston Gazette*, Jan. 20, 1766, *Works*, III, 475–476.
39. Jan. 27, 1766, *ibid.*, 480.
40. *Diary and Autobiography*, II, 59.
41. *Ibid.*
42. *Ibid.*, 58.
43. Oct. 24, 1774, *ibid.*, 156.
44. *Works*, IV, 116.
45. *Ibid.*, 119.
46. *Ibid.*, 122.
47. *Ibid.*
48. *Ibid.*, 127.
49. *Ibid.*, 127–128.
50. *Ibid.*, 146.
51. *Ibid.*
52. *Ibid.*, 177.
53. *Ibid.*
54. *Ibid.*, 174.
55. *Ibid.*, 175.
56. *Ibid.*, 177.
57. J A to Mercy Warren, Nov. 25, 1775, *Works*, IX, 368.
58. Sept., 1775, *Diary and Autobiography*, III, 326.
59. June-Oct., 1775, *ibid.*, 355.
60. *Ibid.*
61. *Works*, IV, 193.
62. *Ibid.*, 194.
63. *Ibid.*
64. *Ibid.*, 195.

65. *Ibid.*, 197.
66. *Ibid.*, 200.
67. *Ibid.*, IX, 376.
68. J A to Joseph Hawley, Aug. 25, 1776, *ibid.*, 434.
69. J A to William Gordon, April 8, 1777, *ibid.*, 461.
70. Feb. 23, 1777, *Diary and Autobiography*, II, 261.
71. March 30, 1778, *ibid.*, 292.
72. Feb. 9, 1779, *Letters of John Adams Addressed to His Wife*, C. F. Adams, ed. (Boston, 1841), II, 43.
73. *Ibid.*, II, 70.
74. May 22, 1779, *Diary and Autobiography*, II, 377.
75. April 25, 1778, *Letters to His Wife*, II, 22–23.
76. May 13, 1779, *Diary and Autobiography*, II, 370.
77. June, 1778, *ibid.*, IV, 123.
78. June 21, 1779, *ibid.*, II, 388.
79. July 18, 1781, *Works*, VII, 445.
80. May 10, 1779, *Diary and Autobiography*, II, 367.
81. *Works*, IV, 216.
82. *Ibid.*, 259.
83. *Letters to His Wife*, II, 68.
84. J A to Secretary Livingston, April 23, 1782, *Works*, VII, 574.
85. *Ibid.*, 151.
86. Nov. 18, 1782, *Diary and Autobiography*, III, 61.
87. Zoltán Haraszti, *John Adams and the Prophets of Progress* (Cambridge, 1952), 144.
88. J A to Thomas Jefferson, Dec. 6, 1787, *Works*, VIII, 464.
89. *Ibid.*, IV, 276.
90. J A to Richard Price, May 20, 1789, *ibid.*, IX, 558–559.
91. *Ibid.*, IV, 279.
92. *Ibid.*, 587–588.
93. *Ibid.*, 285.
94. *Ibid.*, 289–290.
95. *Ibid.*, 290.
96. *Ibid.*
97. *Ibid.*, 292.
98. *Ibid.*, 293.
99. *Ibid.*, VI, 4.
100. *Ibid.*, IV, 300.
101. *Ibid.*, 406.
102. *Ibid.*, 407.
103. *Ibid.*
104. *Ibid.*, V, 432.
105. *Ibid.*, VI, 200.
106. *Ibid.*, 57.
107. *Ibid.*, 115.

108. *Ibid.*, 204.
109. *Ibid.*, V, 30.
110. *Ibid.*, 426.
111. *Ibid.*
112. *Ibid.*, 488.
113. *Ibid.*, 401.
114. *Ibid.*, 492.
115. *Ibid.*, VI, 57.
116. J A to Roger Sherman, July 20, 1789, *Works*, VI, 432.
117. Haraszti, *op. cit.*, 169.
118. *Works*, VI, 239.
119. Oct. 18, 1790, *ibid.*, 417.
120. *Ibid.*, 276.
121. *Ibid.*, I, 460.
122. William Maclay, *Journal*, E. S. Maclay, ed. (New York, 1890), 12, 30, 155, 216.
123. J A to Richard Price, April 19, 1790, *Works*, IX, 563–564.
124. J A to Benjamin Waterhouse, Oct. 29, 1805, *The Selected Writings of John and John Quincy Adams*, A. Koch and William Peden, eds. (New York, 1946), 148.
125. J A to F. A. Vanderkemp, Feb, 16, 1809, *Works*, IX, 609–610.
126. J A to Thomas Jefferson, July 16, 1814, *ibid.*, X, 103.
127. April 15, 1814, *ibid.*, VI, 447.
128. July 13, 1813, *ibid.*, X, 54.
129. *Ibid.*, VI, 451.
130. *Ibid.*, 458.
131. *Ibid.*, 508.
132. *Ibid.*, 461–462.
133. *Ibid.*, 506.
134. *Ibid.*, 490.
135. *Ibid.*, 516.
136. *Ibid.*, 515–516.
137. *Ibid.*, 519.
138. *Ibid.*, 521.
139. July 16, 1814, *ibid.*, X, 101.
140. Nov. 28, 1814, *ibid.*, 106.
141. J A to David Sewall, May 22, 1821, *ibid.*, 399.
142. Haraszti, *op. cit.*, 252.
143. Sept. 14, 1813, *Works*, X, 67.
144. May 3, 1816, *ibid.*, 214.
145. J A to Thomas Jefferson, April 19, 1817, *ibid.*, 255.
146. *Ibid.*
147. J A to Samuel Miller, July 8, 1820, *ibid.*, 389.
148. J A to John Taylor, April 15, 1814, *ibid.*, VI, 454.
149. Hannah Arendt, *On Revolution* (New York, 1963), 168.

CHAPTER IV
AGRARIANISM ✻ *John Taylor of Caroline*

1. John Campbell to David Campbell, June 14, 1814, in Manning Dauer and Hans Hanning, "John Taylor," *Journal of Politics*, VI, 4 (Nov., 1944), 386.
2. J T to T J, March 5, 1795, in Avery O. Craven, "The Agricultural Reformers of the Ante-Bellum South," *American Historical Review*, XXXIII, 2 (Jan., 1928), 305.
3. J T to Aaron Burr, March 25, 1803, A B, *Memoirs*, Matthew L. Davis, ed. (New York, 1838), II, 236.
4. *Arator* (5th ed.; Petersburg, 1818), 54.
5. *An Inquiry into the Principles and Policy of the Government of the United States* (Fredericksburg, 1814), 76.
6. *New Views of the Constitution of the United States* (Washington, 1823), 262.
7. *Inquiry*, 436.
8. *Ibid.*, 143.
9. *Ibid.*, 145–146.
10. *Ibid.*, 510.
11. *Ibid.*, 434.
12. *Construction Construed, and Constitutions Vindicated* (Richmond, 1820), 13.
13. *Tyranny Unmasked* (Washington, 1822), 252.
14. *Inquiry*, 424.
15. *Ibid.*, 159.
16. *Ibid.*, 160–161.
17. *Construction Construed*, 13.
18. *Ibid.*, 14.
19. *Ibid.*
20. *Tyranny Unmasked*, 295.
21. *Ibid.*, 20.
22. *Ibid.*, 253.
23. *Construction Construed*, 186.
24. *Tyranny Unmasked*, 115.
25. *Ibid.*, 116.
26. Thomas Jefferson to Robert J. Garnett, Feb. 14, 1824, T J, *Writings*, A. A. Liscomb and A. L. Bergh, eds. (Washington, 1907), XVI, 14.
27. *Inquiry*, 646.
28. *Tyranny Unmasked*, 347.
29. *Ibid.*, 346.
30. *Inquiry*, 645.
31. *Construction Construed*, 37.
32. *Ibid.*, 46–47.
33. *Inquiry*, 425.
34. *Construction Construed*, 214.
35. *Inquiry*, 511.

36. *New Views*, 20.
37. *Inquiry*, v.
38. *New Views*, 287–288.
39. *Inquiry*, 1.
40. *Ibid.*, 2–3.
41. *Ibid.*, vii.
42. *Ibid.*, 88.
43. *Ibid.*, 85.
44. Quoted in William E. Dodd, "John Taylor of Caroline," *The John P. Branch Historical Papers of Randolph-Macon College*, II, 3–4 (June 1908), 217.
45. *Inquiry*, 175.
46. *Ibid.*
47. *Ibid.*, 194.
48. *New Views*, 127.
49. Thomas Jefferson to Archibald Thweat, Jan. 19, 1821, *Writings*, XV, 307.
50. *Tyranny Unmasked*, 129.
51. *Ibid.*, 80.
52. E R to G W, June 24, 1793, Moncure D. Conway, *Omitted Chapters of History Disclosed in the Life and Papers of Edmund Randolph* (New York, 1888), 152.
53. *Tyranny Unmasked*, 89.
54. *Ibid.*, 52.
55. *Ibid.*, 132.
56. *Ibid.*, 201.
57. *Ibid.*, 207.
58. J T to J M, Oct. 26, 1810, "Letters of John Taylor," *John P. Branch Historical Papers*, 310.
59. *Tyranny Unmasked*, 291.
60. *Arator*, 35.
61. *Ibid.*, 34.
62. *Construction Construed*, 298.
63. *New Views*, 247.
64. *Tyranny Unmasked*, 37.
65. *Ibid.*, 209.
66. *Ibid.*, 120.
67. *Ibid.*, 70.
68. *Arator*, 190.
69. J T, "The Necessities, Competency, and Profit of Agriculture," *Niles' Weekly Register*, Supplement to No. 11, III, Vol. XV (N. S., Nov. 7, 1818), 180.
70. *Arator*, 189.
71. *Ibid.*, 93.
72. J T, *Disunion Sentiment in Congress in 1794*, Gaillard Hunt, ed. (Washington, 1905), 21–23.
73. J T to Vice-President, Oct, 14, 1799, "Letters," *John P. Branch Historical Papers*, 283.
74. J T to J M, Jan. 31, 1811, *ibid.*, 316.

CHAPTER V

TRANSCENDENCE ❈ *Ralph Waldo Emerson*

1. Nathaniel Hawthorne, *The House of the Seven Gables* (Pocket Library, 1954), vi.
2. "Works and Days," 1857, in R W E, *Complete Works*, Edward Waldo Emerson, ed. (Boston, 1903–1904), VII, 177. Hereafter cited as *C W*.
3. D. H. Lawrence, *Studies in Classic American Literature* (Doubleday Anchor, 1955), 93.
4. May 13, 1822, R W E, *Journals and Miscellaneous Notebooks*, William H. Gilman *et al.*, eds. (Cambridge, 1960), I, 133–134. Hereafter cited as *J*, Gilman, ed.
5. March, 1827, R W E, *Journals*, Edward W. Emerson and Waldo E. Forbes, eds. (Boston, 1909–1914), II, 180. Hereafter cited as *J*, Emerson, ed.
6. Oct. 3, 1820, *J*, Gilman, ed., I, 33.
7. Oct. 27, 1831, *J*, Emerson, ed., II, 424.
8. Aug. 11, 1841, *C W*, I, 220.
9. Sept. 21, 1841, *J*, Emerson, ed., VI, 53.
10. Aug. 11, 1841, *C W*, I, 220–221.
11. Octavius B. Frothingham, *Transcendentalism in New England* (New York, 1959), 182.
12. "The Method of Nature," Aug. 11, 1841, *C W*, I, 197.
13. *Nature* (1836), *C W*, I, 24.
14. *Ibid.*, 10.
15. *Ibid.*, 73–75.
16. "Nature," *C W*, III, 178.
17. *C W*, X, 127.
18. "The Method of Nature," Aug. 11, 1841, *C W*, I, 213.
19. *C W*, I, 113.
20. *Ibid.*, 126.
21. *Ibid.*, 127.
22. Ralph L. Rusk, *The Life of Ralph Waldo Emerson* (New York, 1949), 270.
23. *C W*, II, 269.
24. "History," *C W*, II, 10.
25. Quoted in F. O. Matthiessen, *American Renaissance* (New York, 1941), 182.
26. "Spiritual Laws," *C W*, II, 131.
27. Divinity School Address, July 15, 1838, *C W*, I, 124.
28. *C W*, II, 107.
29. *The Conduct of Life* (1860), *C W*, VI, 23.
30. *Ibid.*, 14–15.
31. *Ibid.*, 22.
32. *Ibid.*, 28.
33. "Literary Ethics," July 24, 1838, *C W*, I, 165.
34. "Experience," *C W*, III, 48–49.

35. *C W*, III, 290–291.
36. "The Transcendentalist," Jan. 1842, *C W*, I, 348.
37. *Ibid.*, 349.
38. "The Tragic," *C W*, XII, 415.
39. *Ibid.*, 410.
40. *Ibid.*, 416–417.
41. "Natural History of Intellect," 1848, *C W*, XII, 11.
42. *Ibid.*, 14.
43. "Self-Reliance," *C W*, II, 57.
44. *Ibid.*, 45.
45. *Ibid.*, 84.
46. *Ibid.*, 52.
47. *Representative Men* (1850), *C W*, IV, 4.
48. "History," *C W*, II, 40–41.
49. "The Poet," *C W*, III, 8.
50. *Ibid.*, 16.
51. *C W*, XII, 65.
52. *Ibid.*, 71–72.
53. Jan. 1828, *J*, Emerson, ed., II, 228–229.
54. Nov. 1832, *ibid.*, 528.
55. June 18, 1834, *ibid.*, III, 308.
56. June 24, 1840, *ibid.*, V, 423.
57. Dec. 22, 1834, *ibid.*, III, 404–405.
58. Nov. 1842, *ibid.*, VI, 311.
59. Sept. 23, 1836, *ibid.*, IV, 95.
60. "Politics," *C W*, III, 202.
61. *Ibid.*, 204.
62. *Ibid.*, 208.
63. *J*, Emerson, ed., VII, 148.
64. March 15, 1845, *ibid.*, VII, 12.
65. May(?) 1846, *ibid.*, VII, 206.
66. *Ibid.*
67. May 1846, *ibid.*, VII, 219.
68. *Ibid.*, 222.
69. *Ibid.*, 223.
70. March 1854, *ibid.*, VIII, 449.
71. Feb. 2, 1835, *ibid.*, III, 446–447.
72. Nov. 14, 1839, *ibid.*, V, 324.
73. Oct. 21, 1839, *ibid.*, V, 292.
74. Jan. 25, 1841, *C W*, I, 237–238.
75. *Ibid.*, 242–243.
76. *Ibid.*, 253–254.
77. *Ibid.*, 255.
78. "Lecture on the Times," Dec. 2, 1841, *C W*, I, 277.
79. *Ibid.*, 280.
80. "The Young American," Feb. 7, 1844, *C W*, I, 390.

81. 1844, *J*, Emerson, ed., VI, 535.
82. 1845, *ibid.*, VII, 57.
83. *C W*, IX, 399.
84. 1851, *J*, Emerson, ed., VIII, 186.
85. *Ibid.*, 202.
86. *C W*, XI, 180.
87. *Ibid.*, 208.
88. March 7, 1854, *C W*, XI, 217.
89. Aug. 1852, *J*, Emerson, ed., VIII, 316.
90. *The Conduct of Life*, *C W*, VI, 106.
91. "Historic Notes," *C W*, X, 326.
92. *The Conduct of Life*, *C W*, VI, 249.
93. "American Civilization," Jan. 31, 1862, *C W*, XI, 299.
94. *J*, Emerson, ed., IX, 499.
95. "The Man of Letters," 1863, *C W*, X, 247.
96. Nov., 1863, *J*, Emerson, ed., IX, 557.
97. *C W*, XI, 330.
98. *Ibid.*, 335.
99. Dec. 21, 1822, *J*, Gilman, ed., II, 72.
100. 1822, *ibid.*, I, 352.
101. Dec. 22, 1824, *ibid.*, II, 403–404.
102. July 11, 1822, *ibid.*, 4–5.
103. April 8, 1823, *ibid.*, 115.
104. *Ibid.*, 116.
105. "Literary Ethics," July 24, 1838, *C W*, I, 156.
106. *C W*, III, 37–38.
107. June 1848, *J*, Emerson, ed., VII, 477–478.
108. 1851, *ibid.*, VIII, 226.
109. "The Fortune of the Republic" (1863), *C W*, XI, 515–516.
110. *Ibid.*, 535.
111. July 1865, *J*, Emerson, ed., X, 106.
112. "Resources," Dec. 1864, *C W*, VIII, 142–143.
113. "Progress of Culture," July 18, 1867, *C W*, VIII, 211–212.
114. 1866, *J*, Emerson, ed., X, 144.
115. Feb.(?) 1867, *ibid.*, 195.
116. John Dewey, "Emerson," in M. R. Konvitz and S. E. Whicher (eds.), *Emerson* (Englewood Cliffs, N.J., 1962), 29.
117. Matthiessen, *op. cit.*, xii.
118. Quoted in Newton Arvin, "The House of Pain," *The Hudson Review*, XII, 1 (Spring 1959), 38.
119. Perry Miller, "Jonathan Edwards to Emerson," *New England Quarterly*, XIII (Dec. 1940), 617.

CHAPTER VI

THE DEMONIC ✱ *Herman Melville*

All references to Melville's writings are from Herman Melville, *Works* (Standard Edition; 16 vols.; London, 1922–1924), unless otherwise specified.

1. *Typee*, 3–4.
2. Jay Leyda, *The Melville Log* (New York, 1951), I, 196.
3. *Typee*, 270.
4. *Ibid.*, 18.
5. *Ibid.*, 102.
6. *Ibid.*, 115.
7. Leyda, *op. cit.*, I, 210.
8. *Typee*, 165.
9. *Ibid.*, 166.
10. *Ibid.*, 263.
11. *Ibid.*, 264–265.
12. Leyda, *op. cit.*, I, 248.
13. *Omoo*, 7.
14. *Ibid.*, 371.
15. *Mardi*, I, vii.
16. Newton Arvin, *Herman Melville* (New York, 1957), 99.
17. *Mardi*, I, 198.
18. *Ibid.*, 244.
19. *Ibid.*, 47.
20. *Ibid.*, II, 270.
21. *Ibid.*, 223.
22. *Ibid.*, 243.
23. *Ibid.*
24. *Ibid.*, 245.
25. *Ibid.*, 250.
26. *Ibid.*, 175.
27. *Ibid.*, 222–223.
28. Leyda, *op. cit.* I, 293.
29. H M to Lemuel Shaw, April 23, 1849, *Letters*, Merrell R. Davis and William H. Gilman, eds. (New Haven, 1960), 85.
30. H M to Lemuel Shaw, Oct. 6, 1849, *ibid.*, 91–92.
31. *Redburn*, 259.
32. *Ibid.*, 217.
33. *White Jacket*, 188.
34. *Ibid.*, 189.
35. *Ibid.*, 353.
36. *Ibid.*, 404.
37. *Ibid.*, 502.
38. *Ibid.*, 404.
39. *Ibid.*, 502.

40. R. P. Blackmur, "The Craft of Herman Melville," *The Lion and the Honey-comb* (New York, 1955), 124–144.
41. *Moby-Dick*, I, 1.
42. *Ibid.*, 3.
43. *Ibid.*, 4.
44. *Ibid.*, 270.
45. *Ibid.*, 7.
46. *Ibid.*
47. *Ibid.*
48. *Ibid.*, 73.
49. *Ibid.*, 132.
50. *Ibid.*, 133.
51. *Ibid.*
52. *Ibid.*, II, 26.
53. *Ibid.*, I, 349.
54. *Ibid.*, 60–61.
55. *Ibid.*, 62.
56. *Ibid.*
57. *Ibid.*, 149.
58. *The Piazza Tales*, 136.
59. *Moby-Dick*, I, 257.
60. *Pierre*, 476.
61. *Moby-Dick*, I, 258.
62. *Ibid.*, 78.
63. *Ibid.*, II, 123.
64. *Ibid.*, 83.
65. *Ibid.*, 85.
66. *Ibid.*, I, 48.
67. *Ibid.*, 198; also see II, 1.
68. *Mardi*, I, 19; *White Jacket*, 96.
69. *Moby-Dick*, I, 197.
70. *Ibid.*, 198.
71. *Ibid.*, II, 80.
72. *Ibid.*, 231.
73. *Ibid.*, 310.
74. *Ibid.*, 38.
75. *Ibid.*, I, 190.
76. *Ibid.*, 252–253.
77. *Ibid.*, 183.
78. *Ibid.*, II, 341.
79. *Ibid.*, I, 204.
80. *Ibid.*
81. *Ibid.*, II, 203.
82. *Ibid.*, 361.
83. *Ibid.*, I, 230.
84. *Ibid.*, II, 261.

85. *Ibid.*, 281–282.
86. *Ibid.*, I, 209–210.
87. *Ibid.*, II, 330.
88. *Ibid.*, I, 205.
89. *Ibid.*, 210.
90. *Ibid.*, II, 352.
91. *Ibid.*, 239–240.
92. *Ibid.*, I, 233.
93. *Ibid.*, 207.
94. *Ibid.*, 209–210.
95. *Ibid.*, 222.
96. *Ibid.*
97. *Ibid.*, II, 180.
98. *Ibid.*, 181.
99. *Ibid.*
100. *Ibid.*, 181–182.
101. *Ibid.*, 182.
102. *Ibid.*, 296; italics added.
103. *Ibid.*, I, 286.
104. *Ibid.*
105. *Ibid.*, II, 48.
106. *Ibid.*, I, 357.
107. *Ibid.*, 211.
108. *Ibid.*, II, 119.
109. *Ibid.*, 35.
110. *Ibid.*, 26.
111. *Ibid.*, I, 69.
112. *Ibid.*, 76.
113. *Ibid.*, 107.
114. *Ibid.*, II, 16–17.
115. *Ibid.*, 147.
116. *Ibid.*, I, 93.
117. *Ibid.*, 130.
118. *Ibid.*, 92.
119. *Ibid.*, II, 316.
120. *Ibid.*, 23.
121. *Ibid.*, 33.
122. June 1851, *Letters,* 128.
123. Nov. 1851, *ibid.,* 142.
124. April(?) 16(?), 1851, *ibid.,* 125.
125. "Hawthorne and His Mosses," *Literary World* (Aug. 17 and 24, 1850), *Works,* XIII, 129, 139.
126. June 1851, *Letters,* 129.
127. *The American Whig Review,* Nov. 1, 1852, in Leyda, *op. cit.,* I, 463–464.
128. *Pierre,* 420.
129. *Ibid.*, 421.

130. *Ibid.*, 90.
131. *Ibid.*, 91.
132. *Ibid.*, 125.
133. *Ibid.*, 254.
134. *Ibid.*, 123.
135. F. O. Matthiessen, *American Renaissance* (New York, 1941), 54–55.
136. *Pierre*, 421.
137. *Ibid.*, 385.
138. H M to Evert A. Duyckinck, March 3, 1849, *Letters*, 78–79.
139. *Pierre*, 295.
140. *Ibid.*, 296.
141. *Israel Potter*, 158.
142. Nov. 20, 1856, Nathaniel Hawthorne, *The English Notebooks*, Randall Stewart, ed. (New York, 1941), 432–433.
143. Leyda, *op. cit.*, II, 553–555.
144. *The Confidence Man*, 42.
145. *Ibid.*, 149.
146. *Ibid.*, 250.
147. *Ibid.*, 254.
148. *Ibid.*, 255.
149. *Ibid.*, 263.
150. *Ibid.*, 297.
151. *Ibid.*, 335.
152. H M to John C. Hoadley, March 31, 1877, *Letters*, 260.
153. *Clarel*, Walter E. Bezanson, ed. (New York, 1960), cix.
154. *Clarel*, II, 176.
155. *Ibid.*, 177.
156. *Ibid.*, I, 49.
157. *Ibid.*
158. *Ibid.*, II, 247.
159. *Ibid.*, 248.
160. *Ibid.*, 249.
161. *Ibid.*, 249–250.
162. *Ibid.*, 250.
163. *Billy Budd*, 16.
164. *Ibid.*, 97.
165. *Ibid.*, 29.
166. *Ibid.*, 75.
167. *Ibid.*, 78.
168. *Ibid.*, 86.
169. *Ibid.*, 87.
170. *Ibid.*, 107.
171. *Ibid.*, 99.

INDEX